INTERNATIONAL ORGANIZATIONS ENGAGING THE WORLD

International organizations have always been exclusively seen as vehicles for their member states, exercising delegated powers. This book demonstrates that this picture is seriously outdated: international organizations address a wide variety of social actors, and this needs to be reflected in the way we think about international organizations. The book provides an overview, in distinct chapters, about the sort of actors international organizations engage with; provides empirical examples; investigates potential winners and losers of such interaction; and aims to find ways to come to terms with the realization that international organizations are not solely member state-driven. This title is also available as Open Access on Cambridge Core.

Jan Klabbers is Professor of International Law at the University of Helsinki and is generally regarded as one of the leading scholars in the field of international organizations law. He is the author of *An Introduction to International Organizations Law* and is currently working on a project concerning international organizations and the private sector.

International Organizations Engaging the World

Edited by

JAN KLABBERS
University of Helsinki

CAMBRIDGE
UNIVERSITY PRESS

CAMBRIDGE
UNIVERSITY PRESS

Shaftesbury Road, Cambridge CB2 8EA, United Kingdom

One Liberty Plaza, 20th Floor, New York, NY 10006, USA

477 Williamstown Road, Port Melbourne, VIC 3207, Australia

314–321, 3rd Floor, Plot 3, Splendor Forum, Jasola District Centre, New Delhi – 110025, India

103 Penang Road, #05-06/07, Visioncrest Commercial, Singapore 238467

Cambridge University Press is part of Cambridge University Press & Assessment, a department of the University of Cambridge.

We share the University's mission to contribute to society through the pursuit of education, learning and research at the highest international levels of excellence.

www.cambridge.org
Information on this title: www.cambridge.org/9781009536219

DOI: 10.1017/9781009536202

First published 2025

Cover image: Art by Hilma af Klint, Swedish artist – The Swan, No. 18 (1914–1915) / Bill Waterson / Alamy

A catalogue record for this publication is available from the British Library

A Cataloging-in-Publication data record for this book is available from the Library of Congress

ISBN 978-1-009-53621-9 Hardback

Contents

Acknowledgements

This volume is born out of the PRIVIGO project, 'International Organizations between Mission and Market', generously sponsored by the European Research Council under Grant no. 883417. Most of the papers (with one exception) were first presented at a workshop organized in Helsinki in November 2021, when the world was still somewhat concerned with the outbreak of COVID-19. Travel was possible again, and most of the participants were able to attend in person – quite a relief after the period of lockdowns and restrictions.

I am indebted to Anna van der Velde, at the time the project planner at the Erik Castrén Institute where PRIVIGO is located, and Hannah Ouahmane, then the project's research assistant, for their help in organizing the workshop and their smooth handling of all sorts of practical issues. Beyond this, I am grateful to all participants (also those who ended up not writing a chapter) not only for their intellectual input but also for their patience. This has been a slow process but, it is hoped, eventually a fruitful one. And, as for patience, an enormous 'thank you' also to Marianne Nield and Natasha Burton at Cambridge University Press, who supported this project beyond the call of duty. This volume is dedicated to my children, Johan and Gilda.

erc

European Research Council

Established by the European Commission

Contributors

Helmut Philipp Aust, Free University of Berlin

Fernando Lusa Bordin, University of Cambridge

Orfeas Chasapis Tassinis, University of Cambridge

Jan Klabbers, University of Helsinki

Sebastián Machado, University of Helsinki

Hans-Wolfgang Micklitz, European University Institute

Elisabetta Morlino, Suor Orsola Benincasa University of Naples

Evgenia Ralli, University of Edinburgh

Rebecca Schmidt, University of Oslo

Ukri Soirila, University of Helsinki

Eelco Szabó, independent lawyer

René Urueña, University of the Andes

Dimitri van den Meerssche, Queen Mary University of London

Tleuzhan Zhunussova, University of Helsinki

1

The Vacuum Assumption in International Organizations Law

JAN KLABBERS

1.1 INTRODUCTION

There is a standard joke about two economists being stranded on an uninhabited island with nothing but a can of beans. After a while they get hungry, and realize that they cannot open the can, their only source of food. They fiddle around for a day or two and, with despair growing, one of them has a Eureka moment. She turns to the other and says, 'let's assume that we have a can opener and take it from there'.[1]

Rewarding as it may be to make jokes at the expense of the 'dismal science', it should also be recognized that economists are not alone in using assumptions – academic disciplines generally work on that basis.[2] Scientists, including legal scientists and social scientists, assume certain basic 'facts' about people and institutions in order to allow for further reflection, to allow for modelling, to allow for theory-building, to allow for prediction. Economists may assume such things as 'perfect competition' or 'zero transaction costs'; many International Relations scholars assume that states are the only actors of relevance and that those states are solely interested in power,[3] and international lawyers will often assume that treaties are based on a 'meeting of the minds'.

This chapter has benefited from comments received at seminars at Sorbonne and the European University Institute.

1 On the role of assumptions in economics, see also A. Sen, *On Ethics and Economics* (Blackwell, 1987).

2 For an illuminating discussion of approaches to economics, see A. Klamer, *Speaking of Economics: How to Get in the Conversation* (Routledge, 2007).

3 The role of assumptions and *topoi* in scholarship and political practice is emphasized in the work of Kratochwil. See, e.g., F. Kratochwil, *Rules, Norms and Decisions* (Cambridge

The use of assumptions is not problematic in and of itself, but there is always a risk that those assumptions become their own truths: they move from being heuristic devices to representations of reality and sometimes all the more forcefully so for having been leading assumptions for many generations. The problem then is not with the assumption but with its ossification: disciplinary assumptions need to be re-examined every now and then, both in order to see whether they still hold ('is perfect competition still a reasonable assumption in today's economy?') and with a view to gauging their effects: it is perfectly possible, as we will see, that a fundamental assumption generates all manner of thinking that leads a discipline astray. Put differently, the assumption may represent an earlier 'sliding doors' moment, sending an entire discipline down a path that academically proves to be not very fruitful, having generated a belief rather than understanding.

One of the fundamental assumptions on which the law of international organizations is constructed is the assumption that international organizations only and exclusively interact with their member states.[4] Member states set up international organizations and give them tasks, the performance of which in turn is expected to serve these same member states. This has been the assumption since international organizations were first set up, beginning with the early nineteenth century river commissions: these would do tasks for their member states, on behalf of those member states, on assignment of those member states, and for the benefit of those member states. There was no world around the organization and its member states – the external world simply did not exist. The river commissions were conceived as administrative agencies which just happened to transverse several states, without an external world and even, so to speak, without an internal world. The first river commissions consisted of representatives of member states who would meet every now and then, decide on things and then go home again.[5] These representatives formed their own administration – there was no international civil service just yet, not even in the form of seconded national civil servants. The Rhine

University Press, 1989) and F. Kratochwil, *Praxis: On Acting and Knowing* (Cambridge University Press, 2018).

4 This requires a nuance: it is an assumption within international law (where international organizations law is usually thought to reside) and without prejudice to how domestic legal orders approach international organizations.

5 This helps explain how writers were slow to identify any institutional element beyond the treaty relationship; see, for example, W. J. M. Van Eysinga, *Ontwikkeling en inhoud der Nederlandsche tractaten sedert 1813* (Martinus Nijhoff, 1916), 5–6.

Commission, for example, was set up as an annual conference, with the relevant legal instrument providing that the national commissioners (one per member state) would meet once a year in Mainz, on 1 November.[6]

Much the same applied to the public unions set up in the late nineteenth and early twentieth century: while these may have had a small administration of their own (in contrast to the river commissions, and still usually composed of civil servants seconded from the administration of the host state), they were nonetheless conceived as administrative agencies which just happened to transverse several states. Hence, there was a transboundary element, but otherwise they were not fundamentally different from a national or local administrative agency – an agent doing things for its principal. While the principal was a collective rather than a singular principal, the key factor resided in the nature of that principal–agent relationship: excluding the outside world.

This situation could not but affect the law of international organizations. The law is built around this assumption that only the principal/agent relationship is of any relevance: where states set up agencies to do things for them and on their instructions, it stands to reason that this became the dominant dynamic. To put it graphically, international organizations law is constructed in a vacuum, a vacuum drawn around the relationship between the organization and its member states. Nothing else is able to intervene. This vacuum not only affects the law as it stands but has a broader effect: it also affects the theory underpinning the legal framework. In this framework, the external world – external to the relationship between the organization and its member states – simply does not exist.

The absence of an outside world on this basic level of political thought has serious consequences. If there is no outside world, then there is no relationship to third parties and, thus, it follows that organizations cannot be held accountable for their acts towards that outside world, that is, towards third parties. This is precisely what can be observed. International organizations can be controlled, but only by their member states, with the help of the *ultra vires* doctrine (not very useful, as it happens), or by the unprincipled voting of member states or even by attempts to withdraw or to withhold funding: these can all be seen as mechanisms to hold the organization accountable, however unprincipled perhaps, but only by member states. International organizations cannot in any meaningful way be held to account by outsiders, whether courts

6 1815 Treaty of Vienna, Annex 16 B, article 11. Useful is J. Yao, *The Ideal River: How Control of Nature Shaped the International Order* (Manchester University Press, 2022).

and tribunals or even the court of public opinion, and this finds its origin in precisely the vacuum assumption.

Of course, a certain amount of patchwork can be done and has been done: there is the virtual accountability that can benefit from the International Law Commission's articles on the responsibility of international organizations (ARIO) or the Global Administrative Law approach, but, while these may sometimes work in practice, they are theoretically problematic. They may sometimes work in practice: a court may hold that the ARIO represent the law or that some organization or other should have been held to a commitment it had entered into, but the theory is problematic. It is problematic in that the two main elements of the internationally wrongful act (the international obligation and the attributability of the act[7]) are by no means self-evident, and this in turn finds its cause in the circumstance that the law grew up thinking that international organizations only affected their member states and would not affect third parties. Consequently, they could do no wrong towards third parties. It was only since the moment they actually started to affect third parties negatively, most emblematically with the International Tin Council crisis of the 1980s, that international organizations law devoted attention to the topic. But the structures of the law, one might say, cannot accommodate third party responsibility, and this, in turn, is traceable to the vacuum assumption.[8]

Much the same applies with respect to the position of staff members: these have no place in the theory of international organizations law, as the latter is based on the vacuum assumption. Again, practice has found solutions, ever since the Italian Court of Cassation held, in the early dispute between Mr Profili and the Rome-based International Institute of Agriculture, that the Italian judicial order lacked jurisdiction over staff disputes.[9] As a result, the rights of staff members often find protection in especially established international administrative tribunals. Again though, this tends to be random and ad hoc: it may work but is an odd fit with the system. This calls for a re-thinking of the underlying assumptions.

[7] See, in far more detail, J. Klabbers, 'Sources of International Organizations' Law: Reflections on Accountability', in S. Besson and J. d'Aspremont (eds.), *Oxford Handbook of the Sources of International Law* (Oxford University Press, 2017) 987, and J. Klabbers, 'Responsibility as Opportunism: The Responsibility of International Organizations', in S. Besson (ed.), *Theories of International Responsibility Law* (Cambridge University Press, 2022) 119.

[8] An excellent discussion of the Tin Council crisis is R. Sadurska and C. Chinkin, 'The Collapse of the International Tin Council: A Case of State Responsibility?' (1990) 30 *Virginia Journal of International Law* 845.

[9] See the discussion in Section 1.2.

1.2 THE SILENT DOG

Historically, the vacuum is visible in the long-standing absence of international organizations explicitly being granted international legal personality. Given the overwhelming popularity of the idea that international legal personality depends on the wishes and intentions of their member states as expressed in the constituent instrument or related instruments, the virtual non-existence of international legal personality is striking – and telling.[10]

Going through the constitutions of the classic public unions, one notable element is that they all lack international legal personality and, even as recently as two decades ago, it was noted that 'an express provision on international personality is comparatively rare'.[11] This absence of explicit provision applies, for instance, to the 1875 Meter Convention, establishing the Bureau International des Poids et Mesures. It also applies to the Universal Postal Union (UPU) and the pioneering International Telegraphic Union (ITU). The latter was established in 1865 in Paris, in the rudimentary form of a regulatory convention without much institutional provisions, but already agreeing on the need to revise the regime regularly, and agreeing on the date and place of the next meeting.[12] This next meeting was to be held in 1868, in Vienna, and it was here that a small administrative secretariat (known as the Bureau Internationale des Administration Télégraphiques) was created. This was given the mandate to take measures 'propres à faciliter, dans un intérêt commun, l'exécution et l'application de la Convention' and to that end empowered to centralize information relating to telegraphy, edit telegraphic rates, collect statistics, conduct studies and produce a publication.[13]

As this brief summation indicates, the ITU, like other international organizations, was envisaged to serve its member states – nothing more. And, in this light, the absence of such qualities as international legal personality makes sense. International legal personality was rarely considered necessary or useful in order to allow the organization to act on the international plane, for the excellent reason that the organization was never expected to act on that

10 See the discussion of the so-called will theory in J. Klabbers, *An Introduction to International Organizations Law*, 4th ed. (Cambridge University Press, 2022), 46–50.

11 C. Wickremasinghe, *The Jurisdictional Immunities of International Organisations and Their Officials*. Doctoral Thesis, London School of Economics, 2003, at 23, referring to the constitutions of the African Development Bank, IFAD and ICSID as well as the agreement on privileges and immunities of the International Criminal Court.

12 1865 Convention Télégraphique, article 56.

13 1868 Convention Télégraphique Internationale Révisée à Vienne, article 61. Article 61 was the only article dealing with the Bureau.

international plane – so why endow it with something it does not need and is expected never to be in need of?

There was one seeming exception though, popular for a few years and in particular in Italian legal circles. Thus, there are some writings from the 1930s and even some case-law on international legal personality, but on closer scrutiny this does little to undermine the point that international legal personality was rarely, if ever, explicitly granted, and was rarely, if ever, explicitly granted because it was considered unnecessary to engage in activities on the international plane. The idea informing this Italian approach was different: international legal personality was not something that an organization was explicitly endowed with, but rather something that followed from institutional design. If the organization was considered sufficiently autonomous from its member states, it was considered to possess international legal personality. Decisive was thus not an explicit grant of personality, in this view, but whether the organization would have some independence vis-à-vis its member states.

The argument is sometimes traced to an Italian public law author called Guido Fusinato, writing on the International Institute of Agriculture (IIA) in 1914,[14] and was most explicitly endorsed in the classic *Profili* case, decided in 1931. Mr Profili had been working for the IIA, based in Rome, and upon being dismissed he sued the IIA for compensation. Both the court of first instance and the court of appeal argued they had the jurisdiction to decide, as the IIA was not a subject of international law – it was not a state. The Court of Cassation, however, begged to differ. It characterized the IIA as an autonomous organization, 'removed from the interference of any one State of the Union'. Thus, the IIA was 'free, as regards its internal affairs, from interference by the States composing the Union'. Though the IIA could have subjected itself to some other legal order, for example, with a view to settling labour disputes, it had not done so, with the result that the IIA legal order was

[14] He is referred to by Bederman, noting that Fusinato was 'vigorously arguing' that the IIA possessed international legal personality based on autonomy, prompting an 'equally spirited rebuttal' by Anzilotti. See D. Bederman, 'The Souls of International Organizations: Legal Personality and the Lighthouse at Cape Spartel' (1996) 36 *Virginia Journal of International Law* 275, 347. Both Fusinato and Anzilotti wrote in the *Rivista di Diritto Internazionale* of 1914. Fusinato apparently held that only states could be real persons in international law and, thus, ascribed a kind of quasi-personality ('civil international personality') to the IIA; see R. Portmann, *Legal Personality in International Law* (Cambridge University Press, 2010), 97–98. Portmann does not discuss how Fusinato derived personality but remains content with classifying him in the 'only states are legal persons' group. Fusinato's position was echoed by G. Marchegianno, 'The Juristic Character of the International Commission of Cape Spartel Lighthouse' (1931) 25 *American Journal of International Law* 339–347, esp. 340.

considered to be 'self-contained', to use a word that later gained some traction, and should be in a position to decide on its own labour disputes.[15]

Several points are noteworthy. First, on the substance of the dispute, the Court's solution was awkward: it would mean that staff could only complain to the very authorities with whom they had a dispute. Not surprisingly, therefore, *Profili* is often seen as having provided impetus to the creation of international administrative tribunals. Second though, and more important for the present purposes, the notion of 'international legal personality' at stake in *Profili* was radically different from how that notion is commonly used. In common usage, international legal personality means something like having the possibility to engage in international affairs, and this is very clearly how it is used in the Articles on the Responsibility of International Organizations (ARIO);[16] in *Profili*, this was not of concern at all to the Court of Cassation, which used the phrase as a shorthand for 'autonomy' or, indeed, 'self-contained'.

The semantic confusion was eventually put to rest in 1949, when the ICJ suggested in *Reparation for Injuries* that international legal personality was a threshold for acting internationally.[17] In *Reparation*, the idea of personality as 'autonomy vis-à-vis member states' is completely absent. Instead, the ICJ is at pains to repeat that the UN is engaged in all sorts of activities on the international plane which can only be explained on the basis of the UN having international legal personality – such as the conclusion of treaties.[18] Throughout the opinion, the possibility of being active on the international plane is the topic of discussion when it comes to international personality, and this is even explicitly distinguished from the *Profili* approach. Where the UN, it is true, 'occupies a position in certain respects in detachment from its

[15] *International Institute of Agriculture* v *Profili*, 5 *Annual Digest* 413, at 414–415. See also Wickremasinghe, *Jurisdictional Immunities*, 17, agreeing that what was decisive in *Profili* was the idea of the IIA acting autonomously, independently from member state intervention.

[16] ARIO defines an international organization as an entity with international legal personality and, for the purposes of attributing responsibility to an international organization (if at all . . .), this makes sense; otherwise one has to rely on notions such as 'joint criminal enterprise', used in connection with the criminal responsibility of individuals but difficult to think of in connection with international organizations. Useful is N. Jain, *Perpetrators and Accessories in International Criminal Law: Individual Modes of Responsibility for Collective Crimes* (Hart, 2014).

[17] See also A. Golia Jr and A. Peters, 'The Concept of International Organization', in J. Klabbers (ed.), *The Cambridge Companion to International Organizations Law* (Cambridge University Press, 2022), 25, 35 (viewing personality as a 'precondition' for holding rights and duties).

[18] Never mind that the Court's example was inaccurate: the UN is not, and never has been, a party to the 1946 General Convention on Privileges and Immunities of the United Nations. See *Reparation for Injuries Suffered in the Service of the United Nations*, [1949] ICJ Reports 174, 178.

Members',[19] it also goes further, and is expressly endowed with tasks on the international plane. In the end, the Court concludes, the UN 'could not carry out the intentions of its founders if it was devoid of international personality'.[20]

The very structure of argument in *Reparation* confirms as much. While the Court was not asked about personality but merely about whether the UN could bring a legal claim against a state, it nonetheless felt that it could not answer the questions before it without first addressing personality. Tellingly, it started by first enquiring into whether it could bring international legal action against a member state.[21] One might have thought that this could be decided as an internal organizational matter (this, after all, is what the Italian Court of Cassation had suggested in *Profili*), but the Court held otherwise: to invoke international law presupposes international personality, even vis-à-vis a member state. And this allowed it later to hold *a fortiori* that the UN possessed international personality, allowing it to act against non-members. On this point, the Court famously found that 'fifty States, representing the vast majority of the members of the international community, had the power, in conformity with international law, to bring into being an entity possessing objective international personality ...',[22] that is, personality opposable also against non-members, including the right to bring claims. The logic is clear: international legal personality functions as a threshold condition without which acts under international law are impossible, and is a status granted by the member states of the organization, either expressly ('Organization X shall have international legal personality') or implicitly, for example, by having the organization engage in acts on the international plane.[23]

So, with minor exceptions revolving around a different and inward-focused concept of international personality, the law for decades was clear. International organizations were never considered to need international legal personality: where there is no outside world to engage with, there is no need to establish legal facilities for such engagement either. It was only once the newly created United Nations lost staff in a setting involving a non-member state that the question of acting internationally seriously arose, forcing the International

[19] *Reparation*, 179.

[20] Ibid.

[21] '[T]he Court must first enquire whether the Charter has given the Organization such a position that it possesses, in regard to its Members, rights which it is entitled to ask them to respect. In other words, does the organization possess international personality?' Ibid., 178.

[22] Ibid., 185.

[23] What the Court missed in its construction is the circumstance that if an entity's personality is constituted by activities undertaken on the international plane, personality cannot simultaneously be a threshold condition: it is both declarative and constitutive, to employ language more often associated with statehood in international law.

Court of Justice to come to terms with the international legal personality of the UN in its *Reparation* opinion. And, even then, explicit grants of personality under international law remained rare: even the EEC could only be seen to have international legal personality after the poorly reasoned (nay, non-reasoned) decision of the ECJ in *ERTA*.[24] It was only the messy discussion surrounding the ostensible international legal personality of the EU, after Maastricht, which opened our eyes, with many arguing that, in the absence of a positive provision, the EU actually lacked international legal personality.[25] Surely, it cannot be the case that a newly created EU with a foreign and security policy and a nascent immigration policy would be devoid of international legal personality? That would be a ridiculous, dysfunctional outcome: it would either mean that the EU would be unable to act internationally (rendering its foreign and security policy a dead letter) or that the concept of international legal personality would be meaningless – neither outcome was considered plausible. So, once the EU's international legal personality had been confirmed, it became more common to endow organizations specifically with international legal personality, starting perhaps with the World Trade Organization.

By the same token, few international organizations had been given treaty-making powers: since there was no expectation of engagement with the outside world, there was no need for legal tools such as treaty-making competences to facilitate or channel such engagement either. As noted, though, the UN was in fact engaged in some treaty-making, something the ICJ inductively used as a justification for a finding of international personality.

Still, the first academic studies on treaty-making by international organizations only started to appear in the 1950s, for only after World War II did the realization sink in that the possibility of systematic contact with the outside world could be needed.[26] And it is likewise no surprise that few international organizations have well-developed procedures in their constituent documents with respect to treaty-making – the main exception (and not very representative) is the EU. For, while it is the case that many international organizations nowadays conclude treaties, with few of them is there a clear legal basis for

[24] Case 22/70, *Commission* v *Council (ERTA)*, ECLI:EU:C:1971:32.

[25] For an overview of that discussion, see J. Klabbers, 'Presumptive Personality: The European Union in International Law', in M. Koskenniemi (ed.), *International Law Aspects of the European Union* (Leiden: Martinus Nijhoff, 1998), 231.

[26] Those studies included S. Rosenne, 'United Nations Treaty Practice' (1954) 86 *Recueil des Cours* 275; K. Zemanek, *Das Vertragsrecht der internationalen Organisationen* (Vienna: Springer, 1957); J. W. Schneider, *Treaty-Making Power of International Organizations* (Droz, 1959).

doing so, and with even fewer is there a procedure outlined. It is usually highly uncertain which organ can conclude treaties on behalf of an organization; how consent is to be formed within the organization; whether the organization needs unanimity or majority on the part of its member states, et cetera. Such matters are rarely, if at all, regulated in the constitutions of international organizations, once more signifying that international organizations were never expected to enter regularly into international relations – the vacuum assumption.

Moreover, it became clear that, in some cases, even member states acting in a different capacity could constitute that outside world: peacekeeping, e.g., usually presupposes a mission agreement between the UN and one of its member states (the host state) and, likewise, headquarters agreements typically involve a member state as a treaty partner rather than merely as a member state – a situation which the International Court of Justice had great difficulties coming to terms with in 1980.[27]

In the latter case, it became clear that such a headquarters agreement is not solely a matter internal to the organization, but also implicates general international law. In the case at hand, the WHO could not terminate its agreement with Egypt at will; Egypt's position was protected under general international law through the *pacta sunt servanda* principle, despite the fact that Egypt was also a member state of the WHO. Egypt was both member state and third party (i.e., outside world), and this proved too difficult for the Court to handle. It found a pragmatic way to solve the dispute before it, allowing for termination upon respecting a period of notice, but found no principled answer.

Even the one seeming early exception, the League of Nations, proves the rule. It is not the case that the League was given international legal personality – it was not. Nor was it endowed with explicit treaty-making powers – it was not. But at least there was a glimpse of the outside world visible, possibly as a result of the broad mandate of the League and the idea that it could play a central role in international affairs. That there was an outside world is visible in the security provisions of the Covenant, occasionally envisaging a threat by a non-member state. It is dimly visible in the Article 8 Covenant, which recognizes the dangers posed by private enterprise producing weapons. It is visible in the Article 17 Covenant, addressing disputes with non-members or even amongst non-member states. And it is

[27] *Interpretation of the Agreement of 25 March 1951 between the WHO and Egypt*, advisory opinion, [1980] ICJ Reports 73.

visible in Article 24, suggesting that the existing international bureaux shall be placed in relationship with the League. Then again, Article 20, the supremacy clause, does its best to exclude the outside world, noting that the League of Nations Covenant shall abrogate conflicting treaties, though only in relations between members *inter se*.

This latter point is interesting, for it suggests that the structure of international law, based as it is on sovereign states, offered no other available avenues: the League cannot decide on the legal position of non-members and thus cannot abrogate treaties to which non-members are parties; at best, it can declare such treaties inapplicable as far as its member states are concerned.[28] *Profili* too suggests a world in which only states can act on the international plane and be subjects of international law. Alternative possibilities can only be discussed once the thought to do so has arisen – the unthinkable first has be thought prior to being capable of being reflected in legal instruments. The very structure of international law, revolving around states, created what may loosely be called a 'path dependency': it steered thinking into one direction rather than another.

1.3 THE VACUUM IN ACTION

The vacuum assumption was, to be sure, never a very accurate description of sociological reality. In real life, international organizations occasionally used to engage the outside world (e.g., the International Commission of Cape Spartel Lighthouse joined a convention in the 1930s[29]) and, while explicit grants of international legal personality to international organizations have long been very rare, as the *Profili* case indicates this has not stopped courts on occasion from reading international legal personality into the constitutions: an 'implied grant', derived from the posited autonomy of the organization vis-à-vis its member states.[30]

This reflects, on one level, the fundamentally ambivalent nature of international organizations: they are simultaneously vehicles for member states (agents for their principals) and autonomous, independent actors. The dominant thinking has always stressed the first approach (and this still colours

[28] A recent version of the same problem can be found in article 351 TEU, on conflicts between the obligations of EU members under EU law and under treaties concluded before they joined the EU. For discussion, see J. Klabbers, *Treaty Conflict and the European Union* (Cambridge University Press, 2008).

[29] For more details, see Bederman, 'Lighthouse at Cape Spartel'.

[30] *Profili*.

much of the thinking in International Relations scholarship[31]), but on occasion the second has shone through and is, arguably, shining through more strongly in recent decades.[32] But, for all this, the law has struggled to follow suit. Increased autonomy (autonomy from the member states, that is) implies a fundamental re-orientation of the principal–agent relationship, and entails that legal doctrine come to terms with the increased importance of those parts of organizations where the member states have little traction, in particular the secretariats. After all, typically member states are represented in the other organs (the plenary, the executive where such exists, and various sub-organs and sub-committees), but not so much in the secretariats. Hence, any shift towards the exercise of independent authority by secretariats can be seen (absent strict delegation by plenary or member states acting collectively to the secretariat) as a shift away from member states' authority. Organizational sociology and related scholarship[33] have started to think about this, but international lawyers have thus far been hard-pressed to think about what this means for international organizations law.[34]

If it is clear that international organizations act on the international level, albeit often without a clear mandate, it is also abundantly evident that they do affect the outside world, in manifold ways. They allocate material costs and benefits to companies and industries, for example, and help regulate markets;[35] they set standards for the protection of individuals;[36] they affect

[31] As recently as 2014, Johnson could proudly note to finally introduce IR scholarship to international organizations as something other than only the aggregate of member state preferences. See T. Johnson, *Organizational Progeny* (Oxford University Press, 2014).

[32] This is recognized in recent literature. See, e.g., R. Collins and N. White (eds.), *International Organizations and the Idea of Autonomy* (Routledge, 2011), or J. Klabbers and P. Koutrakos (eds.), 'An Anatomy of Autonomy', (2019) 88 *Nordic Journal of International Law* (special issue).

[33] M. Barnett and M. Finnemore, *Rules for the World: International Organizations in Global Governance* (Cornell University Press, 2004); A. Littoz-Monnet (ed.), *The Politics of Expertise in International Organizations: How International Bureaucracies Produce and Mobilize Knowledge* (Routledge, 2017); O. J. Sending, *The Politics of Expertise: Competing for Authority in Global Governance* (University of Michigan Press, 2017).

[34] Useful descriptive work has been done by J. Mathiason, *Invisible Governance: International Secretariats in Global Politics* (Kumarian Press, 2007) but the relative autonomy of secretariats has yet to leave its imprint on such topics as law-making by international organizations. An attempt is J. Klabbers, 'The Normative Gap in International Organizations Law: The Case of the World Health Organization' (2019) 16 *International Organizations Law Review* 272.

[35] Seminal is C. Murphy, *International Organization and Industrial Change: Global Governance since 1850* (Polity, 1994).

[36] J. Klabbers, 'An Accidental Revolution: The ILO and the Opening Up of International Law', in T. Halonen and U. Liukkunen (eds.), *International Labour Organization and Global Social Governance* (Dordrecht: Springer, 2020), 123.

the space for exercises of authority by local government;[37] they collaborate and compete with each other.[38] But this merely means that there was, and still is, a wide gap between the legal framework and social reality – regardless of how exactly that social reality is described.

Since the law is based on underlying frames which assume the vacuum described in Section 1.1, the law as it stands has few structural possibilities to come to terms with the role of any actor that is not a member state. Whether it concerns the position of non-member states, other international organizations, individuals or companies, cities or other actors, the law is structurally unable to address matters related to the position of these others. And this, in turn, has profound ramifications when it comes to discussing inclusive governance by international organizations, public–private partnerships involving international organizations, the legal protection of staff members against the organization they work for or the accountability of international organizations towards third parties.

So, what to do? A more realistic account of the law of international organizations would have to start by lifting the vacuum assumption. It was probably never all that realistic to begin with, and surely has been by-passed by developments. After all, no doubts exist about the international legal personality of international organizations. There are (muted) debates still ongoing about whence this personality springs, but not about the possibility of personality, and drafters of constituent documents can end all uncertainty by explicitly endowing their creatures with personality. For better or worse: if the constitution of an international organization provides that the organization 'shall have international legal personality', then the matter is effectively closed – even if the organization never actually acts on the international level.[39] What seemed tricky a century ago has become respectable since – it is just that the theory has lagged behind.

Likewise, the capacity of international organizations to conclude treaties is not in doubt, and was recognized, if still necessary, by the conclusion of the 1986 Vienna Convention on the Law of Treaties with or between International Organizations.[40] After all, such a convention would be unthinkable in a world where international organizations lack treaty-making powers. What is often in doubt are the specific treaty-making powers of international

37 M. Tushnet, *The New Constitutional Order* (Princeton University Press, 2003).

38 B. Faude, *Von Konkurrenz zu Arbeitsteilung: Komplexität und Dynamik im Zusammenspiel internationaler Institutionen* (Campus, 2015).

39 This would then constitute yet another dissonance with social reality: the 'empty' legal person.

40 Note also its preambular consideration 'that international organizations possess the capacity to conclude treaties . . .'.

organizations: not all have been granted such powers, and there is an understanding (another assumption perhaps) that they cannot conclude treaties without a proper competence to do so. This competence, moreover, is usually assumed to be limited to the function(s) granted to the organization concerned.

Again, practice has found pragmatic answers. Where a proper treaty-making power is lacking or where the organization wants to engage in collaboration beyond its proper competences, often resort is had to the instrument of the Memorandum of Understanding (MoU). Such MoUs are supposed to be non-legally binding and, thus, so the argument probably goes (it is rarely made explicit), neither require a proper legal basis nor a specific treaty-making competence. Hence, MoUs allow international organizations to engage in all manner of arrangements with states, both member states and third states, as well as other parties, and the landscape of organizational agreements is filled with all sorts of arrangements for which no proper legal basis can be discerned. Not all of these are of great salience. Surely, an agreement between the International Labour Organization (ILO) and the World Trade Organization (WTO) to co-organize a seminar on the relationship between labour issues and trade is not to be considered of great significance: it creates few, if any, obligations or legitimate expectations (whether in law or otherwise),[41] and will be seen by many to perform a useful task. So why bother?

There is one seemingly curious exception to be found in quite a few constitutions of international organizations, and that is a clause that the organization concerned is given the power to cooperate with organizations working in the same or similar policy-domains. An example is article 10 UPU, added, it seems, in 1964:

> Afin d'assurer une coopération étroite dans le domaine postal international, l'Union peut collaborer avec les organisations internationales ayant des intérêts et des activités connexes.[42]

A similar clause can be found in quite a few organizational instruments but does not signify a deep realization of there being a world outside the member

[41] An MoU cannot create legal obligations without becoming self-contradictory, a point lost on most proponents. See, for example, Aust, suggesting that MoUs can generate legal effects through legitimate expectations or estoppel: A. Aust, 'The Theory and Practice of Informal International Instruments' (1986) 35 *International and Comparative Law Quarterly* 787. On the jurisprudential paucity of the concept, see J. Klabbers, 'Governance by Academics: The Invention of Memoranda of Understanding', (2020) 80 *Zeitschrift für ausländisches öffentliches Recht und Völkerrecht* 35.

[42] 'To ensure close cooperation in the international postal domain, the Union may collaborate with international organizations having related interests and activities' (translation, JK).

states; instead, it actually taps into the vacuum assumption, and possibly even strengthens it. It does so by highlighting the need for functional cooperation, as it is invariably limited to collaboration in the same or related policy domains. There is a bureaucratic logic at work here: those with expertise in postal matters can learn from (or teach) those in related domains and so enhance the quality of their own work, and perhaps the old functionalist dream has proved inspirational too, hoping for collaborative spill-over leading to universal peace.[43] But it stops far short from accepting that organizations have effects outside the universe of member states. Yet this is precisely where collective action would be needed and is actively taking place: not so much between the WTO and the World Customs Organization (active in broadly the same policy domain), but rather between the WTO and the ILO, or the WTO and environmental organizations, or the ILO and the International Maritime Organization (IMO) when it comes to labour issues at sea, or the ILO and International Organization for Migration (IOM) on migrant labour. It is this kind of cooperation which requires a proper legal basis.

This requirement partly follows ideational considerations: where the rule of law is cherished, it seems inconsistent to exclude the work of international organizations. But there is more to it: the requirement of a proper legal basis for *inter se* cooperation between organizations follows from the same general logic which so dominates the law of international organizations. The idea is, after all, that the member states instruct the organization – the member states delegate powers and tasks. While it is perfectly acceptable to do so while leaving some discretion to the agent, nonetheless the agent should not be in a position to make up its own instructions, for instance to collaborate with entities active in different domains. Or rather, put differently, in a situation where the agent largely decides on his or her own powers, the very principal/agent model may need reconsideration.

1.4 BEYOND THE VACUUM

A proper understanding of international organizations law, it would seem, needs to break through the vacuum assumption. As it is, the thinking underpinning international organizations law is better seen as ideology than as

[43] This functionalism is usually associated with political scientists, such as D. Mitrany, *A Working Peace System* (Royal Institute for International Affairs, 1943). For a brilliant dissection, see J. K. De Vree, *Political Integration: The Formation of Theory and Its Problems* (Mouton, 1972).

theory.[44] And yet, academic theories are usually expected to have some explanatory value – to be more than ideology. As it stands, the dominant functionalist theory has very little explanatory value and has zero explanatory value when it comes to addressing matters that cannot be directly traced to the relation between the organization and its member states.[45]

So, the vacuum needs to be pierced – that much is clear. Any decent theory of international organizations would have to start by describing the twenty-first century reality that international organizations interact not just with their member states but also with others. It is obvious, for example, that organizations often need to interact with states beyond the circle of members. If the Organization for Economic Cooperation and Development (OECD) wants to have any chance of success with its global tax initiative (the Base Erosion and Profit Shifting initiative), it will need to enlist non-OECD members: its 38 member states cannot on their own create a universal regime. Likewise, UN sanctions demand the cooperation of non-member states and others (such as the EU[46]), something actually envisaged in the UN Charter (Article 2, §6) and given a voice by the ICJ in its *Namibia* opinion, holding that it was 'incumbent' on all states – not just UN-members – to give effect to Security Council resolutions.[47]

International organizations also collaborate with each other, often, as mentioned, through MoUs, and often without a proper legal basis. In some cases, this takes the form of joint ventures – think Codex Alimentarius Commission, Intergovernmental Panel on Climate Change or World Food Programme. More often it assumes ad hoc forms or temporary forms of cooperation (e.g., during crises) but, nonetheless, the lack of attention in the literature is striking.[48]

44 J. Klabbers, 'What Role for International Organizations in the Promotion of Community Interests? Reflections on the Ideology of Functionalism', in E. Benvenisti and G. Nolte (eds.), *Community Interests across International Law* (Oxford University Press, 2018), 86.

45 For lengthy discussion, see J. Klabbers, 'The EJIL Foreword: The Transformation of International Organizations Law' (2015) 26 *European Journal of International Law* 9.

46 See, for example, G. Sullivan, *The Law of the List: UN Counterterrorism Sanctions and the Politics of Global Security Law* (Cambridge University Press, 2020).

47 See *Legal Consequences for States of the Continued Presence of South Africa in Namibia (South West Africa) Notwithstanding Security Council Resolution 276 (1970)*, advisory opinion, [1971] ICJ Reports 16.

48 But see E. Lagrange, 'Les relations entre les organisations internationales', in M. Vellano (ed.), *Il Futuro delle Organizzazioni Internazionali: Prospettive Giuridiche* (Scientifica, 2015) 131; J. Dunoff, 'Is Sovereign Equality Obsolete? Understanding Twenty-First Century International Organizations', (2012) 43 *Netherlands Yearbook of International Law* 99; R. Urueña, 'Interaction between International Organizations', in J. Klabbers (ed.), *The Cambridge Companion to International Organizations Law* (Cambridge University Press, 2022), 222. The

Perhaps most interesting of all is the cooperation with the private sector. This can take several forms. In particular in the medical field this takes the form of so-called public–private partnerships: entities set up with both international organizations and corporations or private foundations as participants – examples include GAVI, the Alliance and the Global Fund, both involving the World Health Organization as well as the Bill and Melinda Gates Foundation.[49] The recent COVAX initiative again involved the private sector, while much of the fund-raising is outsourced to the Coalition for Epidemic Preparedness Initiatives (CEPI), a foundation based in Oslo.

It can also simply involve the acceptance of private donations by international organizations: UNHCR depends on voluntary donations for some 10 per cent of its annual budget (large donors include Proctor and Gamble), while the Bill and Melinda Gates Foundation is one of the most generous contributors to the WHO. The 2022 meeting of the Conference of the Parties to the Kyoto Protocol, moreover (known as COP 27) was sponsored by none other than Coca-Cola, involved in activities often considered environmentally harmful, such as the large-scale use of plastics.

It can also be the case that an organization itself operates on the market and sells products and services. This can be fairly innocent, such as the Christmas cards sold for UNICEF, but can also take on more serious forms: a prime example is that of the IOM offering its services in the field of migration management to member states or, as some would have it, doing the dirty work that its members do not want to do themselves.[50]

It also needs to be acknowledged that the decisions of international organizations can have distributive effects. This helps explain why the tobacco lobby was actively targeting the WHO around the turn of the millennium: the WHO was about to sponsor its 2003 Framework Convention on Tobacco Control – to date the only convention concluded under its auspices.[51] Likewise, pharmaceutical companies know the route to the WHO and

first, as far as I am aware, to devote some attention to relations between international organizations, was F. Morgenstern, *Legal Problems of International Organizations* (Grotius, 1986).

49 See generally L. Andonova, *Governance Entrepeneurs: International Organizations and the Rise of Global Public–Private Partnerships* (Cambridge University Press, 2017); C. Clinton and D. Sridhar, *Governing Global Health* (Oxford University Press, 2017).

50 J. Klabbers,'Notes on the Ideology of International Organizations Law: The International Organization for Migration, State-Making, and the Market for Migration' (2019) 32 *Leiden Journal of International Law* 383.

51 An earlier attempt to sponsor a convention on the marketing of breast milk substitutes came to nothing following industry pressure and eventually became a non-binding recommendation. See Y. Beigbeder, *The World Health Organization* (Martinus Nijhoff, 1998), 75–83.

complain that the WHO is either too quick in announcing a public health emergency of international concern or not quick enough – depending on whether their vaccines are ready to be marketed. By the same token, telecommunications operators participate in some of the work of the ITU,[52] whereas energy companies tend to be represented at meetings of the International Atomic Energy Agency.

The long and the short is that international organizations no longer live in a vacuum, if they ever did. The vacuum assumption, holding that the only relevant concern is the relationship between the organization and its member states, needs to be lifted. It may have had some plausibility a century and a half ago – it is not immediately obvious, for example, why the Bureau International des Poids et Mesures (BIPM) should interact with others. The BIPM is the textbook example, perhaps, of the international organization as a purely administrative agency, engaged in a limited task. But, leaving the BIPM aside, international organizations have always affected third parties and will continue to do so – and of course the standardization work of the BIPM also affects third parties: that is its very point. In such a setting, any theory of international organizations law needs to take this into account.

There are additional elements that a plausible theory should bear in mind.[53] It should take note of the fact that international organizations are not just 'international', but are also 'organizations', and function much like other organizations: they regulate, they monitor and manage and they distribute costs and benefits. Such a theory should start with the function, rather than end with it: all organizations have a *telos*,[54] even states – although in states the function aligns with the community (the nation), something absent in international organizations.[55] It should be historically sensitive, and take into account such events as the decolonization process or the Cold War and its end.[56] It should draw on insights from institutional economics, from ethnography, from public administration and organizational sociology and other academic disciplines. And it should not forget its legal character: the

[52] For a discussion, see J. Klabbers, 'Reflections on the International Telecommunication Union: International Organizations as Epistemic Structures', in A. Bianchi and M. Hirsch (eds.), *International Law's Invisible Frames* (Oxford University Press, 2021) 200.

[53] This draws on J. Klabbers, 'Towards a Political Economy of International Organizations Law' (2023) 20 *International Organizations Law Review* 82.

[54] S. Miller, *The Moral Foundations of Social Institutions* (Cambridge University Press, 2010).

[55] See G. Poggi, *The Development of the Modern State: A Sociological Introduction* (Stanford University Press, 1978).

[56] This is missing from much rationalist theorizing, even the highly sophisticated study by L. Hooghe, T. Lenz, and G. Marks, *A Theory of International Organization* (Oxford University Press, 2019).

world around us is influenced by existing legal structures and in turn influences those structures.[57] One cannot understand the work of international organizations without at least a basic understanding of international organizations law: of how the implied powers doctrine operates, how functional necessity affects the operation of privileges and immunities,[58] how financing takes place, et cetera. Without an understanding of how international organizations are legally structured, the understanding of their work can only be distorted – and, by the same token, a law ultimately based on the vacuum assumption is incapable of generating a solid understanding of international organizations themselves.

1.5 FINALLY

The chapters in this volume can be divided into three groups. A first group discusses the interactions – or aspects thereof – between international organizations and their various partners. These can be non-member states (Fernando Lusa Bordin, Chapter 2), other international organizations (René Urueña, Chapter 3), consultancy firms (Hans-Wolfgang Micklitz and Evgenia Ralli, Chapter 4), cities (Helmut Philipp Aust, Chapter 5) or professional associations (Rebecca Schmidt, Chapter 6). A second group discusses aspects of this kind of relationships, in particular with a view to their role in creating and shaping markets (Elisabetta Morlino, Chapter 7), their market activities (Ukri Soirila, Chapter 8), private sector funding of international organizations (Tleuzhan Zhunussova, Chapter 9) and the distributive or redistributive effects of the work of international organizations (Sebastian Machado, Chapter 10). Finally, a third group aims to connect the worldly activities of international organizations to broader issues: the theory of private law (Orfeas Chasapis Tassinis, Chapter 11), organizational *praxis* (Eelco Szabó, Chapter 12) and ramifications of governance (Dimitri van der Meerssche, Chapter 13). A brief epilogue by the editor concludes the volume.

57 See, e.g., Kratochwil, *Praxis*.

58 Seminal is M. Singer, 'Jurisdictional Immunity of International Organizations: Human Rights and Functional Necessity Concerns' (1995) 36 *Virginia Journal of International Law* 53.

2

How International Organizations Affect the Legal Position of Non-Members

FERNANDO LUSA BORDIN

2.1 INTRODUCTION

International organizations are typically viewed as mechanisms for enhancing cooperation among states that share common goals, such as maintaining international peace and security, protecting and promoting human health or achieving greater prosperity by establishing closer economic ties. By resorting to institutional frameworks where collective decisions can be made and delegating some authority to independent secretariats and dispute settlement mechanisms, states can overcome some of the inefficiencies and costs of unilateral action in a decentralized political system.[1] It is, thus, no surprise that much scholarship focuses on what happens *within* international organizations.

At the same time, in pursuing their purposes and fulfilling their functions those organizations are often required to engage with the outside world by conducting 'external relations' with non-member states and non-member international organizations on the international plane.[2] Those external relations may be sporadic, arising in unexpected ways from the functioning of an organization over time, or they may constitute a core element of the

I would like to think José Alvarez, Julian Arato, Eyal Benvenisti, Kristina Daugirdas, Daniel Halberstam, Sarah Nouwen, Andrew Sanger, and Sandesh Sivakumaran for their valuable comments on drafts of this chapter. All errors remain my own.

[1] For an influential account, see K. Abbott and D. Snidal, 'Why Do States Act through Formal International Organizations' (1998) 42 *Journal of Conflict Resolution* 3.

[2] And, indeed, with other entities, both governmental and non-governmental. The relations with which this chapter is mainly concerned are those of international organizations with non-member states/international organizations or comparable entities. Relations with other entities are covered elsewhere in this volume.

organization's mandate. Either way, by interacting with the outside world, international organizations end up affecting it.

The myriad forms in which organizations relate with non-members on the international plane form a rich universe for sociological, political and legal study. Rather than attempting to provide a systematic account of those relations, let alone a comprehensive one, what I propose to do in this chapter is to offer some reflections on how international organizations may affect the legal position of non-members by either imposing rules on them or exporting rules to them. To borrow José Alvarez's phrase, the chapter considers the 'external ripples' of 'internal law' of international organizations.[3]

To that end, it is convenient to distinguish between universal international organizations (UIOs) and regional international organizations (RIOs), for the size of membership and the character of the goals pursued may determine how the organization engages with the outside world. UIOs may show a tendency to impose rules on non-members in ways that put into question and potentially reshape the structural principles that underpin the international legal system. In contrast, RIOs tend to persuade non-members to adopt rules by enlisting their consent and cooperation, though not without raising specific normative concerns in the process. To substantiate these broad insights, the chapter turns to practices stemming from the United Nations (UN) and the International Criminal Court (ICC) (Section 2.2) and from the Organization for Economic Co-operation and Development (OECD) and the European Union (EU) (Section 2.3).

It must be conceded from the outset that not all or even most UIOs or RIOs maintain significant external relations, let alone attempt to affect the legal position of non-members.[4] The analysis provided here does not seek, therefore, to offer an account of how the average international organization attempts to shape the outside world. Rather, by focusing on organizations that stand out for the ambition of their purposes, the extent of their powers or their capability to engage non-members, I offer some elements for appraising the potential legal and normative impacts of the use of a distinct legal construct, that of the international organization. The value of considering more 'extreme' examples, even when they may seem somewhat unique in the current institutional landscape, is that it allows us to assess the extent that

3 I borrow this term from J. E. Alvarez, *International Organizations as Law-Makers* (Oxford University Press, 2005), 143–146.

4 For a comparative analysis, see F. L. Bordin et al., *Final Report of the ILA Study Group on the International Law of Regional Organizations* (International Law Association, 2024).

collective action through international organizations changes not only international cooperation but also the international legal system itself.

2.2 UNIVERSAL INTERNATIONAL ORGANIZATIONS ENGAGING NON-MEMBERS

2.2.1 *Legal Effects of Decisions of UIOs Addressed at Non-Members*

International organizations of a universal character, when understood as institutions whose 'membership and responsibilities are on a worldwide scale',[5] may have little opportunity to maintain external relations. If they are successful in attracting large swathes of the international community, there are few non-members with whom they can interact on the international plane. Yet, the goal of universal membership is not always straightforward, and, on its way towards it, an organization may have to deal with a considerable number of non-members. In the case of the UN, 51 original members adopted the Charter, leaving several states to seek admission at a later stage.[6] Between 1950 and 1955, due to Cold War politics, no new members were allowed to join the organization, until the 'logjam' was broken with the admission of 16 states, paving the way for the UN to embrace universality of membership in its practice for the years ahead.[7] Moreover, full universality of membership may be impossible to achieve. Even when an organization becomes universal in the sense that it manages to attract (almost) all existing states, a small outside world will remain in the form of new states and other international organizations and entities that do not qualify for membership.

The external relations that UIOs maintain are marked by a particular challenge: how to perform 'responsibilities on a worldwide scale' without

[5] The 1975 Vienna Convention on the Representation of States in their Relations with International Organizations of a Universal Character defines, in Article 2(1)(2), 'international organization of a universal character' as 'the United Nations, its specialized agencies, the International Atomic Energy Agency and any similar organization whose membership and responsibilities are on a worldwide scale'.

[6] It is easy to forget that the UN Charter does not require universality of membership, rather reserving admission to 'peace-loving states which accept the obligations contained in the … Charter and, in the judgment of the Organization', to be jointly exercised by the Security Council and the General Assembly, 'are able and willing to carry out these obligations': UN Charter, Art. 4.

[7] For a comprehensive study of the evolution of thinking and practice within the UN, see T. Grant, *Admission to the United Nations: Charter Article 4 and the Rise of Universal Organization* (Martinus Nijhoff, 2009).

having legal authority over the whole world? In other words, how can they coach non-members into supporting – or at least not impeding – the fulfilment of their universal goals and functions? Article 2(6) of the UN Charter provides a fascinating case study of an UIO identifying and raising this challenge. It prescribes that '[t]he Organization shall ensure that states which are not Members of the United Nations act in accordance with these Principles so far as may be necessary for the maintenance of international peace and security'. In the words of Hans Kelsen, an influential early commentator, '[t]his provision is a consequence of the fact that the purpose of the United Nations ... is not only to maintain peace within the Organisation but within the whole international community, that is to say: to maintain world peace'.[8]

But what can a UIO like the UN legally do to ensure that non-members act in accordance with its principles? The legal effect of Article 2(6) has been the subject of academic debate. Does it impose obligations on non-members, or does it merely create an obligation for the organization itself to take action that ensures that non-members refrain from threatening or using force in international relations and settle disputes peacefully? In either case, does Article 2 (6) provide a legal basis for the organization to use military force against a non-member? Kelsen has provocatively suggested that, if one accepts that Chapter VII action against a non-member is possible, '[t]he Charter attaches a sanction to a certain behaviour of non-Members', thus constituting a 'true obligation of non-Members to observe the contrary behaviour'.[9] But the extrapolation that Article 2(6) creates legal obligations for non-members runs into a major obstacle of principle: it contravenes the *pacta tertiis nec nocent nec prosunt* rule, according to which a treaty does not impose rights or obligations on a third party absent its consent.[10] In a system based on sovereign equality, states cannot make an agreement for the purpose of imposing obligations on third parties.[11] That is why mainstream commentary tends to emphasize that the

8 H. Kelsen, *The Law of the United Nations: A Critical Analysis of Its Fundamental Problems* (Stevens and Sons, 1950), 106.

9 Ibid., 107 (though, as will be seen, Kelsen's position is more nuanced).

10 See Art. 34, 1969 Vienna Convention on the Law of Treaties.

11 As stated in the *Friendly Relations Declaration*, sovereign equality entails that states 'have equal rights and duties and are equal members of the international community, notwithstanding differences of an economic, social, political and cultural systems', and, in particular, that states are 'juridically equal', enjoy 'the rights inherent in full sovereignty', and have 'the duty to respect the personality of other States': UNGA Res 2625(XXV) (1970). From that it follows that, as a default proposition, the legal position of a state may not be affected by majoritarian decision-making.

only addressee of Article 2(6) is the UN itself.[12] A corollary of that proposition is that, in its relations with non-members, the UN is constrained by the rules of general international law.[13] It follows that enforcement action against non-members in cases of individual or collective self-defence would be lawful, but that the proactive use of military force to address threats to international peace and security more generally would be proscribed unless a rule of general international law could be invoked in its support.

This cautious interpretation of Article 2(6) is borne out by the International Court of Justice's advisory opinion in *Namibia*. In Resolution 276 (1970), the Security Council had called upon 'all States ... to refrain from any dealings with the Government of South Africa' that would be inconsistent with its finding that 'the continued presence of the South African authorities in Namibia [was] illegal'.[14] Considering the legal consequences of that resolution for non-member states, the Court found that 'the termination of the Mandate [by the UN General Assembly] and the declaration of the illegality of South Africa's presence in Namibia [were] opposable to all States in the sense of barring *erga omnes* the legality of a situation which is maintained in violation of international law'.[15] That being the case, 'no State which [entered] into relations with South Africa concerning Namibia [could] expect the United Nations or its Members to recognize the validity or effects of such relationship, or of the consequences thereof'.[16] While the Court stated that it was for 'non-member States to act in accordance with those decisions',[17] that was not because the Charter imposed obligations on them. Indeed, the Court emphasized that non-members were 'not bound by Articles 24 and 25 of the Charter'.[18] The basis for the obligation lay instead in general international law. In the words of Judge Onyeama, '[t]he legal consequences for States [were] those which [flowed] automatically, under international law, from the unlawful continuation of South Africa's presence in Namibia'. They would

[12] See, e.g. J. Frowein, 'The United Nations and Non-Member States', (1970) 25 *International Journal* 333, 337–338; K. Widdows, 'Security Council Resolutions and Non-Members of the United Nations' (1978) 27 *International and Comparative Quarterly* 459, 460–461; and S. Talmon, 'Article 2(6)', in B. Simma et al. (eds.), *The Charter of the United Nations: A Commentary* (Oxford University Press, 2012), 252, at 260–262.

[13] Talmon, 'Article 2(6)', 262.

[14] UNSC Res 276 (1970), operative clauses 2 and 5.

[15] *Legal Consequences for States of the Continued Presence of South Africa in Namibia (South West Africa) notwithstanding Security Council Resolution 276 (1970)*, Advisory Opinion, ICJ Reports 1971, para. 126.

[16] Ibid.

[17] Ibid.

[18] Ibid.

not 'extend to enforcement measures which may or may not be adopted by States individually, or the United Nations collectively, to remove South Africa from the Territory or to assert the authority of the United Nations over the Territory, in the absence of treaty provisions or a customary rule of international law requiring such measures to be adopted'.[19]

That said, the practice of the UN Security Council reveals a more complex self-understanding of the legal effects of Article 2(6) than the *Namibia* opinion suggests. Two resolutions close in time to the issuing of the opinion provide an illustration. In Resolution 314 (1972), adopted under Chapter VII, the Council urged 'all States to implement fully all Security Council resolutions establishing sanctions against Southern Rhodesia, in accordance with their obligations under Article 25 and Article 2, paragraph 6, of the Charter of the United Nations'.[20] The Council did not explain what those obligations under Article 2(6) were, but it evidently assumed their existence. In Resolution 418 (1977), also adopted under Chapter VII, the Council went as far as *deciding* that all states were to join an arms embargo against South Africa. A contemporaneous commentator who was sceptical of the view that Article 2(6) imposed obligations on non-members, nevertheless conceded that the language employed in Resolution 418 evinced an intention to bind them.[21]

Also of interest is the UNSC practice in relation to other international organizations, which arguably provide the most important focal point for the application for Article 2(6) nowadays. That those organizations do not qualify for UN membership has not stopped the Council from addressing them. There are no legal difficulties in the Council calling upon 'all States and all international and regional organizations, including the United Nations and its specialized agencies, to act strictly in accordance with [provisions imposing an arms embargo against the Taliban]', or '[encouraging] Interpol to intensify its efforts with respect to the foreign terrorist fighter threat and to recommend or put in place additional resources to support and encourage national, regional and international measures to monitor and prevent the transit of foreign terrorist fighters'.[22]

[19] *Legal Consequences for States of the Continued Presence of South Africa in Namibia*, Separate Opinion of Judge Onyeama, at 148. The Court's opinion in *Namibia* later became a key precedent for the International Law Commission's articulation, in Article 41 of the Articles on the Responsibility of States for Internationally Wrongful Acts, of the obligations of non-recognition and cooperation to put an end to serious breaches of *jus cogens* norms: ILC Yearbook 2001, vol II, Part Two, at 115.

[20] UNSC Res 314 (1972).

[21] Widdows, 'Security Council Resolutions', 462.

[22] UNSC Res 1333 (2000) and UNSC Res 2178 (2014).

But what if the Council were to 'decide' or 'demand' that an organization take a particular course of action?[23] Should that organization be viewed as bound by the UN Charter? In the *Kadi* case, the Court of First Instance of the European Community (now the EU) observed that:

> unlike its Member States, the Community as such is not directly bound by the Charter of the United Nations and that it is therefore not required, as an obligation of general public international law, to accept and carry out the decisions of the Security Council in accordance with Article 25 of that Charter. The reason is that the Community is not a member of the United Nations, or an addressee of the resolutions of the Security Council, or the successor to the rights and obligations of the Member States for the purposes of public international law.[24]

But this may not be the end of the matter, as suggested, for example, by the recent work of the International Law Commission on the law of international organizations. Article 67 of the 2011 Articles on the Responsibility of International Organizations (ARIO) is a saving clause providing that the Articles 'are without prejudice to the Charter of the United Nations'. In the commentary, the ILC observes that 'even if the prevailing effect of obligations under the Charter may have a legal basis for international organizations that differs from the legal basis applicable to States, one may reach the conclusion that the Charter of the United Nations also has a prevailing effect with regard to international organizations',[25] pointing to the Security Council's practice of not distinguishing between states and international organizations in ordering arms embargoes.

What then might be the differing legal basis for the Charter to have such a 'prevailing effect'? One possibility is for the UN to conclude treaties with the other organizations. For example, through Article VII of the Agreement

[23] In this connection, it is noteworthy that the Charter refers, in Chapter VII, to 'regional arrangements or agencies for dealing with such matters relating to the maintenance of international peace and security as are appropriate for regional action'. In particular, Article 53 prescribes that '[t]he Security Council shall, where appropriate, utilize such regional arrangements or agencies for enforcement action under its authority', provided that 'no enforcement action shall be taken under regional arrangements or by regional agencies without the authorization of the Security Council'. What the drafters of the Charter may not have foreseen, forever, is that such regional arrangements would take the form of entities with separate international legal personality which, by application of the normal rules of the law of treaties, could be regarded as third parties in relation to the Charter.

[24] Case T-315/01, *Kadi v. Council and Commission (Kadi I)*, ECLI:EU:T:2005:332, para. 192. On appeal, the European Court of Justice reversed the Court of First Instance's judgment, focusing solely on the question of the compatibility of sanctions with EU law, without pronouncing on the applicability of the Charter to the EU or on the possibility of reviewing UNSC resolutions under international law.

[25] (2011) *Yearbook of the International Law Commission*, vol. II, Part Two, at 104–105.

between the United Nations and the World Health Organization (WHO), the WHO 'agrees to co-operate with the [Security] Council in furnishing such information and rendering such assistance for the maintenance or restoration of international peace and security as the Security Council may request'.[26] But it could be argued more generally that other international organizations must comply with Chapter VII measures for the simple reason that they are entirely composed of UN member states that remain bound by the Charter when they act through those organizations. This view finds some support in the reasoning of the Court of First Instance in *Kadi*, according to which 'in so far as the powers necessary for the performance of the Member States' obligations under the Charter have been transferred to the [EU], the Member States have undertaken, pursuant to public international law, to ensure that the [EU] itself should exercise powers to that end'.[27] Or, as the Court said in another passage from the same judgment, perhaps '[by] conferring those powers on the [EU], the Member States demonstrated their will to bind it by the obligations entered into them under the Charter of the United Nations',[28] so that, even if the EU is not bound by the Charter as a party, it 'must be considered to be bound ... in the same way as its Member States, by virtue of the Treaty establishing it'.[29] The claim that the decision of the UN members to transfer to another organization powers in the field of international peace and security gives rise to an obligation to abide by the Charter under the internal law of that organization, if accepted, would no doubt contribute to ensuring that the organization act in accordance with UN principles in line with Article 2(6). In that scenario, however, the 'prevailing effect' of the Charter would be limited, as the UN has no standing under public international law to demand that other organizations comply with their own internal law. For the 'prevailing effect' to obtain under public international law, it is essential that those organizations owe the UN obligations on the international plane.

Pressure on Article 2(6) may likewise arise from the burgeoning practice of the Security Council to address its resolutions to non-state actors other than international organizations. In Resolution 1244 (1999), for example, the Council demanded that 'the [Kosovo Liberation Army] and other armed

[26] Article VII, Agreement between the United Nations and the World Health Organization (1948). Other relationship agreements are less committed. See, e.g., Article VI, Agreement between the United Nations and the International Monetary Fund (1947) (undertaking to 'have due regard for decisions of the Security Council under Article 41 and 42 of the United Nations Charter' and agreeing to 'assist the Security Council by furnishing to it information').

[27] *Kadi I*, para. 198.

[28] Ibid., para. 200.

[29] Ibid., paras. 192–193.

Kosovo Albanian groups end immediately all offensive actions and comply with the [applicable] requirements for demilitarization'. The International Court scrutinized that resolution in the *Kosovo* advisory opinion, where the question was posed whether the declaration of independence issued in 2008 was in accordance with the legal regime established for Kosovo by the Council. The Court recalled that 'it has not been uncommon for the Security Council to make demands on actors other than United Nations Member States and inter-governmental organizations'[30] but ultimately concluded that Resolution 1244 did not address a prohibition to declare independence to the authors of the declaration.[31] But a tricky question that the Court did not examine was whether the Security Council could have prohibited the authors of the declaration, whom it defined as 'persons who acted together in their capacity as representatives of the people of Kosovo outside the framework of the interim administration',[32] from attempting to secede from Serbia. In other words, may a UNSC Resolution as such create a prohibition on secession? The power of the Security Council to regulate the conduct of non-state actors can be justified as a transfer of jurisdiction from member states to the United Nations in cases where regulating the conduct of persons operating within a state may be required to maintain international peace and security. But what if said non-state actors have established – or are in the process of establishing – a new state? It follows from the reasoning of the Court in *Kosovo* itself that, under international law, the parent state may not make an attempt at secession invalid merely by opposing it.[33] If a member state cannot legally require 'representatives of the people' seeking to create a new state to stop, how can the Security Council presume to do so? Without engaging with those tricky questions, the Court seems to have assumed that the authors of the declaration of independence could have violated Resolution 1244 if only the resolution had been drafted differently.[34]

30 *Accordance with International Law of the Unilateral Declaration of Independence in Respect of Kosovo, Advisory Opinion*, ICJ Reports 2010, para. 116. For a helpful discussion of UNSC practice and the ability to bind non-state actors, see S. Murphy, 'Reflections on the ICJ Advisory Opinion on Kosovo: Interpreting Security Council Resolution 1244 (1999)', in M. Wood and M. Milanovic (eds.), *The Law and Politics of the Kosovo Advisory Opinion* (Oxford University Press, 2015), 134, 161–163.

31 *Kadi I*, paras. 117–118.

32 Ibid., para. 109.

33 Ibid., paras. 79–91 (where the Court concludes that there is no specific prohibition on declarations of independence under customary international law, and that 'the scope of the principle of territorial integrity is confined to the sphere of relations between States').

34 Indeed, the relevant section of the opinion is titled 'The question whether the authors of the declaration of independence acted in violation of Security Council resolution 1244 (1999) or the measures adopted thereunder'.

2.2.2 *Systemic Implications of UIOs' Aspiration to Regulate Non-Members*

The practice of the Security Council and the way it has been received suggest that there is more to the UN Charter and Article 2(6) than meets the eye. While Article 2(6) can be squared with the traditional law of treaties, there is a growing sense that the UN Charter enjoys some sort of special status allowing the Security Council to bind whomever it addresses in its Chapter VII decisions. That intuition shows in a fascinating yet somewhat overlooked decision of Trial Chamber III of the International Criminal Tribunal for the Former Yugoslavia (ICTY) in the *Milutinovic* case. The defence had sought to challenge the jurisdiction of the Tribunal by arguing that, when the alleged crimes were committed, the Federal Republic of Yugoslavia (FRY), today's Serbia, was not a UN member over which the UNSC could exercise authority.[35] The Trial Chamber concluded that, in the relevant period, the FRY could be regarded as a UN member for certain purposes, but also considered the alternative scenario where the FRY was viewed as a non-member. It started its analysis with the disclaimer that it was not 'necessary to pronounce on the general question of the application of the United Nations Charter to non-member States'.[36] The Chamber placed emphasis on the fact that the UNSC had the power to take action at the onset of the conflict in 1991, prior to the breakup of the former Yugoslavia. The main element of its reasoning was that it would be 'odd' if that power had been 'somehow lost in 1993 by the circumstance of the non-membership of the United Nations of any of the States that formerly constituted the SFRY'.[37] In a striking passage, the Chamber added that:

> The constitutional character of the Charter, its near universal membership, the critical importance to the international community of the goal of the maintenance of international peace and security, are all factors that combine to render the Chapter VII resolution establishing the Tribunal applicable to any country that was a part of the former SFRY, irrespective of its United Nations membership at the time of the adoption of that resolution, or at the time of the commission of the offences.[38]

That very much reads as a pronouncement on 'the general question of the application of the United Nations Charter to non-member States' – and one

35 The ICTY was created by UNSC Res 827 (1993).

36 *Prosecutor v Milutinović and others*, Decision on Motion Challenging Jurisdiction, Case No IT-99-37-PT, ICL 63 (ICTY 2003), para 55.

37 Ibid., paras. 55–61.

38 Ibid., para. 62.

which offers a very different account from that of the International Court in *Namibia*. The Charter, the Trial Chamber suggests, enjoys a special 'constitutional' status linked to the 'near universal membership' of the UN and the 'critical importance' of its mandate.

Commentators have tried to grapple with the potentially special status of the Charter in different ways. Bardo Fassbender attempts to explain it by appealing, as the Trial Chamber in *Milutinovic* did, to the Charter's constitutional character: 'the Charter, as the constitution of the international community, is binding on all subjects of international law'.[39] His way around the *pacta tertiis* objection is to propose a 'functional interpretation of the concept of sovereignty', according to which sovereign equality 'depends on a comprehensive prohibition of the use of force in international relations, and a working mechanism to implement and enforce this prohibition' such as that established by the Charter.[40] Another way of making sense of the Charter's special status is to argue, as Stefan Talmon does, that the system of collective security established by the UN Charter now forms part of customary international law. In his words:

> [t]he practice of UN organs . . ., the opinion expressed by member States, and the consistent and uniform practice of non-member states suggest that at least since the 1990s the provisions of the Charter dealing with international peace and security have acquired the status of rules of customary international law that are binding on non-members, both States and non-State actors alike, independently of the Charter.[41]

Neither of these approaches is entirely convincing. While the constitutionalist approach comes across as excessively deductive (Talmon criticises it as an instance of 'law-making by taxonomy'[42]), it is unclear whether treaty rules establishing an organ of an international organization possess the 'fundamentally norm-creating character' required for it to be 'regarded as forming the basis of a general rule of law'[43] or whether the practice of states since the 1990s would meet a rigorous application of the test of *opinio juris*. At the same time, dismissing Security Council practice and its progressive acceptance in the case law and academic commentary would be reductive. The difficulty to

39 B. Fassbender, *The United Nations Charter as the Constitution of the International Community* (Martinus Nijhoff, 2009), 150.

40 Ibid., 111–113.

41 Talmon, 'Article 2(6)', 279.

42 Ibid.

43 *North Sea Continental Shelf Cases (Germany/Denmark; Germany Netherlands)*, Judgment, [1969] ICJ Reports, para. 72.

come up with a clear legal account derives from the fact that, as Kelsen presciently observed in 1950, '[f]rom the point of view of existing international law, the attempt of the Charter to apply to states which are not contracting parties to it must be characterised as revolutionary', so that '[w]hether it will be considered as a violation of the old, or as the beginning of a new international law, remains to be seen'.[44] This appears to remain a situation of uncertainty in the law, even if practice around the Charter does confirm Kelsen's intuition that the Charter attempts to apply to non-members and if, at a time when almost all states are UN members, there seems to be little, if any, appetite to resist that attempt.

Whatever the most plausible legal position may be, Article 2(6) and UN practice vis-à-vis non-members provide a dramatic illustration of an aspiration that is latent in how UIOs engage the world. That is the aspiration to bend non-members to their will – or, in Kelsen's more decorous words, 'the tendency to be the law not only of the United Nations [or *a fortiori* of any other relevant organization] but also of the whole international community, that is to say, to be general, not only particular, international law'.[45] To some degree, every organization that seeks universality shows the potential to become a hegemonic project. The lengths to which they can or will go to impose their rules on the outside world will of course depend on the stakes involved – one does not find, for example, provisions analogous to Article 2 (6) in the constituent instruments of UN specialized agencies with technical mandates. There may also be organizations whose 'membership and responsibilities are on a worldwide scale' but which will neither need nor desire to impose their rules on non-parties, at least overtly. The World Trade Organization's avowed priority, for example, is to establish preferential relationships among 'members of the club' instead of enforcing a unitary trade regime on the whole world.[46] Be that as it may, when a majority of states seriously invested in pursuing a goal that demands universal adherence create an international organization, action geared towards making non-members comply may put pressure on the international legal system, raising the question of whether the rules of the organization apply only among members or whether they rather enjoy a special status, whether 'constitutional' or 'customary'.

44 Kelsen, *Law of the United Nations*, 110.

45 Ibid., 109.

46 Which is not to say that the practice of those organizations may not affect customary international law in meaningful ways. On the impact on custom of *ad hoc* arrangements that are often mistakenly viewed as mere *lex specialis*, see J. E. Alvarez, 'A BIT on Custom' (2009) 42 *New York University Journal of International Law and Politics* 17.

Another interesting (if less straightforward) example of this aspiration is provided by some of the decisions of the International Criminal Court[47] on whether state official immunity posed a procedural obstacle for the parties to the Rome Statute surrendering to the Court Omar al-Bashir, then head of state of Sudan. The question arose because Sudan is not a party to the Rome Statute – the situation had been referred to the ICC by the UN Security Council.[48] Article 27(2) of the Statute prescribes that '[i]mmunities or special procedural rules which may attach to the official capacity of a person, whether under national or international law, shall not bar the Court from exercising its jurisdiction over such a person'. But Article 98(1) provides that

> [t]he Court may not proceed with a request for surrender or assistance which would require the requested State to act inconsistently with its obligations under international law with respect to the State or diplomatic immunity of a person or property of a third State, unless the Court can first obtain the cooperation of that third State for the waiver of the immunity.

That means that, instead of ordering the parties to ensure that non-parties cooperate with the ICC, as Article 2(6) of the UN Charter does for the UN, the Statute directs the parties to respect the rights of third states.[49] That is nicely captured by the decision of Pre-Trial Chamber II in relation to South Africa, where it observed that the rule in Article 27(2) 'applies only to States that have consented to such a regime', whereas 'States that are not parties to the Statute in principle have no obligation to cooperate with the Court and the irrelevance of immunities based on official capacity as enshrined in

[47] Which is (and perceives itself) as an international organization: Decision on the Prosecution's Request for a Ruling on Jurisdiction under Article 19(3) of the Statute, ICC-RoC46(3)-01/18, Pre-Trial Chamber I (2018), para. 48 (affirming the ICC's objective international legal personality in the light of case law and doctrine pertaining to IOs. The Court refers to itself as a 'legal-judicial-institutional entity').

[48] UNSC Res 1593 (2005).

[49] The ICC Statute contains only very modest provisions on external relations. Art. 54, for example, empowers the Prosecutor to '[s]eek the cooperation of any State or intergovernmental organization or arrangement in accordance with its respective competence and/or mandate'. Art. 87 allows the Court to 'invite any State not party to this Statute to provide assistance ... on the basis of an *ad hoc* arrangement, an agreement with such State or any other appropriate basis'; directs the Court to 'inform the Assembly of States Parties or, where the Security Council referred the matter to the Court, the Security Council' if a non-party fails to cooperate; and enables the Court to 'ask any intergovernmental organization to provide information or documents' or 'for other forms of cooperation and assistance which may be agreed upon with such an organization and which are in accordance with its competence or mandate'.

article 27(2) of the Statute has no effect on their rights under international law, which Article 98(1) safeguards'.[50]

In a polemical decision, however, the Appeals Chamber disagreed with that reasoning on the dubious grounds that there is no rule of customary international law recognizing the immunity of heads of state vis-à-vis international courts. The analysis of state practice and *opinio juris* that the Appeals Chamber undertook is less relevant for the present purposes than the assumption that animated it, namely, that international courts and domestic courts have a different character. In the Appeals Chamber's words, '[w]hile the latter are essentially an expression of a State's sovereign power, which is necessarily limited by the sovereign power of the other States, the former, when adjudicating international crimes, do not act on behalf of a particular State or States'.[51] Instead, 'international courts act on behalf of the international community as a whole', which entails that 'the principle of *par in parem non habet imperium*, which is based on the sovereign equality of States, finds no application in relation to an international court such as the International Criminal Court'.[52] It stands to reason that the principle of *par in parem non habet imperium* has no place in the relations between the ICC and its member states, but why must the large section of the international community that did not ratify the Rome Statute accept the ICC as acting on behalf of the international community as a whole?[53] The suggestion that it must seems tied to an institutional self-understanding that the ICC's mission is to combat impunity whenever it has jurisdiction, whatever the rights of third states may be.

50 *Prosecutor v. Omar Hassan Ahmad Al-Bashir*, Decision under article 87(7) of the Rome Statute on the non-compliance by South Africa with the request by the Court for the arrest and surrender of Omar Al-Bashir, ICC-02/05-01/09, Pre-Trial Chamber II (2017), para. 82

51 *Prosecutor v. Omar Hassan Ahmad Al-Bashir*, Judgment in the Jordan Referral re Al-Bashir Appeal, ICC-02/05-01/09 OA2, Appeals Chamber (2019), para. 115.

52 Ibid.

53 The situation is different, of course, when the UNSC refers a situation to the Court under Article 13(b) of the ICC Statute, for, in that case, the obligation to subject to the Statute (including rules dispensing with immunity) comes from the UN Charter itself: see D. Akande, 'The Legal Nature of Security Council Referrals to the ICC and its Impact on Al Bashir's Immunities' (2009) *Journal of International Criminal Law and Justice* 333, 346–348. Indeed, the effects of UNSC Res 1593 (2005) referring the situation of Sudan to the ICC were part and parcel of the ICC's reasoning, so much so that Sarah Nouwen has persuasively argued that 'a close reading' of the Chamber's judgment 'reveals that the Chamber has in fact not gone the "full way" in supporting an "international-criminal-court-exception" because the judgment still depends on the Security-Council-analogous-to-a-state-party-route': S. Nouwen, 'Return to Sender: Let the International Court of Justice Justify or Qualify International-Criminal-Court Exceptionalism Regarding Personal Immunities' (2019) 78 *Cambridge Law Journal* 595, 607–610.

In this connection, the language employed by Pre-Trial Chamber I in the very first decision given on the issue of Al-Bashir's immunity, in relation to Malawi, is revealing: '[t]he Chamber considers that the international community's commitment to rejecting immunity in circumstances where international courts seek arrest for international crimes has reached a critical mass'.[54] If this were read as a Freudian slip, it would betray the notion that once a 'critical mass' of states decides to take a morally valuable course of action other states need to bow down. That is why the ICC's current position on state immunity illustrates the aspiration of organizations that possess or aspire to universality to take over. Were the outside world to acquiesce to this – as it has arguably done in the case of the UN Charter – new structural changes to the international legal system would ensue.

2.3 REGIONAL INTERNATIONAL ORGANIZATIONS ENGAGING NON-MEMBERS

2.3.1 *From International Cooperation to Unilateral Regulation*

Unlike universal organizations, regional international organizations may not have the kind of mandate that fosters an aspiration or tendency to bend the outside world to their will. For one, not every RIO is designed or empowered to maintain external relations with non-members.[55] But the outside world may become crucial to the functioning of RIOs in at least a couple of scenarios.

The first is when the organization, despite being regional (or sectoral) in terms of membership, pursues goals that can only be realized with the cooperation of non-members, that is, goals that could have befitted a UIO. That is the case with the Organization for Economic Co-operation and Development (OECD)'s efforts to develop international tax rules. Alongside the G20, the OECD has been pursuing the ambitious Base Erosion and Profit Shifting (BEPS) project, with the main objective of preventing multinational corporations from taking advantage of 'double non-taxation', that is, from positioning themselves in between two or more jurisdictions in ways that enable them to pay no income tax. The BEPS project comprises 15 proposed actions, including compliance with minimum standards on harmful tax practices, prevention

[54] *Prosecutor v. Omar Hassan Ahmad Al-Bashir*, Decision Pursuant to Article 87(7) of the Rome Statute on the Failure by the Republic of Malawi to Comply with the Cooperation Requests Issued by the Court with Respect to the Arrest and Surrender of Omar Hassan Ahmad Al Bashir, ICC-02/05-01/09, Pre-Trial Chamber I (2011), para 42.

[55] See Bordin et al., *Final Report of the ILA Study Group*.

of tax treaty abuse, and country-by-country reporting.[56] But the 38 current member states of the OECD cannot possibly combat harmful tax practices by creating rules that apply amongst themselves only. There are many non-member states where multinational corporations can seek to benefit from tax loopholes and other regulatory distortions. That is why the organization established the OECD/G20 Inclusive Framework on Base Erosion and Profit Shifting, which has managed to enlarge the group of states and other territories committed to implementing BEPS actions to 143.[57] A high point of the OECD's strategy to engage the wider world in the field of taxation was the adoption of the 2016 Multilateral Convention to Implement Tax Treaty Related Measures to Prevent Base Erosion and Profit Shifting. The Convention modifies thousands of double-taxation bilateral treaties in line with the standards of the BEPS Project for the 81 states (out of 100 signatories) for which it has already entered into force.

A second scenario in which non-members become crucial to the functioning of RIOs is when states make use of those organizations to act on their behalf and pursue their collective interests in international relations. The prime example is provided by the European Union, which has been given wide-reaching competences to engage in external relations in the fields of trade, economic, financial, technical and development cooperation, humanitarian aid, security and defence, and any other subjects falling under its internal policies that have an external dimension. What distinguishes EU external action from the foreign relations of the average state is the organization's willingness and capability to exercise leadership, particularly taking a proactive role in exporting norms to non-members. This institutional self-understanding was captured in a European Commission staff working document from 2007, where it is noted that '[t]here is a window of opportunity to push global solutions forward' and that '[t]he EU is in a good position to take a lead, promoting its modern regulatory framework internationally'.[58]

The EU has thus become very active in global forums such as the World Trade Organization, the International Organization of Securities Commissions, and the Food and Agriculture Organization, where much international regulation is produced. It has also endeavoured to promote its preferred standards by concluding treaties with non-members. Those treaties

56 www.oecd.org/tax/beps/beps-actions/, last accessed 7 August 2023.

57 www.oecd.org/tax/beps/inclusive-framework-on-beps-composition.pdf, last accessed 7 August 2023.

58 European Commission Staff Working Document, 'The External Dimension of the Single Market Review' (2007), at 8.

tend to fall in two main categories.[59] The first are the Partnership and Cooperation Agreements (PCA), which push for EU standards more aggressively. For example, the PCA that the EU concluded with Armenia in 2018 provides that Armenia 'shall take further steps to develop a well-functioning market economy and to gradually approximate its economic and financial regulations and policies to those of the European Union'.[60] The second are the Preferential Trade Agreements (PTAs), which advance EU standards in more subtle ways, nudging non-members in their direction without requiring that they be formally adopted. For example, the PTA concluded by the EU with Colombia and Peru in 2012 commits the parties to '[encourage] its standardisation bodies to cooperate with the relevant standardisation bodies of another Party in international standardisation activities' and makes reference to standards found in global instruments such as the UN Framework Convention on Climate Change and conventions adopted under the auspices of the International Labour Organization.

A more thought-provoking way in which the EU affects the legal position of non-members is by taking unilateral action that causes them to change their rules to adopt (or adapt to) standards favoured by the EU. Three forms of unilateral action are particularly interesting. The first is the adoption of rules that apply to the extra-territorial conduct of foreigners operating abroad. Exercises of extra-territorial jurisdiction not supported by any of the well-accepted jurisdictional bases from international law are rare, but EU practice provides a few significant examples. The so-called Derivatives Regulation, for instance, purports to 'apply to [over-the counter] derivative contracts entered into between third country entities … provided that those contracts have a direct, substantial and foreseeable effect within the Union or where such obligation is necessary or appropriate to prevent the evasion of any provision of [the] Regulation'.[61] This type of action not only affects foreigners operating abroad but also exemplifies how RIO unilateral action can affect the development of custom in core fields of international law.[62] The EU has traditionally

[59] For a helpful description of EU practice, see A. Bradford, *The Brussels Effect: How the European Union Rules the World* (Oxford University Press, 2020), 69–75.

[60] Art. 22(2), Partnership and Cooperation Partnership Agreement between the EU and Armenia (2018).

[61] EU Regulation No 648/2012 on OTC derivatives, central counterparties and trade repositories, Article 11(12).

[62] The possibility of international organizations contributing to the formation of customary international law through their own practice is recognized in Conclusion 4(2) of the ILC's Conclusions on Identification of Customary International Law. For an insightful scholarly account, see K. Daugirdas, 'International Organizations and the Creation of Customary International Law' (2020) 31 *European Journal of International Law* 201.

taken an orthodox approach to the law of jurisdiction, maintaining that extra-territorial exercises of public authority require 'some nexus between the conduct to be regulated and the regulating State'.[63] Yet, the adoption of instruments such as the Derivatives Regulation could be viewed as supporting the so-called effects doctrine, articulated by the United States and traditionally opposed by the EU, according to which there is a nexus between extra-territorial conduct and a regulating entity whenever the effects of that conduct are felt in the territory where the regulating entity operates.[64] Depending on non-members' reactions to those aggressive exercises of extra-territorial jurisdiction, EU practice can have a marked influence on the evolution of the law of jurisdiction.

The second form of unilateral action is a technique Joanne Scott has labelled 'territorial extension'. It happens when '[t]he application of a measure is triggered by a territorial connection' between the entities concerned and the EU, 'but in applying the measure the regulator is required, as a matter of law, to take into account conduct or circumstances abroad'.[65] An example is provided by the General Data Protection Regulation (GDPR), which prescribes that '[a] transfer of personal data to a third country or an international organisation may [only] take place where the Commission has decided that the third country, a territory or one or more specified sectors within that third country, or the international organisation in question ensures an adequate level of protection'.[66] An interesting feature of the GDPR is that it requires not only non-member states but also other international organizations to offer 'an

[63] Brief of the European Commission on Behalf of the European Union as *Amicus Curiae* in Support of Neither Party, *Kiobel v. Royal Dutch Petroleum*, US Supreme Court (2012), at 10 (recognizing, however, the possibility of universal jurisdiction). Similarly, the CJEU has recognized the applicability of principles of customary international law on jurisdiction in EU law: Case C-366/10, *Air Transport Association of America v. Secretary of State*, ECLI:EU:C:2011:864, para. 5.

[64] The possibility that a 'qualified effects test' could ground the extra-territorial application of Council Regulation (EC) No 1/2003 on the implementation of the rules on competition laid down in Articles 81 and 82 of the Treaty was confirmed by the Court of Justice of *Intel v. Commission*, where the Court observed that such a test served the objective of 'preventing conduct which, while not adopted within the EU, has anticompetitive effects liable to have an impact on the EU market': Case C-413/14 P (2017), *Intel v. Commission*, ECLI:EU:C:2017:632, paras. 45–46. For a discussion of the 'effects doctrine' and (early) EU opposition to it, see J. Crawford, *Brownlie's Principles of Public International Law*, 9th ed. (Oxford University Press, 2019), 447–448.

[65] J. Scott, 'Extraterritoriality and Territorial Extension in EU Law', (2014) 62 *American Journal of Comparative Law* 87, 90.

[66] Regulation 2016/679 of the European Parliament and of the Council (General Data Protection Regulation) (2016), Art. 45(1).

adequate level of protection' if they require data from an operator placed under EU jurisdiction.[67] While that is probably permissible under international law because the GDPR applies to data operators over which the EU has jurisdiction, it puts pressure on non-members to regulate data transfers like the EU does (or to the satisfaction of EU organs) and gives rise to concerns of undue intervention. The United Nations, for example, has complained that the GDPR has interfered with the functioning of UN-System organizations by, among other things, making it difficult for them to sign contracts with service providers who are apprehensive of being penalized by the EU.[68] It claims that the application of the GDPR is inconsistent with the privileges and immunities that EU member states – but, notably, not the EU itself – owe to UN-System organizations.[69]

The third form of unilateral action is the phenomenon that Anu Bradford has termed 'the Brussels effect', consisting in the 'EU's unilateral ability to regulate the global marketplace',[70] even when the regulation does not explicitly purport to cover foreign conduct. Whenever the EU is strict in how it, for example, regulates the health and safety of a product, market forces create an incentive for private business to follow the EU regulation wherever it operates because of the cost of having different production lines with different specifications. The unilateral ability to regulate the global marketplace arises when the regulating entity has jurisdiction over a sizeable consumer market and enjoys considerable regulatory capacity that it is willing to deploy to impose stringent rules over producers and products that are inelastic (in that they cannot be easily moved to other jurisdictions) and where production is non-divisible (in that it is not feasible or advantageous to manufacture products with different specifications for each market).[71] This form of external influence through the rippling effects of unilateral regulation may be unwitting in the first instance, but it can be deployed strategically once a regulating entity becomes aware of it.[72]

67 Ibid., Art. 45(5).

68 Comments of the United Nations Secretariat on behalf of the United Nations System Organizations on the 'Guidelines 2/2020 on articles 46 (2) (a) and 46 (3) (b) of Regulation 2016/679 for transfers of personal data between EEA and non-EEA public authorities and bodies' adopted by the European Data Protection Board on 18 January 2020.

69 For a discussion of this controversy, see F. L. Bordin, 'Is the EU Engaging in Impermissible Indirect Regulation of UN Action? Controversies over the General Data Protection Regulation', *EJILTalk!* (2020).

70 Bradford, *Brussels Effect*, 1.

71 See the detailed discussion in Bradford, *Brussels Effect*, 25–65.

72 Ibid., 22–23.

2.3.2 Concerns over Norm Imperialism by RIOs

The external relations of international organizations and their impact on the wider world raise a bunch of normative concerns. For one, they challenge the perception that international organizations are institutions that serve the common good. There has been a progressive realization that international organizations are not always 'harbingers of international happiness', but real-life institutions that can be co-opted by special interests and fall prey to inefficiencies and malfeasance.[73] This invites us to rethink – or at least question – the relative unaccountability that results from the legal autonomy international organizations possess (in particular the assumption that members are not liable for their action[74]); from the difficulty to bring claims against them both on the international and institutional planes; and from the generous immunities that shield them from domestic courts.[75] The core normative tenet of functionalist theories, that international law's priority must be to enable organizations to perform their functions,[76] needs be weighed against other values.

But an aspect of this reckoning, which is of special concern when it comes to RIOs,[77] must be that functionalism can only provide a reason *for members* to enable international organizations to perform their functions and not for the outside world which those organizations engage. While this point may come across as trite, it has sometimes been neglected.[78] Consider Article 51(4) of the ARIO, according to which countermeasures against an international organization are to be taken 'in such a way as to limit their effects on the

[73] J. Klabbers, 'The Life and Times of the Law of International Organizations' (2001) 70 *Nordic Journal of International Law* 287, 288.

[74] Cf Articles on the Responsibility of International Organizations for Internationally Wrongful Acts (2011), Art. 62.

[75] See, e.g. E. Benvenisti, 'Upholding Democracy amid the Challenges of New Technology: What Role for the Law of Global Governance?' (2018) 29 *European Journal of International Law* 9, 16–26.

[76] J. Klabbers, 'The EJIL Foreword: The Transformation of International Organizations Law' (2015) 26 *European Journal of International Law* 9, 11 (describing as 'basic insight' shared by functionalists that 'international organizations are functional entities, set up to perform specific tasks for the greater good of mankind and, as such, in need of legal protection').

[77] Which means the reckoning also applies to UIOs in their relations with non-members. What makes RIOs stand out, however, is that their membership is by definition closed, which in itself affects their ability to make a plausible case to be pursuing the global common good (or at least to do so to the detriment of the interests of their members).

[78] J. Klabbers, 'Sui Generis? The European Union as an International Organization', in D. Patterson and A. Södersten (eds.), *A Companion to European Union Law and International Law* (Wiley, 2016), 3, 5.

exercise by the responsible international organization of its functions'. That provision makes sense in a scenario where it is a member that takes the countermeasure, but why should a non-member be required to take the functioning of the wrongdoing organization into account in its response? By turning our attention to RIOs and how they affect non-members, we can train ourselves to ask *whose* interests the organization is pursuing and how its actions affect stakeholders that are not at all represented in its decision-making.[79] Constituent instruments themselves provide a starting point. The Treaty on European Union, for instance, prescribes that '[i]n its relations with the wider world, the Union shall uphold and promote its values and interests and contribute to the protection of its citizens', and that external action shall be taken in accordance with 'strategic interests and objectives of the Union' to be determined by the European Council.[80] For its part, the Constitutive Act of the African Union includes among the objectives of the organization to 'promote and defend African common positions on issues of interest to the continent and its peoples' and 'establish the necessary conditions which enable the continent to play its rightful role in the global economy and in international negotiations'.[81]

That RIOs pursue the interests of their members according to regional (or sectoral) sensibilities does not mean that they may not have functions and goals of a universal (or at least more generalizable) character. For example, the constituent instrument of the OECD includes among the aims of the organization 'to promote policies designed ... to contribute to sound economic expansion in Member as well as non-member countries in the process of economic development'.[82] Likewise, the Treaty on European Union commits the EU to contributing to 'peace, security, the sustainable development of the Earth, solidarity and mutual respect among peoples, free and fair trade, eradication of poverty and the protection of human rights ..., as well as to

[79] The issue of democratic legitimacy in international organizations is very complex, not least because states serve as proxy representatives for individuals and groups who rarely get to exercise political rights at the international organization level. Moreover, international organizations may pose democratic legitimacy issues even at the level of state representation, as seen in the composition of the UNSC and the special status afforded to the five permanent members. See, for example, Alvarez, *International Organizations as Law-Makers*, and S. Besson, 'Democratic Representation within International Organizations: From International Good Governance to International Good Government' (2022) 19 *International Organizations Law Review* 489.

[80] Compare Arts. 3(5), 21 and 22 of the Treaty on European Union (1992).

[81] Constitutive Act of the African Union (2000), Article 2(d) and (i).

[82] Convention on the Organisation for Economic Co-operation and Development (1960), Art. 1(b).

the strict observance and the development of international law ...'.[83] It also specifies that the EU's

> action on the international scene shall be guided by the principles which have inspired its own creation, development and enlargement, and which it seeks to advance in the wider world: democracy, the rule of law, the universality and indivisibility of human rights and fundamental freedoms, respect for human dignity, the principles of equality and solidarity, and respect for the principles of the United Nations Charter and international law.[84]

But the question arises of how cosmopolitan-minded RIOs are to reconcile, in practice, competing commitments to regional and global interests. Can it ever be expected that regional organizations will, without more, prioritize the outside world over their own members? As Jan Klabbers has noted in respect of the EU, 'one can hold that the European Union contributes to Europe's common good without necessarily also contributing to the global common good'.[85]

Even when regional and global interests align and a RIO can make a plausible case that it is contributing to the common good of the world at large, its action may raise questions of input legitimacy. To return to the example of the OECD/G20 Inclusive Framework on Base Erosion and Profit Shifting, despite the efforts of the OECD to involve non-members, the reality remains that those non-members are being invited to implement standards in the elaboration of which they had little, if any, input. In the case of unilateral regulation with rippling effects such as that adopted by the EU, the concerns are even more serious insofar as rules are indirectly forced upon non-members. Even attempts that the EU makes to export norms by cooperation, especially with neighbouring countries, have led to accusations that the EU is engaging in 'normative imperialism'. In Raffaela Del Sarto's words:

> [T]he conceptualization of the European Union as a normative empire [explains] EU policies toward its borderlands. Thus, it takes issue with a resilient key assumption of 'normative power Europe' approaches: that is, the Union's presumed predisposition to act normatively in world politics because of its specific history and normative construction. Certainly, in essence the EU does not rely on the use of force in its external relations. However ... the 'normative' action of transferring EU rules and practices beyond its borders

83 Treaty on European Union, Art. 3(5).
84 Ibid., Art. 21(1).
85 Klabbers, '*Sui Generis?*', 10–11.

> primarily serves the economic and security interests of the European core vis-a-vis the periphery.[86]

Is the kind of 'normative imperialism' exercised by the OECD and the EU, whether through international cooperation or unilaterally, necessarily a bad thing? À propos the 'Brussels Effect', Anu Bradford ponders that, whether it 'is positive or negative depends on individual preferences that vary across policy areas, individuals' socioeconomic and cultural backgrounds, values and ideologies'.[87] Yet, she cautiously suggests that 'on balance, the Brussels Effect is more likely to generate net benefits that are valuable – even if not uniformly in all instances and for all the people'.[88] While these are difficult assessments to make in times of pluralism and contestation, it is not implausible to suggest that making multinational corporations pay taxes, requiring the private sector to cooperate in the fight against climate change or ensuring that people's data are duly handled potentially reflect global aspirations, even if their realization is promoted through regulation adopted through non-inclusive processes.

The external relations conducted by RIOs invite a comparison with the external relations conducted by states. Everything that has been said here about the ways in which the OECD and the EU have sought to export their rules and values, whether by resorting to international cooperation or by taking unilateral action, could equally apply to any state taking a position of leadership in international relations, such as the United States or China. Which raises an interesting question: does it make a difference that leadership is being exercised by a RIO instead of by individual states? In particular, does the use by states of the legal form of international organization to engage with – and shape – the outside world improve or impoverish the quality of international cooperation? On the one hand, the effort to coordinate the external action of states through institutions that remain creatures of the international legal system may contribute to the adoption of a more cosmopolitan outlook, making it easier for individual states to overcome some of the more parochial pulls of domestic politics that might otherwise stand in the way of desirable courses of action on the international plane. Joanne Scott has suggested that the EU regulates with an 'international orientation', unlike the United States, for example, which is more inward-looking and exceptionalist in its approach.[89] On the other hand,

86 R. Del Sarto, 'Normative Empire Europe: The European Union, Its Borderlands, and the Arab Spring' (2015) 54 *Journal of Common Market Studies* 215, 227. For a thoughtful discussion of eurocentrism that looks specifically into how it colours EU mediation efforts, see S. Nouwen, 'Exporting Peace? The EU Mediator's Normative Backpack' (2022) 1 *European Law Open* 26.

87 Bradford, *Brussels Effect*, 263.

88 Ibid.

89 Scott, 'Extraterritoriality', 114–116.

RIOs provide an instrument for states to pool their resources in ways that may increase the problem of substantive inequality that already prevails among the sovereign equals of today's world. No European state alone would be able to pull its weight as the EU does.[90] Thus far, the practice of using RIOs to engage the outside world has been somewhat timid, with the EU remaining in a league of its own.[91] But if that practice picks up, the significance and implications of groups of states utilizing the legal form of international organization to engage the wider world will become clearer.

2.4 CONCLUDING REMARKS

The external relations of international organizations impact on the legal position of non-members – and the international legal system more generally – in different ways. UIOs such as the United Nations act with a latent aspiration to bend the outside world to their will. That is well exemplified by the Security Council purporting to bind non-members and getting away with it. The RIOs that are set up to pursue goals requiring international operation or to conduct external relations on behalf of their members can also influence the legal position of non-members, both through strategic cooperation or by engaging in unilateral regulation that creates powerful incentives for the outside world to follow suit. While that form of leadership can be (and is) also exercised by individual states, it is arguably amplified by using the legal form of international organization.

The practice of entities such as the UN, the ICC, the OECD and the EU thus speaks to the external ripples of the intensified forms of cooperation that international organizations institutionalize among their members. When states coalesce around UIOs, or empower RIOs to engage the outside world, they put pressure on a decentralized international legal system that remains based on the principle of sovereign equality. The resulting potential for legal innovation and change, which comes with normative implications that may be both desirable and undesirable, deserves close scrutiny.

90 As Bradford puts it, '[i]n the world where the United States projects hard power through its military and engagement in trade wars, and China economic power through its loans and investments, the EU exerts power thorough the most potent tool for global influence it has – regulation': Bradford, *Brussels Effect*, 24.

91 See, e.g., Bordin et al., *Final Report of the ILA Study Group*.

3

Law and the Interaction between International Organizations

RENE URUEÑA

3.1 INTRODUCTION

Almost one year into the COVID-19 pandemic, a ray of hope shone in the form of a set of vaccines that could be potentially rolled out quickly enough to save millions of lives. But rich countries soon cornered the market, empowered by rights under pre-existing contractual arrangements, and enabled by exceptional access to capital in a world ruined by lockdowns.[1] As some of the richest countries effectively hoarded vaccines, and some of humanity's most vulnerable groups were essentially left to die, one of the clearest examples of lack of solidarity at a global scale was crystallizing before our eyes.[2] From the Siege of Melos to the Siege of COVID, in 2021, the rich of the world did what they could, and the poor suffered what they must.

At a bare minimum, international organizations might be expected to play a central role of tackling such challenges to inter-state coordination.[3] And yet, global COVID-19 vaccine governance was characterized by the sidelining of international organizations, mainly for three reasons: first, perhaps as a result of the capital intensive nature of the challenge, much of the multilateral decision-making was privatized, creating in effect a kind of hybrid regulatory

[1] M. Twohey, K. Collins and K. Thomas, 'With First Dibs on Vaccines, Rich Countries Have "Cleared the Shelves"' *The New York Times* (15 December 2020), www.nytimes.com/2020/12/15/us/coronavirus-vaccine-doses-reserved.html, last accessed 17 February 2023.

[2] For a global ethics critique of both 'vaccine nationalism' and 'vaccine cosmopolitanism', see G. Collste, '"Where You Live Should Not Determine Whether You Live": Global Justice and the Distribution of COVID-19 Vaccines' (2022) 15 *Ethics and Global Politics* 43.

[3] In what follows, and following the traditional notation in international law, I will refer solely to inter-governmental organizations as international organizations. This choice excludes from such a rubric private or informal transnational regulatory regimes or institutions.

regime in which private players, like the Bill and Melinda Gates Foundation, played a pivotal role, shadowing international organizations and their public powers.[4] Second, COVID-19 arrived at a peak state-sovereigntist moment, in which the likes of Donald Trump and Jair Bolsonaro were able to play their nationalist tune without much control, undermining multilateralism.[5] And, third, even when international organizations like the WHO, the World Bank, or the WTO strove to act, each of their individual mandates seemed too narrow to tackle the different dimensions of the vaccine challenge – hence, the move to private actors, with deeper pockets and more flexibility.

While leadership in cash-strapped international organizations seemed to have little option but to accept an expanded role of well-funded private actors, and to juggle the tension with Trump and his allies, they were quick to realize that interaction among organizations was something that they *could* do something about. Enter, thus, the Multilateral Leader's Task Force on COVID-19, a joint initiative of the IMF, the World Bank, the WHO, and the WTO, aimed at supporting 'the roll out of COVID-19 tools by leveraging multilateral finance and trade solutions, particularly for low and middle-income countries'.[6]

The intuition behind the Task Force seems reasonable. In a fragmented institutional landscape, attention to inter-institutional interaction, and strategies of coordination, seem paramount. And yet, this challenge is often overlooked by the law of international organizations, which famously focuses on the legal relation between the organizations and its member states, while ignoring its interaction with other actors – such as other organizations.[7] This chapter intervenes in that debate, by exploring the role of law in organizational interaction. In contrast with recent work on international institutional law that seeks to overcome functionalism and make legal sense of interaction,[8]

4 See K. Abbott and B. Faude, 'Hybrid Institutional Complexes in Global Governance' (2022) 17 *Review of International Organizations* 263.

5 See C. Wenham, M. Eccleston-Turner and M. Voss, 'The Futility of the Pandemic Treaty: Caught between Globalism and Statism' (2022) 98 *International Affairs* 837.

6 IMF, WBG, WHO, WTO, 'Task Force on COVID-19 Vaccines, Therapeutics, and Diagnostics' (*World Bank*), www.covid19taskforce.com/en/programs/task-force-on-covid-19-vaccines, last accessed 17 February 2023.

7 See, generally, J. Klabbers, 'The EJIL Foreword: The Transformation of International Organizations Law' (2015) 26 *European Journal of International Law* 9.

8 For an overview of some of such efforts, see J. Klabbers, 'Transforming Institutions: Autonomous International Organisations in Institutional Theory' (2017) 6 *Cambridge International Law Journal* 105, 119–120. My own proposal, reading international institutional law as a theory of normative weights can be found in R Urueña, 'Interaction between International Organizations', in J. Klabbers (ed.), *The Cambridge Companion to International Organizations Law* (Cambridge University Press, 2022), 222.

this chapter argues that interaction among international organizations is a legally constituted phenomena, in two specific senses. First, law constitutes the space of the interaction (that is, their 'organizational ecosystem'). Second, law provides the background norms for organizational autonomy and the vocabulary for the decoupling of the organization's practice and its formal goals. Such a decoupling through institutional law allows international organizations to flexibly interact with each other and adapt to external pressures. Thus, in its dual role, international law provides the building blocks of interaction, playing a crucial role before the need to 'regulate' interaction even appears.

3.2 THE VARYING SIZE AND DENSITY OF THE SPACE OF INTERNATIONAL ORGANIZATION INTERACTION

Interaction among international organizations is the rule, and not the exception, in global governance. It defines a wider sphere of power that goes beyond the independently exercised powers of discrete institutions – a wider analytical lens that has fruitfully been explored by global governance scholars in recent years. Work on 'organizational ecosystems'[9] applies to international relations some of the insights of the 1980s ecological approach in the sociology of organizations, which took as its analytical unit the population of organizations (and not each organization as individual actors).[10] From this perspective, interaction between organizations occurs as they compete for scarce resources: the larger the population, the stronger the competition for those resources. As a result of such competition, the population adapts – mostly by reducing its size, eliminating the weakest organizations or, in the case of international organizations, also by expanding or reducing their areas of activity.[11] Moreover, while competition is the main form of interaction for organizational ecology, this approach does envisage cooperation when international organizations see benefits in suspending competition, while acting in the

[9] For example, in Th Gehring and B. Faude, 'A Theory of Emerging Order within Institutional Complexes: How Competition among Regulatory International Institutions Leads to Institutional Adaptation and Division of Labor' (2014) 9 *Review of International Organizations* 471; K. Abbott, J. Green and R. Keohane, 'Organizational Ecology and Institutional Change in Global Governance' (2016) 70 *International Organization* 247; S. Block-Lieb and T. Halliday, *Global Lawmakers: International Organizations in the Crafting of World Markets* (Cambridge University Press, 2017).

[10] M. Hannan and J. Freeman, 'The Population Ecology of Organizations' (1977) 82 *American Journal of Sociology* 929; M. Hannan, *Organizational Ecology* (Harvard University Press, 1989).

[11] Abbott et al., 'Organizational Ecology and Institutional Change'.

same niche,[12] with the intention of creating more resources or to achieve a wider goal that cannot be attained individually.[13]

Adopting the mindset of a wider space of international organization interaction (or its 'ecosystem') is a step in the right direction, as it leaves behind images of fragmentation or regime collisions[14] that risked obfuscating the fact that, more than a problem to be resolved, such interaction is a particular form through which legal meaning is created[15] and power is exercised.[16] Despite its advantages, such an interactional mindset still provides very little insight into the actual characteristics of interaction. The regulatory space is not static: its form and texture shift constantly as international organizations interact. Even if we posit the existence of an ecosystem of interaction, we know very little about its variation in terms of size and density.

Let us begin by exploring the question of size. The demise of formal international organizations has been greatly exaggerated. While growth rates in the formation of intergovernmental international organizations did decrease by 20% in the first years of the twenty-first century, compared to the previous decade,[17] their growth rate from 2000 to 2022 has kept, at 58.92%, just below the rate of all other international institutions (including non-governmental organizations) in the same period (67.34%).[18] That is, while the growth peak of international organizations between 1980 and 1999 (315%)[19] was indeed remarkable, a lower rate of organizational growth does not mean, by any measure, that we live in a world with less international organizations – or even with a decreasing international organization density. On the contrary, if the current trend continues (and it is a modest trend), we might expect a doubling of international organizations every 50 years or so.

12 Hannan, *Organizational Ecology*.

13 Ch Downie, 'Competition, Cooperation, and Adaptation: The Organizational Ecology of International Organizations in Global Energy Governance', (2022) 48 *Review of International Studies* 364.

14 G. Teubner and P. Korth, 'Two Kind of Legal Pluralism: Collision of Transnational in the Double Fragmentation of the World Society', in M. Young (ed.), *Regime Interaction in International Law: Facing Fragmentation* (Cambridge University Press, 2012), 23.

15 See generally, J. Brunnée and S. Toope, *Legitimacy and Legality in International Law: An Interactional Account* (Cambridge University Press, 2010).

16 See R. Urueña, 'Después de la fragmentación: ICCAL, derechos humanos y arbitraje de inversiones', in A. von Bogdandy et al. (eds.), *El constitucionalismo transformador en América Latina y el derecho económico internacional. De la tensión al diálogo* (Mexico City: Universidad Nacional Autónoma de México Instituto de Investigaciones Jurídicas, 2018), 59.

17 Abbott et al., 'Organizational Ecology and Institutional Change'.

18 Source: Own calculation, with data drawn from *Yearbook of International Organizations* 2021, 'Figure 2.9. Historical overview of number of international organizations by type'.

19 Ibid.

But that is just half of the story. Just as they are created, international organizations also die. Eilstrup-Sangiovanni analysed the population of defunct international organizations and found that, of 561 international organizations created between 1815 and 2005, 218 had ceased to exist by 2015 – that is, 39% of the overall rate of mortality.[20] Since 2000, though, the mortality rate has decreased, stabilizing around 7.6%.[21] Of such rate, almost half implied some kind of organizational continuation (be it succession or merger/absorption by some other international organization), while the other half involves the actual end of activities, under the form of termination or some form of desuetude.[22] Thus, while the space of international organization interaction is indeed growing, such growth is not only the result of new organizations, but also of the underlying dynamics of international organization mortality, which is not uniform at all: global international organizations tend to have a lower mortality rate than regional international organizations which, in turn, have varying mortality rates depending on the time period.[23]

The second question is one of density. Often, the idea of proliferation of international organizations suggests an evenly dense texture of governance; that is, an even distribution of new organizations in the space of governance.[24] However, the opposite is the case. Recent quantitative work has explored overlap as the most intense form of interaction and finds that overlap among international organizations tends to cluster around certain issues and around certain scales of organization. Haftel and Lenz measured the overlap (understood as coincidence of policy competency and membership) among a sample of the 76 most authoritative international organizations developed by the Measure of International Authority project, which is a good indicator to assess

[20] M. Eilstrup-Sangiovanni, 'Death of International Organizations. The Organizational Ecology of Intergovernmental Organizations, 1815–2015' (2020) 15 *Review of International Organizations* 339; Eilstrup-Sangiovanni uses an expanded version of the Correlates of War (COW) datasets, different from the set underlying the *Yearbook of International Organizations*, making it impossible to calculate survival rates between the two. Eilstrup-Sangiovanni does calculate rates in reference solely to COW data.

[21] Ibid., 353.

[22] Ibid., 351.

[23] For example, European international organizations mortality rate peaked for much of the twentieth century until the 1950s, when African international organizations rate peaked. In the 1991–2001 period (the last reviewed on a regional basis), both African and European rates were still higher than the global average. Ibid., 356. Admittedly, such rates are greatly influenced by geopolitical contexts (for example, decolonization or the end of the Cold War) that tend to be flattened out of quantitative calculations.

[24] For example, in O. Young, 'Institutional Linkages in International Society: Polar Perspectives' (1996) 2 *Global Governance* 1.

the overall political relevance of international organizations.[25] The study found that 40 per cent of such international organizations do overlap in either mandate or membership, or both, with overlap roughly doubling from 1970 until today – a trend driven mostly by the expansion of competences, rather than by membership.[26] Most importantly, perhaps, such overlap tends to cluster around particular issues. Confirming what intuition might suggest, the issues in which most overlap seems to occur are financial stabilization, development and humanitarian aid, research policy and human rights, while the issues with less overlap are industrial policy, currency, competition policy, macroeconomic coordination and taxation and, finally (and perhaps unsurprisingly), energy.[27]

Ultimately, then, the ecosystem of international organizations is composed of some densely populated islands of intense interaction, while other islands show low intensity interaction and, finally, other areas no interaction at all. These islands, in turn, shift size constantly – not by increasing or decreasing their membership but rather by expanding the mandate of already existing organizations.

3.3 A *LEGAL* SPACE OF INTERNATIONAL ORGANIZATION INTERACTION

Such a constantly shifting landscape is mostly understood by organizational ecology to be naturally occurring. Seemingly adopting the factual premises of their ecosystem metaphor, interaction among international organizations is often understood to occur in a space of nature, in which organizations interact as naturally occurring organisms in a biological ecosystem. In this reading, law is crucially absent. The size of populations and their density are functions of spontaneous organizational dynamics, and the demand for regulation only appears at a later moment (if at all), when the malfunction of interaction

25 Y. Haftel and T. Lenz, 'Measuring Institutional Overlap in Global Governance' (2022) 17 *Review of International Organizations* 323. On the Measure of International Authority sample, see L. Hooghe, *Measuring International Authority: A Postfunctionalist Theory of Governance. Volume III* (Oxford University Press, 2017). The database is available at 'Measuring International Authority' (MIA), https://garymarks.web.unc.edu/data/international-authority/, last accessed 8 February 2023.

26 Haftel and Lenz, 'Measuring Institutional Overlap', 333.

27 Ibid., Annex 1, Table A.2. For the purpose of overlap, one international organization might be active in several 'issue areas'. Thus, an organization with a wide mandate, such as the UN, might overlap in the issue of 'human rights' with some organizations, while overlapping in 'development aid' with others.

(for example, as incoherence or forum shopping) triggers demands for some kind of top-down ordering principles (such as hierarchy) to the otherwise organic process of interaction.[28]

However, the ecosystem of international organization interaction does not occur in a legal vacuum – it is neither pre-legal, nor independent from the law.[29] On the contrary, it is thoroughly constituted by international law, both in its size and in its density. International lawyers have developed a vocabulary for the wider sphere of governance in which international organizations interact. The image providing more traction here is that of *space*, which has been explored in different contexts. First, as I have argued elsewhere, it is possible to read the interaction among international organizations as part of the 'global regulatory space'[30] – a notion originally suggested in a domestic setting as a reaction against the narrow reading of regulatory processes in terms of conflict between public authority and private interests.[31] Transposing such a notion to global governance, interactions can be seen as part of an emergent 'global administrative space'; that is, 'a space, distinct from the space of inter-state relations governed by international law and the domestic regulatory space governed by domestic administrative law, although encompassing elements of each'.[32] Following a similar line, but in a different context, the non-hierarchical interaction among regimes has been interpreted as a 'legal space' in Europe. Such European legal space 'coalesces what sixty years of Europeanization of domestic public law have achieved, and articulates the specific relationship between the various legal orders as one of mutual

[28] Interestingly, even legal scholars showing how interaction has ius-generative effects, still seem oblivious to the role of (international) law in framing such interaction. See, for example, Block-Lieb and Halliday, *Global Lawmakers*.

[29] In that sense, the organic narrative of interaction mirrors that of the naturally occurring market, which inspired much of the neoliberal approach to regulation. As has been explored at least since Polanyi, the self-regulating market is not a naturally occurring phenomena, but is rather constituted and reconstituted by law and legal institutions, which are in turn obfuscated and demonized by the very political economists that promote the myth celebrating its supposed efficiency and moral virtues. See K. Polanyi, *The Great Transformation: The Political and Economic Origins of Our Time*, 2nd ed. (Beacon Press, 2001). For the place of Polanyi's critique of free market utopianism in contemporary political economy, see F. Block and B. Somers, *The Power of Market Fundamentalism: Karl Polanyi's Critique* (Harvard University Press, 2014), 98–113.

[30] R. Urueña, 'Temporariness and Change in Global Governance' (2014) 45 *Netherlands Yearbook of International Law* 19.

[31] L. Hancher and M. Moran, 'Organizing Regulatory Space', in L. Hancher and M. Moran (eds.), *Capitalism, Culture, and Economic Regulation* (Clarendon Press, 1989), 271.

[32] B. Kingsbury, N. Krisch and R. Stewart, 'The Emergence of Global Administrative Law' (2005) 68 *Law and Contemporary Problems* 15, 26.

structural dependency'.[33] In Latin America, in turn, interactions between the Inter-American Court of Human Rights, domestic courts and other international courts (such as the International Criminal Court) have also been read as reflecting an Inter-American legal space that contributes to the dynamic legal developments that have characterized that region in the last decade.[34]

In all these iterations, the image of a legal space is a step in the right direction. It adopts as its starting point the wider unit of international organization interaction, thus providing a useful alternative to limitations of legal hierarchical order.[35] Moreover, in highlighting its legal nature, the image of the legal space provides a counternarrative to the notion that interaction among international organizations occurs organically, instead emphasizing that the ecosystem is legally constituted, and is thus the outcome of the agency of people in positions of power.

With that in mind, let us go back to the size and density of the organizational 'ecosystem'. As a manifestation of a legal space, the size of the space 'international organization interaction' is a product of legal reasoning. As Sabine Müller-Mall has explained, a 'legal space' can be read as being composed by acts of normative perception, which are necessarily relational: the perception of a particular legal utterance only makes sense in relation to other perceived legal utterances. A particular legal space is thus defined by that constant process of relational observations.[36] The same can be said of international organizations: the limit of the space in which international organizations interact is defined by the relation that the interpreter makes of a particular point of the internal law of that organization (a point in space) with her interpretation of the law of a different organization, and then with the law of another organization and so on. The space defined by that line linking these different legal utterances in reference to different organizations is the space of international organization interaction – the outer limits of the 'ecosystem', as it were.

33 A. von Bogdandy, 'The Idea of European Public Law Today', in P. Huber, S. Cassese and A. von Bogdandy (eds.), *The Max Planck Handbooks in European Public Law: Volume I: The Administrative State* (Oxford University Press, 2017).

34 R Urueña, 'Hacia Un Espacio Jurídico Latinoamericano: El Diálogo Internacional Judicial En La Protección de Los Derechos Humanos En América Latina', in J. Martín y Pérez de Nanclares (ed.), *El diálogo judicial internacional en la protección de los derechos humanos fundamentales* (Salamanca: Universidad de Salamanca, 2019), 419.

35 See, for example, in R. Urueña, 'Interaction as a Site of Postnational Rule-Making: A Case Study of the Interamerican System of Human Rights', in E. Fahey (ed.), *The Actors of Postnational Rule-Making: Contemporary Challenges of European and International Law* (Routledge, 2015), 133. In Europe, see von Bogdandy, 'The Idea', 13.

36 S. Müller-Mall, *Legal Spaces: Towards a Topological Thinking of Law* (Springer, 2013), 65–88.

The space of international organization interaction is thus legally constituted, performative (in the sense that it mobilizes meaning to have an effect) and is always dynamic: the interpreter chooses the particular extension of the legal space with regards to the particular problematic that inspires her approach to interaction, which allows for the meaningful location of a particular set of legal utterances. Ultimately (and this is perhaps not clear enough in prior work on the legal space, with its focus on non-hierarchy) the space of interaction is not 'out there' – it is necessarily performed through interpretations linking legal utterances made in reference to the internal law of two or more international organizations.[37]

A similar thing can be said of the varying density that characterizes the space of international organization interaction. Instead of a naturally occurring process of organic clustering, density of governance is a function of choices expressed through law, which influence how the power of an international organization is clustered around certain issues and not others. A productive way to start thinking about the density of certain clusters of inter-actual governance is to consider them in reference to two different variables: hierarchy between international organizations and mandate differentiation (for example, differentiation in terms of membership, geographical focus or subject-matter competence). Both these variables are constituted by international law, and both have an impact on governance density, as we now turn to see.[38]

To begin with, the densest clusters of governance might emerge from international legal norms that create hierarchy among organizations but establish no clearly differentiated mandates. In that case, international organizations will need to continuously be in contact with each other to define their space of

[37] Admittedly, this argument presents the legal constitution of international organization space as an answer to one level of problematic in global governance (how to make sense of the interaction between autonomous organizations?), which is answered by the performative relation of the law of different organizations. This framing provides no answer to a different level of problematic (how to make sense of the competing images of inter-actual governance produced by contemporary scholarship?), whose answer would feature my idea of the legally constituted space of interaction, not as the structure of the answer but as one of concepts to be connected (together with 'organizational ecosystem', 'global constitution' and so forth) through a different (meta) structure. While some work on international organization interaction intervenes at that level (for example, Klabbers, 'Transforming Institutions'), this is not the intervention in this chapter. On the notion of the problematic used in this sense, see P. Maniglier et al., 'Bachelard and the Concept of Problematic' (2012) 173 *Radical Philosophy* (special issue).

[38] For the mandate/hierarchy matrix, I am following the useful framework presented in C. R. Henning and T. Pratt, 'Hierarchy and Differentiation in International Regime Complexes: A Theoretical Framework for Comparative Research', (2021), www.tylerbpratt.com/s/HenninPratt_Feb252021.pdf (last accessed 1 March 2025).

action, both vertically (in the sense of hierarchy) and horizontally (in the sense of mandate differentiation). That is the case of the peace-keeping and security fields, where the combination of Articles 53 and 103 of the UN Charter gives the UN supremacy over regional organizations with which it might collaborate, but very little is said as to the distribution of competences among them, thus triggering myriad legal problems in terms of responsibility.[39] Lack of differentiated mandates might lead to competition between organizations, which can be tackled by formal legal arrangements among organizations facilitated, in turn, by hierarchy – as has been, in fact, the case with the involvement of regional organizations in peace-keeping and security.[40]

A medium level of density can be expected from legal arrangements creating hierarchical relations and establishing differentiated mandates, which require vertical interaction among international organizations of different hierarchical levels, but little horizontal contact. Despite its apparent lack of hierarchy, that is in practice the system created by Article XXIV of GATT, which regulates the interaction between the WTO and regional economic regimes.[41] Here, we might expect (at least in principle) more cooperation between organizations, expressed in formal institution arrangements that follow hierarchy – such as the notification procedure established in the GATT. A similar level of intensity can be expected from norms that establish non-hierarchical interactions between organizations with non-differentiated mandates, as they must interact horizontally to define their sphere of governance but have no need to horizontally interact with other international

[39] See L. Boisson de Chazournes, 'Les Relations Entre Organisations Régionales et Organisations Universelles' (2010) 347 *Recueil des Cours* 79, 313–329.

[40] For the example of Kosovo and Afghanistan, see A. Herrhausen, *Organizing Peacebuilding: An Investigation of Interorganizational Coordination in International Post Conflict Reconstruction Efforts* (Berne: Peter Lang, 2009). For other examples of formal cooperation agreements, see M. Kamto, 'Le rôle des "accords et organismes régionaux" en matière de maintien de la paix et de la sécurité internationales à la lumière de la Charte des Nations Unies et de la pratique internationale' (2007) 111 *Revue generale de droit international public* 771. For examples of agreements with European security institutions, see A. Novosseloff, 'La coopération entre l'Organisation des Nations Unies et les institutions européennes de sécurité: principes et perspectives' (2001) 2 *Annuaire français de relations internationales* 594.

[41] Article XXIV of GATT tries to bridge the tension between regional economic integration and the multilateral trading system that strived to put the WTO as the centre of the global trading system, by establishing a number of substantive and notification requirements that regional organizations and agreements have to comply with before the WTO. Article 53 of the UN Charter, in turn, provides that, the UN Security Council may utilize such regional arrangements or agencies for enforcement action under its authority, which have included regional IOs. Both these clauses create a system of organizational hierarchy and mandate differentiation that often creates a myriad of coordination problems. On these cases from the IO law perspective, see Boisson de Chazournes, 'Les Relations', 220–237.

organizations. That is the case of the protection and use of plant genetic resources[42] and most of the issues studied by the organizational ecology literature, which focuses on populations occurring in precisely such contexts.[43] In this pattern of interaction we might expect to see more competition, as international organizations reach for the same pool of resources, without a framework of hierarchy.

And, finally, the least dense cluster of governance might emerge when the law establishes no hierarchy and clearly differentiated mandates, as here international organizations have little need to establish links with each other, if at all. In that case, very light interaction is to be expected. That would be the case, for example, of the interaction between the IMF and the WTO on issues of monetary policy and trade – in particular, with regard to the duty on behalf of the WTO's Committee of Balance of Payment Restrictions to consult the IMF on the balance of payments situation of a WTO Member that, facing sharp disequilibrium in its balance of payments, wants to apply import restrictions.[44] Such low density of governance might create incentives for non-binding cooperation, as organizations are not competing for the same resources and might, in fact, adopt a shared goal that boosts each of them in their own area of competence.[45] Of course, in the extreme, total lack of hierarchy and crystal clear mandate differentiation would imply no interaction and, thus, no governance density at all.

3.4 INTERNATIONAL ORGANIZATION INTERACTION AND THE DUAL ROLE OF INTERNATIONAL INSTITUTIONAL LAW

The law of international organizations has a limited vocabulary to account for international organization interaction. Part of the problem, as Klabbers has pointed out, is that the underlying rationale organizing the law of international institutions ('functionalism') provides an account of the relation between members states and the organization, but remains silent on the engagement of the organization with the wider world (for example,

[42] K. Raustiala and D. Victor, 'The Regime Complex for Plant Genetic Resources' (2004) 58 *International Organization* 277.

[43] For more examples, see K. Alter and S. Meunier, 'The Politics of International Regime Complexity' (2009) 7 *Perspectives on Politics* 13.

[44] See V. Thorstensen, D. Ramos and C. Muller, 'The "Missing Link" between the WTO and the IMF' (2013) 16 *Journal of International Economic Law* 353.

[45] N. Kanie et al., 'Introduction: Global Governance through Goal Setting', in N. Kanie and F. Biermann (eds.), *Governing through Goals: Sustainable Development Goals as Governance Innovation* (MIT Press, 2017), 1.

non-member states, private parties and, important for our case, other international organizations).[46] While this observation is accurate,[47] it is not the whole story. The problem is not (only) functionalism. As with any theory, functionalism has proven to be useful for one thing (providing a rationale for the regulation of the principal–agent logic) but not for others. To make sense of the role of law with regards to relations among international organizations, we might need to start looking elsewhere.

As discussed in Section 3.3, interaction is an intensely legal phenomenon: both the outer limits of the space of interaction and its inner dynamics are constituted through law. Obfuscating the legal nature of interaction is, precisely, the main shortcoming of organizational ecology. However, international organization interaction is not only a legal phenomenon. When international organizations interact, such interaction is more than just their underlying legal regimes interacting. International organizations develop organizational autonomy, which is based on law, but goes beyond the relative normativity of their respective constituent document or internal law. It is crucial to focus also on the organization of the law and not just the law of the organization. Providing a legal account of international organization interaction requires, thus, to take seriously the difference between the law of the organization and the organizations itself – without going to the extreme of reifying the organization and considering as existing 'outside the law', as organizational ecology does. As Samantha Besson has rightly put it, international organizations are ruled *and* rule by international law.[48] The limit of functionalism in international organizations law is that it provides a theory for the first dynamic but not for the second, which is the space where interaction occurs.

Perhaps the best way to start going beyond such limitations is to consider international organizations as semi-open entities – that is, to see international organizations as fully structured organizations that are, nonetheless, sensitive to external pressures. Notably, both international organizations law and most work in organizational ecology consider each organization as a closed unit, not able to adapt.[49] Only recently have ecological studies started to account

46 See Klabbers, 'The Transformation'.

47 I explore its accuracy and implications further in Urueña, 'Interaction between International Organizations'.

48 S. Besson, *Reconstruire l'ordre institutionnel international* (Collège de France, 2021), paras. 30–31.

49 Initially, organizational ecology was mostly concerned with issues of entry, permanence and exit of organizations (that is, their birth, life-length and death) and understood each of these events as functions of their environment, without recognizing any internal process of

for processes of organizational openness and adaptation.[50] However, organizational theory has provided a vocabulary to speak of just such phenomena, at least since the 1960s, as a problem of 'decoupling'.[51] Classical organization research took a strict functional view of the formal purposes of an organization, in which formal goals were aligned ('coupled') with their practices. However, critical organizational studies soon began to realize that organizations were open to their environment. And, in that open context, organizational practices were decoupled of formally stated goals – not as a problem of incoherence or lack of compliance with internal regulation, but rather as a way in which the organizations adapted to external pressures, while leaving formal goals unchanged. Decoupling of policy and practice started being read thus not as a problem, but as one of several organizational strategies of adaptation and resilience.

As with any organization, it seems reasonable to expect some level of functional decoupling in international organizations, though there seems to be little research on the matter.[52] For the purpose of international organizations law, though, the decoupling framework, with its underlying concept of a semi-open organization, is a useful starting point to explore the varying roles of

adaptation on behalf of the organization (e.g., Hannan and Freeman, 'Population Ecology'). Latter work on organizational ecology gave more space for adaptation and learning processes by the organizations. Overall, though, ecological international organizations work seems to be draw more from the first mindset than from the second. Underscoring this blind spot in current International Relations scholarship, see Downie, 'Competition, Cooperation, and Adaptation'. On the first phases of organizational ecology as a field, see T. Amburgey and H. Rao, 'Organizational Ecology: Past, Present, and Future Directions' (1996) 39 *Academy of Management Journal* 1265.

[50] Downie, 'Competition, Cooperation, and Adaptation', 7–8. Similarly, underscoring the limits of current organizational ecology approach, Kranke has recently applied an 'open system' framework (that is, 'a relational understanding of organizations as collective actors that interact with and adapt to their environment') to international organization interaction. M. Kranke, 'Pathologies of a Different Kind: Dysfunctional Interactions between International Organizations' (2022) 2 *Global Studies Quarterly* 1, 2. International organizations law seems to have not yet taken that step. See, for example, H. Gött, 'Interactions between International Organizations: Approaching a Neglected Governance Dimension' (2020) 17 *International Organizations Law Review* 75.

[51] The following description of decoupling theory is based on P. Bromley and W. Powell, 'From Smoke and Mirrors to Walking the Talk: Decoupling in the Contemporary World' (2012) 6 *Academy of Management Annals* 483.

[52] For notable exceptions, see M. Kranke, 'Exclusive Expertise: The Boundary Work of International Organizations' (2022) 29 *Review of International Political Economy* 453; M. Stephen, 'Legitimacy Deficits of International Organizations: Design, Drift, and Decoupling at the UN Security Council' (2018) 31 *Cambridge Review of International Affairs* 96 (noting the dearth of international organizations decoupling research, at 105); A. Kentikelenis, Th Stubbs and L. King, 'IMF Conditionality and Development Policy Space, 1985–2014' (2016) 23 *Review of International Political Economy* 543.

law in international organization interaction – beyond functionalism's narrow focus. As mentioned in Section 3.3, international organizations are constituted by law, but are more than legal regimes: they are autonomous organizations that govern through law. Law plays, therefore, two different roles in this context: first, it constitutes international organizations as autonomous actors and, second, it assigns competences and distributes rights and obligations for these organizations to operate.

In its first role, international law serves as the background norm for international organization interaction. This is, for lack of a better word, a 'deep' process of organizational constitution. This is obviously true for notions of statehood and state consent, through which international law constitutes the building blocks of the international 'reality' that create international organizations. More directly related to international organization interaction, international law also creates the doctrinal vocabulary that allows the very existence of international organizations to be taken for granted. In this regard, the background idea of autonomy is key.[53] Through the vocabulary of international law, the ontological existence of international organizations becomes possible, as does the idea of international organizations as autonomous actors, and not, say, organs of a state, parts of decentralized networks or private actors.

To be sure, functionalism seems not to work as a theory for this kind of proto-law of international organizations, as there is no specific function being assigned. Instead, international organizations law seems to play a role here more akin to that of Robert L. Hale which recognized for property rights: the rules that define the rights of property owners are more than recognition of rights to individual actors, but in fact distribute bargaining power between competing interests and, thus, power in society.[54] Similarly, the notion of autonomy distributes bargaining power between the organization, member states and other actors: states get a strong bargaining position, as their consent is required to create the organization but then the idea of autonomy gives the organization an enhanced position, as it is able to increasingly adopt decisions without such consent. Third parties, of course, are given no bargaining power at all.

53 In a register different from that of background norms, Klabbers has argued that ethical and legal debate necessarily require and confirm the autonomy of the organizations, otherwise the debate is just non-sensical. This seems right. J. Klabbers, 'Interminable Disagreement: Reflections on the Autonomy of International Organisations' (2019) 88 *Nordic Journal of International Law* 111.

54 R. Hale, 'Bargaining, Duress, and Economic Liberty' (1943) 43 *Columbia Law Review* 603. This reading of Hale is based on D. Kennedy, 'The Stakes of Law, or Hale and Foucault' (1991) 15 *Legal Studies Forum* 327, 332–334.

The fact that autonomy operates as a background norm, and not as a principle of the institutional 'foreground' norms, is the reason why international institutional law has such difficulty with locating the internal law of the organization (that derives from its autonomy) within the larger landscape of general international law: is the former part of public international law? Or is it akin to the domestic law of a state? To be sure, international organizations tend to defend the autonomy of their own legal system, as in the case of the European Union,[55] or the Andean Community.[56] In contrast, international adjudicators, such as investment tribunals, have been adamant that the internal law of international organizations is not autonomous but part of general international law.[57] When facing that very same question in order to define the relevant law applicable to responsibility emerging from breaches of internal law, the International Law Commission found it difficult to give a clear answer.[58] But this is understandable – it really could not, because the ultimate criteria to define the relevant law (that of autonomy) operates as a background norm.

The second role of law in international organization interactions derives from that legally constituted idea of autonomy and the distribution of

[55] See, for example, the debate arising from the accession of the European Union to the European Convention on Human Rights, in ECJ *Opinion 2/13*, ECLI:EU:C:2014:2454, or the role of UN Security Council Resolutions in EU Law, in ECJ, Case C-402/05 *Kadi v. Commission* ECLI:EU:C:2008:461.

[56] For example, in Case 01-AI-2001, the Andean Court of Justice held that the Andean Community is not bound by WTO law: 'international treaties concluded by Member States on their own initiative, such as the TRIPS Agreement, do not bind the Community, nor have a direct effect in the Community, without prejudice to the binding force that such instruments have in relations between the said Member States and third countries or international organizations'. Ultimately, while the Andean Court has 'an interest in preferring, whenever possible and necessary, an interpretation of (Andean Law) that is compatible with (WTO law), particularly if the international rule has been the source of the Community rule, it still considers it inadmissible for the latter to be replaced by the former and applied in its place' (ACJ, Case 35-AN-2003).

[57] See, for example, *Electrabel S.A. v. Republic of Hungary*, ICSID Case No. ARB/07/19, Decision on Jurisdiction, Applicable Law and Liability, para 4.124; *Eskosol SpA in liquidazione v. Italian Republic*, ICSID Case No ARB/15/50, Decision on Italy's Request for Immediate Termination and Italy's Jurisdictional Objection Based on Inapplicability of the Energy Charter Treaty to Intra-EU disputes (7 May 2019) para 181. Relatedly, the WTO DSB held that neither Argentina nor Brazil could use their MERCOSUR obligations as an argument to wriggle out of their WTO duties, see for the Argentinean case: *WTO, Argentina – Poultry Anti-dumping Duties, Panel Report, Argentina – Definitive Anti-dumping Duties on Poultry from Brazil*, WT/DS241/R (22 April, 2003). For Brazil: *WTO*, Appellate Body Report, Brazil-Measures Affecting Imports of Retreaded Tyres, WT/DS332/AB/R (3 December 2007).

[58] International Law Commission, Commentary to Art. 10, *Yearbook of the International Law Commission* 2011/II, part two, at 64, para. 7.

bargaining power it entails. International law creates the 'foreground' institutional law; that is, it provides the vocabulary for states to create particular organizations and provides the doctrinal tools to define how that particular entity will act in the world – for example, by establishing rules applicable to delegated powers, legal personality, funding, internal structure and internal decision-making powers, among others.

Such a delegation of powers around a particular formal function, though, is only the beginning. As we have seen, international organizations are semi-open entities that need to adapt to their environment (even if their law fails to recognize such a wider environment). In that process, it is likely that their actual practice is decoupled from the formal goals and powers as established, for example, through its constituent document. This process of decoupling does not register in a narrowly functionalist reading of the organization, but it still takes place, through legal means: organ competences are expanded, implied powers are found, international legal personalities are presumed.[59] Overall, the organization takes advantage of the flexibilities provided by the open-ended texture of international law to adapt to its environment by shifting the shape of its practices, while keeping its overall formal function untouched. Again, this is not a problem of non-compliance with the internal law of the organization but rather a process of adaptation that is performed through legal interpretation.

Interaction among international organizations occurs in this space. Part of the stimuli that enters the semi-open organization is the friction with other international organizations, which is also dealt with through law. Once again, explicit delegation of powers is an important starting point: some international organizations have explicit provisions concerning powers to engage in external relations, as in the case of ASEAN, which has explicit treaty-making powers,[60] or the East African Community, which has the explicit power to 'foster co-operative arrangements with other regional and international organisations whose activities have a bearing on the objectives of the Community'.[61] More often than not, though, the friction generated by interactions with other international organizations needs to be internally managed by referring to the flexibility offered by the internal law of the organization, for example, by

59 Alternatively, one could make the opposite argument that this kind of behaviour would be, in fact, fully explained from a wider functionalist perspective, as the function in this case would be organizational survival. For that argument, see K. Daugirdas, 'Review: Advanced Introduction to the Law of International Organizations, Written by Jan Klabbers' (2016) 13 *International Organizations Law Review* 396.

60 Article 41(7) of the ASEAN Charter.

61 Article 130(3) EAC Treaty.

finding the implicit power to engage in external relations, as in the case of the European Union.[62]

Focusing on the organization as created by law, but existing beyond it, allows us to see law operate at both these levels (constitutive and operational). International institutional law provides not only the background norm of autonomy but also both the formal function that defines the organization and the indeterminate vocabulary and flexible mechanisms to perform the decoupling of practice from form, which facilitates the organization's resilience and ultimate survival.

3.5 CONCLUSION

Interaction is the default status of international organizations. It might trigger inconsistencies, undermine state obligations under international law, hinder accountability, and create composite forms of inter-interinstitutional governance that may disproportionately affect states in the Global South. It seems only reasonable that such a common occurrence would have been long considered as part and parcel of mainstream international institutional law. That it has not reveals much about our current thinking about the relation between international organizations and international institutional law as different but intimately linked manifestations of power. International institutional law provides the background vocabulary for the very existence of international organizations as autonomous entities and distributes bargaining power along the different actors involved in their creation. Besides playing this background role, international organizations law also provides a large portfolio of legal doctrines that facilitates the decoupling of form and practice in international organizations – a safety valve that gives international organizations resilience, allowing them to adapt their internal functioning to external pressures, including the paramount pressure of interaction among international organizations.

[62] See P. Koutrakos, *EU International Relations Law* (Hart, 2006), 77–91.

4

Governance Shapers?

The Big Four, International Organizations and the EU

HANS-WOLFGANG MICKLITZ AND EVGENIA RALLI

DISCLAIMER

The plan of the chapter was built on the assumption that it is possible to reconstruct the possible impact of the Big Four consultancy firms on public governance through publicly accessible means through desk research – outside and beyond the rather well researched field of tax and accounting. This turned out to be wrong. There would have been two possible options, either to level the findings up to a more theoretical and abstract analysis based on the rather thin data or give a thorough account of the limited takeaway. We opted for the latter, which led us to the conclusion that our chapter could easily be read as an invitation to draft a research design that complements the picture and that allows for a much more sophisticated analysis.

4.1 THE BLACK BOX: BIG FOUR AND PUBLIC GOVERNANCE

The four leading consultancy firms, the Big Four,[1] are in the spotlight. Their crucial role in providing services in accounting, auditing and law, nationally and globally, to industry and governments is well documented.[2] However, their story

We would like to thank Simona Ciccarini for her excellent research assistance. All the websites and databases referred to under this paper were last visited on 15 August 2022.
The analysis in relation to the state of the law and the relevant literature is dated 15 August 2023.

[1] Deloitte, Ernst & Young, Pricewaterhouse Coopers (PwC) and KPMG.

[2] See, e.g., D. Wilkins and M. Esteban Ferrer, 'The Integration of Law into Global Business Solutions: The Rise, Transformation, and Potential Future of the Big Four Accountancy Networks in the Global Legal Services Market' (2018) 43 *Law and Social Inquiry* 981; W. Wen and A. Sonnerfeldt, 'The Interplay between Global Accounting Firms and National

is not only one of transformation, innovation and dominance of professional services but also one connected to scandals,[3] tax haven networks[4] and organizing power to resist the public advocacy[5] through monitored public procurement contracts or through lobbying strategies and forming advisory groups. Apart from the audit services, the analysis focuses on the provision of different types of services to the public sector. Shifting the focus to the public sector is not only of paramount importance but it fills a research gap. This chapter explores the role of the Big Four in influencing law-making and more generally in public governance with regard to the EU and international organizations.

Mapping the evolution of the Big Four sets the scene. We build on the existing literature which is accomplished through an additional analysis of their global annual reports, their websites and a few other publicly available databases mapping their provision of services or influence exercised towards the EU and international organizations. Secondly, we examine the legal framework in which their activities are embedded, the rules on public procurement and transparency. We start from the premise that the publicly available documentation facilitates an assessment, thereby disclosing gaps for further research. The methodology as well as the sources of information are presented in Section 4.4.

4.2 ECONOMIC AND POLITICAL CONTEXTUALIZATION

How have the Big Four become Big and Four? Their rise does not go together with financialization of the economy. Their history is primarily a history of

Institutional Contexts: The Establishment of the Big Four in China from 1978 to 2007' (2022) 27 *Accounting History* 95.

3 Ch. Shore and S. Wright, 'How the Big 4 Got Big: Audit Culture and the Metamorphosis of International Accountancy Firms' (2018) 38 *Critique of Anthropology* 303, 310 ff.

4 C. Jones, Y. Temouri and A. Cobham, 'Tax Haven Networks and the Role of the Big 4 Accountancy Firms' (2018) 53 *Journal of World Business* 177.

5 M. Kalaitzake, 'Accounting for Success: The Big Four as Allies of Finance in Post Crisis Regulatory Reform' (2019) 21 *Business and Politics* 297; *Financial Times*, 'Big Four Paid Millions to Advise Brussels on Tax Policy', at www.ft.com/content/56f862ee-8392-11e8-96dd-fa565ec55929; Ch. Hurl and A. Vogelpohl (eds), *Professional Service Firms and Politics in a Global Era* (Palgrave MacMillan, 2021); L. Herman, 'Neither Takers nor Makers: The Big-4 Auditing Firms as Regulatory Intermediaries' (2020) 25 *Accounting History* 349; L. Fransen and G. LeBaron, 'Big Audit Firms as Regulatory Intermediaries in Transnational Labor Governance' (2019) 13 *Regulation and Governance* 260; Corporate Europe Observatory, 'Accounting for Influence: How the Big Four Are Embedded in EU Policy-Making on Tax Avoidance', at https://corporateeurope.org/en/power-lobbies/2018/06/tax-avoidance-industry-embedded-eu-tax-policy; B. Momani, 'Professional Management Consultants in Transnational Governance', in L. Seabrooke and L. Henriksen (eds.), *Professional Networks in Transnational Governance* (Cambridge University Press, 2017), 245; M. Boussebaa, 'Global Professional Service Firms, Transnational Organising and Core/Periphery Networks', in L. Seabrooke and L. Henriksen (eds.), *Professional Networks in Transnational Governance* (Cambridge University Press, 2017), 233.

mergers, the Big Eight[6] reduced to the Big Four. Their historical evolution began in 1849, when William Welch founded Deloitte in London.[7] The story of Pricewaterhouse Coopers (PwC) also began in 1849, when Samuel Lowell Price set up a business in London and then in 1865 formed a partnership with Holyland and Waterhouse.[8] Ernst & Young followed in the same year as PwC, first via the establishment of Harding & Pullein joined by Frederick Whinney.[9] In 1891, the story of KPMG starts, when William Barclay Peat assumed leadership of the firm in London where he was working as an accountant and renamed it William Barclay Peat & Co.[10] Legal regulation heavily contributed to their establishment in England.[11] They expanded their services in line with the gradual internationalization of capital and they pioneered the use of information technologies.[12] The financialization, the prominence of multinational companies and the consolidation of the audit market accelerated merger and acquisitions and helped to turn the Big Four into today's global players.[13]

They form an oligopoly in the accounting and auditing market with a revenue of 167.33 billion USD (collectively) in 2021, which almost doubled in the last 10 years, as in 2010 they had a revenue of 95.085 billion USD (collectively).[14] However, their revenue alone does not justify why they are characterized as 'big'. During the same period, the number of their employees (including professional, administrative staff, etc.) has almost doubled

[6] Arthur Andersen, Arthur Young, Coopers & Lybrand, Deloitte Haskins and Sells, Ernst & Whinney, Peat Marwick Mitchell, Price Waterhouse and Touche Ross.

[7] J. Peterson, *Timeline: An Abbreviated History: The Origins of the Big Eight, and How They Shrank to Four* (Emerald, 2017), 305–307.

[8] www.pwc.com/us/en/about-us/pwc-corporate-history.html.

[9] Peterson, *Timeline*, 305–307.

[10] https://home.kpmg/xx/en/home/about/who-we-are/our-history.html.

[11] Peterson, *Timeline*, 305; See also J. J. Glynn, 'The Development of British Railway Accounting: 1800–1911' (1984) 11 *The Accounting Historians Journal* 103.

[12] Shore and Wright, 'How the Big 4 Got Big'.

[13] Ibid.; Herman, 'Neither Takers nor Makers'.

[14] The sources of this information mainly constitute the publicly available global annual reports/reviews and websites of the respective Big Four; For the year of 2010, see www.pwc.ec/es/publicaciones/assets/pdf/global-annual-review-2010.pdf, www2.deloitte.com/content/dam/Deloitte/global/Documents/About-Deloitte/gx-deloitte-2010-gir-cr-report.pdf, https://assets.kpmg/content/dam/kpmg/pdf/2011/03/KPMG-International-Annual-Review-2010.pdf and http://fs.monadnockresearch.com/pubfiles/Ernst_Young_Global_Review_2010.pdf; For the year of 2021, see www.pwc.com/gx/en/about-pwc/global-annual-review-2021/downloads/pwc-global-annual-review-2021.pdf, www2.deloitte.com/content/dam/Deloitte/global/Documents/About-Deloitte/about-deloitte-global-report-full-version-2021.pdf, https://home.kpmg/xx/en/home/media/press-releases/2021/12/kpmg-reports-global-revenues-of-usd-32-billion-for-fy21.html and www.ey.com/en_gl/global-review/value-realized-2021.

(collectively and individually). It has risen from 610,104 in 2010 to 1,189,252 employees in 2021 worldwide (collectively).[15] They operate in more than 140 countries.[16] Most of their revenue originates from auditing/assurance services and consultancy services, but a significant portion originates from tax and legal services.[17] Their entry into the legal services market started in the 1990s. It was triggered by a growing demand for tax services, the declining profitability of accounting services and the fact that the most profitable new areas of services provisions intersected with law, such as corporate restructuring, insolvency, litigation support and forensic accounting services.[18] The websites of the Big Four provide information on the type of legal services at a global level, allowing identification of the relevant legal fields and topics: banking and finance, taxation, corporate, commercial, mergers and acquisitions, competition, employment, migration, legal operation, management, technology, cybersecurity, data protection, entity compliance, governance, sustainability and real estate.[19] The accounting scandals arising out of the 2001 financial crisis or, more recently, the Wirecard scandal,[20] triggered regulatory action in the US and the EU[21] to draw a dividing line between auditing and other – legal – services.[22]

However, despite those reforms, the main concerns about their market power, their continuing growth and the ever-deeper intrusion into the law market remain valid and justify taking a deeper look into the kind of legal services they provide and into the potential influence they exercise on the EU and international institutions.

[15] Ibid.; http://fs.monadnockresearch.com/pubfiles/Ernst_Young_Global_Review_2010.pdf.

[16] Ibid.

[17] PWC, 'Global Annual Review 2021', at www.pwc.com/gx/en/about/global-annual-review-2021/financials.html; Deloitte, '2021 Global Impact Report: Business', at www2.deloitte.com/global/en/pages/about-deloitte/articles/global-impact-report/global-report-business.html; KPMG, 'FY21 highlights', at https://home.kpmg/xx/en/home/insights/2021/12/corporate-reporting-2021-kpmg-at-a-glance.html; Ernst & Young, 'EY Value Realized: Reporting Progress on Global Impact 2021', at www.ey.com/en_gl/global-review/value-realized-2021.

[18] Wilkins and Esteban Ferrer, 'Integration of Law'.

[19] www.pwc.com/gx/en/services/legal.html; www2.deloitte.com/global/en/services/legal.html?icid=top_legal; www.ey.com/en_gl/law; and https://home.kpmg/xx/en/home/services/tax/global-legal-services-kpmg-law.html.

[20] Deutsche Welle, 'The Big Four: Accounting Firms under Scrutiny', at www.dw.com/en/the-big-four-accounting-firms-under-scrutiny/av-62593672.

[21] Directive 2014/56/EU of the European Parliament and of the Council of 16 April 2014 amending Directive 2006/43/EC on statutory audits of annual accounts and consolidated accounts [2014] OJ L158/196; Regulation (EU) No 537/2014 of the European Parliament and of the Council of 16 April 2014 on specific requirements regarding statutory audit of public-interest entities and repealing Commission Decision 2005/909/EC [2014] OJ L158/77.

[22] Wilkins and Esteban Ferrer, 'Integration of Law'.

4.3 BIG FOUR AND PUBLIC GOVERNANCE

The move towards public governance originates from the World Bank's project of social overhead capital starting in the 1950s.[23] The concept pioneered by economists such as Paul Rosenstein-Rodan promoted the financing of the infrastructure in what were then called 'development countries' through internationally funded but nationally planned programmes. However, the emerging tendency to state ownership of key national 'infrastructure' and the severe criticism with respect to efficiency led the World Bank to open up state-run public services to private sector management through Public–Private Partnerships. The Big Four seized the opportunity.

The Big Four exercise their influence upon public governance through multiple channels: formal ones, such as public procurement contracts, interventions in public consultations on envisaged regulatory means or public sector advisory groups, as well as informal ones, such as lobbying, 'revolving doors' (an established proximity of their personnel to the regulators including the swapping of personnel between Big Four and the institutions they advise) or through influence exercised via other interest groups.[24] The lobbying activities revolve around accounting and tax avoidance. In 2011, the Big Four collectively invested 10 million dollars to influence the US Public Company Accounting Oversight Board.[25] Through different means, including financial contributions, they have aimed at influencing the US Securities and Exchange Commission regarding international financial reporting standards.[26] In the EU they targeted the Financial Transaction Tax[27] and the policy responses to tax avoidance[28] and in the UK the Modern Slavery Act through inter alia financial contributions.[29] At a global scale, through engagement with the World Trade Organization (WTO), they lobbied against international standards promoting deregulation at the national level for the accountancy profession.[30] Their policy of 'revolving doors' in the US

[23] N. Hildyard, '"Infrastructure" and the Big 4: Public–Private Partnerships, Corridors, and the Expansion of Capital', in Ch. Hurl and A. Vogelpohl (eds.), *Professional Service Firms and Politics in a Global Era* (New York: Palgrave MacMillan, 2021), 197.

[24] See, e.g., Corporate Europe Observatory, 'Accounting for Influence'; Kalaitzake, 'Accounting for Success'.

[25] Shore and Wright, 'How the Big 4 Got Big', 313.

[26] Herman, 'Neither Takers nor Makers'.

[27] Kalaitzake, 'Accounting for Success'.

[28] Corporate Europe Observatory, 'Accounting for Influence'.

[29] Fransen and LeBaron, 'Regulatory Intermediaries'.

[30] See P. Arnold, 'Disciplining Domestic Regulation: The World Trade Organization and the Market for Professional Services' (2005) 30 *Accounting, Organizations and Society* 299.

Federal Reserve, the UK[31], and the EU[32] or the growing impact on public procurement contracts, on the official provision of services[33] through interventions to public consultations[34] and to established public sector advisory groups are all documented.[35] In essence, the Big Four can be understood as a regulatory intermediary.[36]

4.4 METHODOLOGY: HOW TO OPEN THE BLACK BOX

There is no official database on the nexus between the Big Four, public governance and law-making. Firstly, we examine the legal framework on transparency and public governance. The examination pinpoints the sources and databases where necessary information can be found as well as possible gaps. The focus lies on so-called direct procurement, which involves private suppliers of goods, services or works. Indirect procurement procedures by means of a letter of assist, National Execution (NEX), procedures typical of financial institutions or involving other international organizations and procedures involving private parties as the executors of a function or a task of the organization are not addressed, due to their complex regulatory architecture involving national rules and international agreements.[37] Secondly, we examine the websites of the Big Four concerning their provision of services to EU and international organizations.[38] This exercise has been quite fruitful as the Big Four have used their specific nexus with the EU as a self-marketing exercise for governance-shaping and consultancy. All of them devote specific websites to explaining their co-operation with the EU and its institutions, occasionally also with specific national governments and the United Nations (Deloitte[39]) or the World Economic Forum (Deloitte, PwC, KPMG, Ernst &

[31] Shore and Wright, 'How the Big 4 Got Big'.

[32] Corporate Europe Observatory, 'Accounting for Influence'.

[33] Ibid.; Fransen and LeBaron, 'Regulatory Intermediaries'.

[34] Kalaitzake, 'Accounting for Success'.

[35] Corporate Europe Observatory, 'Accounting for Influence'; Arnold, 'Disciplining Domestic Regulation'.

[36] Ibid.; Herman, 'Neither Takers nor Makers'.

[37] See the detailed analysis in E. Morlino, *Procurement by International Organizations: A Global Administrative Law Perspective* (Cambridge University Press, 2019).

[38] https://home.kpmg/xx/en/home/industries/government-public-sector/eu-services.html; www.ey.com/en_gl/eu-institutions; www2.deloitte.com/be/en/pages/public-sector/topics/eu-institutions-services.html; and www.pwc.com/gx/en/services/european-union.html.

[39] www2.deloitte.com/ch/en/pages/public-sector/solutions/united-nations-and-non-governmental-organisations.html.

Young).[40] A word of caution is needed. These data are the ones the Big Four have made public voluntarily to promote their activities. They do not disclose their revenue per mandate or the frequency of their provision of services per year. Their global annual reports (when available online[41]) from 2010 until 2021 served as a second source of information. Here we can identify specific sectors and cases where the Big Four provided services to the EU and to international organizations.

The data made available by the Big Four are complemented by other databases provided either by the public sector or by research platforms, such as in the EU Transparency Register,[42] opentender.eu[43] and the Financial Transparency System.[44] The EU Transparency Registry lists organizations attempting to influence the law-making and policy implementation process of the EU institutions.[45] It was founded in 2011 by the European Parliament and the European Commission.[46] Specifically,

> [t]he Transparency Registry is a public database holding up-to-date information about interest representatives actively engaged in activities aimed at influencing the formulation or implementation of policies or legislation at EU level. It gives individuals, the media, stakeholders and EU staff the possibility to track interests represented through the EU institutions, find out who is representing those interests on whose behalf, as well as to see what resources are devoted to the related lobbying activities and efforts. It is one of several transparency tools that aims to improve the transparency and openness of the EU decision making process.[47]

With the aim to establish a coordinated approach and broaden the database, in 2021 a new interinstitutional agreement between the European Parliament, the European Commission and the Council of the European

[40] www2.deloitte.com/global/en/pages/about-deloitte/articles/worldeconomicforum.html; www.pwc.com/gx/en/about/contribution-to-debate/world-economic-forum.html; https://home.kpmg/xx/en/home/about/the-world-economic-forum-and-kpmg.html; and www.ey.com/en_gl/wef.

[41] Any gaps are complemented through the annual reports of their corporate headquarters or their websites or other sources such as media news.

[42] https://ec.europa.eu/transparencyregister/public/consultation/search.do?locale=en&reset=.

[43] https://opentender.eu/eu/about/about-opentender.

[44] https://ec.europa.eu/budget/financial-transparency-system/about.html.

[45] https://ec.europa.eu/transparencyregister/public/consultation/search.do?locale=en&reset=.

[46] Agreement between the European Parliament and the European Commission on the establishment of a transparency register for organizations and self-employed individuals engaged in EU policy-making and policy implementation [2011], OJ L191/29.

[47] Annual Report on the functioning of the Transparency Register 2021 (presented by the Transparency Register Management Board to the European Parliament, the Council of the European Union and the European Commission), 2.

Union was signed.[48] One of the new features is that it makes this registry mandatory. According to article 1, the three signatories can decide that 'covered activities'[49] – including many activities of the Big Four – are conditional upon registration in the register. Therefore, the register is still not complete. The column 'Specific activities covered by the Register' includes a list of contributions to 'public consultations 'and 'roadmaps'. This allows us to specifically look for policy areas and regulatory initiatives where the Big Four have intervened, since 24 July 2018. However, this database provides only information concerning the exercise of broad influence by the Big Four upon three EU institutions in theory; the available data primarily concern the European Commission and to a very limited extent the European Parliament.

The opentender.eu platform is a public and open procurement platform run by DIGIWHIST, an EU Horizon 2020 funded project bringing together six European research institutes aiming at the empowerment of the society to combat public sector corruption: the Department of Sociology of the University of Cambridge, Open Knowledge Foundation Germany, Government Transparency Institute, Hertie School of Governance, Datlab and Transcrime (the Joint Research Centre on Transnational Crime of the Università Cattolica del Sacro Cuore of Milan and University of Trento). The data provided

> are procurement data from about 20 various sources. When there is no open data available we [opentender.eu] extract the information from thousands of web pages to arrive at a structured database. After that we [opentender.eu] group together all publications describing each tender and eventually create a final image that most accurately describes the particular tender. Source systems and data differ from country to country, so a tailored piece of software is created for each source separately.[50]

The platform grants access to data concerning contracts awarded by EU institutions to the Big Four between 2009–2021. The data may signal trends and complement qualitative data, namely concerning the types of services provided. They indicate the volume in millions of tenders per year and can only be used to compare the involvement of the Big Four and to identify trends. The data in in the Financial Transparency System and in the

48 Interinstitutional Agreement of 20 May 2021 between the European Parliament, the Council of the European Union and the European Commission on a mandatory transparency register [2021], OJ L207/1.

49 Ibid., articles 3 and 4.

50 https://opentender.eu/eu/about/how-opentender-works.

opentender.eu platform pursue different objectives. The volume represents the total volume in which each of the Big Four have participated. Therefore, they do not represent the total and individual gain or profit of each of the Big Four alone. The EU Transparency Registry covers, in principle, all EU institutions, including agencies.

The Financial Transparency System is managed by the European Commission, more specifically by the Directorate-General for Budget, and provides information on

> ... the beneficiaries funding from the EU budget implemented directly by the European Commission ... and other EU bodies such as executive agencies ('direct management') or implemented indirectly by other international organisations or non-EU countries ('indirect management'), and beneficiaries of the European Development Fund.[51]

The funding types are Grants, Prizes, Public procurement (including provisional commitments and other expenditure), Financial Instruments, Budget Support and External Experts.[52] The scope has been extended over time. Crudely speaking the data cover funding awarded from 2007 (sometimes from 2012/2013) until 2021.[53] According to article 38 Financial Regulation,[54]

> the Commission shall make available, in an appropriate and timely manner, information on recipients of funds financed from the budget, where the budget is implemented by it in accordance with point (a) of the first subparagraph of Article 62(1) ...

According to article 38(2)(2) Financial Regulation, the information concerns the name of the recipient, the amount legally committed and the nature and purpose of the measure in the cases of prizes, grants and contracts which have been awarded as a result of contests, grant award procedures or procurement procedures, and for experts selected pursuant to article 237(2) Financial Regulation. Due to the availability and structure of the search engine we have directed our focus on the amount which is legally committed to the Big Four. This database complements the one on opentender.eu.

In comparison to the multiple European databases, access to information on the consulting activities of the Big Four with international organizations is

51 https://ec.europa.eu/budget/financial-transparency-system/.

52 https://ec.europa.eu/budget/financial-transparency-system/about.html.

53 https://ec.europa.eu/budget/financial-transparency-system/faq.html.

54 Regulation (EU, Euratom) 2018/1046 of the European Parliament and of the Council of 18 July 2018 on the financial rules applicable to the general budget of the Union [2018] OJ L193/1.

scarce. Existing databases have a very narrow focus, for example, procurement in national jurisdictions.[55] As the Big Four do not report about the services they provide to international organizations overall through their websites, our research had to investigate the Big Four's annual reports. Those sources sufficed to identify the United Nations, World Economic Forum, the G20 and the Organization for Economic Cooperation and Development (OECD), which seem to receive services from the Big Four to a greater extent in comparison to other organizations. Theoretically each and every international organization deserves attention. However, we will put the United Nations system in the limelight, which provides publicly available data on procurement or more generally contracts awarded to the Big Four.[56]

Specifically, the Annual Statistical Report on United Nations Procurement (ASR) provides data reported by the participating UN organizations on 'acquisition through purchase or lease of real property, goods or other products (including intellectual property), works or services, as defined by the UN procurement practitioner's handbook'[57] with a total value of 30,000 USD or more from 2000 onwards through the annual statistical reports from 2010 to 2014[58] and from 2015 on the dashboard.[59] The focus rests on the total volume and number of contracts signed between the Big Four and the participating UN organizations. In a few cases the name of the supplier is not reported for security reasons or confidentiality requirements.

4.5 EU LEGAL FRAMEWORK ON TRANSPARENCY OF PUBLIC GOVERNANCE

Comparing the EU to other international or intergovernmental organizations, we would expect that the EU provides better and more stringent rules on transparency, understood as the obligation and the willingness to inform the public at large on the degree to which the EU is using the Big Four in support

55 See, e.g., www.worldbank.org/en/topic/governance/brief/global-public-procurement-database.

56 See www.ungm.org/Shared/KnowledgeCenter/Pages/asr_data_supplier.

57 www.ungm.org/Shared/KnowledgeCenter/Pages/asr_about.

58 www.ungm.org/Areas/Public/Downloads/ASR/2010/Document/ASR_2010.pdf; www.ungm.org/Areas/Public/Downloads/ASR/2011/Document/ASR_2011.pdf; www.ungm.org/Areas/Public/Downloads/ASR/2012/Document/2012_Annual_Statistical_Report_procurement.pdf; www.ungm.org/Areas/Public/Downloads/ASR/2013/Document/ASR_2013.pdf; www.ungm.org/Areas/Public/Downloads/ASR/2014/Document/ASR_2014.pdf.

59 www.ungm.org/Shared/KnowledgeCenter/Pages/asr_data_supplier.

of its constitutional mandate. The presentation of the regulatory framework will be linked to a critical account of its application and enforcement in practice[60] with regard to the Big Four.

4.5.1 *EU as a Forerunner*

Transparency and openness of the decision-making processes towards the citizens in the EU has been a long journey. Over time, transparency evolved from a general principle of public access to a few EU institutions' documents[61] into a right of the individual.[62] The Lisbon Treaty[63] transformed access to documents into a fundamental right under article 42 of the Charter of Fundamental Rights, thereby expanding the addressed EU institutions.[64] Secondary EU law concretizes the requirement through the 2014 Public Procurement Package, but not with regard to EU institutions. Their procurement is regulated by the Financial Regulation.[65] The FOIA Regulation[66] grants 'widest possible access'[67] to documents of the European Parliament, the Council, the Commission and EU agencies.[68] The European Ombudsman is pushing the EU institutions into action. Thanks to its initia-

60 Such as the project carried out at the Erik Castrén Institute at the University of Helsinki: 'Transparency in the EU – From Reaction to Manifesto? (TRUE)'.

61 Declaration on the right of access to information (Maastricht Treaty, Annex 17).

62 Article 255 TEC (Treaty of Amsterdam). See further, B. Neamtu and D. Dragos, 'Freedom of Information in the European Union: Legal Challenges and Practices of EU Institutions', in D. Dragos, P. Kovac and A. Marseille (eds.), *The Laws of Transparency in Action: A European Perspective* (Palgrave MacMillan, 2019), 11.

63 European Commission, Explaining the Treaty of Lisbon (2009) MEMO/09/531; M. Hillebrandt, 'The Big Lesson after Ten Years of EU Transparency Reforms? You Will Never Get It Right' (*Open Government in the EU*, 14 January 2020), at www.eu-opengovernment.eu/?p=1064.

64 Neamtu and Dragos, 'Freedom of Information'; see also especially articles 1, 11(2) and (3) and 15(3) TEU.

65 See note 54.

66 Regulation (EC) No 1049/2001 of the European Parliament and of the Council of 30 May 2001 regarding public access to European Parliament, Council and Commission documents [2001] OJ L145/43; Concerning the regulatory overlap and relationship between EU procurement law and law regarding the access to documents, see A Sanchez-Graells, 'Transparency in Procurement by the EU Institutions', in K.-M. Halonen, R. Caranta and A. Sanchez-Graells (eds.), *Transparency in EU Procurements* (Edward Elgar Publishing, 2019), 82.

67 P. Leino, 'Transparency, Participation and EU Institutional Practice: An Inquiry into the Limits of the "Widest Possible" EUI Working Paper Law 2014/3'.

68 K. Lenaerts, '"In the Union We Trust": Trust Enhancing Principles of Community Law' (2004) 41 *Common Market Law Review* 317, 321.

tive,[69] the European Court of Auditors, the ECB and European agencies adopted particular rules governing access to their documents.[70] EU citizens may launch complaints with the Ombudsman or seek judicial review before the Court of Justice of the EU in case access to the documents is denied.[71]

This regulatory evolution towards further transparency with a focus on tackling corruption is going to be further accelerated taking into consideration the recent so-called Qatargate scandal. At this stage, this is indicated by the European Parliament's Resolution,[72] which calls for the adoption of several measures enhancing transparency at EU level and particularly at the European Parliament's level, for example, the establishment of an EU ethics body, the introduction of a cooling-off period for former Members of the European Parliament to avoid the negative effects of the phenomenon of revolving doors, the strengthening of the EU transparency register with the aim to become mandatory or the revision of the Staff Regulations.[73]

4.5.2 *Stock-Taking: EU Commission, Court of Auditors, COE and EurActiv*

Maarten Hillebrandt stated that 'the European institutions sullenly seem to have reached the conclusion that they apparently can never do anything right. The mantra seems "damned if you do, damned if you don't"'.[74] In fact, the practice of the EU institutions is subject to strong criticism.[75]

The Corporate Europe Observatory in 2018[76] and EurActiv in 2021[77] attacked the over-reliance of the EU institutions upon the Big Four. They

[69] 616/PUBAC/F/IJH, OJ C44/9, 1998.

[70] P. Craig, *EU Administrative Law*, 3rd ed. (Oxford University Press, 2018); See also D. Curtin and P. Leino, 'In Search of Transparency for EU Law-Making: Trilogues on the Cusp of Dawn' (2017) 54 *Common Market Law Review* 1673.

[71] Curtin and Leino, 'In Search of Transparency for EU Law-Making'.

[72] European Parliament Resolution of 15 December 2022 on suspicions of corruption from Qatar and the broader need for transparency and accountability in the European institutions (2022/3012(RSP)).

[73] Ibid.; see also EURACTIV with Reuters, 'EU Parliament Head Sets out Transparency Plan in Response to "Qatargate" Scandal' (*EURACTIV*, 12 January 2023), at www.euractiv.com/section/justice-home-affairs/news/eu-parliament-head-sets-out-transparency-plan-in-response-to-qatargate-scandal/.

[74] Hillebrandt, 'The Big Lesson'.

[75] See, e.g., Erik Castrén Institute, 'Transparency in the EU – From Reaction to Manifesto? (TRUE)' Research Project, at www2.helsinki.fi/en/erik-castren-institute/transparency-in-the-eu-from-reaction-to-manifesto-true and all research output listed.

[76] Corporate Europe Observatory (n. 5).

[77] J. Valero, 'EXCLUSIVE: Commission's Ballooning Bill with Consultancy Firms Revealed' (*EURACTIV*, 18 March 2021), at www.euractiv.com/section/economy-jobs/news/exclusive-commissions-ballooning-bill-with-consultancy-firms-revealed/.

criticized their increasing influence on law-making, in fields which either address the Big Four directly (e.g., international accounting standards) or their clients (e.g., tax, competition, financial law). EurActiv revealed that the 'European Commission spent more than €462 million between 2016 and 2019 in contracts with PWC, KPMG, Deloitte and Ernst & Young, known collectively as the Big Four'.[78] It is no coincidence that the information was disclosed at a time when the European Court of Auditors was about to investigate the activities of the European Commission.[79] The report triggered significant reactions from multiple EU institutions and bodies, the European Parliament, the European Court of Auditors and the European Commission. The European Court of Auditors[80] informed Euractiv that it examines hundreds of millions worth of contracts the European Commission had concluded with external consultants.[81] The European Parliament told Euractiv that it will investigate the Commissions' bill to consultancy firms[82] and a number of MEPs wrote a letter to the Commission precisely on this matter.[83] The European Commission was initially quite defensive. The Big Four were said to be more cost-efficient in terms of human resources, with transparent public procurement, and the Commission remains responsible for using or rejecting the information. At the same time the European Commission declared that it would follow the European Ombudsman's recommendation and propose amendments to the Financial Regulation, such as the obligation for those who reply to the public tender to disclose conflicting interests.[84] This

[78] Ibid.

[79] European Court of Auditors, 'Timeline – Special Report 17/2022: External Consultants at the European Commission', at www.eca.europa.eu/Lists/ECATimeline/Timeline-SR-22-17/Timeline-SR-22-17_EN.pdf.

[80] According to article 285 TFEU, the Court of Auditors shall carry out the Union's audit. Specifically, it shall examine the accounts of all revenues and expenditure of the Unions and its respective bodies, etc.

[81] J. Valero, 'EU Court of Auditors Looking into Commission's Contracts with Consultants' (*EURACTIV*, 19 March 2021), at www.euractiv.com/section/economy-jobs/news/eu-court-of-auditors-looking-into-commissions-contracts-with-consultants/.

[82] J. Valero, 'Parliament to Look into Commission's Multi-million Bill with Consultancy Firms' (*EURACTIV*, 14 April 2021), at www.euractiv.com/section/economy-jobs/news/parliament-to-look-into-commissions-multi-million-bill-with-consultancy-firms/; Parliamentary Question 'Special Relationship between the EU and Consultancy Firms' E-005496/2021 (9.12.2021), at www.europarl.europa.eu/doceo/document/E-9-2021-005496_EN.html.

[83] J. Valero, 'MEPs Grill Commission about Growing Expenditure in Consultancy Firms' (*EURACTIV*, 30 March 2021), at www.euractiv.com/section/politics/news/meps-grill-commission-about-growing-expenditure-in-consultancy-firms/.

[84] https://portal.ieu-monitoring.com/editorial/eu-commissions-use-of-private-consultancy-firms-answer-to-a-written-question.

was in fact realized through proposed targeted adjustments to the Financial Regulation announced in May 2022.[85]

Roughly 1 year later the European Court of Auditors published its special report 17/2022 on 30 June 2022 according to article 287(4)(2) TFEU.[86] Remarkably, the Court of Auditors acknowledged that its assessment on the use of external consultants by the European Commission is incomplete as it did not have full knowledge of the facts. The Report is nevertheless telling: there is an increasing use of external consultants to perform various advisory and support services, mainly in implementing the EU's neighbourhood and enlargement policies, international partnerships, foreign policy instruments, environmental and climate actions.[87] The European Court of Auditors identified gaps in the regulatory framework with regard to potential risks related to the concentration of service providers, overdependence and conflicts of interest which are not sufficiently monitored and expressed doubts in the added value of the consultants' input. Those observations ended in a call for improving the management of external consultants and increasing transparency by reporting more regularly and accurately. In reaction, the European Commission confirmed that it will implement the recommendations by the end of 2023.[88] The latest developments document convincingly the burdensome and painful process on the role and function of the Big Four in the daily work of the European Commission. Despite the efforts to avoid a 'Qatargate' 2 scandal, tackle corruption and enhance transparency,[89] it will be a long way down the road before the administrative reality might be aligned with the ambitious wordings of the Treaties.

85 European Commission, 'Proposal for a Regulation of the European Parliament and of the Council on the financial rules applicable to the general budget of the Union (recast)', COM (2022) 223 final.

86 European Court of Auditors, 'Special Report: External Consultants at the European Commission: Scope for Reform' (30 June 2022), at www.eca.europa.eu/en/Pages/DocItem.aspx?did=61461.

87 The European Court of Auditors acknowledged that its report covers only the services of external consultants financed by the EU budget and contracted by the European Commission between 2017 and 2019, and recorded by the Commission as consultancy, study, evaluation or research. However, IT consultancy services are not covered and included in the report's results.

88 European Commission, 'Replies of the European Commission to the European Court of Auditors' Special Report', at www.eca.europa.eu/Lists/ECAReplies/COM-Replies-SR-22-17/COM-Replies-SR-22-17_EN.pdf.

89 See Corporate Europe Observatory, 'Qatargate: Lobby Watchdog Says the European Parliament Needs to Close All Loopholes', at https://corporateeurope.org/en/2023/01/qatargate-lobby-watchdog-says-european-parliament-needs-close-all-loopholes, criticizing the recent proposals of the President of the European Parliament.

4.6 GOING BEYOND: BIG FOUR SHAPING PUBLIC GOVERNANCE AND LAW-MAKING?

The websites of the Big Four provide for a first idea of the types of services they offer: policy analysis and advice, auditing, financial resources and risk management, technology consulting and implementation, human resources and even financial management related to the EU budget.[90] They provide the same type of services with regard to sustainability, digitalization, auditing and education, but there are also differences.[91] Ernst & Young and Deloitte are not involved in financial management relating to the EU budget and the internal public sector's accounting standards. Public procurement, border control and security are in the hands of PwC and Deloitte, services related to space, financial services (independent professional services) and economic growth are provided by PwC only and services related to health are given by Deloitte only, whereas services related to corruption, fraud detection and criminal justice are managed by Deloitte and KPMG. The Big Four's reports from 2010 to 2021 confirm *grosso modo* the findings.[92] Specifically, the provision of services such as policy advice and analysis, technology consulting and implementation could be verified. The same is true with regard to services in relation to borders and security by PwC, in relation to auditing/financial reporting by PwC, Deloitte and KPMG, sustainability by PwC, Deloitte and Ernst & Young and financial services by PwC. However, the annual reports do not provide for a full picture about the relevant topics and areas and the types of services provided, let alone the respective topics and areas. If any, specific examples are highlighted, obviously more in a self-marketing perspective than with the intention to inform the public any deeper of what they are doing, why and with what intention towards whom and with what objective.

4.7 THE EU TRANSPARENCY REGISTRY

It seems that the added value of the EU Transparency Register is quite limited and does not go much beyond what the websites and the reports are telling, in particular when the differing categories are linked together (e.g., climate can be associated with sustainability, gender equality with education focusing

90 See https://home.kpmg/xx/en/home/industries/government-public-sector/eu-services.html; www.ey.com/en_gl/eu-institutions; www2.deloitte.com/be/en/pages/public-sector/topics/eu-institutions-services.html; www.pwc.com/gx/en/services/european-union.html.

91 Ibid.

92 See the Annex for references.

mainly on human resources and finally trade with economic growth).[93] However, the data do not match when it comes to the question of which of the Big Four is engaged in what kind of services. This is hardly surprising as the Transparency Registry does not include data concerning all EU institutions but primarily only the European Commission. The websites and the annual reports of the Big Four disclose the information they are willing to give away. The information is not limited to the EU and to what they have done but includes services they could offer in the future. Under the registry the Big Four are obliged to provide at least some of the information on specific lobbying activities towards the three signatories (namely the European Commission, the Council and the European Parliament in principle).

4.8 THE OPENTENDER.EU PLATFORM

Deloitte[94] was involved in 177 tenders in total from 2009 to 2021, with a volume of 2,212.9 million. Those tenders concern multiple sectors of business: law, marketing, consulting, recruitment, printing and security (88), IT services (32), research, development and related consultancy services (29). PwC[95] was involved in 112 tenders in total from 2010 to 2021, with a volume of 906.7 million. Similarly to Deloitte, PwC has been involved in law, marketing, consulting, recruitment, printing, security (52), research,

[93] PWC (name: PwCIL, registration number 60402754518-05) provides services in areas/topics such as auditing, taxation (e.g. Fighting the use of shell entities and arrangements for tax purposes), corporate governance/financial sustainability/finance (e.g. Strengthening the quality of corporate reporting and its enforcement), climate (Carbon Border Adjustment Mechanism) and digitalization/technology/data/AI (e.g. Digital Education Action Plan). Ernst & Young (name: Ernst & Young Core Business Services BV, registration number 04458109373-91) provides services in areas/topics such as auditing, taxation (New EU system for the avoidance of double taxation in the field of withholding taxes), corporate governance/financial sustainability/finance (e.g. Strengthening the quality of corporate reporting and its enforcement) and digitalization/technology/data/AI (e.g. Requirements for Artificial Intelligence). Deloitte (seven different registrations under seven different names, e.g. Name: Deloitte & Associés, registration number: 419726214834-51) provides services in areas/topics such as auditing, taxation (e.g. Digital Levy), corporate governance/financial sustainability/finance (e.g. Revision of Non-Financial Reporting Directive) and digitalization/technology/data/AI (e.g. Cyber Resilience Act). KPMG (name: KPMG, registration number 65515368730-59) provides services in areas/topics such as auditing, taxation (e.g. Fighting the use of shell entities and arrangements for tax purposes), corporate governance/financial sustainability/finance (e.g. Action Plan on anti-money laundering) and climate (e.g. Updating the EU Emissions Trading System).

[94] Based on the search engine of opentender.eu, Deloitte is 'registered' under 103 different companies.

[95] Based on the search engine of opentender.eu, PwC is 'registered' under 58 different companies.

development and related consultancy services (24) and IT services (18). Clearly, KPMG[96] participated in much fewer tenders between 2009 and 2021, namely 62 in total, most of them were related to law, marketing, consulting, recruitment, printing, and security (37). The total volume of those tenders comes up to approximately 714.6 million. KPMG seems to go for larger tenders, as the major difference in numbers does not affect the volume. Finally, Ernst & Young[97] has been involved in twice the number of tenders in comparison to KPMG from 2009 to 2021, namely 120/121 tenders but of which the total volume is 758.6 million, which is quite close to KPMG's. Following a similar pattern with the rest of the Big Four, most of the tenders relate to law, marketing, consulting, recruitment, printing and security (63), research, development and related consultancy services (29). These are the predominant ones amongst the Big Four, IT services ranking second particularly in the cases of PwC and Deloitte. Those findings seem to confirm the qualitative data from the websites and the annual reports.

4.9 THE FINANCIAL TRANSPARENCY SYSTEM

The Financial Transparency System[98] by and large confirms EURACTIV's estimations. The latter observes the amount of 462 million in comparison to 435 million based on the Financial Transparency System between 2016 and 2019. This amount almost doubled between 2014 and 2021 as the Big Four collectively were contracted by the European Commission for 817.49 million. Moreover, we do observe that clearly PwC has had by far the smallest commitments contracted and consumed in terms of volume and Deloitte has had the biggest but without a huge difference in terms of volume with Ernst & Young and KPMG.

4.10 INTERIM CONCLUSION

The analysis so far tells us much more about the impact of the Big Four on the European institutions than their possible impact on shaping public

96 Based on the search engine of opentender.eu, KPMG is 'registered' under 39 different companies.

97 Based on the search engine of opentender.eu, Ernst & Young is 'registered' under 85 different companies.

98 https://ec.europa.eu/budget/financial-transparency-system/about.html; Based on the database of the Financial Transparency System, PwC is 'registered' under six different companies/partnerships et cetera; Ernst & Young is 'registered' under 45 different companies/partnerships et cetera; Deloitte is 'registered' under 30 different companies/partnerships et cetera; and KPMG is 'registered' under 32 different companies/partnerships et cetera.

governance. Somewhat overstated, we know the total amount spent and the fields of activities in which the Big Four are contracted. The total amount sounds rather small in comparison to the overall budget of the European Commission or the European Parliament, but it might be large if compared to the total amount of money the European institutions spent on external advice in forms of studies and research projects equally tendered and undertaken by Brussels consultancy companies and academic institutions. Conversely, the total amount does not tell us anything about the impact of the consultancy, the degree to which the Big Four succeeded in pre-shaping and predetermining EU legal policies in the respective business sectors. A clear picture would require much more detail on the rather broad categories, the reasons that triggered the mandating and the interaction between the European institutions and the Big Four during the consultation. It would require looking into all the tenders, the reports which have been prepared to meet the tender, and the concrete legislative action which stands behind the tender. It is not difficult to add even more questions.

These findings clash dramatically with the bombastic language in the Treaties and casts a shadow on the democratic understanding of the European institutions. Without pressure from the outside, mainly and most importantly through the media, through a kind of investigative journalism together with the European Court of Auditors and other national authorities taking into account the recent 'Qatargate' scandal, the European institutions do not seem to be ready to move and make a serious effort to inform the public at large about the degree to which they rely on and follow the advice provided by the Big Four in the core of what holds the EU together – the internal market. The legal framework as it stands shields the European institutions against critique from the outside world. The analysis of the role of the Big Four underpins such an assessment.

4.11 INTERNATIONAL ORGANIZATIONS

According to the annual reports of the Big Four,[99] the showcased international organizations are the UN, the World Economic Forum, the G20 and the OECD. The topics and areas to which the Big Four have contributed, engaged and worked with those organizations focus on sustainable economic growth and development, corruption, gender equality, ethical business conduct, the future role of civil society, of work and future of regulation broadly, tax transparency, Environmental, Social and Governance (ESG) metrics and

[99] See the Annex.

non-financial reporting standards. There are other well-known institutions to which the Big Four are providing services such as the World Bank, Financial Stability Board, International Monetary Fund, Asia-Pacific Economic Cooperation Forum and the World Trade Organization, as well as specialized private sector associations such as the World Business Council on Sustainable Development, the International Federation of Accountants, the International Organization of Securities Commissions, the International Forum for Independent Audit Regulators, the International Integrated Reporting Committee and International Organization of Employers.

Comparing the data with those of the EU, they are not specifying, enlarging or clarifying the field of activities. The services and the fields are by and large the same and breathe the same spirit – rough data on all sorts of policy fields coloured through examples, the value of which is hard to assess without analysing the context and without knowing the reasons for their choice.

4.12 THE CASE OF THE UNITED NATIONS SYSTEM

International law is not built on transparency but on secrecy, opacity and confidentiality. Only recently has transparency begun to play an important role in global governance.[100] However, there is still not one international legal framework on transparency. Instead, each international organization has developed its own internal rules on transparency policies and on procurement through references in funding treaties, in specific procurement rules included in financial regulations and administrative circulars or manuals, mainly addressed to the staff of the organizations.[101] Despite the patchy legal framework, legal scholarship seems to agree that there is an overall evolution towards codification, proceduralization and publicization.[102] This has been

[100] I. Koivisto, 'The IMF and the "Transparency Turn"', (2016) 25 *Minnesota Journal of International Law* 381, 381–383; A. Gupta, 'Transparency under Scrutiny: Information Disclosure in Global Environmental Governance', (2008) 8 *Global Environmental Politics* 1, 6.

[101] See Morlino, *Procurement by International Organizations*, providing an extensive presentation and examination of the legal framework regarding procurement by international organizations. See also A. Grigorescu, 'Transparency of Intergovernmental Organizations: The Roles of Member States, International Bureaucracies and Nongovernmental Organizations', (2007) 51 *International Studies Quarterly* 625; M. Donaldson and B. Kingsbury, 'Power and the Public: The Nature and Effects of Formal Transparency Policies in Global Governance Institutions', in A. Bianchi and A. Peters (eds.), *Transparency in International Law* (Cambridge University Press, 2013), 502.

[102] Morlino, *Procurement by International Organizations*, 47–95; A. Peters, 'Towards Transparency as a Global Norm', in A. Bianchi and A. Peters (eds.), *Transparency in International Law* (Cambridge University Press, 2013), 534.

the case of the United Nations system since the mid-1980s.[103] This is also reflected by the Annual Statistical Report on UN Procurement (ASR), which was first presented in 1984,[104] and by Resolution 39/220,[105] under which the need for regular reporting of the procurement data was recognized by the General Assembly and organizations of the United Nations system were encouraged to participate in this reporting exercise. However, contrary to the EU institutions, individuals (whether companies or citizens) do not enjoy rights to access information held by international organizations.[106] In this regard, international law relies on states as those who may invoke rights, if at all. Judicial review *stricto sensu* of transparency policies and procurement would require a different legal order.[107]

According to the annual reports of the Big Four[108] and the United Nations' database, the Big Four have been constantly providing services to the United Nations system[109] between 2010 and 2021. Collectively they have contracted for 513,283,709.69 USD [half a billion] (PWC[110]: 214,188,842.41, Deloitte[111]: 129,352,569.43, KPMG[112]: 93,448,152.29 and Ernst & Young[113]: 76,294,145.56), providing services on Education and Training, Finance and Insurance, Politics and Civic Affairs, Management and Admin,

[103] Morlino, *Procurement by International Organizations*, 91–92, where it is mentioned that 'UN Financial Rules and Regulations and the UN Procurement Manual are probably the most complete example of procurement rules set by an international organization for its own procurement activities, and have been adopted as parameters for the other agencies within the UN family, many of which have their own financial rules and regulations and procurement manuals . . .'.

[104] www.ungm.org/Shared/KnowledgeCenter/Pages/asr_about.

[105] UNGA Res 39/220 (18 December 1984) UN Doc A/RES/39/220.

[106] See A. Tzanakopoulos, 'Transparency in the Security Council', in A. Bianchi and A. Peters (eds.), *Transparency in International Law* (Cambridge University Press, 2013), 367.

[107] Morlino, *Procurement by International Organizations*.

[108] See the Annex.

[109] Specifically, 26 out of the 38 funds, programmes, UN specialized agencies, other entities and bodies and related organizations which are of the UN system (at www.un.org/en/about-us/un-system), e.g., International Fund for Agricultural Development (IFAD), International Labour Organization (ILO), International Telecommunication Union (ITU), Organization for the Prohibition of Chemical Weapons (OPCW), United Nations Development Programme (UNDP), World Meteorological Organization (WMO). Six more organizations or bodies not included under the above list were reported and included under the database, namely United Nations Office at Geneva (UNOG), Pan American Health Organization (PAHO), United Nations Volunteers (UNV), United Nations Procurement Division (UNPD), United Nations Economic Commission for Africa (UNECA), United Nations Office at Nairobi (UNON).

[110] PWC was searched under the names 'PWC' and 'Pricewaterhousecoopers'.

[111] Deloitte was searched under the name 'Deloitte'.

[112] KPMG was searched under the name 'KPMG'.

[113] Ernst & Young was searched under the names 'ERNST&YOUNG', 'ERNST AND YOUNG' and 'EY'.

Transportation, Storage and Mail, Engineering and Research, Environment, Public Order and Security, Public Sector, Healthcare, Industrial Clearing, Editorial, Design and Graphic, Building and Maintenance, Accounting, Auditing, Human Resources, Business and Corporate Management, Technology, Software Maintenance and Support, Personnel Services, Monetary Systems and Issues, Consultancy, Training, Evaluation, IT Consultancy, Studies and Research, Nutrition and Social Mobilization.

4.13 INTERIM CONCLUSION

Comparing the EU institutions with the United Nations system, collectively the Big Four have contracted for a much smaller amount of money with the latter. Between 2010 and 2021 they have contracted for 513,283,709.69 USD, although in the case of the EU only from 2014 to 2021 according to the Financial Transparency System the Big Four have been the beneficiaries of funding of 817,490,000.00 EUR from the EU budget and the European Development Fund and according to the opentender.eu platform they have been involved in contracts awarded by the EU institutions from 2009–2021 with a volume of 4,592.8 million or in other terms 4.5 billion EUR. Taking into consideration the plurality of international organizations to whom the Big Four provide services and the fact that the 4.5 billion EUR does not signal the total amount of money awarded only to the Big Four since, in the respective tenders, other companies/entities et cetera participate as well, the comparison suggests that most probably the Big Four are making more money at the level of international organizations than at the EU level. The topics dealt with are almost the same with respect to international organizations and the EU, with the exception of Engineering and Research Services, Industrial Clearing, Building and Maintenance Services. The Annual Statistical Report on UN Procurement uses different wording, but the services can quite easily be identified.

The differences in the respective legal frameworks of the EU and the UN are not mirrored in the quality, accessibility and concentration of data. Overall, the degree of transparency is low. One notable exception at the EU level is the opentender.eu platform which, however, is not run by EU institutions.

4.14 THE WAY FORWARD

The only way forward seems to be to engage in a much deeper analysis which could only be executed with participation of the Big Four, the EU institutions and the United Nations system. What remains to be done and what could be done at the EU level is to analyse the tenders, check when the Big Four have won the tender, search for the final report on the website of the EU – provided it is available – and then dive deep into the respective legislative means in order to find out whether and to what extent the EU institutions have been following the advice from the Big Four. However, while such a research design might reveal the involvement of the Big Four in what the EU institutions call research projects, this might be different from the policy advice on which the current paper focused.

ANNEX

The reports of the Big Four relied on, and insofar not referenced elsewhere in this chapter, can be found at the following sites (in lieu of a very lengthy footnote):

PWC:
www.pwc.ec/es/publicaciones/assets/pdf/global-annual-review-2010.pdf;
http://fs.monadnockresearch.com/pubfiles/PwC_2011_Annual_Review.pdf;
www.pwc.com/gx/en/annual-review/2012/assets/pwc-global-annual-review-2012.pdf;
www.pwc.com/gx/en/annual-review/2013/assets/pwc-global-annual-review-2013.pdf;
www.pwc.com/gx/en/global-annual-review/assets/pwc-global-annual-review-2014.pdf;
www.pwc.com/gx/en/about-pwc/global-annual-review-2015/campaign-site/pwc-global-annual-review-2015.pdf;
www.pwc.com/gr/en/about-us/assets/pwc-global-annual-review-2016-making-a-difference.pdf;
www.pwc.com/sk/en/global-annual-review-2017.html;
https://ub.unibas.ch/digi/a125/sachdok/2018/BAU_1_3651209_2018.pdf;
https://nairametrics.com/wp-content/uploads/2019/11/PwCs-revenues.pdf;
https://michaelhannadesign.com/wp-content/uploads/2020/06/GAR2019_Print.pdf;
www.pwc.com/gx/en/about-pwc/global-annual-review-2020/downloads/pwc-global-annual-review-2020.pdf;
www.pwc.com/gx/en/about-pwc/global-annual-review-2021/downloads/pwc-global-annual-review-2021.pdf.

Deloitte:
Global Reports from 2010–2017 are available at
www2.deloitte.com/bd/en/pages/about-deloitte/articles/gx-global-reports-archives.html;

Global Impact Reports from 2018–2021 are available at www.deloitte.com/global/en/about/governance/global-impact-report/gx-global-reports-archives.html.

KPMG:
International Annual Reviews from 2010–2018 are available at
https://home.kpmg/xx/en/home/about/previous-international-annual-reviews.html;
https://assets.kpmg/content/dam/kpmg/pe/pdf/global-annual-review-2019.pdf;
https://assets.kpmg/content/dam/kpmg/dk/pdf/dk-2021/02/KPMG_Annual_%20Report_%202020_web.pdf;
https://assets.kpmg/content/dam/kpmg/uk/pdf/2021/3/uk-members-report-financial-statements-2020.pdf;
https://corporatereporting.kpmg.nl/FbContent.ashx/pub_1000/downloads/v220107105554/KPMG_Integrated_report_2020-2021.pdf;
https://assets.kpmg/content/dam/kpmg/uk/pdf/2022/02/uk-members-report-and-financial-statements-2021.pdf.

Ernst & Young:
http://fs.monadnockresearch.com/pubfiles/Ernst_Young_Global_Review_2010.pdf;
https://fdocuments.in/document/ey-global-review-2013-5584b58060a7e.html?page=8;
https://issuu.com/eyfsoconsulting/docs/global_review_2014;
https://weblogibc-co.com/wp-content/uploads/2017/12/EY_Global_review_2015.pdf;
http://cdn.ey.com/echannel/gl/en/about-us/global-review-2016/assets/doc/EY-GR16-press-release.pdf;
https://assets.ey.com/content/dam/ey-sites/ey-com/en_uk/topics/assurance/annual-reporting-in-2016-17-broad-perspective-clear-focus/ey-annual-reporting-in-2016-17.pdf;
www.ey.com/en_hu/global-review/2017;
www.ey.com/en_hr/global-review/2018;
www.ey.com/en_it/global-review/2019;
www.ey.com/en_uk/global-review/2020;
www.ey.com/en_gl/global-review/value-realized-2021.

5

Towards an Urban Internationalism?

Cities and International Organizations in the Interwar Era

HELMUT PHILIPP AUST

5.1 INTRODUCTION

Among the many partners with which international organizations engage in today's system of global governance, cities and their networks play an odd role, at least if they are considered from the perspective of international law. Despite a growing attention for the local–global dynamics that such interactions trigger,[1] international law practice and scholarship still find it difficult to accommodate international or global forms which involve sub-national actors.[2] From the perspective of public international law, cities and local governments are first and foremost state organs. As such, their conduct can be attributed to their respective home state, either for the purpose of establishing state responsibility for wrongdoing or, potentially, also for productive forms of the development of international law through state practice.[3]

It would be misleading, however, to reduce cities to this role of mere state organs, even though this is a perspective that might gain more currency again with the rise of authoritarian and highly centralized states like the People's Republic of China, which arguably does not leave its cities much leeway for independent action.[4] But, in parallel with the growing number of national

1 See the contributions in H. P. Aust and J. Nijman (eds.), *Research Handbook on International Law and Cities* (Edward Elgar, 2021).

2 G. Nesi, 'The Shifting Status of Cities in International Law? A Review, Several Questions and a Straight Answer' (2021) 30 *Italian Yearbook of International Law* 17, 35–36.

3 H. P. Aust, *Das Recht der globalen Stadt: Grenzüberschreitende Dimensionen kommunaler Selbstverwaltung* (Mohr Siebeck, 2017), 148–154.

4 S. Jiang, 'Serving the National on the Global Plane: Disentangling Chinese Cities' Practice of International Law' (2022) 15 *Urban Research & Practice* (online first, https://doi.org/10.1080/17535069.2022.2133477).

governments which project outright hostility to ideas of multilateralism, it is both subnational actors as well as international organizations which see value in their cooperation. We can identify multiple attempts by cities and their networks to reach out to international organizations in order to gain recognition as internationally relevant actors. At the same time, international organizations increasingly observe that it is useful for them to establish direct links with subnational actors. This dynamic was presciently analysed in one of the foundational texts of the international law literature on cities by Yishai Blank in 2006, when he wrote that it was time to rethink a prevailing dyadic understanding of international order (states and international organizations) and rather conceptualize it as trinity, with cities also in the mix.[5]

A good 15 years after Blank formulated this argument, it seems to have fallen in fertile soil in the practice of cities and international organizations, but has also run into opposition from various corners, in particular states which view an empowerment of their local governments with a good measure of scepticism. These rivalling trends can be illustrated, on the one hand, by the prominence that cities and other sub-national actors play in the current philosophy and policy outlook of the United Nations Secretary General, Antonio Guterres, who has repeatedly claimed that it is high time to adopt a concept of 'networked multilateralism' in which cities could play their part.[6] Empirical research by political scientists also shows a constant rise of urban topics in United Nations (UN) fora, both with respect to cities as actors as well as sites of global governance issues.[7] But, at the same time, it is still the case that cities and their networks run into several barriers when it comes to a direct representation of local governments at the UN level. This became noticeable, for instance, in the context of debates about the reform of UN-Habitat, the UN agency charged with questions of housing and urban development more broadly. When Secretary General Guterres appointed a high-level panel for UN-Habitat reform after the adoption of the 'New Urban Agenda' (NUA) in Quito 2016, this panel suggested not just minor reforms of UN-Habitat, but the creation of an Urban Assembly as well as a new body with the name of UN Urban, to function as cross-cutting institution to connect the various loci in

5 Y. Blank, 'The City and the World' (2006) 44 *Columbia Journal of Transnational Law* 875, 881–83.

6 'Secretary-General Stresses Need for More Networked, Inclusive Multilateralism, in International Day of Diplomacy Message', Press Release, UN Doc. SG/SM/20699 (23 April 2021).

7 A. Kosovac, M. Acuto and T. L. Jones, 'Acknowledging Urbanization: A Survey of the Role of Cities in UN Frameworks' (2020) 11 *Global Policy* 293.

which the UN is engaged in urban issues.[8] When the suggestions were discussed, several states voiced discomfort, with the Russian Federation most openly speaking out against any erosion of statehood which might be implied by such a development.[9] This state of play is captured very well in the recent analyses by Jacob Katz Cogan, emphasizing the simultaneity of the seemingly unstoppable rise of cities to an internationally relevant actor and the persistence of the existing structures of the law of international organizations, leaving cities very much in shadow of international institutional law.[10]

The relationship between states, cities and international organizations can be a useful prism to assess broader trends of the development of the international system. With a view to the overarching themes of this volume and the question of how international organizations engage with the world, such debates are also useful indicators for the fundamental tension which runs throughout much of what international organizations (can) do. On the one hand, they are empowered to pursue certain objectives and to do this in a fairly independent manner, as evidenced by their separate legal personality which sets them apart from ad hoc initiatives like conferences and coalitions in which states retain a more formal grip over what is happening. But still, international organizations are heavily contingent on their member states which control them in various ways, ranging from decision-making processes in representative or executive organs to the issue of financing. Engaging with sub-national actors like cities and their networks and associations brings a further level of complexity to this constant tug-of-war between an international organization's independence and the preferences that member states have with respect to the work of the international organization.

What this chapter aspires to do is to provide some background to these current debates by turning to an earlier episode in which this relationship between states, cities and international organizations was already negotiated along strikingly similar lines. It was in the context of the League of Nations that the issue of a growing international role of cities was negotiated. Turning back to this historical episode might not equip us with straightforward 'lessons'

[8] 'Report of the High-Level Independent Panel to Assess and Enhance Effectiveness of UN-Habitat' (1 August 2017) UN Doc. A/71/1006.

[9] M. Acuto, 'Cities Are Gaining Power in Global Politics: Can the UN Keep Up?' *The Conversation*, 14 September 2017, available at https://theconversation.com/cities-are-gaining-power-in-global-politics-can-the-un-keep-up-83668 (last visited 26 October 2022).

[10] J. K. Cogan, 'Cities in the Shadow of International Institutional Law' (2021) 18 *International Organizations Law Review* 133; J. K. Cogan, 'International Organizations and Cities', in H. P. Aust and J. Nijman (eds.), *Research Handbook on International Law and Cities* (Edward Elgar, 2021), 158.

for today. But it might help us to take a more nuanced and informed perspective on current debates about international institutional reform and the promise that cities and their associations and networks can play in this regard. Accordingly, this paper will re-introduce us to these debates of the 1920s, which have received some attention in historiographical and (less so) legal scholarship, but whose significance remains undervalued. Section 5.2 will accordingly detail the background to these debates, beginning with the formation of the 'Union Internationale des Villes' (UIV) in 1913 and how it became embroiled in debates in the League Assembly in the 1920s, but also managed to establish some more modest ties with the International Labour Organization (ILO). This section will also shed some light on further 'partners' involved in this set-up, that is, philanthropical foundations which took a keen interest in the global role of local governments. Section 5.3 draws out some of the implications these debates might have for current developments before the chapter will offer some concluding observations and pointers for further research (Section 5.4).

5.2 URBAN INTERNATIONALISMS IN THE INTERWAR ERA

The attempts at establishing some kind of formal ties between cities and international organizations in the interwar era is set against the story of the founding of the UIV in 1913, the first international city association in the modern sense. In parallel to its slow operational beginnings in the early 1920s, some states began to make suggestions to strengthen international forms of intermunicipal cooperation, first in the context of the Pan-American conferences and then at the League of Nations. As we will see, this cooperation also took place in close coordination with the work of philanthropic organizations (Section 5.2.4).

5.2.1 *A First International City Network: The Union Internationale des Villes*

You are from France, Germany, Great Britain and Holland; you have come from farther afield: from Italy, Spain, Russia and Scandinavia; and from farther still: from North and South America, from Japan and China, from Egypt and from Southern Africa. All of you fulfil similar functions in cities – be they large, medium-sized or small – where you have been entrusted with the exercise of local public office; functions for which the citizens who live in the community of urban centres have made you responsible: to watch over their safety and their health, the prosperity of their affairs, the education of their children and the enjoyment of their leisure pursuits. You have come together to deliberate for several days on the major problems that arise from the universal nature of the conditions of present-day life, which are more or less the same anywhere.[11]

With these words, the Mayor of the City of Ghent opened the founding assembly of the Union Internationale des Villes in the margins of the 1913 World Exhibition. This event heralded the beginning of institutionalized cooperation between cities and local governments of different countries. The invitation to the congress underlines its purpose, which was the exchange of knowledge relevant to the cities:

> The general progress of civilization and the progress achieved by the most backward nations have resulted in the same questions preoccupying the administrations of major cities throughout the world today. The solutions found by one of these cities can also be used by the others, if not in the same form, then at least after the necessary adaptions.[12]

In contemporary parlance one could describe this endeavour as one of defining best practices. The history of the UIV can only be briefly outlined here.[13] Though its founding came at an inopportune moment, namely, in 1913, shortly before the outbreak of the First World War, it managed to establish itself as the first and for a long time most relevant international association of cities. Later it came to be rechristened the 'International Union of Local Authorities' (IULA), before morphing into 'United Cities and Local Governments' (UCLG) in 2004.[14] In its early days, UIV/IULA membership was open to national associations of cities as well as to single cities and municipalities; the membership structure was subsequently reformed on a quasi-federal basis whereby exclusively national associations of cities and municipalities were awarded membership.[15] The actual strength of the organization is not easy to determine. According to UIV/IULA's

[11] Cited after P. Y. Saunier, 'Sketches from the Urban Internationale, 1910–1950: Voluntary Associations, International Institutions and US Philantropic Foundations' (2001) 25 *International Journal of Urban and Regional Research* 380.

[12] Cited after H. Revers, *IULA 1913–1963. The Story of the First Fifty Years of International Municipal Co-operation* (International Union of Local Authorities, 1963), 19.

[13] For a more comprehensive view of the first 50 years of the organization, see ibid.

[14] Regarding the motivation behind this merger, see P. Y. Saunier, 'Introduction', in P. Y. Saunier and S. Ewen (eds.), *Another Global City. Historical Explorations into the Transnational Municipal Movement* (Palgrave Macmillan 2008), 1, 17.

[15] R. Payre and P. Y. Saunier, 'A City in the World of Cities. Lyon, France; Municipal Associations as Political Resources in the Twentieth Century', in P. Y. Saunier and S. Ewen (eds.), *Another Global City. Historical Explorations into the Transnational Municipal Movement* (Palgrave Macmillan 2008), 69, 70.

archives, by 1926 UIV membership comprised 52,000 cities in 30 different states.[16] At the 1932 UIV Congress held in London, membership was estimated at 50,000 cities representing more than 190 million people.[17] Above and beyond these impressive figures, however, it is difficult to ascertain how active the respective cities were in this movement and to what extent – as the organization itself claims of itself – they identified with the goal of 'intermunicipalism'.[18]

This term is, however, an essential slogan for the ideological and historical significance of the UIV/IULA movement. The organization signals a departure from municipal reformers to cross-border cooperation. The movement was initially associated with an earlier development originating in the latter part of the nineteenth century, the objective of which was to establish international collaboration in the field of science and statistics. In their attempt to forge international contacts, local government reformers were keen to establish an exchange on what may be called municipal science.[19] Through contact with local administrators from other countries, urban planners and public health experts sought to address the problems of large-scale urbanization considered critical throughout Europe.[20] Hence, the emergence of intermunicipal exchange across national borders constituted a variant of the more general phenomenon of a growing contemporary international congress system.[21] This was owing, not least, to the concentration of efforts of both internationalist-minded local administrators and those interested more generally in scientific international cooperation in Belgium and above all in Brussels. A pivotal role was played by Belgian librarian and 'universal scholar' Paul Otlet, who succeeded in persuading King Leopold II to support the founding of a central office of international institutions in Brussels.[22] This

[16] Compare Saunier, 'Sketches' 384.

[17] P. Dogliani, 'European Municipalism in the First Half of the Twentieth Century: The Socialist Network' (2002) 11 *Contemporary European History* 573, 587.

[18] See further the instructive description of the absence of activities as well as the general lack of identification on the behalf of the Mayor of Lyon during the interwar period. Payre and Saunier, 'A City in the World of Cities', 74–75, 79, 83.

[19] O. Gaspari, 'Cities against States? Hopes, Dreams and Shortcomings of the European Municipal Movement, 1900–1960' (2002) 11 *Contemporary European History* 597, 598; Payre and Saunier, 'A City in the World of Cities', 70.

[20] On the problems raised by this surge of urbanization, see F. Lenger, *Metropolen der Moderne. Eine europäische Stadtgeschichte seit 1850* (Beck, 2013), 51ff.

[21] Cf. also M. Schulz, 'Internationale Institutionen', in J. Dülffer and W. Loth (eds.), *Dimensionen internationaler Geschichte* (Oldenbourg, 2012), 211, 216ff on the forerunners of 'modern' international organizations.

[22] A. Wright, *Cataloging the World: Paul Otlet and the Birth of the Information Age* (Oxford University Press, 2014), 73.

new central office was to be at the forefront of a rapidly developing, worldwide system of formalized exchange across all fields of science.[23] Otlet identified a general trend towards greater international exchange. Disappointed by the Hague Peace Conferences, he also saw in this development a more promising avenue for achieving world peace.[24] The historian Marz Mazower summarized the motive behind Otlet's views as follows:

> What internationalism offered in particular was the possibility of carving out a politics-free zone where men of science could meet, setting aside the factionalism of nations and treating the world and its peoples as the whole they really were.[25]

Alongside Otlet, instrumental for the foundation of the UIV, was the Belgian international lawyer, Henri La Fontaine – a member of the Institut de Droit international, who was awarded the Nobel Peace prize in 1913 for the role he played in the European Peace Movement[26] – and the younger Belgian legal expert and local politician, Emile Vinck, a close friend of Otlet's who was to remain Secretary General of the UIV/IULA until 1948.[27] This constellation of personnel is revealing insofar as it establishes the connection between the general political ideals of peace and cooperation in the sphere of science while emphasizing the role of local governments. Thus, both with respect to personnel history and intellectual history, it underscores the connection between intermunicipal cooperation and broader trends of internationalization.[28]

The work of the UIV and its protagonists ranged from administrative and dry technical matters to utopian goals.[29] Otlet even drafted a plan to make Brussels the 'international city' par excellence, a focal point in which all

[23] M. Mazower, *Governing the World: The History of an Idea* (Penguin, 2012), 104–105.

[24] Wright, *Cataloging the World*, 67.

[25] Mazower, *Governing the World*, 95–96.

[26] Cf. www.nobelprize.org/nobel_prizes/peace/laureates/1913/fontaine-facts.html (last visted 28 October 2022).

[27] Revers, *IULA 1913–1963*, 52ff; Payre and Saunier, 'A City in the World of Cities', 70.

[28] On these connections, see also E. Rosenberg, 'Transnationale Strömungen in einer Welt, die zusammenrückt', in E. Rosenberg (ed.), *Geschichte der Welt 1870–1945: Weltmärkte und Weltkriege* (Munich: CH Beck, 2012, Zettel transl.), 815, 951–952.

[29] The same holds for the emergence of international organizations towards the end of the nineteenth and beginning of the twentieth century: J. Klabbers, 'The Emergence of Functionalism in International Institutional Law: Colonial Inspirations' (2014) 25 *European Journal of International Law* 645, 646–647; J. Klabbers, 'The EJIL Foreword: The Transformation of International Organizations Law' (2015) 26 *European Journal of International Law* 9, 36ff. on the interplay between functionalism and the 'salvation of mankind' in the thought on international cooperation.

activities of scientific and political exchange would be concentrated[30] – in some senses an anticipation of Brussels as the undisputed yet also incomplete capital of the European Union.[31] The path to reaching this utopia was, in turn, intimately linked to the belief in the means of scientific exchange between experts: by way of direct exchange between experts an escalation of national interests would never arise.

The situation for UIV activities was to change decisively in the aftermath of the First World War. With the League of Nations, there was now an international organization which, in accordance with its statutes, could legitimately claim to address all relevant questions of an international nature.[32] The work of the UIV soon expressed the desire to contribute to achieving the League of Nations' objectives at the municipal level.[33] At the same time, the UIV also sought recognition for its role under the auspices of the League of Nations and other international organizations.

5.2.2 *Pan-American Openings*

Article 24 of the League of Nations provided for the incorporation of already existing or future international organizations into the League of Nations.[34] Aside from the question as to whether the UIV was an international organization according to this provision, attempts were made to establish and formalise cooperation between the UIV and the League of Nations. Such efforts proved successful to varying degrees. Following a Cuban initiative, a discussion took place within the League of Nations about whether it ought to promote and recognize cross-border cooperation between cities and municipalities.[35]

30 P. Otlet, 'Un projet grandiose' de Cité Internationale', in W. Whyte (ed.), *Ghent Planning Congress 1913: Premier Congrès international et exposition comparée des Villes* (UIV, 1913), 237; see further Gaspari, 'Cities against States', 605; Wright, *Cataloging the World*, 124ff.

31 A further comparison suggests itself in relation to The Hague as the self-proclaimed 'legal capital of the world', see further, P. Van Krieken and D. McKay (eds.), *The Hague: Legal Capital of the World* (Springer, 2005).

32 See Mazower, *Governing the World*, 116ff.

33 Something that played a role, for example, at the Amsterdam Congress in 1924. See Revers, *IULA 1913–1963*, 31.

34 Covenant of the League of Nations; see on this provision, D. Pulkowski, 'Structural Paradigms of International Law', in T. Broude and Y. Shany (eds.), *The Shifting Allocation of Authority in International Law* (Hart, 2008), 51, 68–69.

35 With respect to the Cuban initiative, one should not lose sight of the fact that Cuba was under considerable US influence at the time in question, see, in particular, W. Smith and D. R. Kaplowitz, 'Cuba', in J. Krieger (ed.), *The Oxford Companion to Politics in the World* (Oxford University Press, 1993), 206, 207.

This initiative originated in a resolution of the Pan-American Union, the forerunner of the Organization of American States (OAS), in 1923. The resolution, approved at the Fifth Conference of American States[36] and endorsed by 18 states, advocated the development of relations between cities from different states.[37] This resolution was also based on a motion from Cuba. Vidal Caro, President of the Cuban Delegation at the Fifth Conference, justified the initiative on the grounds that, as he put it, cooperation between cities and municipalities could potentially make a valuable contribution to achieving Pan-American ideals:

> if this field of action be enlarged beyond the frontiers, it is evident that such greater area of action will be the means of forming a greater source of wealth for the national development of the countries which adopt the principles of Inter-Municipality.[38]

In his statement to Congress, Caro was quick to anticipate the concern that this may infringe on traditional principles of foreign policy and diplomacy. Cooperation between cities

> does not try to adopt prerogatives that encroach on the faculties assigned to the Consular and Diplomatic Corps, but only to establish an independent labor for the drawing together of nations which noble purpose cannot but inspire general applause. Inter-Municipality does not play a part within the plan of diplomatic or consular relations devoted to international practices inasmuch as it is only formed for promoting congeniality outside of the official spheres of the State, by means of unrestricted association of public corporations, which as a result of a constant exchange of ideas regarding their experience and the fulfilment of their official duties, are bound to attain perfection in the administration of matters entrusted to them.[39]

In relation to classic diplomacy these efforts amount to, at best, 'effective auxiliaries'.[40] With no substantive debate, the Assembly finally adopted a resolution recommending that governments facilitate cross-border networking among their local authorities.[41]

36 About the Congress in general, see J. B. Scott, 'The Fifth International Conference of American States' (1923) 17 *American Journal of International Law* 518.

37 U. Borsi, 'Municipalisme et internationalisme', in *Mélanges Hauriou* (Sirey, 1929), 81, 84.

38 Verbatim Record of the Plenary Sessions of the Fifth International Conference of American States, Santiago de Chile 1923, Vol 1, 481.

39 Ibid., 481–482.

40 Ibid., 482.

41 Ibid., 483.

5.2.3 *The Turn to the League of Nations*

In 1923, the Cuban delegation introduced a draft resolution at the Assembly of the League of Nations intended to render the proposals of the Pan-American Conference 'universal': 'The more relations between the principal cities of the world are developed the easier it will be to secure international co-operation for the attainment of the desired end.'[42] The assembly opted to postpone discussion of this proposal until reconvening the following year.[43] In 1924, a discussion was held on the Cuban initiative. The Cuban delegate and appointed Rapporteur, M. Patterson, initially tabled a draft resolution that would generally acknowledge intermunicipal cooperation. This would amount to a new form of cooperation between peoples that would contribute significantly to the spread of the ideals of the League of Nations.[44] However, during the ensuing discussion, opposition was voiced among some delegations who argued that such a recognition of intermunicipal cooperation was too great a threat to national sovereignty, a position advanced by the delegations of Italy, Romania, Uruguay and the Kingdom of Serbs, Croats and Slovenes. In contrast, the French delegate remained unconvinced that intermunicipal cooperation could pose a threat to national sovereignty. In a letter to the competent Fifth committee, the Rapporteur Patterson had already sought to anticipate these concerns by pointing out that intermunicipal cooperation was 'entirely non-political and confined to purely municipal matters'.[45] Owing to the concerns expressed by the mentioned delegations, a slightly revised draft of the resolution was nevertheless adopted, which stated:

> Recognising that the establishment of direct relations between major local authorities of the different countries, within the strict limits of the sovereignty of states, constitutes a new form of co-operation between the peoples which will contribute to the dissemination of ideals that have led to the creation of the League of Nations and has inspired its activity.[46]

Hence, the discussions led to greater emphasis on national sovereignty, the limits of which would need to be respected by intermunicipal cooperation.[47]

42 *Journal de l'Assemblée de la Société des Nations*, Vol. 4 (1923), 234.
43 Ibid., 235.
44 *Journal de l'Assemblée de la Société des Nations*, Vol. 5 (1924), 145.
45 Report of the Fifth Committee to the Assembly, Rapporteur: His Excellency M. G. Patterson (Cuba), 18 September 1924, Doc. A.74.1924.IV, 1.
46 *Journal de l'Assemblée de la Société des Nations*, Vol. 5 (1924), 146, 180, 210.
47 Saunier, 'Sketches', 393.

The League of Nations Assembly returned to the issue the following year. In the meantime, growing scepticism became apparent among the states concerning the threats posed to their sovereignty by intermunicipal cooperation.[48] The discussion no longer focused on international cooperation, but increasingly on cooperation between cities within states. It is remarkable, furthermore, that the French delegation, which a year earlier had expressed no reservations about respecting national sovereignty, now reversed its position.[49] Eventually, a significantly weaker resolution than that of the previous year was adopted, the most decisive part of which stated:

> The Assembly … (d)ecides to call the attention of the different Governments to the advantages which closer co-operation, national and international, between the municipalities, within the strict limits of national sovereignty, present from the point of view of the aims of the League of Nations.[50]

In any case, the optimism of the previous year's discussion was all but gone.[51] Several delegates emphasized, furthermore, that institutional duplication should be avoided. At this point, the UIV came into play, which would now not be brought into a more close-knit relationship with the League of Nations, as had been hoped. Yet, quite to the contrary, its very existence was cited as the reason why no new institutional steps would have to be taken, simply because the UIV already existed.[52] The result was a decidedly mixed message: international cooperation between cities – yes, please. But no formalized ties of the association with the League!

In the contemporaneous academic literature, there is no significant echo of these discussions. One single contribution can be found, however, in a 1929 *Festschrift* contribution by Italian administrative law scholar Umberto Borsi, who supported the more recent restrictive perspective among states endorsing the borders of national sovereignty:

> Sans prétendre élever les Communes à la qualité de sujets de droit international, la doctrine de l'intermunicipalité admet l'efficacité de leur volonté

48 *Journal de l'Assemblée de la Société des Nations*, Vol. 6 (1925), 231.

49 Ibid.

50 Ibid., 231–232.

51 It appears that Cuba also ceased to vigorously pursue the earlier initiative. This coincided with the transition of government in 1925, in which the notorious President Gerardo Machado assumed power, cf. A. F. Lowenfeld, 'Cuba', in *Max Planck Encyclopedia of Public International Law*, para 11.

52 According to the French and Belgian delegates, United Kingdom delegates were likewise pleased that 'the report did not suggest the formation of any new international body', *Journal de l'Assemblée de la Société des Nations*, Vol. 6 (1925), 230–231.

> hors du territoire de leurs Etats respectifs et, par conséquent, indépendamment de la capacité que leur concède la législation de ces derniers. Mais une telle conception coincide forcément avec une amoindrissement de la souveraineté de l'Etat.[53]

Borsi went so far as to contend that any form of internationalization of the field of action at the municipal levels would dramatically alter the traditional understanding of the relationship between state and municipality:

> Municipalisme et internationalisme ne peuvent se lier directement sans que soient altérés le caractère de la Commune et celui de l'Etat et sans que leurs rapports soient construits sur le souvenir d'un passé qui n'est plus ou sur l'hypothèse d'un avenir qu'aucune donnée n'autorise jusqu'à présent à prévoir.[54]

However, the UIV did not in every respect prove as unsuccessful as it did when seeking to establish its contacts with the League of Nations. The International Labour Organization (ILO) appeared somewhat more open to formalizing cooperation with the UIV.[55] Following several discussions between the Executive Boards of the ILO and the UIV,[56] the two organizations began regularly exchanging information on housing, hygiene, the fight against unemployment and other issues deemed to be of interest for local governments.[57] Moreover, ILO and UIV wished to concentrate on unifying standards, which would result in greater comparability of municipal statistics. The objective was by no means modest, albeit primarily a technical and administrative issue:

> Un tel effort pour fixer dans les différents domaines à la fois la terminologie et les bases aussi bien de la statistique que de l'information documentaire, paraît

[53] Borsi, 'Municipalisme et internationalisme' 90. 'Without aiming to elevate communes to the status of subjects of international law, the doctrine of inter-municipality recognizes the effectiveness of their will outside the territory of their respective states and, consequently, irrespective of the capacity granted by legislation of the latter. But such a conception coincides strongly with a diminishing of state sovereignty' (translation, JK).

[54] Ibid., 91. 'Municipalism and internationalism cannot be directly connected without altering the character of the commune and that of the state and without their connections being constructed on the memory of a past that no longer is or on the possibility of a future that no one with given authority has thus far foreseen' (translation, JK).

[55] See further Saunier, 'Sketches', 395.

[56] See the letter from Emile Vinck to Edgard Milhaud of 8 January 1925 and the memorandum on the meeting between Milhaud, Vinck and other ILO and UIV representatives of 17 December 1924, ILO Archives S/01/2032/1. I warmly thank Pierre-Yves Saunier for kindly providing this and the following documents from the ILO archives to me.

[57] ILO report to their representatives in Washington, DC from January 1926, ILO Archives I 1061/6/15, 1.

> devoir servir de la façon la plus efficace, par la surêté, la comparabilité et la valeur des informations, les intérêts du progrès social.[58]

The focus of the envisaged cooperation between the UIV and the ILO in the areas of documentation and statistics – to some extent already initiated – forms part of a broader trend during the interwar period. As Mark Mazower observed, the League of Nations succeeded in breaking new ground in the field of technical and scientific cooperation. At this stage, governments and public administrations had become accustomed to being consulted by international organizations and providing data for the statistical work of the international bureaucracy.[59] In a sense, the League of Nations also adopted the ideas of Otlet, who sought the centralization of knowledge and, thus, in his zeal for data collection, in many respects appears to have been a forerunner of contemporary notions of Big Data.[60]

With respect to anchoring intermunicipal cooperation at the international level, the UIV/IULA went on to achieve a success of sorts after the Second World War, albeit that in doing so it also considerably undermined the status of cross-border cooperation between cities. The IULA was granted observer status in the UN Economic and Social Council (ECOSOC) as well as in the World Health Organization and UNICEF.[61] Its status, however, was that of a non-governmental organization (NGO). It thus found itself on the same level as civil society institutions and, therefore, the special character of cities and their associations as *public* actors gets lost somehow.[62] Even though this classification is understandable from the perspective of the UN system and sovereignty concerns that member states might hold, the ambitious programmatic outlook of the early debates on intermunicipal cooperation recedes into the background.

5.2.4 *Relations with Foundations and Actors in Civil Society*

This raises the question as to whether the lack of success with respect to the organization's formal recognition by the League of Nations or the ILO played

58 Ibid., 5. 'Such an effort to establish in the different fields both the terminology and the bases of both statistics and documentary information, seems to serve in the most effective way, through the security, comparability and value of information, the interests of social progress' (translation, JK).
59 Mazower, *Governing the World*, 149.
60 For a comprehensive discussion, see Wright, *Cataloging the World*, 8, 295ff.
61 Revers, *IULA 1913–1963*, 16.
62 See also M. Betsill and H. Bulkeley, 'Cities and the Multilevel Governance of Climate Change' (2006) 12 *Global Governance* 141, 148 on the erroneous conclusion that city networks should be classified as NGOs.

a role in the increased cooperation with charitable foundations. As Pierre-Yves Saunier pointed out, the UIV and other associations of cities founded at the time – such as the International Union of Garden Cities – attracted the attention of American charitable foundations in the 1920s. The Carnegie, Rockefeller and Ford Foundations began initiating research projects aimed at spreading American ideals of public administration in what they perceived to be backward Europe:

> American activities within the Urban Internationale were connected with a conscious, organized desire for worldwide dissemination of ways of seeing, thinking about and managing the city that suited the American liberal project. Here we are witnessing a symbolic conquest of the world of the urban, carried forward in the name of the universal.[63]

This programme could be easily aligned with that of the UIV. Once again, here, too, there are revealing personal and institutional links. The Carnegie Foundation was instrumental in financing the central institute of international institutions planned by Paul Otlet. The 1913 Congress in Ghent, at which the UIV was founded, was largely financed by the Carnegie Foundation.[64] Saunier drew attention to the fact that a change took place once the Rockefeller Foundation began funding the project. Unlike the Carnegie Foundation, whose support was more broadly directed at internationalization and the promotion of world peace, the Rockefeller Foundation sought to disseminate a certain model of public administration that was, above all, rational and efficient. Supported by economists and administration scientists at the University of Chicago, 'the gospel of the new social sciences, government efficiency and expertise' was to be spread throughout the world.[65]

5.3 IMPLICATIONS FOR CURRENT DEVELOPMENTS

When considering the development of inter-municipal cooperation over the course of the twentieth century, it is clear that the ambitious objectives of the UIV founders were not initially fulfilled. The state has retained its central position in the international system and was simply supplemented by international organizations that were, in turn, based on acts of state creation. The international dimension of intermunicipal cooperation, by contrast, would

[63] Saunier, 'Sketches', 387; P. Y. Saunier, 'Les voyages municipaux américains en Europe 1900–1940. Une piste d'histoire transnationale' (2003) 15 *Jahrbuch für Europäische Verwal tungsgeschichte* 267, 276.

[64] Saunier, 'Sketches', 387–388.

[65] Ibid., 389.

become increasingly marginalized. While the founding fathers of the UIV may have been concerned with technical-administrative issues, nevertheless their activities also contained utopian potential. The realization of world peace was always a more or less clearly expressed ideal, in part connected with socialist ideas of a brotherhood of classes extending beyond the boundaries of nation states.[66]

As always, it does not seem opportune to draw too easy inferences from a historical experience for today's developments. At the same time, a brief glance at the interwar debates on international cooperation between cities and their relation to international organizations can underline that sometimes overblown claims of newness of the urban turn of global governance and the urban age in which we are all supposedly living should be taken with some caution.[67] This is all the more important insofar as the 'global cities' discourse in other social sciences has been conducted in a decidedly ahistorical manner for quite some time.[68] As the historian Pierre-Yves Saunier has observed, the global role of cities that has emerged since the early 1990s has often been presented as a complete novelty.[69] More recent historical research has shown, by contrast, that there have been several phases of international involvement by cities and municipalities, a finding also supported by research in the field of global history, which places greater emphasis on earlier processes of international interdependence than has long been acknowledged.[70]

In any case, a perspective on cities and their attempts at international cooperation facilitates developing new perspectives on the formation of international institutions. Thus, the intermunicipal movement of the interwar period is a revealing parallel history on the formation of international organizations. As the opening statement of the Mayor of Ghent and the invitation to the first UIV congress reproduced in Section 5.2.1 underline, the project of intermunicipal cooperation also shared a considerable amount of civilizational rhetoric and belief in a linear form of progress with the general

66 Cf Dogliani, 'European Municipalism' 585–586; Payre and Saunier, 'A City in the World of Cities', 70.

67 For very optimistic assessments of the urban future, see B. Barber, *If Mayors Ruled the World: Dysfunctional Nations, Rising Cities* (Yale University Press, 2013); for a critical assessment of this book, see H. P. Aust, 'Shining Cities on the Hill: The Global City, Climate Change and International Law' (2015) 26 *European Journal of International Law* 255.

68 M. P. Smith, *Transnational Urbanism: Locating Globalization* (Blackwell, 2001), 56; Payre and Saunier, 'A City in the World of Cities', 69.

69 Saunier, 'Introduction', 5ff.

70 For an overview, see S. Conrad, *Globalgeschichte* (Beck, 2013), 22; for a specific focus on cities in global history, see J. Osterhammel, *Die Verwandlung der Welt: eine Geschichte des 19. Jahrhunderts* (Beck, 2009), 366ff.; Rosenberg, 'Transnationale Strömungen', 951.

trajectory towards international cooperation.[71] Seen from this perspective, the development of a form of international cooperation between cities is thus not necessarily an alternative route to the forms of cooperation between states in and through international organizations. Rather, the two phenomena are closely interlinked and for whatever historical reasons the intermunicipal track has – for the longest time – not taken off in the same way as has the idea of international cooperation through international organizations. Remembering that early stages of the history of international organizations shared the same civilizational rhetoric with the nascent city networks can imbue us with a sense of caution when today representatives of cities and their networks make all too sweeping statements on what cities can deliver (as opposed to states, as it is alleged in some instances).[72]

A retrospective glance, furthermore, also helps better to grasp why the UIV's efforts were not crowned with success. The insistence, by some states within the League of Nations, that bolstering international cooperation between cities would endanger state sovereignty may help clarify why, according to a traditional understanding of international law, cities and municipalities have yet to be allocated roles as independent actors. One might ask, furthermore, as to whether the lack of 'recognition' at the intergovernmental level has opened the door to greater influence by private actors. Attempts by US-based foundations to exert influence at the intermunicipal level were also coupled with the hope that public administration could be more effectively modernized than has otherwise been the case at the diplomatic intergovernmental level. In today's various forms of international entanglement of cities in networks consisting of international organizations, states and private actors, remnants of this development can be seen. Approaching development issues at the local level may have readily apparent benefits for actors in the international development community. But it is possibly also true that the local level can be compromised in various ways if it proves too open for supposedly beneficial outside influences. When US foundations, for instance, set up programmes with shiny names such as '100 resilient cities', it is hard to disagree that the pressing needs of many cities, particularly in the Global South, will make such programmes attractive. But if the same programmes serve to embed consultants in city administrations, questions of democratic legitimacy should also be put on the table.[73]

71 See Saunier, 'Sketches' and Revers, *IULA 1913–1963*, respectively.

72 See Barber, *If Mayors Ruled the World*.

73 On some of these issues, see H. P. Aust and A. Rodiles, 'Cities and Local Governments: International Development from Below?', in R. Buchanan, L. Eslava and S. Pahuja (eds.), *The Oxford Handbook on International Law and Development* (Oxford University Press, 2023), 207.

5.4 CONCLUDING OBSERVATIONS

From the perspective of international law, the idea of international cooperation between cities may at first sight seem to be somewhat of a dead end. The more recent developments of cities becoming more and more accepted as internationally relevant actors suggest that this was a mere temporary impasse and, thus, perhaps, more of a 'quiet side street' of international institutional developments now on the verge of expansion.[74] When such side streets open up and displace a previously shared feeling that a certain development ran into a cul-de-sac, it is illuminating to revisit the debates which first seemed to lead us into a dead end. With the growing awareness about the significance of what cities do on the international level, it is a sobering experience to see that very similar debates to today's questions were already put on the table of the League of Nations Assembly almost 100 years ago.

[74] For a statement in favour of the investigation of 'sleepy side streets' and 'cul-de-sacs' in the history of international law, S. Kirmse, 'Sleepy Side Alleys, Dead Ends and the Perpetuation of Eurocentrism' (2014) 25 *European Journal of International Law* 307.

6

Climate Action in Sports

The UN Climate Change's Sports for Climate Action Initiative and Its Implementation in the Wider Sports Sector

REBECCA SCHMIDT

6.1 INTRODUCTION

This chapter assesses the United Nations Framework Convention on Climate Change (UNFCCC) Secretariat's (UN Climate Change) Sports for Climate Action Initiative (S4CA), which is part of a complex web of climate actions by private actors facilitated and managed by UN Climate Change. This chapter will first outline the implementation efforts of the International Olympic Committee (IOC) as one of the co-drafters of the Initiative before assessing the commitment and contribution of three professional leagues – England's Premier League (EPL), the Deutsche Fußball Liga (DFL) and the National Basketball Association (NBA). By depicting the wider web of public and private actions related to the S4CA framework, it illustrates how international organizations apply direct and indirect interactions with private actors (in this case in the sports sector) to achieve the goals set through public international treaties. Here, the pull factor of what is being termed a 'pioneer or leader organization',[1] namely organizations with the power and reach to achieve broader change in a specific issue area (in this case sports), will be studied.

The S4CA, with its integration of a diverse set of sports actors, is an example of public–private interaction in the pursuance of publicly set goals. It falls within a broader trend of involving private actors directly in the execution of

This chapter is based on research conducted between 2022 and 2023, but updated with the newest numbers where relevant.

[1] R. Wurzel, D. Liefferink and D. Torney, 'Pioneers, Leaders and Followers in Multilevel and Polycentric Climate Governance' (2019) 28 *Environmental Politics* 1.

transnational governance.[2] This trend is particularly prevalent in the context of climate change regulation, where private actors are traditionally closely involved. For example, the UNFCCC states that the Conference of the Parties (CoP) should 'seek and utilize, where appropriate, the services and cooperation of, and information provided by, competent international organisations and intergovernmental and *non-governmental bodies*'.[3] Over time, private actors have become increasingly relevant in international efforts to address the dangers of climate change. In 2014, the CoP 20 UN Climate Change and the Peruvian government initiated the Non-State Actor Zone for Climate Action (NAZCA) portal. It has since been renamed the Climate Action Portal.[4] The Portal tracks climate actions by different actors and includes cooperative initiatives, such as the S4CA framework.[5] In a similar spirit, leading to the Paris Conference, the Lima-Paris Action Agenda was created to orchestrate and mobilize actors from all areas of society. In the end, more than 10,000 commitments by non- and sub-state actors came together.[6] It is therefore not surprising that the Paris Conference in 2015 agreed on a stronger mobilization of non-party actors. Decision 1/CP.21, which also includes the Paris Agreement, mentions several non-state actors and their commitments.[7] On this basis, private non-party engagement has been constantly growing. At the time of writing, 43,152 actors are listed on the Climate Action Portal, of which only 14,937 are state or sub-state actors. The vast majority of the rest are privately organized.[8]

In legal scholarship, direct engagement with such polycentric interactions is less pronounced. A simple reason for this is possibly the orientation towards the more traditional and hierarchical structures of law and legal systems. Even though we do find exceptions in the context of EU law,[9] as well as in the

[2] K. Abbott et al. (eds.), *International Organizations as Orchestrators* (Cambridge University Press, 2015); J. Green, *Rethinking Private Authority: Agents and Entrepreneurs in Global Environmental Governance* (Princeton University Press, 2014).

[3] Article 7 2(l) UNFCCC. Emphasis added.

[4] Th Hale, 'The Role of Sub-State and Non-State Actors in International Climate Processes' (2018) *Chatham House Research Paper*, www.chathamhouse.org/sites/default/files/publications/research/2018-11-28-non-state-sctors-climate-synthesis-hale-final.pdf: at 7. See also the portal at: https://climateaction.unfccc.int.

[5] https://climateaction.unfccc.int.

[6] Hale, 'Role of Sub-State and Non- State Actors', 7. See also K. Bäckstrand et al., 'Non-State Actors in Global Climate Governance: From Copenhagen to Paris and Beyond' (2017) 26 *Environmental Politics* 561.

[7] 1/CP.21 for instance in the preamble, in para 106, 109, 117, etc. See also UN Climate Change, History of Non-Party Stakeholder Engagement, available at: https://unfccc.int/climate-action/introduction-climate-action/history-non-party-stakeholder-engagement.

[8] https://climateaction.unfccc.int/Actors.

[9] E. Partiti, 'Orchestration as a Form of Public Action: The EU Engagement with Voluntary Sustainability Standards' (2019) 25 *European Law Journal* 94.

context of climate change law,[10] from a traditional international law perspective, most of these interactions fall simply in the 'soft law' category. However, setting these interactions aside as just 'soft law' misses the intricate ways in which international organizations operate today and in which transnational regulation comes about. For this reason, the present chapter will analyse the S4CA framework's myriad interplays between public and private actors, as well as the legal structures that underpin them. To achieve this, the following structure is adopted. First, a theoretical background for an analysis of public–private regulatory interactions will be provided (Section 6.2). This will be predominantly based on international relations and governance literature, where this phenomenon has become more prevalent in recent decades. However, the importance of the law and legal literature will also be outlined. Section 6.3 will then introduce the S4CA framework in more detail, and Section 6.4 will depict its application by several sports actors. A discussion of the empirical developments based on our understanding of complex regulatory interactions in or based on international legal frameworks is provided in Section 6.5. Section 6.6 concludes.

6.2 THE COMPLEXITY OF PUBLIC–PRIVATE REGULATORY INTERACTIONS: THE THEORETICAL FRAMEWORK

Traditionally, in both international law and relations, the literature has focused on horizontal state interactions.[11] Yet, for decades, we have been able to observe scholarship broadening this focus.[12] We now find a significant body of research that investigates the role of non-state actors, whether they be private, NGO-based or sub-state entities.[13] A strand of literature has been concerned with the role that international organizations can play in these interactions. Thus, Abbott, Genschel, Snidal and Zangl have created a two-by-two matrix setting of four modes of interaction: hard, soft, direct and indirect (Table 6.1).[14]

[10] D. Bodansky, J. Brunnée and L. Rajamani, *International Climate Change Law* (Oxford University Press, 2017), ch. 8.

[11] J. L. Brierly, *The Law of Nations*, 6th ed. (Clarendon Press, 1963) 63; R. Keohane, *After Hegemony: Cooperation and Discord in the World Political Economy* (Princeton University Press, 1984); S. Krasner (ed.), *International Regimes* (Cornell University Press, 1983).

[12] Ph Jessup, *Transnational Law* (Yale University Press, 1956).

[13] For example, A.-M. Slaughter, *A New World Order* (Princeton University Press, 2004); T. Börzel and Th Risse, 'Governance without a State: Can It Work?' (2010) 4 *Regulation and Governance* 13.

[14] K. W. Abbott et al., 'Introduction', in Abbott et al. (eds.), *International Organizations as Orchestrators* 1–2.

TABLE 6.1 *Modes of interaction*

	Direct	Indirect
Hard	Hierarchy	Delegation
Soft	Collaboration	Orchestration

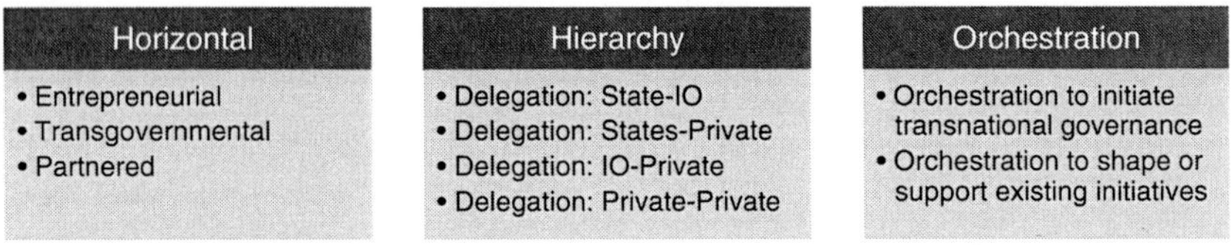

FIGURE 6.1 Modes of governance
Hale and Roger (2014)

More specifically for the context of climate governance, Hale and Roger created a typology of the varieties of relationships between different types of actors. These roughly align with the matrix in Table 6.1 in the way that horizontal interactions refer to collaborative versions, hierarchy refers to forms of delegation and finally orchestration is an independent category in both settings (Figure 6.1),[15]

To better understand what these individual categories entail, let us look a bit more closely at how they play out in regulatory practice and look for ways in which these interactions enter the legal literature.

The first form of horizontal interaction in Table 6.1 is labelled 'entrepreneurial'.[16] It refers to private actors, whether NGOs or firms or a combination of the two engaging in regulatory activities (often standard setting) without direct public participation.[17] They are entrepreneurial in the sense that they become active in areas where they perceive a lack of public initiative. In the context of climate regulation, Roger and Hale mention the Greenhouse Gas Protocol,[18] which also plays an important role in the S4CA framework. However, private regulatory initiatives are common across many regulatory domains, from forestry and fisheries,[19] to financial

[15] Th Hale and Ch Roger, 'Orchestration and Transnational Climate Governance' (2014) 9 *Review of International Organizations* 59, 62ff.

[16] Green, *Rethinking Private Authority*; Hale and Roger, 'Orchestration and Transnational Climate Governance'.

[17] Green, *Rethinking Private Authority*.

[18] https://ghgprotocol.org.

[19] S. Carodenuto and B. Cashore, 'Can Non-State Regulatory Authority Improve Domestic Forest Sustainability? Assessing Interactive Pathways of Influence in Cameroon', in S. Wood

markets[20] and new technologies.[21] These phenomena have also been captured by legal scholars engaged in transnational private regulatory processes.[22] Here, focus has often been on contractual arrangements which are used by these private regulators to implement and enforce their regulatory regimes;[23] the resemblances to public law instruments;[24] and the way in which public regulators may have responded to such initiatives.[25]

The second group listed in the horizontal column is collaborations between sub-state domestic actors. These could be regulatory agencies and other bureaucratic units or regions and cities. Pathbreaking in the context of such trans-governmental networks has been the work by Anne-Marie Slaughter dating back to 2004.[26] In the context of climate regulation, cities have been particularly active in creating such transnational networks.[27]As we will see, their role is important in the sports context, as many large sporting events take place in major cities. Legal scholarship, too, has started to focus on the role of regional and local authorities and cities in particular in international law when emphasizing their growing involvement in international soft law processes while still not being recognized as international legal actors.[28] Finally,

et al. (eds.), *Transnational Business Governance Interactions: Advancing Marginalized Actors and Enhancing Regulatory Quality* (Edward Elgar, 2019), 207; L. Gulbrandsen and G. Auld, 'Contested Accountability Logics in Evolving Nonstate Certification for Fisheries Sustainability' (2016) 16 *Global Environmental Politics* 42; E. Meidinger, 'Forest Certification and Democracy' (2011) 130 *European Journal of Forest Research* 407.

20 M. Borowicz, 'Contracts as Regulation: The Isda Master Agreement' (2021) 16 *Capital Markets Law Journal* 72; J. Biggins and C. Scott, 'Resolving the Gaps: Embedding Isda in States' Responses to Systemic Risk', in Nicholas Dorn (ed.), *Controlling Capital, Public and Private Regulation of Financial Markets* (Routledge, 2016), 157; M. Andenas and I. H.-Y. Chiu, *The Foundations and Future of Financial Regulation: Governance for Responsibility* (Routledge, 2014).

21 IEEE AI technologies standards.

22 Among many others: F. Cafaggi, 'New Foundations of Transnational Private Regulation' (2011) 38 *Journal of Law and Society* 20.

23 Among others: Borowicz, 'The Isda Master Agreement'.

24 E. Meidinger, 'The Administrative Law of Global Private–Public Regulation: The Case of Forestry' (2006) 17 *European Journal of International Law* 47.

25 L. Gulbrandsen, 'Public Sector Engagement with Private Governance Programmes: Interactions and Evolutionary Effects in Forest and Fisheries Certification', in A Nollkaemper et al. (eds.), *Smart Mixes for Transboundary Environmental Harm* (Cambridge University Press, 2019), 211.

26 Slaughter, *A New World Order*.

27 Hale and Roger, 'Orchestration and Transnational Climate Governance', referring to T. Lee, 'Global Cities and Transnational Climate Change Networks' (2013) 13 *Global Environmental Politics* 108, and N. Toly, 'Transnational Municipal Network in Climate Politics: From Global Governance to Global Politics' (2008) 5 *Globalizations* 341.

28 C. Swiney, 'The Urbanization of International Law and International Relations: The Rising Soft Power of Cities in Global Governance' (2020) 41 *Michigan Journal of International Law*

from a more theoretical angle, we can refer to the Global Administrative Law project, which explicitly included 'administration based on collective action by transnational networks of cooperative arrangements between national regulatory officials' and distributed administration conducted by national regulators under treaty, network or other cooperative regimes[29].

The final horizontal mode of interaction is partnered governance, which Hale and Roger define as 'mixtures of sub-state and non-state actors who come together to achieve some governance goal'.[30] The S4CA initiative on which this paper focuses is, to a degree, a good example of such a partnered form of governance. It brings together a treaty body, UN Climate Change and private actors, among them the IOC, to achieve better climate protection mechanisms in the field of sports. However, such partnered approaches are not new, especially not in the sports context, where, as early as in the 1990s, we observed collaboration between the IOC and the United Nations Environmental Programme (UNEP).[31] Such partnerships are more common than one might think;[32] and have in recent years also received more attention in legal literature.[33]

The second column in Hale and Roger's typology covers hierarchical forms of interactions and here in particular delegation, which refers to the 'grant of authority from a principal to an agent'[34]. Unlike with horizontal relationships, here it is clearly the principal that initiates and designs the interaction. The agent is furthermore held to account by the principal and there may be forms of punishment for violation or failure to properly implement the agreement.[35]

(2020) 227; Y. Blank, 'The City and the World' (2006) 44 *Columbia Journal of Transnational Law* 875; Y. Blank, 'Localism in the New Global Legal Order' (2006) 47 *Harvard International Law Journal* 263; M. Ruffert, 'Transboundary Cooperation between Local or Regional Authorities', in *Max Planck Encyclopedia of International Law* (Oxford University Press).

29 B. Kingsbury, N. Krisch and R. Stewart, 'The Emergence of Global Administrative Law' (2005) 68 *Law and Contemporary Problems* 15, 20.

30 Hale and Roger, 'Orchestration and Transnational Climate Governance', 63.

31 See Memorandum of Understanding between UNEP and the IOC from 1994 (on file with the author). See furthermore, R. Schmidt, 'Protecting the Environment through Sports? Public–Private Cooperation for Regulatory Resources and International Law' (2017) 28 *European Journal of International Law* 1341–1366.

32 K. Abbott, 'Public Private Partnership', in *Max Planck Encyclopedia of International Law* (Oxford University Press).

33 D. Aziz, 'Global Public–Private Partnerships in International Law' (2012) 2 *Asian Journal of International Law* 339; R. Schmidt, *Regulatory Integration across Borders: Public Private Cooperation in Transnational Regulation* (Cambridge University Press, 2018).

34 D. Hawkins et al., 'Delegation under Anarchy: States, International Organizations and Principal–Agent Theory', in D. Hawkins et al. (eds), *Delegation and Agency in International Organizations* (Cambridge University Press, 2006), 3.

35 Hale and Roger, 'Orchestration and Transnational Climate Governance', 64.

Delegation was traditionally spoken of in the context of states allocating tasks to international organizations.[36] In the context of transnational environmental regulation, delegation from states, or groups of states, as well as from international organizations to private actors – transnational delegation – has increased in the past three decades.[37] One reason for this development is seen in the increased complexity of environmental treaties that employ multi-stakeholder forms of governance.[38] As will be subsequently depicted in this article, this complexity also leads to other types of delegation. In particular, delegation between private actors might take the form of sub-delegation as well as even forms of delegation from private to public actors, as is the case in the sports context between the IOC and host cities.[39]

The final column in Hale and Roger's matrix addresses orchestration. Orchestration was originally defined by Abbott et al. as 'one actor (or set of actors), the orchestrator, [who works] through a second actor (or set of actors), the intermediary, to govern a third actor (or set of actors), the target'.[40] Originally, this research started out with the goal of understanding the way in which international organizations engage in this mode of governance; the focus was therefore put on public actors – (states or) international organizations which in one way or another engage private organizations, often NGOs, as intermediaries.[41] However, as previous literature showed, states or international organizations engage in orchestration and many actors can be intermediaries, from private actors to networks to states or other NGOs. Especially in the context of climate, governance orchestration rose since the late 1990s;[42] with UN Climate Change taking on a more prominent role in recent years.[43] Reasons for why actors engage in orchestration are manifold, but it is generally believed that a combination of factors encourages it. First, the inability to achieve goals via traditional intergovernmental cooperation; second, the fact that sub-state and non-state actors have capacities and the interest to address a

36 Ibid., 63.

37 Ibid.; J. Green, 'Transnational Delegation in Global Environmental Governance: When Do Non-State Actors Govern?' (2018) 12 *Regulation and Governance* 263, 275.

38 Green, 'Transnational Delegation in Global Environmental Governance', 275.

39 R. Schmidt, 'The Carbon Footprint of the Games: International Climate Change Law and the Olympics' (2020) 114 *AJIL Unbound* 362.

40 Abbott et al., 'Introduction', 4.

41 Abbott et al. (eds.), *International Organizations as Orchestrators*; Hale and Roger, 'Orchestration and Transnational Climate Governance'.

42 Hale and Roger, 'Orchestration and Transnational Climate Governance'.

43 K. Bäckstrand and J. Kuyper, 'The Democratic Legitimacy of Orchestration: The UNFCCC, Non-State Actors, and Transnational Climate Governance (2017) 26 *Environmental Politics* 764–788.

regulatory problem but face obstacles to do so, for example, collective action problems; third, the orchestrators possess attributes that help overcome the aforementioned problems.[44] Those attributes are given if the orchestrator is a so-called anchor organization or 'natural focal institution'; if they have convening power; if they possess public legitimacy, as well as material and intellectual resources and organizational culture.[45] Again, one can also observe these elements with UN Climate Change, which possesses qualities of an anchor organization; the details of this will be discussed in more detail in the rest of this chapter.

From the short overview of governance interactions that we just saw, it is easy to imagine that one might have difficulty drawing a straight line between the different modes of interaction. Abbott et al. described this in the following manner:

> [the modes of interactions] are mixed and blended into hybrid forms. Rather than treating the direct–indirect and hard–soft distinctions ... as categorical, then, they should be regarded as the extreme points of continua. Thus, there are degrees of '(in)directness' in governance. For instance, direct collaboration in professional self-regulation may blend into indirect orchestration when governments promote the creation of professional associations that serve as independent middlemen between government and targets.[46]

We thus find multifaceted combinations of interactions within the same regulatory issue area and sometimes even within the same regulatory framework. This is especially the case in climate governance, in which the post-Paris Agreement has become an exemplar case of polycentric governance,[47] that is based on interactions between the different actors therein.

Before turning to an examination of these phenomena through a close assessment of the S4CA framework, let us analyse the role that individual actors may play in these interactions. The literature on governance interactions often, though not always, starts from the perspective of public actors such as states, international organizations or subnational entities. However, it might also be the initiatives of private actors that lead to the development of novel regulatory approaches to fostering change in a certain regulatory field. In the context of climate governance, the role of so-called leaders and pioneers

44 Hale and Roger, 'Orchestration and Transnational Climate Governance', 67–68.
45 Ibid.
46 Abbott et al., 'Introduction', 10.
47 S. Oberthür, 'Reflections on Global Climate Politics Post Paris: Power, Interests and Polycentricity' (2016) 51 *International Spectator* 80. A. Jordan et al., 'Governing Climate Change Polycentrically: Setting the Scene', in A. Jordan et al. (eds.), *Governing Climate Change: Polycentricity in Action?* (Cambridge University Press, 2018), 3.

has been discussed.[48] According to Wurzel, Liefferink and Torney, 'pioneership/leadership refers either to actors who are first to introduce and/or propagate a certain policy measure or who exhibit the highest level of ambition'.[49] Leaders are usually distinguished from pioneers in that they 'seek to attract followers', something that pioneers do not.[50] Leaders or pioneers can be different actors, international organizations, single countries, business actors, NGOs, etc.[51] In Section 6.3, we will look at this intersection between governance interactions and the role of regulatory pioneers and leaders in the context of the Sports for Climate Action framework. As will be shown, these complex interplays are at the centre of a comprehensive approach to climate change regulation.

6.3 THE SPORTS FOR CLIMATE ACTION FRAMEWORK

Questions about the environmental impact of sports have been prominent for at least three decades. The 1992 Winter Olympics in Albertville, for instance, was considered 'an environmental disaster' and led to widespread global concern about the impact of such mega-events.[52] As a result, the IOC had to put in place environmental policies for the Olympic Games specifically and the movement generally.[53]

The Paris Agreement set out to hold 'the increase in the global average temperature to well below 2°C above pre-industrial levels'.[54] The provision only binds those states that are signatories to the agreement. However, to successfully tackle climate change, it is understood that a broader societal effort is necessary. Non-state actors can be involved by states in their climate action plans.[55] To this end, UN Climate Change launched the Global Climate Action Portal, which lists climate change commitments (actions) by actors from all segments of society. Non-state actors can determine their own

48 Wurzel et al., 'Pioneers, Leaders and Followers'.
49 Ibid., 8.
50 Ibid.; D. Liefferink and R. Wurzel, 'Environmental Leaders and Pioneers: Agents of Change?' (2017) 24 *Journal of European Public Policy* 951.
51 Wurzel et al., 'Pioneers, Leaders and Followers', 15.
52 H. Cantelon and M. Letters, 'The Making of the IOC Environmental Policy as the Third Dimension of the Olympic Movement' (2000) 35 *International Review for the Sociology of Sport* 294, 300.
53 For further information, see Schmidt, 'Protecting the Environment through Sports?'.
54 U.N. Doc. FCCC/CP/2015/L.9/Rev/1, article 2(a); Sports for Climate Action Framework, paras 5 and 12.
55 U.N. Doc. FCCC/CP/2015/L.9/Rev/1, article 2(4); D. Wei, *Linking Non-State Action with the U.N. Framework Convention on Climate Change* (Center for Climate and Energy Solutions, 2016).

contributions to tackling climate change by, for instance, reducing emissions by a certain date. At the time of writing, 43,152 actions were listed, the vast majority of which are non-state actors.[56] One campaign that is also found on GCAP and particularly important to the present example is the Race to Zero (R2Z) campaign, which was established in 2020. It is described as 'the UN-backed global campaign rallying non-state actors … to take rigorous and immediate action to halve global emissions by 2030 and deliver a healthier, fairer zero carbon world in time'.[57]

Before this background, UN Climate Change, the IOC and other leading sports organizations started the S4CA initiative in 2018. Its goal, as stated in Section 6.1, is to foster the commitments made in the Paris Agreement in the sports sector.[58] Numerous sports actors, such as federations, clubs and actors from the sports industry, have signed up to it, totalling 280 participants at the time of writing.[59] UN Climate Change published a support document, the so-called Sports for Climate Action framework, which asks signatories to develop a climate action agenda based on five principles: first, to undertake systematic efforts to promote greater environmental responsibility; second, to reduce overall climate impact; third, to educate for climate action; fourth, to promote sustainable and responsible consumption and, fifth, to advocate for climate action through communication.[60]

Principle 2 establishes the central goal of achieving climate neutrality.[61] There is a two-step process foreseen by the framework to achieve climate neutrality. First, participating organizations should 'measure and understand',[62] by gathering information on current activities to establish a baseline climate footprint. Through this, the overall climate impact of the organization is established. These data then guide decision-makers in implementing the second step,[63] where organizations must mitigate their carbon footprint through a hierarchical five-stage process that starts with avoidance measures (1), then reduction (2) and substitution (3) of emissions. Finally, compensation through

56 See https://climateaction.unfccc.int/Actors. Those also include public initiatives such as those by cities or regions but not by states.

57 https://climatechampions.unfccc.int/Initiatives?id=Race_to_Zero.

58 https://unfccc.int/climate-action/sectoral-engagement/sports-for-climate-action; for further information on the implementation of this framework in the context of the Olympic Movement, see Schmidt, 'Carbon Footprint of the Games'.

59 https://climateaction.unfccc.int/Initiatives?id=Sports_for_Climate_Action.

60 Sports for Climate Action Framework, available at: https://unfccc.int/sites/default/files/resource/Sports_for_Climate_Action_Declaration_and_Framework_0.pdf, para 18.

61 Ibid., para 22.

62 Ibid., paras 23–25.

63 Ibid., para 25.

TABLE 6.2 *Five step table*

Step	Starting Line	Leadership Practice
Pledge	- Reach (net) zero GHGs by 2050 at the latest - Reach the interim target of 50% global reduction of CO_2 by 2030 - Targets must cover all GHG emissions, including all three scopes of the Greenhouse Gas Protocol Corporate Standard.[64]	- Target absolute zero or net negative emissions - Adopt inclusive boundaries - Twin targets for reduction and removal - Specific targets for short-term reduction of methane and other GHGs - Protect nature - Contribute to 2030 breakthroughs
Plan	- Transition plan within 12 months of joining, includes actions taken within 12 months, 2–3 years and by 2030	- Support a just transition - Integrate nature - Empower stakeholders
Proceed	- 'Immediate action through all available pathways toward achieving (net) zero' emissions	- Contribute beyond own value chain - Prioritize emissions-intensive sectors - Scale up climate solutions - Empower ecosystems
Publish	- Public reporting of progress	- Activate the ambition loop - Mainstream (net) zero alignment
Persuade	- Align external policy and engagement to halving emissions by 2030 and the net zero goal by 2050	- Activate the ambition loop - Mainstream (net) zero alignment

UNFCCC recognized mechanisms (4) for those emissions not covered by stages (1)–(3) is foreseen. Beyond the mitigation steps, step two also requires the reporting of the climate footprint and mitigation actions.[65]

The Sport for Climate Action framework also links to the R2Z campaign, to which several sports organizations, such as the IOC or the EPL, have already subscribed.[66] R2Z also consists of a five-step plan that overlaps to a degree with

64 The three scopes derive from the Greenhouse Gas Protocol, a global framework to measure greenhouse gas emissions. The framework classifies the scopes in the following way: 'Scope 1 emissions are direct emissions from owned or controlled sources. Scope 2 emissions are indirect emissions from the generation of purchased energy. Scope 3 emissions are all indirect emissions (not included in scope 2) that occur in the value chain of the reporting company, including both upstream and downstream emissions'. https://ghgprotocol.org/sites/default/files/standards_supporting/FAQ.pdf.

65 Ibid., para 26.

66 https://climateaction.unfccc..int/Initiatives?id=Sports_for_Climate_Action.

TABLE 6.3 *Four-step version*

Step	Action
Pledge	- Pledge by the head of the organization which includes commitments to reach (net) zero by 2040
Plan	- Within 12 months of joining, signatories will be expected to submit plans to UN Climate Change outlining the actions they will take toward achieving their climate pledges (especially in the short term (2030 target)) - These plans will likely be iterative
Proceed	- Take immediate action toward climate goals - Reflect the urgency of rapid emissions reductions - Each organization can choose how to approach emission reduction audits (different starting lines)
Report	- Annual public reporting from 2021 onwards

the S4CA principles, yet it does provide some more concrete targets (Table 6.2). The five steps are divided into starting-line criteria, which all members must meet, and leadership practices, which map out potential pathways for leadership in a net zero economy.[67]

The S4CA has in recent years aligned its own framework with the targets of the R2Z campaign and, as mentioned, some signatories of the S4CA have also joined the R2Z.[68] The S4CA has invited all participants to adopt the following targets. First, reduction of GHG emissions by 50 per cent by 2030 at the latest, either using a 2019 baseline or the latest year for which data is available; second, net zero GHG emissions by 2040; third, targets should be inclusive of scopes 1, 2 and 3 of the Greenhouse Gas Protocol[69]; and, fourth, organizations for which Scope 3 represent 40 per cent or more of total emissions generated by the organization to model Scope 3 emissions and set Scope 3 targets.

Furthermore, to ensure a consistent process and to incentivize action, all Sports for Climate Action signatories are requested to adhere to a four-step version of the R2Zs 5-step plan (Table 6.3).[70]

In the following we will look at the implementation of the S4CA framework by different sports actors. We will start with the IOC itself and then look at for-profit sports organizations that are not themselves part of the Olympic orbit. Examples of the latter will be two football leagues (the EPL and the First and

67 https://climateaction.unfccc.int/Initiatives?id=Race_to_Zero.

68 Cf Schmidt, 'Carbon Footprint of the Games' (at the time of writing that article the R2Z scheme had not been in place yet).

69 See n. 67.

70 See https://unfccc.int/climate-action/sectoral-engagement/sports-for-climate-action.

Second German Bundesliga under the umbrella of the DFL) as well as the NBA.

6.4 CLIMATE ACTION BY SPORTS ACTORS

6.4.1 *Climate Action by the IOC*

The IOC has a history of environmental policy that has reached back over three decades. Climate action is a more recent activity.[71] It was the IOC that, together with UN Climate Change, co-initiated the S4CA. Internally, its own climate policy started with its sustainability strategy in 2017.[72] The strategy was in line with Agenda 2020, a reform process adopted in 2014,[73] and included the pledge to achieve carbon neutrality by 2030, which was to be achieved through a combination of reducing and compensating for direct and indirect emissions.[74] However, at least 50 per cent of this should be achieved through reductions.[75] In the course of the recent Olympic Agenda 2020+5 process, another list of sustainability objectives for the timeframe of 2021–2024 was added. Five criteria are to guide these objectives, among them the criteria to 'reflect the IOC's commitment to be a climate positive organisation by 2024 and for all Games to be climate positive from 2030 onwards'.[76]

Importantly, the IOC is only responsible for a fraction of the Olympic Movement's GHG emissions. Thus, the Tokyo Olympics, even though held under pandemic conditions, produced 1.962 million t-CO_2 emissions,[77] whereas the IOC's emissions in 2018, for example as the year where they were highest, only amounted to 60,630 tonnes.[78] To account for this, the sustainability strategy uses three spheres of responsibility: the IOC as an organization, the IOC as the owner of the Olympic Games and the IOC as the leader of the Olympic Movement.[79]

71 The current section builds on Schmidt, 'Carbon Footprint of the Games'.

72 IOC, Sustainability Strategy, available at: https://olympics.com/ioc/sustainability.

73 https://olympics.com/ioc/olympic-agenda-2020.

74 IOC, Sustainability Strategy, available at: http://extrassets.olympic.org/sustainability-strategy/2-1, 42.

75 https://olympics.com/ioc/sustainability/climate-positive-commitment.

76 Sustainability Report, available at: https://stillmed.olympics.com/media/Documents/News/2021/12/IOC-Sustainability-Report-2021.pdf?_ga=2.96718367.1665806811.1656500530-1116173954.1656500530, 25.

77 Tokyo 2020, Sustainability Post-Games Report, available at: www.tokyo2020.jp/ja/image/upload/production/Sustaiability%20Post-Games%20Report.pdf, 26.

78 See IOC, The IOC's Climate Positive Commitment, available at: https://olympics.com/ioc/sustainability/climate-positive-commitment.

79 IOC, Sustainability Strategy, 4.

Based on this threefold division, we find several climate-related objectives in the new Agenda 2020+5. Thus, the IOC as an organization is to reduce its 'CO_2 emissions in line with the Paris Agreement, with a 30 per cent reduction in our travel emissions by 2024 and additional measures targeting our digital activities, buildings and catering'.[80] With regards to the IOC as owner of the Olympic Games, the new objectives prescribe that the IOC assists and accelerates 'the transition to climate positive Olympic Games through the development of guidance and expertise . . . and the revision of relevant existing operational requirements'.[81] These goals are in line with the requirements provided by the S4CA or R2Z schemes.

With the caveat that this is a moving target, with the IOC's sustainability strategy being in flux, let us now look at the implementation level of climate actions in the context of the Olympics. This happens at the host city level and a crucial document here is the Host City Contract's Operational Requirements. The latest version of this document was published in 2018. It contains a Sustainability and Legacy section, which requires host cities to implement their own sustainability strategies that are compatible with the IOC's.[82] Crucially, it needs to include the following requirements from 2026 onwards:

- [Organizing Committees of the Olympic Games] OCOGs and host cities [are] to minimize the Olympic Games' carbon emissions;
- OCOGs [are] to compensate for their 'direct'/'owned' emission;
- OCOGs and host cities [are] to promote low-carbon solutions for and through the Olympic Games in the host country; [and]
- Candidate cities, OCOGs and host cities [are] to take into account the potential consequences of climate change when selecting Olympic Games locations.[83]

How is this implemented? As mentioned, OCOGs must develop their own sustainability strategies. These must be accompanied by an implementation plan,[84] as well as by a sustainability management system based on the ISO 20121:2012 on Sustainable Events Management.[85] To depict the host city's progress on this front, OCOGs must prepare three sustainability reports (two before and one after the Games).[86]

80 Sustainability Report, 26.
81 Ibid., 26.
82 IOC, Host City Contract: Operational Requirements, June 2018, SUS 01, 166.
83 IOC, Sustainability Strategy, Annex 3, 54.
84 IOC, Host City Contract: Operational Requirements, June 2018, SUS 02, 166.
85 Ibid., SUS 04, 167
86 Ibid., SUS 06, 167.

More specifically, regarding climate actions, OCOGs are required to develop a specific carbon management plan with the goal of measuring and ultimately minimizing carbon emissions.[87] To this end, the IOC has developed the Carbon Footprint Methodology Guideline. This technical document provides methodological principles and technical guidance on how to measure and calculate carbon footprints.[88] The methodology used in the Guideline is based on the aforementioned Greenhouse Gas Protocol, ISO 14064 and the European Commission's Organization Environmental Footprint.[89] Based on this framework, OCOGs are also required to implement an iterative process. First, they need to estimate the carbon footprint of their Games using planning documents and assumptions. On this basis, a carbon management plan is then developed and an initial carbon footprint report is published. The second step consists of the creation and implementation of a carbon footprint reduction plan, followed by a revised carbon footprint report. After the Games, in the final step, OCOGs measured the actual footprint of the Games and reported it.[90]

6.4.2 *Professional Leagues and Climate Action*

Unlike the Olympic Movement, which has a decades-long history of challenges around the interplay between environmental protection and sports mega-events, many professional leagues have only recently faced more significant environmental and sustainability demands.[91] This brought with it new challenges that leagues now need to tackle to a greater degree. To date, the S4CA framework includes a large and growing number of professional associations and teams that are not directly within the Olympic orbit as signatories. These actors, just as the IOC, subscribed to the same requirements outlined. However, as will be discussed in Sections 6.4.2.1–6.4.2.3, in most cases, they are still less advanced in the development and implementation of relevant policies.

87 See, e.g., Paris 2024 Delivering Carbon Neutral Games, available at: www.paris2024.org/en/delivering-carbon-neutral-games/.

88 IOC, Carbon Footprint Methodology for the Olympic Games (December 2018).

89 Ibid., 12, and 17.

90 Ibid., 20.

91 T. Walters, 'The Football Industry Needs to Wake Up to the Climate Emergency', *The Guardian*, available at: www.theguardian.com/football/2020/aug/04/the-football-industry-needs-to-wake-up-to-the-climate-emergency.

6.4.2.1 English Premier League

Football is a truly global industry, one of significant size, and it is estimated that its carbon footprint is too. Around 0.3–0.4 per cent of all carbon emissions worldwide could stem from it.[92] The travel of teams and fans is one of the main sources. However, for the longest time, climate change and sustainability in general were not high on the agenda of those leading the industry.[93]

The EPL joined the S4CA framework on 4 November 2021. With its signature, it is committed to reducing its emissions by 50 per cent by 2030 to achieve net zero emissions by 2040. In line with the S4CA frameworks, this is achieved through adhering to the five principles outlined in Table 6.2.[94] The EPL published its sustainability strategy in 2025. The strategy outlines plans to reduce climate impact and cooperate with relevant stakeholders.[95] Central to the League's ambitions are not surprisingly EPL clubs. Currently, a number of clubs in the EPL have also signed onto the S4CA framework.[96] The first one to do so was Arsenal FC, which has set the target of reducing emissions by 50 per cent in 2030 and achieving climate neutrality by 2040.[97] It took a variety of measures to achieve these goals, such as switching to 100 per cent green electricity. Furthermore, it also engages in educational activities, such as a sustainability module that can be delivered to local schools.[98] Another club that signed the framework is Tottenham Hotspur. Its signature in January 2021 is building on several initiatives that the club has already engaged in. One is the 10:10 initiative, which asks individuals and organizations to cut their emissions by 10 per

92 https://sancroft.com/2022/03/22/a-more-beautiful-game-sustainability-in-football-comes-of-age/.

93 www.theguardian.com/football/2020/aug/04/the-football-industry-needs-to-wake-up-to-the-climate-emergency.

94 League commits to UN Sports for Climate Action Framework, 4 November 2021, available at: www.premierleague.com/news/2327983.

95 https://premierleague.com/news/4266971.

96 Ibid.

97 See 'Arsenal Joins with UN to Tackle Climate Change', 16 November 2020, available at: www.arsenal.com/news/arsenal-joins-un-tackle-climate-change. Sport + Positive Leagues, which provides a ranking of environmentally sustainable clubs, states that climate neutrality is to be achieved by 2040, but the club itself still lists 2050 on its website, see: www.sportpositiveleagues.com/pl-2021/.

98 UNFCCC, 'Four Premier League Clubs Taking Climate Action', 26 February 2021, available at: https://unfccc.int/blog/four-premier-league-clubs-taking-climate-action; and www.sportpositiveleagues.com/pl-2021/. See, furthermore, Arsenal Media, 'Arsenal Joins with UN to Tackle Climate Change'.

cent in 1 year.[99] Another project in which the club is a founding member is Count Us In. The goal of this initiative is to mobilize one billion people to take 16 steps to mitigate carbon pollution.[100] Liverpool is the third team that signed the S4CA framework. It is also committed to halve greenhouse gas emissions by 2030 and to achieving net zero by 2040. To achieve this, the club developed the Red Way strategy, which bundles all sustainability initiatives. The strategy concretely helped the club set off 435 tons of CO_2 and thus become carbon-neutral in its direct activities.[101] Another club having signed onto the S4CA framework early is Southampton. Their actions are bundled in the Halo Effect, which was launched in January 2021. According to this strategy, the club aims to be carbon neutral by 2030. Via the S4CA framework, there is an obligation to achieve carbon neutrality by 2040 at the latest.[102]

6.4.2.2 German Football League Association

The German Football League Association (DFL), which operates the First and Second Bundesliga, has also joined the S4CA framework. It implemented a binding sustainability directive in 2021, which will bind first and second Bundesliga clubs and took effect on 1 January 2023.[103] This step was preceded by the inclusion of sustainability as a goal of the DFL in its statutes.[104] In the future, clubs need to demonstrate their alignment with the requirements of the directive during the licensing process.[105] The goal of the directive is to provide a uniform framework for the existing individual commitments of Bundesliga clubs. One challenge in implementing the directive is that different clubs have different economic, structural and personnel starting points.

99 'Passionate about Our Planet', available at: www.tottenhamhotspur.com/the-stadium/passionate-about-our-planet/.

100 UNFCCC, 'Four Premier League Clubs Taking Climate Action'; https://unfccc.int/news/four-premier-league-clubs-taking-climate-action.

101 Liverpool, 'Our Planet', available at: www.liverpoolfc.com/theredway/our-planet; Liverpool, 'The Red Way', available at: www.liverpoolfc.com/news/community/422474-the-red-way-points-to-sustainability; UNFCCC, 'Four Premier League Clubs Taking Climate Action'.

102 Southampton, Environmental Responsibility, available at: www.southamptonfc.com/~/link.aspx?_id=B9728B7AA0364AD199F18FDFE5C3BF4D&_z=z.

103 'Anhang XIV: Nachhaltigkeitsrichtlinie', available at: https://media.dfl.de/sites/2/2022/06/Anhang-XIV-zur-LO-2022-05-31-Stand.pdf; DFL, 'Clubs der Bundesliga und 2. Bundesliga beschließen erstmals Nachhaltigkeitskriterien für Lizenzierungsordnung', available at: www.dfl.de/de/aktuelles/clubs-der-bundesliga-und-2-bundesliga-beschliessen-erstmals-nachhaltigkeitskriterien-fuer-lizenzierungsordnung/.

104 DFL, 'Clubs der Bundesliga und 2. Bundesliga beschließen erstmals Nachhaltigkeitskriterien für Lizenzierungsordnung'.

105 Ibid.

To this end, the directive foresaw a multi-stage implementation model consisting of three categories of minimum standards and extended criteria:[106]

- Minimum criteria I: Fulfilment must be fully demonstrated by licence applicants from the Third league by 1 March 2023 and from the First and Second Bundesliga by 15 March 2023;
- Minimum criteria II: Fulfilment must be fully demonstrated by licensees by 1 September 2023;
- Extended criteria: Fulfilment or response can be demonstrated and financially and non-financially incentivised by licensees by 1 September 2023.[107]

The minimum criteria can be assigned to three subject areas of sustainability: 'Club management and organization', 'Environment and resources' and 'Stakeholder groups'. In the second category, we find CO_2 emission management. Here are the minimum criteria required:

> Proof of biennial recording of the greenhouse gas emissions caused by the club's business activities in Scopes 1 and 2 of the GHG Protocol as well as club-relevant components in Scope 3.
>
> Minimum components for Scope 3 are: (1) mobility of employees, (2) business trips (including sports and function teams), (3) fan mobility, and (4) emissions from club stadium use under leases.[108]

Minimum Criteria II for now contains questions to the clubs regarding their emission reduction goals and measures to achieve such reductions.[109]

Besides the DFL itself, two Bundesliga clubs – 1. FC Köln and VFL Wolfsburg – were early signatories of the S4CA framework. VFL Wolfsburg is usually mentioned as a model actor when it comes to climate action. It was the first football club to sign onto the S4CA framework and has since implemented significant and detailed measures to reduce emissions. Currently, the goal is to achieve net zero emissions by 2025. It has determined its climate footprint using the GHG model and has put concrete measures into place to reduce and offset its emissions.[110]

[106] https://media.dfl.de/sites/2/2022/06/Anhang-XIV-zur-LO-2022-05-31-Stand.pdf, p. 1.
[107] Ibid.
[108] Ibid., p. 13.
[109] Ibid.
[110] VFL Wolfsburg, 'Moving Together, Sustainability Report of the VFL Wolfsburg 2020', available at: https://static-typo3.vfl-wolfsburg.de/user_upload/Medien/Dokumente/210425-VfL-Wolfsburg-Sustainability-Report.pdf, p. 55.

6.4.2.3 National Basketball Association

The third example of a professional league's engagement with the S4CA framework is the NBA. The NBA was the first professional sports league to sign onto the S4CA in 2019.[111] With its signature, the NBA also agreed to halve its emissions by 2030 and to achieve net zero emissions by 2040. However, to date, there is at least no publicly available sustainability policy, even though the NBA has engaged in several activities to mitigate emissions.[112] These mainly centre around creating awareness and green buildings. Ten teams have already received Leadership in Energy and Environmental Design (LEED) certifications.[113]

A major source of emissions for the NBA, like other sports leagues, is carbon emissions through (air) travel. There are estimates that, in 2018, the four major North American leagues emitted 122,000 tons of CO_2 for 7.5 million kilometres of travel in total.[114] The NBA is said to have had the largest footprint. As a result, meaningful commitments to reduce emissions need to address air travel. This has also been acknowledged by NBA Commissioner Adam Silver in a recent statement made at the Aspen Ideas Festival.[115] As a response, the NBA announced on 17 August 2022 that it had adjusted the playing schedule in such a way that travel would be reduced by 5 per cent or 90,000 fewer kilometres.[116] Regarding teams, Portland Trail Blazers are frequently mentioned as particularly progressive, even though they have not signed up the S4CA framework. The team has adopted a sustainability plan called 'livegreener' which, among other areas, also contains a policy on energy usage. Here, the team states that the carbon footprint/event-day-person was cut by 25 per cent since 2008. The current goal is to reduce this footprint by an additional 15 per cent by 2025 and to continue offsetting 100 per cent of electricity and natural gas use. Together with EnergyTrust of Oregon, the

[111] https://greensportsalliance.org/nba-signs-on-to-uns-sports-for-climate-action-framework-whos-got-next/.

[112] See https://cares.nba.com/programs/nba-green/.

[113] LEED is a rating system which is developed by the US Green Building Council and which rates buildings according to carbon, energy, water, waste, transportation, materials, health and environmental equality. Information available at: www.usgbc.org/leed.

[114] S. Wynes, 'Covid-19 Disruption Demonstrates Win–Win Climate Solutions for Major League Sports' (2021) 55/23 *Environmental Science & Technology* 15609, 15609.

[115] Interview available at Angie Lassman, 'NBA Commissioner Talks about League's Efforts toward Sustainability', www.nbcmiami.com/news/local/changing-climate-south-florida/nba-commissioner-talks-about-leagues-efforts-toward-sustainability/2758589/.

[116] R. Del Bello, 'The NBA Takes Action to Reduce Its Carbon Footprint', *Le Monde*, 24 August 2022.

team completed 53 energy-related projects.[117] To date, few of the teams of the NBA have joined the S4CA framework.

6.5 DISCUSSION: THE COMPLEXITIES OF PUBLIC–PRIVATE INTERACTION IN THE S4CA FRAMEWORK

The previous sections depicted both the S4CA framework and the implementation of climate change measures by four actors in the sports context: the IOC itself, the EPL, the DFL and the NBA. In this section, the focus will be directed towards both the types of interactions that characterize the S4CA and the underlying legal framework(s).

Let us begin with the role of the IOC. It is fair to say that, in the 1990s, when the first environmental policies were developed, the IOC took a leadership position in the Olympic realm and possibly a pioneering role regarding the wider sports orbit.[118] The policies developed became binding on future host cities and impacted actors, such as local Olympic committees and sports federations. At the time, cooperating with the UNEP seemed a logical step, given the new territory that the IOC was entering, its own lack of expertise in the field and the fact that UNEP had plenty of it and was furthermore considered a legitimate actor.[119] Back then, the relationship could be described as more cooperative. Since the 1990s, a lot has changed and engagement with the UN and the integration into broader projects backed by the UN has become more commonplace for the IOC.[120] At the same time, engagement with various private actors has also become more commonplace for UN institutions.

It is therefore not surprising that the cooperation between UN Climate Change and the IOC regarding the S4CA framework stands on a different footing. At first, we can detect parallels: The IOC cooperates with a UN institution to develop a framework to improve environmental protection in the sports sector. The IOC then enforces these rules within its own regulatory

[117] Trail blazers, livegreener committed to making a big difference, with a small footprint, available at: www.nba.com/blazers/livegreener/.

[118] However, we must also note that the IOC itself was inspired by the work done in host cities, in particular Lillehammer, see R. Schmidt, 'Local Practices: Transnational Solutions? The Role of Host Cities in the Cyclic Process of Environmental Regulation in the Context of Sports', in S. Wood et al. (eds.), *Transnational Business Governance Interactions* (Edward Elgar, 2019), 77.

[119] Schmidt, *Regulatory Integration across Borders*, 180–189.

[120] Ibid., 194–197.

framework, for example, requiring adoption by host cities. On the other hand, cooperation with the UN Climate Change displays a number of crucial differences. First, this time, it was not the IOC alone but a broader set of representatives from the sports sector both from within the Olympic orbit (federations and host cities) and beyond (Forest Green Rovers Football Club, World Surfing League) that were involved.[121] With regard to the R2Z campaign, the IOC even states to have 'joined it', thus taking on a role as a mere participant rather than one of a developer.[122] Second, from the UN Climate Change's perspective, involving the private sector has become a common process. Thus, the Climate Action Portal lists 43,152 actors active in climate initiatives, of which a majority are non-state or sub-state actors.[123] The S4CA only lists 280 participants on the Portal, thus only a small number of the overall commitments; it is also only one of many other cooperative initiatives.[124] UN Climate Change has become a facilitator for a significant variety of private actor commitments and cooperation. Its role has also received backing from decisions of the CoP and individual state practice, which have again emphasized the role of private actors.[125] Thus, the role of UN Climate Change's is one of nuances. It partners (collaborates) with private actors to develop specific regulatory frameworks. Even though it would probably go too far to characterize its relationships with the private sector as one of delegation, we can see hierarchical features at play. Thus, UN Climate Change sets targets for private engagement, which are ultimately based on the Paris Agreement's goals. Finally, we can also detect elements of orchestration. This becomes particularly visible in the example of the DFL. By joining the S4CA, the DFL has made commitments that are now becoming mandatory through its sustainability directive. These requirements affect the current Bundesliga clubs, but also prospective ones moving up from lower leagues. Similarly, the IOC requires alignment with the S4CA goals of the host cities and other actors in the Olympic orbit. Though none of those interactions fit neatly into a specific category of Hale and Roger's table, they form an intricate web of interactions which are based on international treaty law, then transmitted through a combination of soft law

[121] UNFCCC; 'Sports for Climate Action Framework, 2.0', available at: https://unfccc.int/sites/default/files/resource/Sports_for_Climate_Action_Declaration_and_Framework_0.pdf, para 13; World Athletics, 'UN Sports for Climate Action Initiative Launched at COP24 in Katowice', 11 December 2018, available at: www.worldathletics.org/news/news/un-sports-for-climate-action-initiative-launc.

[122] https://olympics.com/ioc/news/sport-sets-pace-for-climate-action-as-ioc-and-other-sports-organisations-join-race-to-zero-campaign.

[123] https://climateaction.unfccc.int/Actors.

[124] https://climateaction.unfccc.int/Initiatives.

[125] Decision 1/CP.21.

commitments and private contractual stipulations. Together, these give UN Climate Change a much wider and more direct reach than it would have as a simple facilitator of state action.

Regarding the substance of the requirements, we can observe a harmonization of what climate change measures and carbon reduction mean in the private (sport) sector. This is facilitated through a complex multilevel (soft) law and contractual framework in which the commitments in the Paris Agreement provide the benchmark. UN Climate Change then facilitates non-state commitments towards the same goals. As we can see, with the implementation of the R2Z campaign, original obligations might be adapted over time to achieve more coherence or commitment. Cooperative initiatives such as the S4CA provide a framework for serious commitments by non-state actors and provide an easily accessible framework for actors from this specific sector. Up to this point, we are dealing with soft law commitments that are not legally enforceable in themselves. However, they might overlap with the legal requirements in the countries in which they are located. Furthermore, enforceability might also change once we go one level down and look at the implementation at the signatory level. Here, we can in particular point to the IOC and the DFL. As outlined in Section 6.4.1, the IOC's own framework is very advanced and, on paper, fulfils the requirements of the S4CA and the Race2Zero framework. In its own regulatory domain, it acts as an intermediary by fostering its own commitments through contractual measures (host city contracts) and laws of association (wider Olympic family). Similarly, the DFL uses its licensing procedures to require Bundesliga clubs to implement sustainability actions that are clearly measurable. In the context of climate change, this involves measures that are in line with the S4CA and R2Z frameworks. Thus, we can observe a stringent and serious commitment by both actors, which also includes their wider orbit of actors. The DFL is acting in a leadership role here. The EPL has now published its sustainability policies and it will be interesting to see how far the commitments therein are also extended directly to EPL clubs. Several clubs have already committed to the S4CA framework themselves. There are expectations that the trend of going green will continue as demands from the general public are rising.[126] On the other hand, we are also observing that professional clubs are struggling to find meaningful ways of reducing emissions, especially when those emissions are linked to their

[126] B. Weston, 'Football Must Do More to Tackle Climate Change: This Is How Clubs and Fans Can Help', *The Guardian*, 6 May 2022.

main operations, for example, travelling to matches.[127] From here, there is also only a small step towards accusations of tokenism and even greenwashing.[128] Given that most of the clubs' actors analysed here only recently signed up with the S4CA framework, it is too early for a final evaluation. Time will tell whether it is possible to implement the ambitious goals of the S4CA framework in the sports context more broadly.

6.6 CONCLUSION

This chapter provided an assessment of the sports sector's involvement in global climate action steered by UN Climate Change. It started with a description of the S4CA framework, which was developed by UN Climate Change, together with diverse sports actors, most notably the IOC. The framework now provides a backdrop for wider commitment from the sports sector. In the first step, the example of the S4CA was used to depict and entangle the intricate web of (public and) private interactions linked to its development and implementation. This showed how IOs can use direct and indirect engagement with the private sector to facilitate public goals, as defined in public international treaties. Importantly, the chapter also demonstrated that state support for these initiatives, whether directly through state action or through treaty mandates, facilitates these effects.

The chapter also analysed the role those different actors took within such an interactive framework. Here, the role of UN Climate Change was first characterized as being located between a hierarchical and a collaborative actor. UN Climate Change sometimes takes on the role of a delegator; it actively cooperates with private actors and engages in orchestration. The role of private actors is similarly heterogeneous. Some actors, such as the IOC or the DFL, take on a leadership and pioneering position that strongly affects their wider orbit. Contractual and statutory instruments are used here in particular. The commitments of other actors are still more at an infancy level, and we find rule-takers that orient themselves towards established paths of achieving climate goals.

[127] R. del Bello, 'The NBA Takes Action to Reduce Its Carbon Footprint', *Le Monde*, 24 August 2022.

[128] Ibid.

7

International Organizations and the Market

ELISABETTA MORLINO

7.1 INTRODUCTION

Buyers and sellers, producers and consumers, investors and traders: all these entities can be defined as market actors in as much as they play a role in the market by interacting with each other to exchange goods, services, works, financial instruments and information. This interaction may result in determining, conditioning or influencing the supply and demand, the prices and, more in general, the market dynamics and efficiency, the distribution of benefits and costs and ultimately the very existence or behaviour of other market actors.

Whereas, however, the role played by states, firms or individuals in shaping the market has been extensively researched and studied, there is virtually no research and speculation on the hypothesis that international organizations can be market actors and have an impact on the market and on the single entities which are part of it.

The immediate objection to this last statement is, of course, that there are international organizations that have as institutional and primary mission, precisely that of regulating markets – the World Trade Organization among others – or of providing rules for regulating market exchanges (the UNCITRAL, for instance) and that these organizations, as well as the function performed by them, have been analysed and discussed in the literature.[1]

[1] See *inter alia* P. Van den Bossche, *The Law and Policy of the World Trade Organization*, 5th ed. (Cambridge University Press, 2021); M. Matsushita et al., *The World Trade Organization. Law, Practice, and Policy*, 3rd ed. (Oxford University Press, 2015); I. Bantekas et al., *UNCITRAL Model Law on International Commercial Arbitration: A Commentary* (Cambridge University Press, 2020).

Indeed, it is not these organizations, nor their specific institutional mission that are the primary focus of this chapter, although they will be part of the analysis.

Rather, the scope of the chapter is transversal and includes international organizations *in general*, so also those whose institutional mission does not pertain to markets at least *prima facie* and, rather, is guided by a wider range of political and social objectives, in addition to the economic ones, that international organizations may pursue, from peace and security to humanitarian aid, from environmental protection to food security.

In line with an approach more sensitive to the economic aspects of international organizations,[2] the questions that this chapter aims to address are, thus, first and foremost, whether there is a connection between international organizations and the market – including those organizations that do not have institutional objectives directly related to the market; and, more precisely, whether international organizations can be considered to be market actors and to what extent they have an impact on the market and on other market actors. If this is ascertained, the following question should be how international organizations shape the market; in other words, what are the means and mechanisms through which international organizations inform the behaviours of other market players? Finally, if the impact on the market is significant or at least non-negligible, a problem of accountability emerges which needs to be discussed: are international organizations accountable in shaping the market?

These questions do not stem from a theoretical and generic hypothesis about the connection between international organizations and the market, possibly based on an analogy between international organizations and governments (and their influence on the market). Rather, they originate from the empirical observation of a growing but overlooked phenomenon, that of the relationships between international organizations and private businesses, mainly for procurement purposes, that is, to procure goods, services and works for, directly or indirectly, carrying out the international organizations' mission.

Procurement by international organizations has been, in fact, the subject matter of some studies.[3] These have provided an analysis from the point of view of the relationships between international organizations and private subjects, assessing the extent of the rights and duties originating from this relationship.

[2] As in J. Klabbers, 'Towards a Political Economy of International Organizations Law' (2023) 20 *International Organizations Law Review* 82.

[3] See E. Morlino, *Procurement by International Organizations: A Global Administrative Law Perspective* (Cambridge University Press, 2019).

The present contribution intends to build on these analyses and enrich those findings by adding a different perspective, that of the market. The aim is to bring the conceptualization of international organizations a step further, adding a new dimension to the existing analyses and exploring the role of international organizations as market actors, beyond the specific institutional mission of some of them.

In order to do that, the chapter is structured into three parts. Section 7.2 discusses the existence of a relationship between international organizations and the market, laying down its main features and identifying the different roles played by international organizations vis-à-vis the market. Section 7.3 explores the means and tools through which international organizations shape the market. Section 7.4 deals with the problem of accountability and assesses the effectiveness of the mechanisms through which international organizations are held accountable when shaping the market. Section 7.5 then provides some conclusions and suggests a way forward.

7.2 INTERNATIONAL ORGANIZATIONS AND THE MARKET: AN UNEXPECTED RELATIONSHIP

International organizations such as the World Trade Organization, the World Customs Organization and the United Nations Conference on Trade and Development, but also the International Organization for Standardization or the International Maritime Organization, have as institutional mission to, directly or indirectly, promote and facilitate free international trade. They remove tariffs and barriers to trade by setting common rules and standards globally or regionally and, in some instances, by providing fora to resolve conflicts related to protectionist domestic policies. The idea underlying these organizations is an evolution of the liberal economic theories that connect free trade policies with higher productivity and economic well-being and, ultimately, with peace and security.

In order to carry out their institutional mission, however, all international organizations – and not only those committed to specifically promoting free trade – go on the market to procure goods, services and works. To do so they deal with private businesses following a set of rules and procedures that have been gradually and slowly developed and codified since the 1980s, and that only recently have acquired external relevance and publicity. In this way, international organizations create markets for certain type of goods, services, and works, and for businesses worldwide or established in some specific geographical area.

These institutional and legal phenomena, that is, first, the establishment, existence and functioning of specific international organizations whose institutional mission is to regulate the market and, second, the procurement by all international organizations, are the two main ways through which international organizations create a link with the market, influencing, conditioning or determining the behaviour of other market actors.

We could define the first type of relationship between organizations and the market as a *direct institutional relationship*, in that it is based on the institutional mission of the organizations and is directed to have an impact on the market, and the second type as an *indirect instrumental relationship*, being a consequence of an instrumental activity of the organizations, that of procurement and having an indirect impact on the market.

The relationship between international organizations and the market has, thus, two main manifestations which differ in several respects, namely the function of the international organization vis-à-vis the market, the market players that are involved in the relationship, the values and interests guiding this relationship and its economic impact. It is worthwhile to identify and discuss these differences.

7.2.1 *Function: International Organizations as Market Creators, Regulators and Adjudicators*

With regard to the function,[4] three main functions of the relationship between international organizations and markets can be identified: international organizations can create the market *ex novo*, can regulate it and can adjudicate disputes arising from the regulations.

International organizations whose institutional mission is to ensure and facilitate free trade mainly perform a market regulatory function and, some of them, a conflict resolution function. These organizations provide for principles, rules and procedures to facilitate trade and set the conditions for free markets. At the same time, some of them also add to this a function of resolving disputes arising from a possible violation of those standards, rules and

[4] A preliminary consideration is needed. The term ‘function’ is used here with a different meaning than is usually referred to in the literature on international organizations. Indeed, we do not refer here to the concept of ‘function’ as institutional mission, often used to justify international organizations’ immunities and limitations to their accountability. Rather, we refer to a more specific concept of function related to the relationship between international organizations and the market. In other words, what function do international organizations perform with respect to the market? Do they create it? Do they regulate it? Expanding it or shrinking it? Both?

procedures. In relation to the market, the function of these organizations is not to create a market *ex novo*, but to ensure that the market, potentially created by the interaction between individuals and companies from different states, functions in a certain way and under certain conditions, namely those of free trade. In other words, it opens up and expands markets that were there already, even if not fully accessible. Thus, the function is not related to the creation of a market but to the manner in which market dynamics are regulated and shaped; and to the compliance with the rules and procedures ensuring these dynamics. In this way, the function of creating the market remains in the hands of states and companies, while the function of regulating it is partly delegated to international organizations.

In contrast, in international organizations that do not have an institutional mission directly related to the market, the link between the organizations and the market responds to two different, yet interrelated, functions. As mentioned in Section 7.1, organizations turn to the market to obtain goods, services and works needed to carry out their institutional mission, whatever that may be. In doing so, they *create* a market, that of public procurement, which goes beyond state boundaries and is untied, at least apparently, from state decisions. Thus, international organizations create new market sectors as a by-product of their own procurement needs. The new market sectors, moreover, are regulated by the organizations themselves: they set the procurement rules and procedures and, in so doing, also define the way these sectors of the market operate. For example, they may be competitive or, conversely, driven by preferential or protectionist goals. A secondary function is, hence, to regulate these market sectors and provide market opportunities for local enterprises or, on the contrary, for enterprises incorporated in the countries financing the organizations. All international organizations, therefore, to a different extent, perform a creative function *stricto sensu*, that is they create a market sector and a regulatory function, restricting or expanding the commercial opportunities related to such sector.

In this type of relationship, however, regulation is not directed at states, as in the first type of relationship, but is addressed at the organization itself (and the bodies responsible for implementing procurement) as well as at companies or individuals.

Also, states intervene only indirectly in the rulemaking phase, as opposed to the other type of relationship in which market regulation is shaped by states themselves within the international fora of debate and negotiation.[5]

[5] On the 'agora function' of international organizations, see J. Klabbers, 'Two Concepts of International Organization' (2005) 2 *International Organizations Law Review* 277.

Finally, a dispute resolution function is very rarely attached to this type of relationship. As we shall see in Section 7.4, very few organizations have established judicial or para-judicial bodies competent to oversee compliance with rules and procedures and, thus, indirectly also to ensure that organizations provide market opportunities consistent with those rules and procedures.

7.2.2 *Market Players*

Turning to the market players involved in the relationship between international organizations and markets, it has been mentioned that, in both types of relationships, the direct institutional relationship and the indirect instrumental relationship, international organizations, states and private actors are involved. The role played by each and their reciprocal dynamics, however, changes in the two relationships.

In the *direct institutional relationship*, the organization acts as a catalyst for states and their economic and trade policy options, defining shared standards, rules and procedures and, to some extent, ensuring compliance mechanisms to which states themselves are bound. Given the highly political and economic relevance of the subject matter of regulation, the rulemaking phase formally takes place within the organizations but substantially is the result of the negotiations between representatives of the states.[6] Furthermore, the implementation of the relationship between organizations and the market takes place through the activity of states.

On the one hand, states formally cede sovereignty to organizations in the definition of standards, rules and procedures, and this cession of sovereignty is consistent with the very object of regulation, namely the market: the goals of increasing market opportunities and making possible trade between companies incorporated in different states explain the necessity of an international forum for rulemaking.

On the other hand, states retain, on their own territory, a significant margin of discretion in the implementation of those standards, rules and procedures. The conflict resolution mechanisms set up in the organizations aim precisely at controlling the exercise of this discretion and ensuring that it is exercised within the framework of the standards, rules and procedures set up.

Finally, companies and individuals are the recipients and, in theory, also the ultimate beneficiaries, of market policies and rules, set by international organizations and implemented by states. The cross-border nature of trade obviously also creates a wide-ranging system of extraterritorial

6 Ibid.

implementation: the implementation by states of these market standards, rules and procedures has an impact not only on the private entities incorporated in the state itself, but also on foreign private entities.

In the *indirect instrumental relationship*, the actors are, again, the organization, states and companies or individuals, but with different roles and scopes of activity. The organizations dictate rules and procedures, the implementation of which pertains to the direct responsibility of the organizations in direct procurement and of the states (but supervised by the organizations) in indirect procurement.

In this type of relationship, states and, in particular, the major funding states, certainly have an influence in the rule-making phase. Rulemaking, however, is formally the product of the international organization and their secretariats.

Furthermore, the role of states in the implementation phase of the rules and procedures is not institutionalized, at least in direct procurement. In indirect procurement, the implementation phase is entrusted to the states but is guided by the principles set forth by the organizations. That is to say, the relationship between international organizations and private entities is immediate, and not mediated: the rules and implementation by international organizations have an impact on private entities and on the market that is not formally mediated by states.

It should, however, be added that there are informal and primarily political forms of influence by states both in the rulemaking phase and in the implementation of procurement rules and procedures, and that these influences have the effect of widening or narrowing the market, making it more competitive or conversely more protectionist. So, while the impact that organizations have on the market is formal and direct, and, as seen, can create the market as well as regulate it, it cannot be ignored that states play a substantive and informal role in setting the direction of procurement policies and, thus, of the market.

Thus, comparing the role of the institutional actors, and in particular international organizations and states, similarities and differences can be detected. In the direct institutional relationship, where the market is already created by the states and they aim mainly to regulate it and eventually open it, it is the states that retain decisive decision-making power, albeit such power is exercised within an international forum and is subject to negotiation. The international organization maintains a role as a facilitator of confrontation and dialogue among states, as well as a role as a body that formally adopts standards, rules and procedures based on the legitimacy derived from its international nature and the delegated authority from states.

When, on the other hand, the organizations create a market from scratch and then regulate it, as in the case of the indirect functional relationship, the role of states is less obvious and takes place mostly 'behind the scenes'. It is possible, however, to distinguish two stages. The market creation stage is almost entirely the result of an internal determination of the international organization: the market, as mentioned in Section 7.1, arises from a need for the international organization to function. In this stage, states have, if anything, a preliminary role in the moment they give their funding to the organization, enabling the organization to operate. In the market regulation phase, created by the operational needs of organizations, the source of regulation remains the organization. However, states exercise forms of influence, mainly through non-formal channels of representation. Rule-making takes place in collegial fora where the administrative officials of the organizations sit. These fora, even where they do not house formal state representatives, are nevertheless not impervious to state influences. States retain *de facto* power in guiding the direction towards which regulation might tend. Their influence is, moreover, present in the implementation phase of both direct and indirect procurement. By the implementation phase, we mean the phase during which contracts are awarded. The awarding of contracts is conditioned, within a certain extent and especially with reference to contracts of greater economic value, by the indications of certain states, in particular the financing states.

7.2.3 *Values and Interests*

Different values and interests underlie the two types of relationships between international organizations and the market. The direct institutional relationship is linked to the mission with which international organizations are entrusted. The underlying idea of these organizations is that a global market, with harmonized rules, without internal barriers or with barriers allowed only exceptionally, can contribute to increasing collective material well-being by giving firms opportunities for trade and exchange across national borders. These opportunities come from the aggregate of consumers pertaining to foreign states, whereas in the indirect functional relationship trade opportunities come from the organization itself. Of course, these guiding values may be counterbalanced by the interests of states that, from time to time, in specific circumstances or for certain sectors, prefer to maintain protectionist policies.

The values and interests underlying the indirect instrumental relationship, on the contrary, are not necessarily those of the free market. Instead, at least three different set of values and interests can be identified. The first is closely related to the operating needs of the organizations. In carrying out their procurement activities, there are internal interests that drive the organizations and have an impact on the market: economy of resources and efficiency of administrative action generally have a restrictive impact on the market. Economy and efficiency, in fact, result in faster, less publicized, non-competitive and hard-to-access procedures, and the market is, thus, limited and accessible to few companies.

These underlying interests, however, pertain to the international organization as an administration. When one shifts the focus from international organizations as administrations to international organizations as political entities and institutions promoting policies for growth and development, then one also sees how, in procurement and in the market created by procurement, administrative interests combine with institutional and political values. Indeed, the values underlying the regulation of the market derived from procurement are infused with those deriving from the mission carried out by the international organization. For example, in some cases procurement procedures are regulated in such a way as to favour market access of local economic operators through preferential treatment. In this way, employment of the population and development of the area should be promoted, at least in theory. This is the so-called domestic preference in procurement contract award.

Values related to the organizations' institutional mission then intersect with the economic interests of the actors involved, including the organizations themselves. For them the need to exist and operate plays a determining factor; and this possibility depends on funding from member states. It becomes, therefore, crucial to secure the support and funding of some states. At the heart of this type of relationship between organizations and the market are, therefore, again the states, particularly the funding states. Their interests are to ensure that the market created by the organization guarantees a return on the funding and translates into business opportunities for their companies. For example, making a contractor selection process highly competitive can favour large companies from developed countries over small local companies from developing countries. But the opposite can also happen, that is, carrying out opaque procedures to favour companies from donor countries.

The market, created by the organizations, is thus regulated within this triangle of influences in which the values associated with the mission of the organizations can be distorted by the varying synergies between the autonomous administrative interests of the organizations, the interests of the organizations related to state funding and the interests of the funding states. The picture is, therefore, much more articulated, nuanced and dynamic than in the direct institutional relationship.

7.2.4 Economic Impact

Another of the dimensions of the relationship between international organizations and the market is the economic impact the former produce on the latter. Of course, economic impact is a varied concept that can include the movement of monetary flows and the complex of business opportunities for individuals and firms, but also the conditioning on the operations of companies.[7]

Thus understood, the economic impact of international organizations on the market differs depending on whether it is a direct institutional relationship or an indirect instrumental relationship.

With reference to the first type of relationship, the economic impact that organizations have on the market is broad, varied and difficult to measure. There are, however, attempts to quantify this impact. For example, if one takes the WTO, the overall economic impact will be given by the economic and trade policies that each of the member states has adopted in response to the international organization's rules on barriers to trade. So, the measurement of the impact comes from comparing economic flows before and after each state joined the organization. Research by the UK Department of International Trade,[8] for example, highlighted how all WTO member states, albeit with differences, experienced significant economic growth subsequent to joining the organization:

> [f]rom 2000 to 2016, the overwhelming majority (79%) of WTO members experienced a significant decrease in trade (export and import) costs as a result of WTO membership. . . . For a sample of 43 WTO members all these countries saw increases in both relative (compared to the rest of the world) aggregate exports and aggregate welfare as a result of WTO membership. The average increase in exports for this sample as a result of membership was 35%, from a high of 129% (Mexico) to a lower bound with 4% (Lithuania).[9]

The economies that have benefited most from the organization's membership have been those of developing countries, while those most resistant to the organization's economic impact are the economies of former Soviet countries and small states.

The WTO is, of course, only one example, although one of the most relevant given its wide and varied membership and significant effects on the

7 A. Bradford, *The Brussels Effect: How the European Union Rules the World* (Oxford University Press, 2020), 2.

8 UK Department of International Trade, *Valuing the Impact of the World Trade Organization (WTO)*, 25 August 2022, 4.

9 Ibid.

economy. Studies have been devoted to the economic impact of the European Union, even beyond the borders of the member states. Adopting a broader perspective, the theory of the 'Brussels effect'[10] argues that European rules, in addition to creating a single market among member states, also shape the international business environment. Of other supranational organizations, as well as of development banks, something similar can be hypothesized, although to a lesser extent.

In general, the economic impact related to the direct institutional relationship has at least two main features.

The first is that the genesis of such economic impact is varied and multifactorial. Indeed, on the one hand, some studies have succeeded in drawing a causal link between the organization and market, measuring the impact of the former on the latter. On the other side, this impact is always produced in the context of a concomitance of factors that are also external to the international organization and that are decisive in enhancing or reducing its effect. As mentioned, WTO membership led to significant economic effects in developing countries but was almost irrelevant for former Soviet countries. In this first type of relationship, therefore, the impact of the organization is not autonomous: its effectiveness depends on competing factors pertaining *inter alia* to state size, the policies adopted by states and their macroeconomic choices.

The second feature is related to the first and pertains to the role of states. The impact on the economy of the direct institutional relationship has at least two generative factors, neither of which is in isolation sufficient to produce that impact: the first is the regulatory role of markets played by the international organization, the second is the implementation role by states, which are both advocates of their own economic policies and recipients of the effects produced by the policies of other states. The latter is crucial to ensuring the effectiveness of the former.

Shifting to the indirect instrumental relationship, it should be noted that the economic impact of this second relationship is, first of all, more easily measurable. Indeed, it can be hypothesized that it corresponds to the organizations' expenditure on both their direct and indirect procurement. This expenditure is intended to be channelled through contracts concluded by international organizations or by states under the organizations' supervision. It, therefore, corresponds to the set of business opportunities offered to companies and individuals by the organization (or states under the organization's supervision) and, thus, to the market sector created.

[10] Bradford, *Brussels Effect*.

In numerical terms, from 2012 to 2022, the United Nations agencies, for example, overall went from spending more than $15.3 billion on goods and services to spending $29.6 billion[11], a constant increase that followed a similar trend in the previous decade. Statistics also show which market has taken most advantage of the organizations' resources. In 2022, for example, the companies that benefited the most from resources channelled through procurement of UN agencies were, in order, from the United States ($2.4 billion), Belgium ($1.7 billion), the United Kingdom ($1.3 billion), Denmark ($1.3 billion) and Switzerland ($1.1 billion)[12]. In addition, the market sectors that got expanded by agency procurement were health, which remains the largest procurement sector of the UN system and obviously peaked in 2021 due to the COVID-19 response) ($7.6 billion), food and farming ($4.2 billion), construction, engineering and science ($3.5 billion)[13].

In contrast, the market created by indirect procurement, that is, procurement conducted by states under the supervision of the international organization and in compliance with its rules, is linked to individual projects funded by the organizations. For the World Bank, for example, the companies that benefitted most from the resources distributed by the Bank between 2000 and 2019 were Chinese companies, followed by Indian companies and Brazilian companies.[14] About half of the resources allocated to Indian companies went to companies in the United Kingdom and the United States, which are the fourth and fifth largest markets[15] after China, India and Brazil. Although, therefore, indirect procurement seems to create significant market slices, mainly in large developing countries, it also creates significant market space for some developed countries, such as the United States and the United Kingdom.

So, overall, the economic impact of the indirect instrumental relationship has been positive especially for developed country markets that have benefitted from direct procurement and some, United States and United Kingdom, also from indirect procurement.

In this sense, the two features defining the economic impact of the direct institutional relationship are shaped differently in the indirect instrumental relationship.

[11] See UNOPS, 2022 *Annual Statistical Report on United Nations Procurement*, 2023, which collects data of 31 UN agencies.

[12] Ibid.

[13] Ibid.

[14] See World Bank, *Summary Report by Fiscal Year & Supplier/OECD Country (US$ 000) – FY 2000 to 2019*, 2020.

[15] Ibid.

The first feature, the one pertaining to the genesis of economic impact, is much easier to identify because it is mono-factorial, or at least weakly multi-factorial, in the indirect instrumental relationship. In other words, while for the direct institutional relationship the impact of the organization on the market depends on the organization but also on many other factors connected to the state and inter-state relations, in the indirect instrumental relationship it is first and foremost the organization, its functional and operational needs and its internal policies that create, define and direct the market, especially in direct procurement.

The second characteristic, namely that pertaining to the role of states, is much more nuanced in the indirect instrumental relationship. In the direct institutional relationship, the reach of the economic impact of the organization is defined explicitly primarily by the states and their autonomous implementation policies. In the indirect instrumental relationship, on the contrary, the power that states have over the organization travels indirect paths and manifests itself in terms of influence, rather than as an autonomous determination of the policies that regulate the market. This influence is related to the type of relationship each state has with the organization: as the above statistics show, in direct procurement, and to some extent also in indirect procurement, the largest funding states are also those where the organization's positive economic impact is mostly produced. In indirect procurement, the influence of the funding states is mixed and combined with that of the large developing economies, which, while not among the major funders of the organizations, claim their portion of the market by virtue of the institutional objectives of the organization; in the case of the World Bank, for example, growth and development of disadvantaged areas (Table 7.1).

7.3 HOW INTERNATIONAL ORGANIZATIONS SHAPE THE MARKET?

Mention was made in Section 7.2 of the tools that international organizations use to create and regulate the market. It is worthwhile, however, to dwell on this point because the analysis of these tools and the understanding of how they work are useful with respect to the reflection on the accountability of organizations in their market relationships.

The distinction between direct institutional relationship and indirect instrumental relationship is central also in the identification of tools and their functioning: the two relationships the instruments put in place, while having a common basis, differ in their legal sources, structure, actors involved, effects, nature and content.

TABLE 7.1 *International organizations and the market*

	Direct institutional relationship	Indirect instrumental relationship
Function	• IOs as market regulators • IOs as market adjudicators	• IOs as market creators (*ex novo*) • IOs as market regulators • IOs as market adjudicators (limited)
Market players (and their role)	• States – formal and *de facto* leading role • IOs – facilitating role	• States – *de facto* influential role • IOs – formal decision maker role
Values and interests	• Free market (and other market related interests)	• IOs' economy and efficiency • Institutional values (other than free market) • Interests linked to funding
Economic impact	• Multi-factorial genesis • States' leading role	• Single-factorial (or weakly multi-factorial) genesis • States' influential role

These tools have one common feature: they are set forth and regulated by rules, which translate policies. However, if we look at the *sources of the rules* we can identify some differences: in the direct institutional relationship the rules providing for these tools are included in the founding treaties of the organizations – market regulation is indeed one of the institutional objectives, set in the international agreements that eventually implement the institutional objectives and in the state rules that implement the international rules.

In the indirect instrumental relationship, on the other hand, the rules are set in secondary and internal regulatory sources of the organizations, such as, for example, financial rules and regulations and procurement manuals. In addition to these sources, there are no state legal sources in direct procurement. Within a certain extent, there may be state rules in indirect procurement but these can be applied only insofar as they are compatible with the principles and disciplines of the organization and under the organization's supervision.

The difference is relevant from the perspective of transparency and accountability. Primary rules, such as treaties and international agreements, tend to be formed and decided in international fora, with the participation of states and the publication of both the preparatory works and the final outcomes. The same cannot be said of rules produced internally by the organizations: they are shaped in the context of meetings, whose proceedings are not made public, and which are composed of officials of the organizations without formal state representation.

Thus, in the direct institutional relationship rule-making for the market is characterized by greater transparency *vis-à-vis* the public, and by inter-institutional accountability, guaranteed by the representations of the states. In contrast, rule-making for the market that originates from the indirect instrumental relationship appears more opaque and more untethered from accountability mechanisms.

Looking then at the *structure of regulation*, this takes the form of a double layer structure in the direct institutional relationship and single layer in the indirect instrumental relationship. In the first type of relationship, in fact, market regulation is the result of a double layer of rules: those dictated by the international organization and those adopted by states to fulfil the obligations arising from membership in the organizations. In the second type of relationship, there is a single layer of rules that are dictated by the organization. It is possible, as mentioned, that in indirect procurement there is a double layer of rules, those of the organization and of the states receiving funding, but the latter are not adopted to implement the organization's rules. Rather they are pre-existing domestic rules that the organization allows us to use but only insofar as they are compatible with the organization's principles and discipline.

The double layer of rules in the direct institutional relationship allows for different forms of democratization of the rule: the international rule is the result of negotiation between representatives of member states, delegated on the basis of a democratic albeit very indirect mechanism; the domestic rule that implements the international rule should, *a fortiori*, result from the activity of democratic legislative procedures.

In contrast, the single layer structure of the indirect instrumental relationship falls outside the democratic circuit, being entirely internal to the international organization and unaccompanied by state-level implementing legislation that would have some democratic legitimation.

From the legal sources and structure, it is also possible to deduce who are the *actors* involved in the rulemaking that governs the relationship between organizations and the market. In the direct institutional relationship, although it is the organization that formally adopts the discipline, it is the states, through their representatives, that take part in the negotiations from which the rules then emerge. States, then, are also the recipients of these rules and the filter that allows the discipline to become effective and to produce effects on the market and, therefore, on companies. In parallel, in the indirect instrumental relationship, organizations produce the rules, but these rules are directed at regulating the activities of the organizations themselves, and their interactions with other market actors. Insofar as they are produced by and directed to the organizations, one would be inclined to think that the transparency and accountability of these rules are secondary issues. This, moreover, is one of the justifications implicitly underlying the lack of transparency and accountability in the rulemaking process.

The criterion for assessing the adequacy of existing transparency and accountability mechanisms, however, is not only the subjects towards whom the rule is directed, that is, the subjects to whom the rule dictates certain requirements, but globally all the subjects on whom the rule produces its direct and indirect *effects*. If a norm impacts on other economic actors and the market, although it is a norm produced by the organization for itself, transparency and accountability of these norms and their enforcement practices should also be ensured with respect to non-institutional actors and, thus, to economic actors and the market more generally.

Finally, if we look at the *nature* of these rules, a distinction can be drawn between substantive and procedural rules. In the direct institutional relationship, the rules contained in treaties and related international agreements are predominantly substantive in nature and relate, often, to free market objectives. There is also a procedural component, but it remains at a general level, especially in treaties. In the indirect instrumental relationship, on the contrary, the procedural component is dominant and takes the form of detailed rules, designed to regulate the activities of international administrations.

The substantive and procedural character of the rules is not, however, the only element that differentiates their nature. The other element is their bindingness, understood as the ability to conform a conduct. In the direct institutional relationship, bindingness should be ensured by a system of horizontal controls between states that provides for the possibility of sanctions and retaliation measures. In some cases, judicial or para-judicial bodies, established by the organization, can judge on the violation of these norms, such as for instance the appellate body of the WTO. There is almost no need to say that the existence of a control system or judicial bodies can be more or less effective, but nevertheless they are in place.

In contrast, there are no bodies of an adjudicative nature, nor systems of control, except merely internal (intra-administrative), in the indirect instrumental relationship. Very few organizations have established bodies of a quasi-jurisdictional nature, for example the European Space Agency, but the para-judicial review mechanisms are rudimental. The monitoring of compliance is conducted by bodies within the administration that are hierarchically superordinate to the procuring entity and are scarcely accessible for economic operators through more or less informal bid protest procedures. This has also led in practice to a high level of non-compliance with the rules and a significant hiatus between the rules and practice.

7.3.1 *The Rules and Practices in the Indirect Instrumental Relationship and their Impact on the Market*

While the substance of the rules and practices affecting the market in the direct institutional relationship has been the subject matter of general studies regarding specific organizations, such as the WTO, less explored is the content of the rules and practices that influence the market in the indirect instrumental relationship.

Rules and practices in the direct institutional relationship pertain primarily to the removal of barriers to trade and the related implementation policies adopted by states. Their analysis has been the object of analysis and critique, although not under the specific lens of the relationship between international organizations and the market. Instead, it is worth focusing on the content of the rules and practices adopted by organizations in the indirect instrumental relationship because these and their impact on the market have been overlooked.

One of the characteristics of these rules is that they are primarily procedural in nature, and they pertain mainly to the vendors' selection phase.

The regulation and enforcement practice of vendor selection procedures affect the market and economic operators in several ways, such as the choice of the procurement method, waivers, splitting contracts, extension of long-term agreements and domestic preference. First, the size of the market created by the organization depends on the *procurement method* chosen. Traditionally, for example in the public procurement of European Union member states, three types of procurement procedures are set: open, restricted and negotiated procedures.[16] Open procedures are tenders open to any operator who is interested and wants to submit its offer.[17] Restricted procedures are those in which any economic operator may request to participate but whereby only those economic operators invited by the procuring entity may

[16] EU procurement directives also include competitive dialogue among the basic procurement procedures.

[17] Directive 2014/24/EU, art. 27; Directive 2014/25/EU, art. 45; WTO Government Procurement Agreement, art. I(m).

submit an offer.[18] Negotiated procedures are procedures in which the contracting authorities consult companies of their choice and negotiate the terms of contract with one or more of these.[19] The EU public procurement regulation for member states prescribes as basic procedure the open one, in order to ensure the widest possible competition.

On the contrary, rules governing direct procurement of the organizations with the highest volume of procurement, such as the UN, World Food Programme, or UNICEF, prescribe the restricted procedure as the basic procedure for vendor selection, not including an open procedure among the options. Furthermore, they identify specific circumstances and thresholds that allow for direct contracting and sole source. Thus, the basic procurement procedure is not the open one but, rather, a procedure that, right from the outset, can limit the scope of the market, as well as competition within such a market. In the restricted procedure the organizations choose how many and which vendors to invite. Thus, it is always for the organizations to filter and scale the degree of competition to be applied to the market.

The rules governing procurement procedures also provide for the possibility of *waivers*. Under certain circumstances, specified by the procurement manuals, organizations may select vendors without opening a competitive process. The conditions under which this can take place are, however, often laid down broadly and indefinitely and organizations are left with a wide discretion in this regard. This has led, in direct procurement, to practices of recurring use and sometimes abuse of waivers. The consequence is the creation of an uncompetitive market or of a market whose scope corresponds to a few companies chosen by the organization itself.

Moreover, even when the rules do not provide for the possibility of anticompetitive choices, international organizations find ways to avoid competitive procedures *tout court* and, as a result, limit the breadth of the market. The practice of *splitting contracts* is, for example, often used by international organizations for the purpose of avoiding the implementation of competitive procedures for vendor selection. The activation of some procurement methods, such as the open or restricted procedure, is often linked to certain thresholds of contract value. It is not uncommon that large procurement volumes, usually requiring competitive procedures, are artificially broken up so that they do not meet the thresholds above which these procedures must be activated.

[18] Directive 2014/24/EU, art. 28; Directive 2014/25/EU, art. 46; WTO Government Procurement Agreement, art. I(q); art. IX(4)-(6).

[19] Directive 2014/24/EU, art. 29, art. 32; Directive 2014/25/EU, art. 47, art. 50; WTO Government Procurement Agreement, art. I(h), art. XIII.

Also, with the primary aim of saving internal resources by avoiding cumbersome procedures, international organizations make use of the *extension of long-term agreements* (LTAs). LTAs are framework agreements between the organization and a company that relate to a certain time frame, within which the organization can make repeated purchases of specified goods or services at a fixed price. Competition is not completely eliminated because, in order to award an LTA, the organization must, as for other types of contracts, issue a call for tenders and undertake a competitive procedure. However, the frequency of competitive procedures undertaken by the organizations decreases: once the LTA is concluded, the same vendor can provide repeated goods or services over an agreed period of time, with no need for the administration to initiate a competitive procedure when the procurement need arises. In addition to this, the organizations can extend existing LTAs so that competition and the market is further limited. The combination of these elements has resulted in quite extensive usage of LTAs in organizations within the United Nations system and, to a lesser extent, in EU institutions[20] and in a recurring pattern of extending existing LTAs.

In indirect procurement, although restricted and negotiated procedures are also among the tools provided to states by the procurement guidelines, the basic procedure is rather the open procedure. So, organizations generally seek to ensure that states create more open markets, with some exceptions that we will see below. This trend is understandable considering the goals that move international organizations in indirect procurement. Open procedures guarantee the widest participation, including the participation of foreign companies – thus, for instance, companies from countries funding the organization. Competition is, thus, necessary to pursue not only the organization's interest in economy and efficiency, but also to ensure a return to the states who finance the organization.

Consistent with this, although the possibility of waivers is provided for in the guidelines governing indirect procurement, it is little used in practice. Moreover, when national administrations implement the international organizations' projects, international organizations monitor and authorize the use of waivers by the national administration. So, the possibility of making an exception to competition is always controlled and perhaps limited by the organizations.

Similarly, in indirect procurement the practices of splitting contracts as well as the usage and extension of existing LTAs are less recurring. Since these are

20 Joint Inspection Unit, *Review of Long-Term Agreements in Procurement in the United Nations System*, JIU/REP/2013/1, 2013, para 10.

anti-competitive practices, international organizations tend to limit their spread either through *ex ante* controls over procurement needs or through *ex post* checks over the implementation of vendor selection procedures.

The tools discussed so far refer to the pre-bid phase. International organizations, however, can determine the scope and competitiveness of the market, even at the bid evaluation stage. The rules governing the international organizations' indirect procurement, in fact, sometimes provide that calls for tenders may include evaluation criteria that give *preference to local companies*.

By favouring domestic suppliers, international organizations may aim to foster local development, job creation, and capacity building within the countries where they operate. Moreover, procuring goods and services locally may sometimes be more cost-effective and less risky in terms of logistics, transportation, and regulatory compliance. So, domestic preference may be motivated by external economic and social objectives as well as by efficiency objectives.

Domestic preference can, however, result in market-distorting effects. Indeed, domestic preference policies can distort market dynamics by artificially inflating demand for domestic goods and services, potentially leading to inefficiencies and higher costs for the procuring organization.

Also, by limiting the pool of potential suppliers to domestic ones, international organizations reduce competition in procurement processes. This can result in higher prices, lower quality and less innovation compared to what might be available from a broader, global pool of suppliers. It is, however, a trade-off between social objectives and market goals or, to put it in another way, it is the (legitimate) cost of social objectives.

A different trade-off is found when one looks at preferential evaluations in direct procurement and sometimes indirect procurement as well. The so-called *tied procurement*[21] is a practice often used by the organizations, but rarely provided by the rules, where contracts are awarded subject to conditions that require the works, goods or services to be purchased from a particular country, that is according to the donor country criterion. Usually, the country is one financing the organization or a certain programme or project sponsored by the organization.

Thus, the donor funding criterion is directly tied to a specific state. This also means that the same organization may apply varying levels of competition for similar procurement activities, depending on the funding source – whether from a single state or from the general budget. When funding originates from

[21] In general, on tied aid procurement, see A. Lachimia, *Tied Aid and Development Aid Procurement in the Framework of EU and WTO Law: The Imperative for Change* (Hart, 2013).

a single state, the donor funding criterion embodies formal or informal tied aid. While this criterion is explicit in certain organizations, it exists, albeit not explicitly stated or only briefly mentioned, in others.

States are, of course, highly influential in tied procurement as they can define the scope of competition, even eliminating competition from the process when a single vendor is preselected — typically a vendor from the financing state.

In such cases, administrative decisions may even exclude vendors due to political tensions between the financing state and the vendor's home country or due to differing standards adopted by these states. Both political and technical factors can play a role in restricting competition.

Thus, the procurement process operates on a hierarchy of interests associated with different international public actors. While the principle of competition is primarily intended to secure the best value for the international organization, it takes a backseat when it clashes with the political and economic interests of the financing state.

7.4 ACCOUNTABILITY IN SHAPING THE MARKET

Through norms and practices, international organizations are able to create, regulate and influence some sectors of the market, and they have an impact, and not a negligible one – especially for economies in transition, on the economies of individual states and their companies. Given this impact, the question that, therefore, arises is to what extent are organizations accountable in exerting this influence? And, more specifically, what are the mechanisms, if any, that ensure accountability with respect to this specific function? And are these mechanisms effective?

Again, the distinction between *direct institutional relationship* and the *indirect instrumental relationship* is relevant and helps to identify the various components of accountability in the relationship between international organizations and the market.

In the *direct institutional relationship*, accountability is primarily inter-institutional and refers to both the rule-making and implementation phases. As mentioned earlier, states participate in rulemaking in international fora that allow for confrontation, dialogue and negotiation. In this sense, there are physiological checks that states can exert through the participation of their institutional representatives in the rule-making process of the international organization.

Moreover, in the implementation phase of market policies, there is often horizontal accountability, activated by states on other states, which is intertwined with legal accountability ensured by the organization itself. In the context of the WTO this is the case of the Appellate Body that hears appeals in disputes brought by WTO members. Although these accountability mechanisms have weaknesses and shortcomings, nevertheless the formal presence of states at the core of the accountability mechanism allows all states to have opportunities to monitor the compliance with the policies and principles set by the international agreements governing the market.

In contrast, accountability mechanisms in the *indirect instrumental relationship* are less developed and effective. The accountability framework within international organizations for procurement comprises three fundamental components: external controls, internal controls and mechanisms for private sector appeals against the actions and decisions of procurement entities.

These components serve multiple critical purposes. Firstly, they aim to ensure that member states, representing taxpayers and participating businesses, are well-informed about the procurement activities of the organizations. Secondly, they aim to maintain the awareness of the organization's administrative heads regarding the actions of procurement officials and any deviations from principles and rules. Lastly, they are intended to provide private parties with opportunities to assert their rights against international organizations and states.

Of these components, accountability to states is the most extensively realized. Member states exercise oversight through various bodies such as Executive Boards, Boards of Auditors, and the Joint Inspection Unit (for the organizations of the UN family). These bodies evaluate different aspects of procurement activity and provide information to states. Additionally, legislative bodies of organizations decide whether to implement reforms in response to oversight findings.

However, internal controls in direct procurement have notable shortcomings. Increased procurement volume and decentralization have exacerbated issues in delegation of authority and responsibility. Even when lines of authority are clear, practices of evading responsibility are not uncommon. Moreover, controls by bodies independent from the procuring entity and implementation of the relative recommendations are still subject to the political will of states. As the final decision still always rests with the contracting administrations, controls by independent bodies can also indirectly weaken the legal position of companies, in particular their interest in being registered in the vendors rosters and participating in tender procedures, without giving them guarantees of due process.

In indirect procurement, a variant of internal controls is inter-institutional controls between the international organization and national administrations.

Unlike what happens in direct procurement, here the oversight methods are more effective. Financial institutions, the European Commission and also some organizations that engage in indirect procurement (UNDP, UNHCR etc.), carry out general controls aimed at determining, over longer periods of time, whether project implementation and, thus, also procurement, are being handled according to the organization's objectives, principles and rules. Moreover, financial institutions and the European Commission carry out specific controls on the acts and decisions adopted during the tender procedure, for example, the call for tenders, the bid evaluation, the award decision, but also on the activity performed in execution of the contract. In this way, as it pursues its own interest in effective management of the resources granted, the international organization also becomes the guarantor of private subjects' rights, as defined in the guidelines.

The third component of accountability includes the mechanisms that make international organizations and national administrations accountable to private subjects during the vendor selection phase and execution of the contract. Within this component as well, there is a significant difference between direct and indirect procurement. In the former, although there have been significant developments compared to the past, the degree of accountability and its effectiveness are still decided by the international organizations. Bid protest mechanisms are scarcely proceduralized and mostly managed by the administrations and consist in hierarchical appeals or protests before the same body that adopted the decision. With the exception of ESA, EU institutions and some UN agencies, the bodies to whom a protest can be presented do not yet provide sufficient guarantees of independence and, while they have the power to annul the procedure, they lack the power to order compensation for damages.

On the contrary, in indirect procurement, the mechanisms for accountability vis-à-vis private subjects take advantage of the tripartite nature of the relationships among international organizations, national administrations and private subjects. The organization scrutinizes the handling of complaints by the national procuring entity; it may intervene by blocking an award decision or requiring to cancel and revise the bidding procedure; it may provide a further debriefing if the vendor is not satisfied with the answer provided by the national procuring entity; it may conduct investigations based on a private party's allegations of fraud and corruption against national administrative officials or other private parties who participated in the bidding procedure. In all cases, the international organization has the power of financial retaliation against the financed state. Moreover, in the case of EU institutions it is also possible to file a complaint against the supranational administration itself, asserting failure to properly supervise.

Finally, in executing the contract, while private parties are guaranteed the opportunity of appeal to impartial bodies to protect their legal positions through recourse to arbitrators rather than judicial bodies within organizations, the effectiveness of this protection is nevertheless undermined by the inherent international public nature of the organizations, which can always invoke immunity from execution.

An overall analysis of accountability in the *indirect instrumental relationship*, thus, underscores two aspects. The first regards the ties between each of the three components, and more in particular the influence that external oversight has on the other two types of oversight and on the limited effectiveness of public procurement principles. The external controls described show that states have a detailed awareness of how resources are managed and procurement activity is carried out. Thus, in direct procurement, regulatory limits and application practices that deviate from the principles of competition, transparency and integrity, the shortcomings of the system of internal controls, and the only partial protection of the private parties' legal position during contractor selection and contractual execution are not the result of the states' lack of information, but rather their lack of will, or at any rate their tolerance, dictated by a particular dynamic of interests between international organizations and states.[22] Proof of this is that, when the balance of interests shifts, as occurs in indirect procurement, the two components of internal controls and accountability to private parties function more effectively. The dynamic of interests is, however, a 'covert operative'. The noble justification for the lack of accountability is the exercise of the public function: 'ubi maior, minor cessat', where the 'maior' is the higher public interest ensured by the exercise of the institutional function and the 'minor' is whatever can hamper such interest, namely the interests and legitimate expectations of private actors. In this way, the functionalist approach has worked as a useful conceptual shield to protect the *status quo*.[23]

The second aspect regards the contract. Although, in fact, unlike some national legal systems, there is no administrative judge who settles on contractual disputes, the neutrality of the judicial body does not guarantee that both parties to the contract are equally accountable to each other. In this

[22] On how states' economic interests shape the functioning of international organizations in general, see R. Stone, *Controlling Institutions: International Organizations and the Global Economy* (Cambridge University Press, 2011). On how states' economic interests shape procurement of international organizations, see Morlino, *Procurement by International Organization*, 376ff.

[23] On the evolution of functionalism, see J. Klabbers, 'The EJIL Foreword: The Transformation of International Organizations Law' (2015) 26 *European Journal of International Law* 9.

sense, the privileged legal position of the international public body does not come from having a special jurisdiction, as in some domestic legal systems, because, except for a few organizations, the system does not offer this component. Rather, the privilege consists of activating immunities that allow the international organization to jeopardize the effectiveness of the accountability mechanisms even when they are entrusted to neutral and impartial bodies.

7.5 CONCLUDING REMARKS: A NEW ETHOS FOR INTERNATIONAL PUBLIC POWERS

This analysis on the relationship between international organizations and the market stemmed from a number of questions that are worth recalling: first, the preliminary question of whether there is a relationship between international organizations and the market; then, if the first question was answered in the affirmative, what are the mechanisms through which organizations impact the market; and finally, whether in exerting this impact on the market, international organizations are accountable.

The analysis that developed around these questions allows for some general considerations.

The answer to the first question is partially as expected: yes, there is a relationship between international organizations and the market. And yet, already this first part of the answer has revealed unexpected aspects. While the relationship stemming from the market-related mission of some organizations has been the subject matter of attention and research by specialized studies, there is another type of relationship that has not been analysed and conceptualized from the perspective of the market: the activity carried out by international organizations to procure goods, services and works. At the state level, this conceptualization is so well known that public procurement is strategically employed as a market policy. In contrast, it has never been formulated in these terms with reference to international organizations.

In this sense, the distinction that has been proposed between direct institutional relationship and indirect instrumental relationship has not only the sense of a taxonomy that systematizes reality, but the objective of bringing awareness on the meaning and implications that a certain activity of international organizations has. Meaning and implications, in fact, transcend the needs related to the functioning of the organizations, and show a broader and more significant impact on the market; and, as such, must be treated and regulated. In this respect, a transition of the procurement activity can be observed from a mere activity instrumental to the functioning of organizations to an activity that integrates functional profiles with those of market policies.

Here, I come to the second consideration. Weak forms of accountability have so far been attached to procurement of international organizations. The reasons for this are rooted in the dynamics of interests between international organizations, states and private parties. These reasons were justifiable in light of an originally modest number of partnerships between international organizations and private actors, of a scarcely significant procurement activity of the international organizations, of an exclusive functional relationship between the organizations and their procurement (i.e. procurement was primarily an activity that enabled the operation of the organization) and of an underdeveloped legal environment with reference to accountability mechanisms of public powers.

The conditions under which, however, international organizations operate have changed profoundly. The rise of global public–private partnerships[24] and the increase in procurement activities lead to the reconceptualization of procurement activities as activities having a market impact. Moreover, at the state level the legal framework governing relations between public powers and individuals has profoundly changed in the direction of greater transparency, participatory or at least informed decision-making tools, penetrating accountability mechanisms. In other words, the ethos of public powers is undergoing a deep transformation.

Considering this reconceptualization and the changes of the context, preserving and tolerating a dynamic of interests that maintains the *status quo*, and protects the 'function' at the expenses of accountability, creates a temporal dissonance between international organizations and their context[25] that can further undermine the already fragile legitimacy of the organizations. This is all the more so in a globally fragmented context in which states and national policies are regaining relevance and influence.

[24] On this, see L. Andonova, *Governance Entrepreneurs. International Organizations and the Rise of Global Public–Private Partnerships* (Cambridge University Press, 2017).

[25] On the temporal dissonance of international organizations and the factors creating it, see E. Morlino, 'Engaging with International Organizations: A Tale of Love and Darkness' (2024) 21 *International Organizations Law Review* 460. A similar concept with reference to the European Union is used in J. H. H. Weiler and A. P. Müller, 'Everything Must Change so that Everything Can Remain the Same (G. Tomasi di Lampedusa): The CJEU and the Temporal Dissonance of Europe "Then" and "Now"'. Paper presented at the *Public Law Workshop Series*, New York University School of Law, 2 April 2024.

8

International Organizations as Sellers of Goods and Services

UKRI SOIRILA

8.1 INTRODUCTION

International organizations engaging in entrepreneurial activities by selling goods and services remains an understudied subject. It is a well-known, although often-ignored, fact that many international organizations run their gift shops and cafés, lease their premises and charge for parking. It is also commonly emphasized that international financial institutions make revenue through their loan and investment activities. And it is a curious anecdote that UN Postal Administration makes revenue by selling stamps and UNICEF by selling greeting cards. But little else has been written about the topic.[1]

Yet, many international organizations engage in various types of entrepreneurial activities daily. Some of the entrepreneurial organizations (or bodies of organizations) are little-known even within the field of international organizations law, but others are traditional institutions, such as the Universal Postal Union and the International Civil Aviation Organization. Many international organizations experimenting with entrepreneurial activities remain firmly tied to the mandatory contributions of their member states, but some – such as the World Intellectual Property Organization and the International Organization for Migration – make such a significant part of their revenue by selling services (or more rarely goods) that they have become almost financially self-reliant. In fact, at least two entities, namely the United Nations Office for Procurement Services, which is a subsidiary organ of the UN General Assembly, and the European Patent Office have been designed to be entirely

[1] See, however, H. G. Schermers and N. Blokker, *International Institutional Law: Unity within Diversity*, 6th ed. (Martinus Nijhoff, 2018), paras 1050–1063.

financially independent and are thus entirely dependent on their market activities.

In engaging in entrepreneurial activities, international organizations challenge the fundamental assumptions of the law of international organizations that these creatures interact only with their member states and that they perform technical tasks set by said member states, acting as a collective principal. Although entrepreneurial international organizations do sell their services most commonly to their member states, these commercial relationships often change the dynamics between the organizations and their principals by making international organizations more dependent on the individual member states that are willing to pay for services than on the collective will of the members. In other words, international organizations start to do the bidding of their 'clients', the individual interests of which do not necessarily match those of the majority of the member states. Furthermore, there are many cases of international organizations selling their services to 'third parties', such as non-member states, other international organizations and even to private sector actors, thus entirely severing the principal–agent relationship.

This chapter takes some first steps towards an analysis of the entrepreneurial activities of international organizations by providing examples of international organizations selling goods and services and mapping their legal powers to do so. The three main sections of the chapter focus on international organizations selling goods and services to member states (Section 8.2); to other public actors, namely non-member states and other international organizations (Section 8.3); and to private actors, including non-governmental organizations, companies and individuals (Section 8.4). Section 8.5 concludes. While the chapter remains mostly descriptive, its motivation is to complicate the assumption about international organizations simply fulfilling the technical tasks set by their member states, acting as a collective principal. In line with this, the chapter also seeks to demonstrate that international organizations are not blessed entities, acting always for the salvation of humankind, but complex actors that have their own internal agendas. In this way, then, the chapter points towards the need to start rethinking the theory of the law of international organizations.

8.2 SELLING TO MEMBER STATES

Many of the business activities of international organizations conform to the fundamental assumptions of the law to the extent that they consist of these entities selling goods or services to their member states. Yet, as this section seeks to demonstrate, the commercial relations between international organizations and their individual member states may also fundamentally challenge the assumed principal–agent dynamic between the collective of member states and the international organization.

That said, oftentimes the entrepreneurial relations between international organizations and individual member states differ quite little from the assumed activities of international organizations and are in fact organized in such a way that they are difficult to distinguish as commercial transactions. Commonly in these cases, the transaction is arranged around voluntary member state contributions.

Many international organizations have special funds for voluntary contributions or technical cooperation. When states want specific services tailored just for them, they make contributions to these funds to cover the costs of the service and overheads. For example, the work of the International Atomic Energy Agency (IAEA) can be divided into two areas, its regular programme, funded by mandatory member state contributions, and the Technical Cooperation Programme, which is funded by precisely this type of voluntary contribution. The programme provides tailored services to states, helping them to safely utilize nuclear technologies to address local needs.[2] In exchange for these services, the recipient state makes a contribution to the Technical Cooperation Fund,[3] although it must be noted that the cooperation might also be funded by an external funder, for example through IAEA's Peaceful Uses Initiative – a practice that became very relevant during the COVID-19 pandemic as many target states ran out of funds.[4]

The power of the IAEA to provide technical assistance is provided in the Statute of the IAEA. According to Article IX of the Statute, any member state may request the assistance of the organization in projects related to the development or practical application of atomic energy for peaceful purposes or for the securing of financing for such projects and they may also ask the IAEA to supply materials and services for the project. According to paragraph F of the Article, if the IAEA approves the project, it shall enter into an agreement with the member state or group of states. The agreement sets forth the terms and conditions of the project and also stipulates, in accordance with subparagraph 3, the price of materials, services or equipment provided by the IAEA (if applicable).

2 www.iaea.org/services/technical-cooperation-programme/about (accessed 30 January 2022).
3 IAEA, Technical Cooperation Report for 2018, GC63/INF/4 (2019), 34.
4 IAEA, Technical Cooperation Report for 2020, GC65/INF/4 (2021), 5–6.

Interestingly, the Statute also grants the IAEA the power to provide atomic energy materials, services and equipment to its member states. According to Article XIV(E), the IAEA may set charges for such goods and services. Unlike most international organizations engaging in entrepreneurial activities, the IAEA may even make a profit in this way. Indeed, Article XIV(E) continues by stating that the scale of the charges shall be designed so as to produce sufficient revenue for the Agency to carry out its functions related to said material, equipment and services. According to the paragraph, 'the revenue shall be placed in a separate fund which shall be used to pay members for any materials, services, equipment, or facilities furnished by them' and to meet other expenses incurred by the Agency itself. Another important passage regarding profit is in paragraph F, which provides that if the IAEA makes any *excess* revenue through the aforementioned activities, this shall be placed in a general fund which may be used as the Board of Governors determines. It is this passage that confirms that the IAEA may make a profit, even though the profit goes to the Technical Cooperation Fund and is used for future projects. However, it must be noted that in practice the paragraph has been of little relevance: while the drafters of the Statute anticipated that selling nuclear materials would form an important part of the IAEA's activities, this has actually never come to be, for nuclear material supplies have remained plentiful and the IAEA has therefore never achieved the position in the markets that the drafters envisioned.[5]

Another international organization that sells its services in the form of technical cooperation is the International Civil Aviation Organization (ICAO). Much like the IAEA, the ICAO also has a Technical Cooperation Programme, run by its Technical Cooperation Bureau. Through the Programme, the ICAO provides a wide range of services to its Members States. It, for example, reviews the national civil aviation institutions, helps with air navigation plans, supports remedial action resulting from safety and security audits and facilitates capacity building. Just like in the case of the IAEA, states and donors in essence pay for tailor-made services by making contributions to the Programme. The vast majority of the contributions are provided by countries that finance their own technical cooperation projects but development banks, regional organizations, funding institutions and the aviation industry also fund some projects supporting developing states.

The foundations of the ICAO's technical cooperation are set in its constitutional document, the 1944 Chicago Convention on International Civil Aviation. According to Article 71 of the Chicago Convention, member states

[5] Schermers and Blokker, *International Institutional Law*, 6th ed., para 1052.

can request the ICAO Council to provide, staff, maintain and administer any of its airports and other air-navigation facilities. In such situations, the Council can, under the same article, specify reasonable charges for the use of the facilities. Furthermore, Article 74 states that, when the ICAO Council provides airports or other facilities, the arrangement can, with the consent of the state, include technical assistance related to the operation of the airports and other facilities. The Article also stipulates that, in such situations, (part of) the revenue made by operating the airport or facility may be used to cover the operation expenses of the airport or facility, as well as interest and amortization charges. Technical cooperation was given a clearer legal framework in 1954 when the ICAO adopted its Financial Regulations. Regulation 9.3 states that the costs of the administration and operation of the technical cooperation shall be met by the government, organization or other entity cooperating with the ICAO. Nowadays a special position is however granted to the United Nations Development Programme (UNDP), for charges for UNDP projects shall be determined in cooperation with the UNDP, whereas otherwise the charges are based on the estimate of the ICAO of the costs incurred by it for the implementation of the project. According to Regulation 9.4, the funds received as charges for the projects shall be put into the ICAO's Administrative and Operational Services Cost Fund, which is used to meet the full costs of the administration of the projects and to support the ICAO's technical cooperation in general. This suggests that the ICAO may charge overheads that are not linked directly to the expenses of a given project but that are related to maintaining its technical cooperation in general.

The Universal Postal Union (UPU), too, has a specific funding mechanism for services provided for states, although these are not branded as technical cooperation. The UPU is financed through three 'pillars', out of which the first one consists of regular member state contributions to the UPU's regular budget and the third one of the sale of products and commercially oriented services. The second pillar is the most relevant here, however (the third pillar will be discussed in Section 8.4). It consists of member state contributions to UPU affiliated cooperatives and bodies for their services.[6] These cooperatives and bodies include the EMS Cooperative, which consists of 178 postal operators that work together to provide an express mail service; the Telematics Cooperative, which promotes cooperation, infrastructure and services related to new postal communication and information technologies; and the UPU Clearing User Group, which provides its members a low-cost and efficient system for settling their international postal accounts. All of the

6 www.upu.int/en/Universal-Postal-Union/About-UPU/Finance (accessed 25 January 2022).

entities fully participate in the UPU mission, enjoy support from the organization's International Bureau and are under direct oversight of the UPU leadership. These entities are not legal entities or companies under private law but fully part of the UPU.[7]

The operation and financing of the cooperatives and similar bodies are not really regulated by the UPU Constitution, but by internal rules. The Articles coming the closest to touching the issue in the Constitution are perhaps Articles 1 and 18. Article 1(2) states that the purposes of the UPU include the improvement of postal services, whereas paragraph 3 adds that the UPU 'shall take part, as far as possible, in postal technical assistance sought by its member countries'. Article 18 holds that the 'Postal Operations Council (POC) shall be responsible for operational, commercial, technical and economic questions concerning the postal service'. The Constitution does not provide anything else related to the cooperatives or similar bodies, however; nor did the General Regulation or the Rules of Procedure of the Council of Administration (CA) and the POC – for a long time. The bodies were therefore created on an *ad hoc* basis to respond to new challenges and opportunities, particularly related to technological developments, without any coherent policy or legal framework. If any legal justification was thought of or considered necessary, it was most likely seen to be derived from the Constitution on the basis of the implied powers doctrine.

To respond to this legal gap, then, the 2008 Congress in Geneva ordered the CA to study the issue. Following the study, the 2012 Doha Congress added Article 152 to the UPU General Regulations to establish clearer decision-making between the permanent bodies of the UPU related to voluntarily funded subsidiary bodies.[8] According to the first paragraph of the Article, the POC may, with the approval of the CA, establish aforementioned bodies 'in order to organize operational, commercial, technical and economic activities' which fall within the POC's competence under article 18 of the Constitution. According to the second paragraph of the Article, the POC shall, in so doing, also establish the legal framework of the body, including its mandate, constituency and financing. Furthermore, Article 26(3)(b) of the UPU Financial Regulations now states that one of the ways of financing the Voluntary Fund of the UPU is through 'tied voluntary contributions governed by special agreements' and Annex 2 of the Regulations regulates the mechanism more closely. According to Article 2(1), the services provided by the UPU

7 Ibid.

8 Commentary to Article 152 of the UPU General Regulations, Constitution and General Regulations Manual with Commentary by the UPU International Bureau, 2018.

must be in accordance with its purpose, and according to Article 3(3) the precise terms and conditions of such voluntary contributions shall be agreed by a signed contract between the parties. The bodies have therefore been given a legal framework retroactively.

A slightly different example of an international selling services to its member states is Eurocontrol, which collects central route charges on behalf of its member states and provides other services in exchange for a fee. Eurocontrol is a civil–military organization tasked to support European aviation, aviation service providers and airports. Although it is not an EU agency, the EU has delegated parts of its sky regulations to it, turning it into the central organization for air traffic control in Europe. Eurocontrol's centralized system – operating through its Central Route Charges Office – makes the collection of the charges easier and more efficient for its members, which include all EU member states and the EU itself.[9] Following its Multilateral Agreement relating to Route Charges, Eurocontrol takes care of billing and collecting on a monthly basis and then disburses the route charges to the member states. It also offers similar services for terminal navigation charges and communication charges,[10] as well as cross-border air navigation services, managing the upper airspace over the Netherlands, Belgium, Luxembourg and north-west Germany through its Maastricht Upper Area Control Centre.[11]

The power of Eurocontrol to collect route charges is set directly in its constitutional document, the Eurocontrol Convention. Article 2(1)(j) of the amended convention grants Eurocontrol the power to collect route charges levied on users of air navigation services, assist member states in designing and setting up air traffic facilities and services and to provide and operate such services on behalf of the member states. Furthermore, according to the same Article, the member states may also ask Eurocontrol to assist them in air flow management and air navigation services, as well as in the collection of other charges than the aforementioned route charges. The collection of route charges is further regulated by the Multilateral Agreement relating to Route Charges, which, in Articles 1(2) and 8, reaffirms the task of Eurocontrol to collect the charges, in addition to further clarifying the framework of the route charges system.

9 There is, however, a series of domestic legal cases raised against Eurocontrol, challenging its practices in the collection of route charges. See J. Wurm, 'Asking National Courts to Correct Over-Flight Charges of Eurocontrol', in A. Reinisch (ed.), *Challenging Acts of International Organizations before National Courts* (Oxford University Press, 2010), 157.

10 www.eurocontrol.int/crco (accessed 27 February 2022).

11 www.eurocontrol.int/muac (accessed 27 February 2022).

The examples provided so far do not yet challenge in any fundamental way the principal–agent dynamic of international organizations theory, although they do complicate and blur it, given that international organizations engage in closer cooperation with those member states that are willing to pay for their services. There are, however, other organizations (or bodies within them) that take the entrepreneurship much further. Although these, too, interact with the typical partners of international organizations – the member states – they are far from merely fulfilling direct orders of their collective principal (as international organizations do in most 'realist' accounts) or imposing rules on and disciplining their unruliest members (as often described in more critical analyses), instead at times operating almost like private companies. The two organizations or bodies that embody this trend most clearly are the International Organization for Migration (IOM) and United Nations Office for Procurement Services (UNOPS). I will use the case of IOM to illustrate the challenge that these organizations pose to the law of international organizations,[12] whereas UNOPS will be discussed in more detail in Section 8.3, it being one of the few institutions that sell services (also) to international organizations.

The IOM sells its member states various migration-related services, ranging from visa processing and voluntary repatriation of migrants to border management and humanitarian services, oftentimes packaged as discrete projects.[13] Seeking assignments much like a private market actor, the IOM prides itself on providing tailor-made solutions, adapting efficiently to its clients' wishes,[14] and 'getting things done', taking full advantage of its flexible constitution[15] and position at the outskirts of the UN family.[16] It has also been very successful in carving out niches and filling out gaps wherever it has seen business opportunities, most recently rebranding itself as an humanitarian actor – albeit one without an official humanitarian mandate (which is one of the factors increasing its flexibility).[17]

The IOM's identity as a service provider is already engrained in its Constitution. The first preambular recital of the IOM Constitutions notes

[12] For a more detailed discussion, see J. Klabbers, 'Notes on the Ideology of International Organizations Law: The International Organization for Migration, State-Making, and the Market for Migration' (2019) 32 *Leiden Journal of International Law* 383.

[13] M. Bradley, *The International Organization for Migration: Challenges, Commitments, Complexities* (Routledge, 2020), 6.

[14] www.iom.int/speeches/message-director-general-antonio-vitorino-iom-staff.

[15] Klabbers, 'Notes on the Ideology', 390–391; Bradley, *International Organization for Migration*, 8.

[16] Bradley, *International Organization for Migration*, 18–25.

[17] Ibid., 8.

that the 'provision of migration services at an international level is often required to ensure the orderly flow of migration movements throughout the world', whereas Article 1 begins by stating that a function of the organization is the 'organized transfer' of migrants, refugees, displaced persons and others. The key passage is, however, Article 1(1)(c) which tasks the organization to provide, at the request of any member state, a set of specific migration services from processing and selection to recruitment and medical examination. The passage therefore presents the IOM as a service provider for member states, rather than as a cosmopolitan guardian of humanity. Furthermore, the third paragraph of Article 1 holds that both the admittance standards and numbers of migrants are within the domestic jurisdiction of states. The service provider characteristic of the IOM is also clearly expressed in the Constitution's provisions on the financing of the organization. Article 20 distinguishes between the administrative and operational costs of the organization. Whereas the former are subject to a regular membership fee, the latter are paid on a voluntary basis and may be made subject to different terms and conditions set by the paying state. Hence, the IOM has to enter the market for migration services to gain anything but the most minimal funding. Indeed, the IOM has virtually no core budget and is almost entirely dependent on overheads from the projects it undertakes, those overheads covering for example almost all of the headquarter expenses as well as some of the migration policy programmes that it is best known for.

As Jan Klabbers has demonstrated, the financially self-reliant IOM selling its services on the market, and thus acting at least partly according to the market logic, jars against the notion of international organizations following the aims and wishes of their collective principals.[18] Because the IOM's financial well-being, if not existence, is reliant on attracting states as its clients, it has to focus on projects that are financially profitable, rather than maximizing its mission (which is rather vague, at any rate). This simultaneously flies against the principal–agent theory or legal functionalism and provides an extreme case of it; one that twists it to an almost unrecognisable form. At the same time as the IOM has almost unprecedented 'independence' from the collective wish of its member states – the organization following the market logic rather than the wishes of its collective principal – the market logic also makes it much more tied to the desires and orders of those individual members that purchase their services than an ideal type an international organization would be.

Moreover, the IOM also differentiates from an ideal type international organization in that it influences what its client states are doing and how they

[18] Klabbers, 'Notes on the Ideology'.

are shaped, thus distorting the principal–agent relationship.[19] Klabbers gives the example of the IOM's Border and Identity Solutions Unit, which can be hired to evaluate the technical needs of member states and provides them expert advice and different training services. As Klabbers notes, the role of the Unit means that 'whatever the IOM says becomes influential: it is the IOM's definition of "technical needs" that comes to prevail; it is the training provided by IOM which dictates how states end up operating'.[20] And the Unit is no curiosity in this regard but reflects the nature of much of the IOM's work. As services and suggestions are systematized and generalized in the various manuals and handbooks published by the organization and studied closely by national authorities, the outcome is 'a continuous loop of mutual direction and influence', which is surprisingly efficient at softly disciplining states and their activities.[21]

8.3 SELLING TO NON-MEMBER STATES AND INTERNATIONAL ORGANIZATIONS

The majority of the services sold by international organizations are sold to member states. Selling services to non-member states is much rarer; perhaps because at least the larger international organizations have such near-universal membership that all states that want to interact with them are already members. The most likely exceptions to this rule are regional organizations. Indeed, one example of an international organization selling services to non-member states is Eurocontrol. Section 8.2 discussed Eurocontrol collecting route charges on behalf of its member states and providing other air navigation related services. But Eurocontrol also markets air navigation charge services to non-member states that are willing to pay for them. According to Eurocontrol, their services provide states several benefits, including high recovery rates and timely billing, ensuring stable cash flow, compliance with ICAO rules, efficient and professional service and permanent monitoring of payments.[22] In 2016, Eurocontrol concluded a Comprehensive Agreement on wide-scale service provision with two non-member states, Morocco and Israel.[23] By virtue

[19] See, more generally, G. F. Sinclair, *To Reform the World: International Organizations and the Making of Modern States* (Oxford University Press, 2017).

[20] Klabbers, 'Notes on the Ideology', 395.

[21] Ibid.

[22] www.eurocontrol.int/service/bilateral-agreements-terminal-and-air-navigation-charges (accessed 17 June 2022).

[23] www.eurocontrol.int/our-member-and-comprehensive-agreement-states (accessed 17 June 2022).

of the Agreements, Morocco and Israel are now fully integrated into Eurocontrol's working structures and enjoy the full range of Eurocontrol provided services. Eurocontrol has also concluded bilateral agreements with Belarus, Uzbekistan and Egypt regarding the collection of air navigation charges.[24]

A bit more common (though still rare) case than international organizations having commercial relations with non-member states is them, or their bodies, selling services to other international organizations or bodies. A peculiar such example – that is explored in more detail in Eelco Szabó's Chapter 12 – is GAVI's Partner Engagement Framework. GAVI provides funding for its target states, which can then select the organizations or companies they wish to work with. Common partner organizations include, for example, the World Health Organization (WHO) and UNICEF. After winning their contracts through competition, the organizations are also required to report their activities to GAVI.

A more straightforward example of international organizations selling services to each other is the case of the United Nations Humanitarian Air Service (UNHAS), which operates under the World Food Programme (WFP). The UNHAS delivers humanitarian actors – both public and private sector organizations – to and from crisis and conflict areas where commercial airlines do not fly, or where flights are difficult to find or very expensive. Some of the most frequent users of the UNHAS services include, for example, the UNHCR, WHO and IOM (in addition to the WFP itself).[25] Chartering the airplanes from commercial airlines, the UNHAS charges a fee from the users of its services, at least partly planning its business according to market conditions,[26] although an important part of its funding comes from donor contributions. Indeed, a hint of entrepreneurial attitude is detectable, for example, in the fact that the FAO's financial committee has observed that the UNHAS managed to make yearly 'profit' in the sense that its actual expenditure has often been lower than the budget and the ticket sales have funded activity also for future budget years.[27]

[24] Eurocontrol Central Route Charges Office, Report on the Operation of the Route Charges System in 2019, 5, 8, available at www.eurocontrol.int/sites/default/files/2020-04/eurocontrol-crco-report-2019.pdf (accessed 18 June 2022).

[25] FAO Financial Committee, Report of the External Auditor on air transport services, FC 181/7, 2020, Annex 4.

[26] For example, in 2019, the prices varied significantly from 90 USD for flights in Nigeria to 500 USD in The Democratic Republic of the Congo. FAO Finance Committee, Report of the External Auditor on air transport services, 2020, NC753/e, para. 122.

[27] FAO Finance Committee, Report of the External Auditor on air transport services, 2020, NC753/e, para. 53.

The legal foundation for the UNHAS activities can be found in the WFP General Regulations and General Rules. According to Article II(2)(d) of the document, the purposes and functions of the WFP include providing 'services to bilateral donors, United Nations agencies and non-governmental organizations for operations which are consistent with the purposes of WFP and which complement WFP's operations'. The UNHAS can be interpreted as one such service, the transportation of humanitarian actors to crisis areas fitting the purposes of emergency and refugee relief under subparagraphs (b) and (c) of the same Article. Accordingly, the WFP established the predecessor of the UNHAS, the WFP/Air Service, in the 1980s to carry its food and non-food items, and soon the service also started serving a larger community.[28] The actual mandate for the UNHAS – a service catering for the entire humanitarian community –however came much later, in 2003, when the UN High-Level Committee on Management came to an inter-agency administrative agreement to assign the WFP the management of all UN humanitarian air operations.[29] Nevertheless, although the UNHAS is the result of this decision, it remains a generic name for a common support service provided by the WFP, with vague guidelines, rather than a clearly regulated institution.[30]

Another example that can be considered as international organizations (or parts of them) selling services to each other is the case of the United Nations Development Programme (UNDP), which receives billions of dollars yearly in voluntary contributions, distributing the money to participant organizations in the form of projects. When the UNDP carries out a development programme, it hires specialized agencies to implement it, and the agencies can therefore be seen as selling their services to the UNDP. Since the UNDP is a common activity of participating organizations, it is perhaps misleading to describe the situation as a commercial transaction, but the gist is nevertheless an organization receiving funds from another organization in exchange for its services.[31]

Perhaps the most interesting example of (a body of) an international organization selling services to other international organizations (or their bodies) is however the case of the UNOPS. Established in its current form

[28] A. Dorn and R. Cross 'Flying Humanitarians: The UN Humanitarian Air Service', in A. Dorn (ed.), *Air Power in UN Operations: Wings for Peace* (Ashgate, 2014), 101.

[29] Joint Inspection Unit, Review of the United Nations Humanitarian Air Service (UNHAS), prepared by Tadanori Inomata, JIU/Note/2003/3, paras 13–15. See CEB/2002/5, 8 October 2002, paragraph 23 and CEB/2003/3, June 2003, paragraph 13.

[30] Joint Inspection Unit, Review of the United Nations Humanitarian Air Service (UNHAS), prepared by Tadanori Inomata, JIU/Note/2003/3, paras 17–18.

[31] Schermers and Blokker, *International Institution Law*, 6th ed., para 1063.

by a General Assembly resolution in the mid-1990s,[32] after beginning its life as part of the UNDP,[33] the UNOPS is a subsidiary organ of the UN General Assembly, listed on the UN website as one of the 'other entities or bodies' established by the UN.[34] The purpose of the UNOPS is to provide a range of operational services, from procurement of goods, such as medical supplies and equipment, to construction and infrastructure projects. It can be hired either to execute or implement projects. In the former role it is responsible for the management of an entire project, including its goals and objectives, whereas as an implementor its role is limited to certain subcontractor services (such as procurement) within a more general project, as specified in a Project Agreement between the UNOPS and the contractor.

What makes the UNOPS particularly interesting here is that it is financially fully self-dependent and thus entirely reliant on the projects it sells to its clients. It is therefore not surprising that it is perhaps the main competitor to the IOM in business-mindedness, constantly comparing itself to private companies and emphasizing its competitiveness. Although a large portion of the UNOPS projects are now conducted for UN member states, the UNOPS and its predecessors were explicitly established to provide procurement and project services for other UN entities, and recently the UNOPS has provided lots of services for other international organizations as well. Since 2017, for example, it has worked on World Bank financed infrastructures programs in Yemen, restoring urban services such as schools, roads, water services, solar power and electricity supply.[35] And in Zimbabwe it helps the country to recover from Cyclone Idai, rehabilitating water and sanitation services, schools, roads and irrigation networks, again with World Bank funding.[36]

The external relations of the UNOPS to its clients are specified through agreements. According to the UNOPS's Financial Regulation 7.02, the Executive Director has the power to enter into such written contractual arrangements as are necessary to undertake UNOPS activities, whereas Regulation 7.04 states that UNOPS shall agree with its clients on services

[32] General Assembly decision 48/501, available at Resolutions and decisions adopted by the General Assembly during its 48th session. Volume 2, 24 December 1993–19 September 1994. A/48/49 (Vol. II), 1994, p. 59 (GAOR, 48th sess., Suppl. no. 49 A).

[33] See D. Dijkzeul, 'Not Just States or the Secretary-General: The Emergence of UNOPS as a New UN Organization', in J. Oestreich (ed.), *International Organizations as Self-Directed Actors: A Framework for Analysis* (Routledge, 2012), 195.

[34] www.un.org/en/about-us/un-system (accessed 21 May 2022).

[35] www.unops.org/news-and-stories/stories/finding-light-amid-yemens-darkest-times (accessed 25 April 2022).

[36] www.unops.org/news-and-stories/stories/supporting-post-disaster-recovery-in-zimbabwe (accessed 25 April 2022).

through a project agreement. Rules 107.01 and 107.02, which specify the Regulation, further stipulate that the agreement should contain, inter alia, the rights and responsibilities of the client and UNOPS, arrangements for the suspension or termination of activities and settlement of disputes. The agreement must also include such provisions which ensure that the privileges and immunities of the UN and UNOPS are not compromised.

All in all, then, international organizations do not sell their services only to their member states, but also to non-member states and other international organizations, thus distorting further the fundamental assumptions about international organizations interacting only with their member states. Furthermore, as Section 8.4 demonstrates, international organizations also do an increasing amount of business with the private sector.

8.4 SELLING TO PRIVATE ACTORS

In addition to selling their goods and services to member states and other public sector actors, international organizations also sell to private actors, including non-governmental organizations, companies and individuals. Some examples of this have already been mentioned in this chapter, such as the selling of stamps and souvenirs or the collection of parking charges. The UNHAS also sells the same flights to humanitarian NGOs as it sells to international organizations, some of its main clients including, for example, the International Rescue Committee, Danish Refugee Council, World Vision, Médecins Sans Frontières and Save the Children.[37] Furthermore, the UNOPS's services are also, at least in theory, available to private sector actors. It is only a moderate exaggeration to say that these examples merely form the tip of the iceberg.

Very common commercial activities of international organizations involving the private sector are international organizations selling courses and publications. Examples of the former include, for example, the little-known World Customs Organization (WCO) running the WCO Academy, which is an e-portal selling customs-related courses to the private sector and the academia, and the World Tourism Organization (abbreviated UNWTO to distinguish it from the more famous WTO) selling courses to the tourist sector through its Tourism Online Academy. Selling publications is even more common. As Schermers and Blokker note, '[m]ost international organizations

37 FAO Financial Committee, Report of the External Auditor on air transport services, FC 181/7, 2020, Annex 4.

sell documents and other publications',[38] including the aforementioned WCO, which has a bookstore that sells books for businesses and other private actors.

A scroll through WCO's constitutional document, namely the Convention Establishing a Customs Co-operation Council (which is what the WCO was called before it was renamed in 1994), WCO's other regulations or its website does not reveal what it bases its power to sell its bookstore products or courses on. However, the General Terms and Conditions of its bookstore (which are similar in its key points to those of the Academy and other terms and conditions), available on the bookstore website,[39] suggest that its relations to its customers are regulated by a combination of international law, EU law and Belgian law (Belgium being the state where WCO has its headquarters). According to a notice on the cancellation rights at the beginning of the terms and conditions, the customer has a 14-day cancellation period, in accordance with the Belgian Law of 6 April 2010 on marker practices and consumer protection. Article 11.2 of the General Terms and Conditions states that all orders will be invoiced exclusively of value added tax, since, according to an EU directive, 'the WCO shall be regarded as non-taxable person in respect to the activities or transactions in which it engages as public authority'. Article 19.1 states that the rights and obligations of the WCO and its customers 'shall be governed by these Terms and Conditions and, in the second place, by Belgian laws'. Paragraph 2 of the same Article states that '[g]iven the WCO's capacity as an international organization and in particular its jurisdictional privileges', any dispute between the customer and the WCO shall be settled by an arbitration process, determined by a decision of WCO (annexed to the document); although paragraph 3 provides the exception that if the customer is a member state of the WCO, the dispute shall be settled amicably. Paragraph 4 further clarifies that none of this should be construed as a waiver of the privileges and immunities of the WCO or its customers.

To give another example, the sale of the ICAO products and services is coordinated though its Ancillary Revenue Generation Fund, which, although not matching the organization's regular programme budget or the technical cooperation programmes, is nevertheless an important source of revenue. In 2018, the Ancillary Revenue Generation Fund made a revenue of 25.5 million Canadian dollars and a profit (when business-related expenses were taken into account) of over 11 million Canadian dollars (CAD) through different business activities. The printing of training materials is the most

[38] Schermers and Blokker, *International Institutional Law*, 6th ed., para 1058.

[39] www.wcoomdpublications.org/en/article/terms-and-conditions (accessed 25 June 2022).

important one, representing 30–35 per cent of ICAO's external revenues. In 2018, almost 5 million CAD of profit was made through publications, and almost 3 million CAD was profit from licensing. Delegation and conferences also made a profit of about 1.5 million CAD, whereas training and events profited almost 700.00 CAD each, and new products close to half a million CAD.[40] One example of new products is the ICAO TV, which was launched in 2020 and provides online access to video content and disseminates ICAO information.[41] Indeed, the ICAO puts much effort in advertising its products and services. During 2018, for example, the ICAO distributed over 2.4 million marketing emails to increase awareness of the ICAO products and services. The ICAO also deployed a new events app and launched the ICAO Instagram channel, which accumulated over 5,000 followers in under six months.[42]

A more curious case is international organizations selling software and other such products. The aforementioned WCO engages in this activity as well, selling a product called the WCO trade tools, which helps actors in international trade to classify their products and support the exporting and importing of goods. But the UPU is perhaps the strongest example in this regard. As mentioned in Section 8.2, the UPU has based one of its three funding pillars on the sale of products and commercially oriented services. And the pillar is in no way insignificant for the UPU's overall budget. In 2019, the UPU's revenue from the sale of products and services was almost one third compared to the funding it received through statutory member state contributions and matched the sum of voluntary contributions. Most of the revenue came from the sale of the UPU's International Financial System (IFS) and International Postal System (IPS) Lines of Products and related products.[43] The IFS products are software designed for operations and the accounting of electronic postal payments, as well as for the tracking of postal payments, whereas the IPS products are 'integrated international mail management applications that combine mail processing, operation management and … messaging into one application'.[44] These products are sold to post offices and

40 ICAO, Financial Statement and Reports of the External Auditor for the Financial Year Ended 31 December 2018, ICAO Doc 10129 (2019), para. 3.26. See also note 3.2, paras 126–127, in the same Statement.

41 www.icao.int/annual-report-2020/Pages/supporting-strategies-finances-revenue-generating-activities.aspx (accessed 15 January 2022).

42 www.icao.int/annual-report-2018/Pages/supporting-strategies-finances-revenue-generating-activities.aspx (accessed 15 January 2022).

43 www.upu.int/UPU/media/upu/documents/Finance/dfiEtatsFinanciers2020En.pdf, Note 20 (accessed 25 January 2022)

44 www.upu.int/en/Postal-Solutions/Technical-Solutions/Products/IPS-Line-of-products (accessed 25 January 2022).

other postal actors, many of which are now private actors. Other revenue through the selling of UPU products and services include, for example, revenue from addressing different postal and barcode services, internet relay chat services and services provided by the Telematics Cooperative.[45] Under Article 21(2)(a) of the UPU's Financial Regulations, this revenue can be used, for example, to maintain the UPU's Reserve Fund.

In some rare cases, selling services to private actors can even form the majority of the revenue of an international organization. This is the case with the World Intellectual Property Organization (WIPO) and the European Patent Office (EPO), both of which charge fees for intellectual property applications. The WIPO administers the Patent Cooperation Treaty (in addition to processing the international registration of trademarks and acting as a depository for internationally deployed industrial designs and as a registry for applications for appellations of origin). In this role, it processes 'international patent' applications, governed by the Treaty. The 'international patent' is actually not a patent but a pre-patent that can establish the patentability of the invention. However, once the 'international patent' application criteria have been met, there will be no subsequent requirement for amending the application when it is filed in (designated) Member States to the Treaty.[46]

Partly similarly, a European Patent granted by EPO is not a uniform patent for all Member States. But it goes further than the 'international patent' in that the granting of the patent implies that the patent will be treated as if it had been granted by the national authorities of the Member States. It does not therefore demand a national patent application process at all but forms a kind of series of parallel patents (although in a more limited number of jurisdictions than the 'international patent').[47]

The WIPO and EPO services are therefore highly valuable to businesses applying for patents. Hence, although both have to compete with other intellectual property application services, they do very well in that competition. The WIPO may, depending on the year, make over 90 per cent of the organization's total revenue through fees charged for intellectual property applications, whereas the EPO is entirely financed in this way. Because the demand for the service depends on the demand for intellectual property titles,

[45] www.upu.int/UPU/media/upu/documents/Finance/dfiEtatsFinanciers2020En.pdf, Note 20 (accessed 25 January 2022)

[46] C. May, *The World Intellectual Property Organization: Resurgence and the Development Agenda* (Routledge, 2007), 42–44.

[47] A. Reinisch, 'Decisions of the European Patent Organization before National Courts', in A. Reinisch (ed.), *Challenging Acts of International Organizations before National Courts* (Oxford University Press, 2010), 137, 137.

it is dependent on the performance of the global economy, investment in research and development, new technological discoveries, as well as exchange rate fluctuations.[48]

Another, much less known, international organization charging private sector actors for intellectual property applications is the International Union for the Protection of New Varieties of Plants (UPOV). UPOV shares headquarters with the WIPO and WIPO's Director General is the Secretary-General of UPOV, but the two are nevertheless separate organizations. The UPOV was established in 1961 by the International Convention for the Protection of New Varieties of Plants, with the mission 'to provide and promote an effective system of plant variety protection ... for the benefit of society'.[49] The UPOV Convention encourages the breeding of new plan varieties by granting the breeders 'a breeder's right', which enables its propagation for commercial purposes. To facilitate the applications, the UPOV has created an on-line tool called UPOV Prisma, charging a fee for each application through the software.[50] This business is much less lucrative than that of the WIPO and EPO, but nevertheless forms another peculiar example of an international organization selling services to private actors. Furthermore, the UPOV also runs a plant variety database called Pluto. Although users are able to search and display results for free, the UPOV charges a fee for the premium service which has more and better functions and features.[51]

In the case of the WIPO, EPO and UPOV, the power of the organization to sell services is clearly established in their constitutions. The power of the WIPO to gather finances by rendering legal-technical assistance is set in Article 11(3)(b)(iii) of the Convention Establishing the WIPO. The actual legal framework for the international patent system and the WIPO's power to administer it are set in the Patent-Cooperation Treaty. Furthermore, Article 11(2)(b)(iii) of the Convention Establishing the WIPO also gives the organization the power to gather funds by selling publications, and 11(2)(b)(v) by collecting rents and interests. Article 51 of the European Patent Convention states that the EPO 'may levy fees for any official task or procedure carried out under [the] Convention' and, according to Article 21(1)(c) of the 1991 UPOV Convention, the revenue of UPOV shall be made, inter alia, by charging payments for services rendered.

[48] Schermers and Blokker, *International Institutional Law*, 6th ed., para 1061.

[49] www.upov.int/portal/index.html.en (accessed 29 January 2022). On the birth of UPOV, see K. Raustiala and D. Victor, 'The Regime Complex for Plant Genetic Resources' (2004) 58 *International Organization* 277, 284–288.

[50] www.upov.int/upovprisma/en/fees.html (accessed 29 January 2022).

[51] www.upov.int/pluto/en/fees.html (accessed 29 January 2022).

8.5 CONCLUDING REMARKS

The entrepreneurial activities described in this chapter challenge the idea that international organizations interact only with their member states, following the (collective) principal–agent relationship. In selling goods and services, international organizations engage in commercial relations with various actors, from non-member states and other international organizations to private sector actors, including individuals, companies and non-governmental organizations. Although in some cases the international organizations have been equipped for these interactions with constitutional powers from the very beginning, in many cases the activities developed ad hoc and over time and are therefore regulated, if at all, through internal rules and the implied powers doctrine. Furthermore, even though most of the services sold by international organizations are sold to their member states – oftentimes through arrangements that veil the commercial relationship – these interactions complicate the fundamental assumptions of the law of international organizations in significant ways. Since the services are rendered to individual member states, in engaging in entrepreneurial activities, international organizations distort the image of them acting under the control and in the interest of their collective principals. Instead, they are increasingly doing the bidding of individual member states that have the will and means to pay for their services, sometimes packaged as discrete projects.

Although a historical account of the birth and development of the entrepreneurial activities of international organizations is beyond the scope of this article, it would seem that such activities have steadily increased, especially following the budgetary problems of international organizations and the rise of managerial mindsets – in particular the New Public Management thinking – from the late 1980s onwards. It seems therefore likely that the phenomenon is going to continue expanding and become more important in the near future, raising questions about its implications for the law of international organizations, not least in terms of accountability and immunities. These questions indicate a need to rethink the theory of international organizations law.

9

Corporate Philanthropy in the UN Development Sector

TLEUZHAN ZHUNUSSOVA

9.1 INTRODUCTION

With the end of the Cold War and the revival of international cooperation, the mandates of international organizations have expanded dramatically, requiring more and more funding to sustain the newly developed activities. While originally international organizations were mostly funded through mandatory contributions from their member states, the 1990s saw a sharp rise in voluntary donations, including from private actors.[1] This trend is particularly notable in the United Nations (UN) development sector, where around 80 percent of the budget consists of voluntary earmarked contributions from governments, private foundations, academic institutions, NGOs, and business enterprises.[2]

In particular, the UN's cooperation with the business sector has come to be seen as an important instrument in advancing the UN development goals in the past two decades, making corporate philanthropy a widespread phenomenon in the field. Major companies, including Apple, Goldman Sachs, Gucci, IKEA, Mercedes Benz, and others not only contribute frequent one-time donations to the organization but also establish long-term partnerships with various UN agencies aimed at improving access to water, health,

[1] E. R. Graham, 'Money and Multilateralism: How Funding Rules Constitute IO Governance' (2015) 7 *International Theory* 162, 176–187.

[2] See Dag Hammarskjöld Foundation and the United Nations Multi-partner Trust Fund Office, *Financing the UN Development System: Time to Walk the Talk*, September 2020, p. 40, available at www.daghammarskjold.se/publication/unds-2020. The report indicates that, in 2010, voluntary earmarked contributions amounted to 66 percent of the budget while in 2018 this figure reached 79 percent. For different categories of donors, see, for instance, the UNDP Funding Compendium 2020, pp. 21–31, available at www.undp.org/funding.

and other basic needs in developing countries.[3] This trend is likely to continue, as is clear from the General Assembly's adoption of the 2030 Agenda for Sustainable Development, which among its 17 objectives provides for further strengthening of the role of private sector partnerships in the development field.[4]

While cooperation with corporate actors has notable advantages, such as allowing the UN to mobilize necessary financial resources, expertise, and technology for its development activities, it may also lead to serious reputational risks for the organization. Close association of the UN with business enterprises engaged in illegal or controversial activities may run the risk of compromising the organization's image as an objective and credible actor. In fact, the UN has already been criticized in the past by different civil society actors for its poor judgment in partnering up with notable human rights and environmental standards violators such as Coca-Cola, Chevron, Nike, Nestle, Novartis, Shell, and others.[5]

Against this background, this chapter will take stock of these issues by critically assessing the role and the impact of corporate philanthropy in the UN development sector, with a specific focus on the activities of the UN Development Program (UNDP) as one of the most active UN bodies when it comes to private sector collaborations.[6] In doing so, this contribution will first provide an overview of the evolution of the corporate philanthropy in the UN system. This will be followed by exploration of different forms of corporate funding at the UN, including direct contributions to the organization; indirect contributions through the establishment of a charitable foundation; and public–private partnerships. The chapter will conclude with an assessment of the mechanisms that were put in place by the UN as a whole and the

[3] B. Adams and J. Martens, *Fit for Whose Purpose? Private Funding and Corporate Influence in the United Nations* (Global Policy Forum, 2015), 49–51. See also J. Laurenti, 'Financing', in T. G. Weiss and S. Daws (eds.), *Oxford Handbook on the United Nations*, 2nd ed. (Oxford University Press, 2018), 250, 274–275; J. K. Cogan, 'Financing and Budgets', in J. K. Cogan, I. Hurd and I. Johnstone (eds.), *Oxford Handbook of International Organizations* (Oxford University Press, 2016), 903, 910–914.

[4] General Assembly Resolution 'Transforming Our World: The 2030 Agenda for Sustainable Development', A/Res/70/1, September 25, 2015, Goal 17.

[5] CorpWatch, 'Tangled Up in Blue: Corporate Partnerships at the United Nations', September 1, 2000, available at www.corpwatch.org/article/tangled-blue. For a detailed account of the UN partnership controversies, see A. Zammit, *Development at Risk: Rethinking the UN–Business Partnerships* (South Centre, 2003), 63–68.

[6] United Nations International Children's Emergency Fund (UNICEF) is another notable example. While the definition of private sector may also include NGOs, charitable foundations, and academic institutions, in this chapter the terms "private sector," "business actors," "corporate entities," and "companies" will be used interchangeably.

UNDP in particular to mitigate the reputational risks associated with the business sector cooperation.

9.2 EVOLUTION OF CORPORATE PHILANTHROPY AT THE UN

Until the late 1990s, the business sector mainly perceived the UN as a hostile environment, due to the claims of a New International Economic Order and the associated neo-Marxist ideas that were prevalent in some UN bodies in the 1960s and 1970s.[7] This dynamic radically changed when Kofi Annan was elected as the UN Secretary-General in 1997. Many scholars maintained that it was Annan's business degree and his previous involvement with the business sector that shaped his vision of the organization as collaborating closely with private actors.[8] Since the very beginning of his tenure, Annan saw close cooperation with the private sector as an essential means to advance the goals of the organization and to revive its image in the era of globalization.[9] In his report to the General Assembly on the role of the UN in the twenty-first century, he emphasized the urgency of including private actors in tackling the challenges of the new millennium:

> Today, global affairs are no longer the exclusive province of foreign ministries, nor are states the sole source of solutions for our small planet's many problems. Many diverse and increasingly influential non-state actors have joined with national decision makers to improvise new forms of global governance. The more complex the problem at hand … the more likely we are to find non-governmental organizations, private sector institutions and multilateral agencies working with sovereign states to find consensus solutions.[10]

Speaking at the World Economic Forum in Davos several years earlier, he stressed in particular that "market forces are essential for sustainable development" and constitute "the dominant engine of growth … and the source of

7 B. Bull, M. Bøås and D. McNeill, 'Private Sector Influence in the Multilateral System: A Changing Structure of the World Governance?' (2004) 10 *Global Governance* 481, 484; S. Tesner with G. Kell, *The United Nations and Business: A Partnership Recovered* (Macmillan, 2000), 1–2.

8 Bull et al., 'Private Sector Influence', 485; L. Andonova, *Governance Entrepreneurs: International Organizations and the Rise of Global Public–Private Partnerships* (Cambridge University Press, 2017), 70; Tesner, *The United Nations and Business*, 31–32.

9 Andonova, *Governance Entrepreneurs*, 75.

10 'We the Peoples: The Role of the United Nations in the Twenty-First Century', Report of the Secretary-General to the UN General Assembly, the Millennium Assembly of the United Nations (54th session), UN Doc. A/54/2000, March 27, 2000, para. 315. See also paras. 46–47; Andonova, *Governance Entrepreneurs*, 75–76.

the largest financial, technological, and managerial resources," warranting a close partnership between the UN and the private sector.[11] To realize his vision, Annan created the Office of the Assistant Secretary-General for Strategic Planning within the UN Secretariat, charged with the tasks of developing specific initiatives for closer collaboration between the organization and the private sector and generating support for these among member states, UN agencies, and the private actors.[12] One of the main initiatives proposed in Davos was "a global compact of shared values and principles, which will give a human face to the global market."[13] Since then the Global Compact has become the world's largest corporate social responsibility initiative, which encourages business actors to comply with 10 principles related to human rights, labor, environment, and anti-corruption.[14] Business entities participating in the initiative are supposed to bring their policies and operations in line with the Compact's 10 principles, as well as to take strategic initiatives to advance the UN Sustainable Development Goals, by forming partnerships between the UN and the private sector and engaging in other types of corporate philanthropy.[15]

While Annan's leadership was crucial in bringing the organization and the business sector together, larger factors that made this paradigmatic shift possible were also at play. Among these factors was an ideological shift that occurred with the end of the Cold War, marking the victory of economic liberalism and accordingly, a preference for market-based solutions also in the public domain.[16] In addition to this, while private finances in the development sector were on the rise, the UN's own financial resources had been under continuous strain.[17] After the end of the post-Cold War enthusiasm in international relations, the United States and other major donors started to reduce their contributions to the organization, unsatisfied with its inefficiency in dealing with new societal challenges.[18] In 1997, the UN suffered the largest budgetary deficit in its history, when the US Congress failed to allocate the annual contribution to the organization, amounting to 30 percent of its

[11] UN Secretary-General, Address to the World Economic Forum, Davos, Switzerland, January 31, 1998, Press Release SG/SM/6153, available at www.un.org/press/en/1997/19970131.sgsm6153.html (visited 1 August 2022). See also Tesner, *The United Nations and Business*, 32.

[12] Andonova, *Governance Entrepreneurs*, 75.

[13] UN Secretary-General, Address to the World Economic Forum.

[14] The UN Global Compact website, at www.unglobalcompact.org/what-is-gc. On the history of the Global Compact, see Andonova, *Governance Entrepreneurs*, 88–104.

[15] The UN Global Compact website, at www.unglobalcompact.org/what-is-gc/mission.

[16] Bull et al., 'Private Sector Influence', 484; Tesner, *The United Nations and Business*, 2.

[17] Andonova, *Governance Entrepreneurs*, 71.

[18] Ibid.

budget.[19] As a response to this, Ted Turner, an American philanthropist and a founder of the CNN and other television networks, decided to singlehandedly compensate for this shortage and donate one billion USD to the organization in the course of 10 years. This unprecedented gesture became a turning point in the history of corporate philanthropy at the UN, giving the Secretariat an opportunity to introduce a number of institutional changes, starting with the creation of the UN Fund for International Partnerships (UNFIP) to act as a liaison between the organization and Ted Turner's charitable body, the UN Foundation.[20] While initially created for this purpose, UNFIP became the first gateway for brokering partnerships between the UN and the private sector more generally.[21] In 2006, UNFIP was incorporated into the UN Office for Partnerships (UNOP) that currently represents the central platform for facilitating partnerships between public and private actors.[22] In addition, almost every UN agency has a separate office responsible for engagement with the private sector, including the UNDP's Division for Business Partnerships, indicating the latter's prominent role in the organization. As cooperation with the business sector has been evolving, new legal arrangements were required to accommodate corporate donations and companies' direct involvement in UN development initiatives. The respective rules and policies will be discussed in Sections 9.3 and 9.4.

9.3 MODES OF CORPORATE PHILANTHROPY IN THE UN DEVELOPMENT SECTOR

As a starting point, the UN Financial Regulations and Rules allow voluntary contributions, gifts, and donations from both states and private actors, provided that their purpose is consistent with the policies, aims, and activities of the United Nations.[23] In addition, the regulations provide that the contribution should not entail any additional financial liabilities to the organization, except when explicitly authorized by the General Assembly.[24] In all the other

[19] Ibid., 76–77.

[20] Ibid.

[21] For a detailed account of the diffusion of public–private partnerships at the UN, see ibid., 80–88.

[22] UNOP website, at www.un.org/partnerships/content/what-we-do-1 (visited 1 August 2022). In addition to UNFIP, UNOP incorporates the Partnership Advisory and Outreach Service and the UN Democracy Fund, created in 2005 to fund projects aimed at strengthening national democratic processes worldwide.

[23] Financial Regulations and Rules of the United Nations, Secretary-General's Bulletin, ST/SGB/2013/4, July 1, 2013, Regulation 3.12.

[24] Ibid.

cases when the approval of the General Assembly is not required, the receipt of contributions, gifts, and donations by the UN is still subject to the approval of the Secretary-General.[25]

Further, the UN Guidelines on Cooperation between the United Nations and the Business Sector, first adopted in 2000, identify three main modalities of corporate funding in the organization: direct contributions by business partners to the organization; indirect contributions through the establishment of a charitable foundation; and sponsoring a particular project by entering into a public–private partnership with the organization.[26] Each of these arrangements will be discussed in turn.

The first obvious form of corporate philanthropy is the direct donations from a business enterprise to a UN agency. In terms of legal arrangements, the UN financial regulations distinguish between earmarked and non-earmarked contributions: while the former are set as trust funds or special accounts, the latter are treated as miscellaneous revenue.[27] The overwhelming majority of the direct contributions fall in the first category, being allocated for a specific project or a thematic priority chosen by the donor. An illustration of this is a three million USD donation from Coca-Cola to the UNDP to one of the organization's thematic priorities in 2020.[28]

The second modality is when a business partner donates money to the UN indirectly through the establishment of a charitable organization or to an already existing one. The primary example in this regard is the United Nations Foundation, which, as mentioned in Section 9.2, was created by Ted Turner in 1997 as a public charity body in domestic law to channel his one billion dollars donation into the organization. The interaction between the UN Foundation and the UNFIP, which represents the organization, is regulated by a special agreement, laying out the terms of the projects' financing, the use of the UN's name and emblem, privileges and immunities of the organization, liability of the parties, and settlement of disputes.[29] In particular, when it comes to the procedure for the identification of the projects that

[25] Financial Regulations and Rules of the United Nations, Secretary-General's Bulletin, ST/SGB/2013/4/Amend.1, December 4, 2018, Rule 103.4. (a).

[26] 'Towards Global Partnership: Co-operation between the United Nations and All Relevant Partners, in Particular the Private Sector', Report of the Secretary-General to the General Assembly, 56th session, Guidelines for Cooperation between the United Nations and the Business Community, Annex III, UN Doc. A/56/323, October 9, 2001, para. 18.

[27] Financial Regulations and Rules of the United Nations, Regulations 3.13 and 3.14.

[28] See the UNDP Funding Compendium 2020, 30.

[29] Agreement between the United Nations and the United Nations Foundation, Inc., of June 12, 1998, United Nations Fund for International Partnerships, Report of the Secretary-General, A/53/700, November 24, 1998, Annex.

receive funding, the agreement stipulates that the UNFIP will submit grant proposals to the Foundation from different UN agencies and programs, with the Foundation having a final say on which projects to sponsor in line with its thematic priorities.[30] The thematic priorities are identified in consultation with the UNFIP and have most recently included global health; women empowerment; climate change and environment, data, and technology; and peace, human rights, and humanitarian causes.[31] The agreement between the UN Foundation and the UNFIP has been renewed twice, most recently in 2014 for the period of another 10 years.[32] The 2014 agreement also established the Joint Coordination Committee, co-chaired by the UN and the UN Foundation, to ensure an effective coordination of common initiatives.[33]

The Foundation made its mission to not only dispense Turner's gift but also to mobilize further resources for the UN and to advocate for the organization's cause in both US political and business circles.[34] Among the contributors to the UN Foundation are Amazon, Barclays, Chevron, Coca-Cola, Ericsson, Google, Goldman Sachs, Mastercard, Nestle, Proctor & Gamble, and other corporate giants.[35] Overall, the initiative proved very successful as in the period from 1998 to 2020, the UNFIP received 1.47 billion USD from the UN Foundation, including 0.45 billion USD from Ted Turner's original gift and other additional funds mobilized by the UN Foundation from corporate actors and private individuals.[36] These funds allowed for implementation of a total of 676 projects in 128 countries, involving 48 UN partners.[37] The two main recipients of the Foundation's grants within the UN system were UNICEF and the WHO, having secured more than 500 million USD each in the period between 1998 and 2019.[38] While prominent, the UN Foundation is not the only example of the corporate philanthropic foundation in the field of development. To illustrate, among the 10 top private sector contributors to the UNDP are

[30] Ibid., Part III.

[31] UN Foundation website, https://unfoundation.org/what-we-do/issues (visited 1 August 2022).

[32] Program Budget for 2021: UN Office for Partnerships, Report of the Secretary-General, A/76/218, July 23, 2021, para. 54, table 4.

[33] Program Budget for the Biennium 2014–2015: UN Office for Partnerships, Report of the Secretary-General, A/70/202, July 27, 2015, para. 5.

[34] UN Foundation website, https://unfoundation.org/who-we-are/our-mission (visited 1 August 2022). See also, Andonova, *Governance Entrepreneurs*, 77–79.

[35] UN Foundation website, https://unfoundation.org/who-we-are/our-partners/more-of-our-partners (visited 1 August 2022).

[36] Program Budget for 2020: UN Office for Partnerships, Report of the Secretary-General, A/75/230, July 24, 2020, para. 2; Program Budget for 2021, para. 55, table 5.

[37] Program Budget for 2021, para. 55, table 5.

[38] Program Budget for 2020, annex I, figure A.

such philanthropic organizations as the Bill and Melinda Gates Foundation, the Nigerian Aliko Dangote Foundation, the Palestinian Paltel Group Foundation, the Swiss Stiftung Auxilium, and other entities whose funding derives from corporations or wealthy business owners.[39]

The third funding modality is when a business enterprise enters into a partnership with the UN. What separates this form of funding from other types of contributions is that a business entity not only finances the project but is also frequently involved in its design and implementation by providing staff and expertise or serving as a forum for UN goals advocacy. The UN defines partnerships as "collaborative relationships between various parties, both public and non-public, in which all participants agree to support a common cause or to achieve a common purpose, and to potentially share risks, responsibilities, resources and benefits."[40] UN-business partnerships in the field of development vary in their composition, scope, and objectives. Some comprise only the UN agencies and business entities, whereas others also include governmental institutions and civil society actors. Partnerships can be time-bound or without a specific end-date; they can be local, regional, or global in their reach.[41] When it comes to their governance structures, they can be based on a formal or an informal agreement (normally a memorandum of understanding), operate as a project, or even be constituted as a distinct entity.[42] To provide a few examples, the Angola Enterprise Program that took place from 2002 to 2007 was a public–private partnership co-funded by the UNDP (one million USD) and ChevronTexaco (five million USD).[43] The program, set as a UNDP-managed project, aimed at promoting the development of the small and medium enterprise sector in the country. In addition to financing the bulk of the project, Chevron was actively involved in the implementation of the project through its participation in the Partnership Board and the joint Management Committee, which met on a regular basis to provide the direction and oversight of the joint project.[44] A more recent example is a multi-stakeholder partnership between the governments of Japan and South Africa, Toyota South Africa Motors, and the UNDP for training and re-skilling young

39 See the UNDP Funding Compendium 2020, 30.

40 United Nations Global Compact, *UN–Business Partnerships: A Handbook*, 6, available at www.unglobalcompact.org/library/361 (visited 1 August 2022).

41 For an overview, see ibid., 12.

42 On this point specifically, see ibid., 25–27.

43 Memorandum of Understanding between the United Nations Development Program and the Chevron Texaco Corporation, November 25, 2002, Art. II, para. 2(1), available at https://info.undp.org/docs/pdc/Documents/AGO/Memorandum_of_Understanding_UNDP__ChevronTexaco.pdf (visited 1 August 2022).

44 Ibid., Art. II, para. 2(3).

South African men and women in the post-COVID economic recovery in the country.[45] In this case, the UNDP and Toyota signed a memorandum of understanding in December 2021, providing for the opening of a company-led manufacturing academy in one of the local colleges.[46]

9.4 MANAGING REPUTATIONAL RISKS IN UN–BUSINESS PARTNERSHIPS

As is clear from the examples in Section 9.3, an obvious positive side of partnering with the private sector is that it allows the organization to mobilize the necessary financial resources, as well as technology and expertise to achieve the UN development goals.[47] In addition, the other often cited benefit of closer cooperation with the private sector is an opportunity for the UN to promote its goals and values in business communities, thereby raising the organization's profile in wider circles.[48] At the same time, such cooperation raises a number of concerns. The main issue often expressed by the UN member states and civil society actors is that a close association of the UN with business partners – especially those with a controversial reputation – may compromise the image and credibility of the organization.[49] This may happen, for instance, when the organization chooses to partner up with a business entity that has been involved in human rights violations or other dubious activities. In particular, allowing that business partner to use the organization's logo and other symbols for the duration of the partnership may give an impression to third parties that the UN endorses the company's actions and policies.[50] Other reputational risks may be associated with granting a business partner precedence or exclusive access to information on an organization's procurement opportunities and other cases of conflict of interests.[51] Finally, other concerns relate to the lack of accountability and effectiveness in the design and implementation of the UN–business

45 www.undp.org/africa/news/japan-south-africa-undp-and-toyota-sa-launch-automotive-project-advance-youth-development (visited 1 August 2022).

46 Ibid.

47 See also 'Towards Global Partnership: Co-operation between the United Nations and All Relevant Partners', para. 16, para. 8.

48 Ibid., para. 17.

49 Ibid., para. 24. Another concern expressed during the General Assembly debate on the UN's cooperation with the private sector was that the increase of private funding in the organization would lead to undue corporate influence in the UN decision-making, see ibid., para. 9. For lack of space, this issue will not be covered here.

50 Ibid., para. 26.

51 Ibid.

partnerships that could cast a shadow on the convening power of the organization in the future.[52]

In light of the above-mentioned considerations, there was a shared understanding among the UN member states and the Secretariat that proper rules and policies were required to mitigate the potential risks to the UN reputation. To this end, in 2000, the Secretariat presented its first "Guidelines on Cooperation between the United Nations and the Business Sector," which were subsequently revised in 2009 and 2015.[53] The guidelines introduced the conditions on the use of the UN's name and emblem by organization's partners, as well as the criteria for their selection.[54] As to the former, the document states that a business partner is allowed to use the name and the emblem of the organization on a non-exclusive basis as long as its main objective is to promote the goals and activities of the UN. This includes mobilizing funds for the organization, even if it involves incidental profit-making for the business entity.[55] Furthermore, the guidelines provide that the use of the name and the emblem in each single case should be authorized in writing by the UN Office of Legal Affairs.[56]

When it comes to the choice of the business partners, the document contains various criteria that have been continuously revised as a result of pressure from the General Assembly and civil society actors for greater care and transparency in the selection process.[57] As the first condition, the guidelines provide that the UN will only engage with business entities that "demonstrate responsible citizenship by supporting United Nations causes and core values as reflected in the Charter and other relevant conventions and treaties."[58] In addition, the document states that the organization will not cooperate with businesses that "contribute to or are otherwise complicit in human rights abuses, tolerate forced or compulsory labor or the use of child labor, are involved in the sale or manufacture of anti-personnel mines or cluster bombs, or that otherwise do not meet relevant obligations or

[52] Ibid., para. 27.
[53] Ibid., annex III.
[54] Ibid., annex III.
[55] Ibid., annex III, para. 16 (c) and (d).
[56] Ibid., annex III, para. 16 (b), (e), para. 17.
[57] See, for instance, 'Towards Global Partnership: A Principle-Based Approach to Enhanced Cooperation between the United Nations and All Relevant Partners', General Assembly Resolution A/Res/68/234, December 20, 2013, paras. 13, 27. See also, Andonova, *Governance Entrepreneurs*, 93–94, 102–103.
[58] Guidelines on a Principle-Based Approach to the Cooperation between the United Nations and the Business Sector (2015), available at www.unglobalcompact.org/library/3431 (visited 1 August 2022), para. 15 (a).

responsibilities by the United Nations."[59] Since 2009, the guidelines have also stated that the UN will not collaborate with corporations that violate the UN Security Council sanctions.[60]

In addition, the guidelines designate the UN Global Compact as the main point of reference for choosing a business partner.[61] As previously mentioned, the UN Global Compact is currently the world's largest corporate social responsibility initiative, which endorses 10 principles related to human rights, labor, environment, and anti-corruption that companies are invited to follow in their policies and day-to-day operations.[62] The UN guidelines state that the organization will "not partner with business sector entities that systematically fail to demonstrate commitment to meeting the principles of the United Nations Global Compact," except for the cases where the partnership in question specifically aims at improving business actor's compliance with the initiative.[63] Instead, to be chosen as a UN partner, a company "should have demonstrated a commitment to meeting or exceeding the principles of the Compact by translating them into operational corporate practice."[64]

However, despite the central role given to the Compact in the selection of UN business partners, the nature of the initiative makes it ill-suited for this purpose. This is because, in the words of the UN Secretariat, the Global Compact is a "learning network," as opposed to a robust corporate code of conduct accompanied by an effective enforcement mechanism.[65] In fact, as emphasized in the Compact's policies, its main *raison d'être* is to "facilitate the adherence to the principles of the Compact through openness and enhanced communication."[66] To this end, the initiative aims to be all-encompassing, with very minimal entry requirements. To clarify, any company that is not involved in the production of landmines, bombs, or tobacco manufacturing,

59 Ibid., para. 16 (a).

60 Ibid., para. 16 (b).

61 Ibid., para. 15. In 2015, the Global Compact has been joined by the UN Guiding Principles on Business and Human Rights, unanimously adopted by the Human Rights Council in 2011, as the other point of reference for expected conduct by a UN business partner, see para. 7. Because of lack of space, a detailed analysis of the Guiding Principles will not be provided.

62 The UN Global Compact website, at www.unglobalcompact.org/what-is-gc (visited 1 August 2022).

63 Guidelines on a Principle-Based Approach to the Cooperation between the United Nations and the Business Sector (2015), para. 17.

64 'Towards Global Partnership: Co-operation between the United Nations and All Relevant Partners', Annex III, para. 12(b).

65 'Towards Global Partnership: Co-operation between the United Nations and All Relevant Partners', para. 86.

66 Global Compact Integrity Measures FAQ, United Nations Global Compact, 2, available at www.unglobalcompact.org/library/1831 (visited 1 August 2022).

as well as not present on either the UN Ineligible Vendors or the UN Security Council sanctions list may join the Global Compact.[67] In order to do so, a company simply needs to send an official letter to the UN Secretary-General pledging its commitment to implement the 10 principles of the Compact and to report on its progress by submitting an annual "Communication on Progress" (the "CoP").[68] The CoPs are then published on the Global Compact website and are accessible to media, civil society, and the wider public to facilitate dialogue and social vetting.[69] Yet, according to the 2020 Global Compact "Building on Twenty Years of Progress" report, two-thirds of the Compact's participants maintained that the CoP reporting mechanism has had no real-life impact on how the issues of human rights, labor, environment, and corruption are implemented on the ground.[70] The main reason for this outcome, as repeatedly emphasized by the Compact's critics, is the fact that there is no effective monitoring system in place that would ensure compliance with the 10 principles.

This is notwithstanding the fact that, in 2005, the Global Compact Board adopted the so-called integrity measures precisely to mitigate this criticism and to protect the initiative's reputation.[71] The measures introduced included delisting the participants who failed to submit the CoP for two consecutive years, as well as a mechanism for handling the allegations of "systematic or egregious abuses" of the Compact's aims principles. However, the latter procedure has little impact, being reserved exclusively for very grave violations, such as murder, torture, deprivation of liberty and forced labor, serious environmental damage, and blatant corruption.[72] Moreover, the mechanism does not amount to a legal remedy for such violations but is rather focused on dialogue facilitation between the company and a third party.[73] If the company refuses to engage in the dialogue within a two-month period, it may be considered "non-communicating" and in the case of a prolonged inactivity, eventually

[67] United Nations Global Compact Joining Policy, January 2022, available at www.unglobalcompact.org/participation/join/application (visited 1 August 2022)

[68] www.unglobalcompact.org/participation/join/application/business.

[69] United Nations Corporate Partnerships: The Role and the Functioning of the Global Compact, Joint Inspection Unit Report, JIU/Rep/2010/9, at 12, footnote 26.

[70] Uniting Business in the Decade of Action: 'Building on Twenty Years of Progress', DNV GL and the United Nations Global Compact Report, January 2020, 123.

[71] United Nations Corporate Partnerships: The Role and the Functioning of the Global Compact, para. 65.

[72] Global Compact Integrity Measures FAQ, 2.

[73] Ibid., 2–3.

removed from the Global Compact.[74] In addition, the Global Compact Office – after consulting the Global Compact Board – may de-list the company in question as the measure of last resort when it has admitted to having committed the abuse or has been found guilty of doing so by a court of law.[75] According to the Global Compact Annual Report, in 2021 there were only 10 instances in which a third party raised an allegation of the abuse of the Compact principles (compared to 13 in 2020), out of which only two were deemed acceptable for the dialogue facilitation process.[76] While no further reasons were provided in the report, it appears that the Global Compact Office frequently uses its right to refuse the claims on the ground that they are better suited to being resolved by another entity, such as a court, an administrative organ, or any other dispute resolution mechanism.[77]

In light of the inefficiency of the Global Compact to mitigate risks to the UN's reputation, it is essentially up to the individual UN agencies to conduct a proper due diligence check on the potential partners.[78] While there is a significant disparity between different UN agencies, a few have developed their own rules and policies to regulate their cooperation with the private sector, in addition to the UN Guidelines and the Global Compact standards.[79] UNDP is one of these agencies, having several detailed regulations on the private sector partnerships, including a designated due diligence policy and a risk assessment tool.[80] In a nutshell, the UNDP's due diligence procedure is based upon differentiating between three risk levels: the "highest risk," "significant risk," and "lower risk."[81] In the "highest risk" category are the business entities falling within the UN-wide and the UNDP-specific exclusionary criteria. The former

74 Ibid., 4. However, the company in question has the right to be reinstated if it convinces the Global Compact Office that it has taken appropriate actions to mitigate the violation and has otherwise brought its actions in line with the Compact principles.

75 Ibid., 3.

76 United Nations Global Compact 2021 Annual Report, UN Global Compact, March 2022, 65.

77 Global Compact Integrity Measures FAQ, 3. An example of such claim provided in the FAQ is a dispute between the company and its employees or their respective trade unions, at 3.

78 This, in fact, is encouraged by the UN Guidelines themselves, see Guidelines on a Principle-based Approach to the Cooperation between the United Nations and the Business Sector (2015), paras. 19–22.

79 The United Nations System – Private Sector Partnerships Arrangements in the Context of the 2030 Agenda for Sustainable Development, Joint Inspection Unit Report, JIU/Rep/2017/8, para. 35.

80 These include the Main policy on Private Sector Partnerships, the UNDP Policy for Due Diligence and Partnerships with the Private Sector (2013), the Policy on Cooperation between UNDP and Private Sector (2009), Risk Assessment Tool (2017). All the documents are available at https://popp.undp.org/SitePages/POPPSubject.aspx?SBJID=391&Menu=BusinessUnit (visited 1 August 2022).

81 UNDP Policy for Due Diligence and Partnerships with the Private Sector, 2–3.

include enterprises that manufacture and sell weapons and tobacco; those that are complicit in human rights abuses, use forced or compulsory labor, or child labor; and those that violate UN Security Council sanctions or are found on the UN Ineligible Vendors list.[82] To these criteria, common to all the UN agencies, the UNDP also adds companies that are involved in gambling, the production and distribution of pornography, as well as entities that sell phase-out substances and endangered species of fauna and flora.[83] The second risk level, "significant risk," includes companies that are involved in "significant controversies" concerning governance, labor issues, environment, and others, as evidenced by the court cases against them or criticism expressed by media, governments, or civil society actors.[84] In addition, the UNDP guidelines identify several high-risk sectors where such "significant controversies" are most likely to occur, prompting for extra caution in the company's assessment. These sectors include oil and gas; metals and mining; utilities provision; large infrastructure construction; production of timber, pulp, and paper; the alcohol industry; manufacture of chemicals and pharmaceuticals; production of clothing, toys, and domestic electronic appliances; and the fast food and high sugar drinks industry. Finally, the third level, "lower risk," comprises all the commercial enterprises that do not fall under the exclusionary criteria or the "significant controversies" category.[85]

With these three levels of risk in mind, the UNDP country office that is considering a partnership first conducts a pre-screening to establish whether the potential business partner falls under the exclusionary criteria.[86] If this is the case, then the UNDP will abstain from entering into a partnership, subject to a few exceptions.[87] If the opposite is true, the unit proceeds with the second stage, which is identifying if the company is involved in any "significant controversies." If major controversies are found in several areas, the local unit should not engage with the company.[88] If there are issues but they are

82 Ibid., 4–5.

83 Ibid., 4.

84 Ibid., 2.

85 Ibid.

86 For the summary of whole due diligence process, see ibid., 11, figure 1.

87 Some exceptions are made in the case of indirect involvement of the company in the exclusionary criteria activity through a subsidiary, a parent company, or a supply chain partner, and/or when the annual revenue from the said activity is below a certain threshold, e.g. 5 percent. For more details, see ibid., 3–5. In these exceptional cases, the company moves on to the next level of the screening process but the decision is 'escalated' to the UNDP headquarters: ibid., 11.

88 Ibid., 11. What qualifies as a 'major controversy' depends on the subjective assessment by the initiating unit.

regarded to be of a lesser concern, the business entity may still be eligible for partnership but the case needs to be referred to UNDP headquarters.[89] If no major controversies are found, the local UNDP office continues with the last stage of the screening process, which involves the evaluation of the company's performance in the UN Global Compact, the Environmental, Social, and Governance ("ESG") indices, as well as various sustainability certifications.[90] This is followed by the assessment of the business entity's commitment to human rights, labor, environmental, and good governance standards. Lastly, other risks, together with the benefits of the potential partnerships, are examined at this final stage. Based on this comprehensive three-stage assessment, if no exclusionary criteria and major controversies are found, and the company's ESG commitments are deemed adequate, the UNDP can make a positive decision regarding the partnership. In situations where the company's ESG commitment is found to be satisfactory but some controversial issues have been identified, the decision regarding the partnership is reviewed by the inter-bureau technical committee that, based on all the due diligence information available, makes a recommendation to the senior UNDP management who makes the final decision.[91] Overall, it seems that the UNDP managed to develop its own thorough due diligence process to protect the agency from reputational risks associated with partnerships, in light of the shortcomings of the UN Secretariat efforts in doing so.

9.5 CONCLUSION

To sum up, the analysis undertaken in this chapter demonstrates how in just over two decades the role of the private sector at the UN has evolved significantly, making business entities prominent actors in the organization's development initiatives. The cooperation between the two progressed from occasional one-time donations to elaborate partnership schemes involving their own budgets, governing bodies, and innovative forms of business involvement. A further scaling-up of the UN and private sector collaboration is expected with the adoption of the 2030 Agenda for Sustainable Development, which, in the words of the UN Secretary-General, "presents a historic opportunity for the United Nations ... to unlock the full potential of those partnerships."[92]

[89] Ibid.
[90] Ibid.
[91] Ibid., 9.
[92] Enhanced Cooperation between the United Nations and All Relevant Partners, in Particular the Private Sector, Report of the Secretary General, A/72/310, August 10, 2017, 16.

However, as UN–business partnerships increase in numbers and complexity, the organizational rules and policies that regulate this interaction remain inadequate, especially when it comes to managing risks to the organization's reputation. As illustrated, in the absence of proper due diligence mechanisms, both the Secretariat's Guidelines on Cooperation between the UN and the Business Sector and the Global Compact fall short of ensuring that all the UN's business partners adhere to accepted human rights and environmental standards. While these shortcomings are partially compensated by proper due diligence procedures set up by some UN agencies, including the UNDP, this is not the case with other UN entities with less resources and fewer manpower.[93] In order to counter this discrepancy, the organization needs a coordinated approach to cooperation with the private sector, including viable operational tools that would safeguard the integrity and impartiality of the UN as a whole.[94]

93 For comparison between different UN entities, see 'The United Nations System – Private Sector Partnerships Arrangements in the Context of the 2030 Agenda for Sustainable Development', paras. 35–67.

94 This is also one of the main recommendations made by the Joint Inspection Unit in its Report, see ibid., 23.

10

The WHO and the A1H1 Flu: Fine-tuning for Pandemic Responses

SEBASTIÁN MACHADO

10.1 INTRODUCTION

Traditional scholarship on international institutional law tells us that an organization, in principle, maintains relations only with its member states.[1] This follows a simple line of reasoning: if the legal personality of organizations is, in principle, subjective, then it is, in principle, opposable only to those who have accepted its existence as a matter of law – its members.[2] The life of international organizations, however, shows us that the legal fiction of subjectivity is imprecise as a matter of fact. Organizations routinely engage, affect or regulate activities in which *others* – either non-members or just third parties, public and private – are affected to a greater or lesser extent.[3]

One way of dealing with this nuance has been to relativize the form of engagement, that is, to distinguish between effects of institutional actions and other forms of direct legal relationships (such as procurement).[4] Affecting

[1] See, for example, H. G. Schermers and N. Blokker, *International Institutional Law: Unity within Diversity*, 5th ed. (Martinus Nijhoff, 2011), para 1687.

[2] J. Klabbers, *An Introduction to International Institutional Law*, 2nd ed. (Cambridge University Press, 2009), 38–39.

[3] In the field of financial regulation, for example, it has become commonplace for relevant organizations to regulate third-party activity. See, for example, Article 11(12) of EU Regulation 648/2012 related to derivatives contracts, which applies to 'third country entities'; or the OECD's Base Erosion and Profit Shifting (BEPS) Project whose scope of application far exceeds OECD membership, amongst others.

[4] The so-called Brussels Effect is a good example of this. See A. Bradford, *The Brussels Effect: How the European Union Rules the World* (Oxford University Press, 2020). It is also noteworthy that the EU has relied on this nuanced distinction for much of its regulation, e.g. through the 'qualified effects case' or the 'implementation test' in antitrust matters. See, e.g., case C-413/14 P, *Intel v. Commission*, ECLI:EU:C:2017:632.

third parties can then be theorized in terms which are not necessarily tied to membership, recognition or subjectivity, but rather in the language of political economy. In this way, it is not necessary to be blind to the different forms of transactions through which organizations exist and operate and can bring otherwise background tones to the forefront. It makes an inquiry into the extent to which the existence of international organizations – and all the different activities performed during the course of their operation – have the potential of reshuffling the costs and benefits of third parties possible. At the heart of this inquiry lies a tension between constituent powers and organizational teleology; between mission and market, so to speak.

To this end, in this chapter I undertake a case-study of the World Health Organization's ('WHO') handling of the 2009 'Swine' influenza pandemic ('A1H1 Pandemic'). The objective is to discuss some ways in which the WHO's response to the 2009 A1H1 Pandemic had powerful redistributive effects that can be theorised in the context of this tension between mission and market, in order to import notions of political economy which are legally meaningful. In this vein, Section 10.2 begins by framing the legal context under which the WHO and its different organs reacted to the A1H1 Pandemic. In Section 10.3, I discuss some of the concrete economic impacts of the discussions and decisions emanating from the WHO in order to contain the A1H1 influenza, followed by some of the backlash to these determinations in Section 10.4. In Section 10.5, I offer some remarks on the legacy of the WHO's handling of the A1H1 virus and its impact on the COVID-19 pandemic, while I make some broader conclusions on the topic in Section 10.6.

10.2 LEGAL CONTEXT

After the highly disruptive COVID-19 virus it might seem quaint to reflect on its distant cousin: the A1H1 Pandemic. After all, any comparison in death toll and economic loss reveals that both situations are in different orders of magnitude.[5] The relatively small scale of the A1H1 Pandemic, however, offers its own advantages: the more modest radiating effect of the health-related decision-making makes it a manageable case-study to reflect on its legacy for international institutional law.

[5] The WHO reports that the official death toll of the Swine Flu was 18,499 people, although latter studies suggest that the real number is closer to 200,000. See F. S. Dadwood et al., 'Estimated Global Mortality Associated with the First 12 Months of 2009 Pandemic Influenza A H1N1 Virus Circulation: A Modelling Study' (2012) 12 *The Lancet Infectious Diseases* 687.

There was already a long tradition of treaty-making in the field of public health before the World Health Organization's constitution entered into force on 7 April 1948.[6] The regime of 'international health law' has a history which points to similar anxieties to those we live with today, mostly rooted in the need for international cooperation from Western states to coordinate quarantine and isolating measures to protect themselves from 'Asiatic' diseases (such as cholera, plague or yellow fever).[7]

The drafting of the WHO constitution, however, did not follow the collaborative frameworks established by its predecessor, the International Sanitary Convention of 1926. It is worth noting that, before the WHO, international cooperation on public health issues was grounded on the International Sanitary Convention of 1926, a successor to the International Sanitary Convention of 1892. Interestingly, the language and different obligations enshrined in the Sanitary Convention already show a concern with the potentially disruptive effect that health measures can have on international trade. For example, Part II of the Convention deals only with special provisions related to regulatory measures in the Suez Canal. Instead, the drafters believed that the technical nature of disease control and prevention would permit harder mechanisms of enforcement which would not be prone to the arbitrariness of international politics and endowed the WHO with a 'quasi-legislative process that was, at the time of WHO's origins in the late 1940s, a radical approach to international law'.[8] Even by today's standards, the explicit, constitutional treaty-making capacity and mandatory regulatory powers that the WHO enjoys make it a comparatively powerful organization.

In addition to the broad powers vested in the WHO constitution, both the Director-General and the Executive Board enjoy far-reaching authority in cases of public health emergencies. Pursuant to Article 28(j) of the constitution, the Executive Board may:

6 See J. E. Alvarez, *The Impact of International Organizations on International Law* (Martinus Nijhoff, 2017), 190–194.

7 Ibid., 191.

8 D. Fidler, 'The Future of the World Health Organization: What Role for International Law?' (1998) 31 *Vanderbilt Journal of Transnational Law* 1079, 1088. Fidler is referring to articles 21 and 22 of the WHO constitution, according to which the organization can adopt binding regulations on all of its members in five different areas: sanitary and quarantine requirements; disease nomenclature; international standards for diagnostic procedures; the safety of biological and pharmaceutical products; and the advertisement and labelling of relevant products in global trade. It is important to note that Fidler considers that the creation of the WHO represents a genuine break in the history of international public health by merging the collective security system of the UN with a human rights regime.

> take emergency measures within the functions and financial resources of the Organization to deal with events requiring immediate action. In particular it may authorize the Director-General to take the necessary steps to combat epidemics, to participate in the organization of health relief to victims of a calamity and to undertake studies and research the urgency of which has been drawn to the attention of the Board by any Member or by the Director-General.

These emergency powers should be read in conjunction with the International Health Regulations ('IHR') – a robust set of binding obligations related to the implementation of WHO actions – relied on during the A1H1 outbreak. The ambitious wording of the constitution, coupled with a tradition of teleological interpretation of its own powers, gives the WHO (and the Director-General in particular) some unusual and overarching regulatory capacity in the international arena.[9] The preamble of the WHO constitution is remarkably ambitious for its time. The final pre-ambulatory paragraph establishes that 'Governments have a responsibility for the health of their peoples which can be fulfilled only by the provision of adequate health and social measures'. For a document written in 1948, it contrasts with other attempts at internationalizing what was considered an essentially domestic matter, such as the regulation of non-international armed conflicts of common Article 3 to the Geneva Conventions or the Additional Protocol II adopted 30 years later. This is probably one of the most significant changes in the regime of international public health, as the Sanitary Conventions of 1926 or 1892 were only concerned with inter-State phenomena. Furthermore, most of the decisions emanating from the WHO and its organs tend to be about life and death, which has led to scholars referring to the Director-General as the 'second most difficult job in the world'.[10]

It is in this context that the WHO and its organs have the power to intervene in the international arena and directly bind 194 States of the world community. The pressure is significant and its recent history is riddled with claims of being constitutionally conservative,[11] historically neglectful of international

[9] Much of the criticism directed to the WHO is not based on the liberal interpretation of its constitutional powers bur rather the opposite: a perceived timidness to act to the fullest of its potential under a human rights paradigm. Fidler, for example, considers that '[s]ince 1948, the potential for international legal activity created by the WHO Constitution has remained untapped'. See Fidler, 'The Future', 1089; Alvarez, *The Impact*, 257.

[10] J. Klabbers, 'The Second Most Difficult Job in the World: Reflections on COVID-19' (2020) 11 *Journal of International Humanitarian Legal Studies* 270.

[11] Alvarez, *The Impact*, 198.

law[12] and with periods 'of decline, weak leadership, allegations of corruption at all levels, and paranoid defensiveness when any kind of external scrutiny was conducted'.[13]

It is thus safe to say that the WHO operates in a tense context. Its institutional architecture and organizational practices have made it prone to scathing critique. Moreover, the Director-General who was leading the Organization at the time of the A1H1 outbreak, Margaret Chan, had been elected and re-elected in a particularly controversial, drawn-out process.[14] It is in this context that the A1H1 flu arrived on stage in 2009: the first epidemic of the twenty-first century. In addition to the structural difficulties in operating the WHO to which I have alluded, it is noteworthy that this first pandemic occurred soon after the adoption of the IHR.[15] After decades of being called to adopt generic and binding regulations, the A1H1 outbreak made for an immediate test of the efficiency and impact of the newly adopted set of obligations pursuant to Articles 48 and 49 of the IHR which provide for the composition and procedure of Emergency Committees.[16]

In all these respects, the handling and decision-making at the WHO as a response to the A1H1 virus of 2009 represented a watershed moment in the history of international health policy and the organization itself. This importance of its response is not only marked by the suitability of the newly adopted IHR (in 2005) but due to the additional stress put on the technocratic vocation of the organisation. The WHO, as a model specialised agency of modern international law, was designed as if it were supposed to act above international politics and exclusively in the medical interest of the world community.

Yet the breadth of its mission and its constitutional powers have all too often remained unused. It is not just the failure to adopt any meaningful reform for over 70 years, but the coy approach to its 'hard' powers.[17] During its lifetime,

[12] Fidler, 'The Future', 1082.

[13] 'The Brundtland Era Begins' (1998) 351 *The Lancet* 381.

[14] H. Brown, 'And the Next Director-General of WHO Is . . .' (2006) 368 *The Lancet* 1757.

[15] The scope of application of the IHR is generic and not reserved for any specific disease, unlike any of its predecessors. Article 2 states: 'The purpose and scope of these Regulations are to prevent, protect against, control and provide a public health response to the international spread of disease in ways that are commensurate with and restricted to public health risks, and which avoid unnecessary interference with international traffic and trade.'

[16] D. Fidler, 'The Swine Flu Outbreak and International Law', *ASIL Insights*, 27 April 2009, www.asil.org/insights/volume/13/issue/5/swine-flu-outbreak-and-international-law#_edn1, accessed 23 August 2021.

[17] The power to make binding decisions at moments of urgency pursuant to Article 28(j) of the WHO constitution often gets compared to the powers that the Security Council has under chapter VII of the UN Charter. See, for example, Alvarez, *The Impact*, 198.

the WHO has witnessed the 'Asian' Flu of 1957, the 'Hong Kong' Flu of 1968, the 1976 'Swine Flu', the 1977 'Russian Flu', the 1997 'Avian Flu', as well as the 2009 'Swine Flu' and 2019 COVID pandemics. During all this time, however, the Organization had recourse to its powers under Article 19 of its constitution (the adoption of conventions within the scope of the organization) only once – for the adoption of the Framework Convention on Tobacco Control – and only twice adopted regulations pursuant to Article 21 with lacklustre effects,[18] until the IHR came to effect in 2007.[19]

All in all, it is fair to say that the WHO has not operationalized its powers to the full extent of its constitutional capacity.[20] The lofty ideal of placing technocracy above politics has never been fully realized and, in some cases, the opposite seems to be true.[21] This does not mean, however, that the softer forms of decision-making surrounding the WHO's participation in global pandemics do not have a powerful impact. The economic magnitude of pandemics highlights the astronomical stakes at which any related institutional decision can have. Indeed, it is estimated that, during the twentieth century, pandemic losses amounted to 0.7–4.8 per cent of the global GDP,[22] while pre-COVID (2019) modelling suggests that there was a 10 per cent

[18] A. Taylor, 'Controlling the Global Spread of Infectious Diseases: Toward a Reinforced Role for the International Health Regulations' (1997) 33 *Houston Law Review* 1327, 1341–1346.

[19] To be fair, there are good reasons to suspect that there have been some structural limitations to a broader role for the WHO, as illustrated by the failed attempt at getting an Advisory Opinion from the International Court of Justice on the legality of the use of nuclear weapons. In that case, the Court considered that '[t]he question put to the Court in the present case relates, however, not to the effects of the use of nuclear weapons on health, but to the legality of the use of such weapons in view of their health and environmental effects. Whatever those effects might be, the competence of the WHO to deal with them is not dependent on the legality of the acts that caused them. Accordingly, it does not seem to the Court that the provisions of Article 2 of the WHO Constitution, interpreted in accordance with the criteria referred to above, can be understood as conferring upon the Organization a competence to address the legality of the use of nuclear weapons, and thus in turn a competence to ask the Court about that.' On the other hand, this might very well be attributed to the high political stakes of the request rather than a conservative notion of the WHO's scope and constitution.

[20] Fidler, for example, considers '[t]he structural and public health reasons behind the need for international law, combined with WHO's historical neglect of international law, produce arguments that WHO should dramatically change its attitude toward international law'. See D. Fidler, 'International Law and Global Public Health' (1999) 1 *University of Kansas Law Review* 1, 57–58.

[21] See: M. Kavanagh, R. Singh and M. Pillinger, 'Playing Politics: The World Health Organization's Response to COVID-19', in S. Greer et al. (eds.), *Coronavirus Politics* (University of Michigan Press, 2021), 34.

[22] W. McKibbin and A. Sidorenko, 'Global Macroeconomic Consequences of Pandemic Influenza', https://cama.crawford.anu.edu.au/sites/default/files/publication/cama_crawford_anu_edu_au/2021-06/26_mckibbin_sidorenko_2006.pdf, accessed 25 August 2021.

chance that the average losses in this century will be more than $120 billion per year.[23]

It is in this context that the WHO's Executive Board and Director-General must make decisions that can, quite literally, make or break health-related firms.[24] This much seems to have been clear to the drafters of the IHR, which explicitly states as the purpose of the instrument (Article 2) to 'prevent, protect against, control and provide a public health response to the international spread of disease in *ways that are commensurate with and restricted to public health risks, and which avoid unnecessary interference with international traffic and trade*' (emphasis added). Coupled with the fact 'that international organizations, their structures, activities, and decisions generate distributive or redistributive effects',[25] it is worth asking: who wins and who loses when the WHO intervenes in pandemic scenarios?

In Section10.3, I will address this question in the context of the 2009 A1H1 virus. There are a few reasons why this pandemic can provide some insight as a case-study. On the one hand, the events are recent enough to have unfolded under the purview of the 2005 IHR while, on the other hand, they are distant enough to permit some dispassionate critique. Considering the disruptive impact of the 2019 COVID-19 pandemic and the increased probability of health-related emergencies becoming more and more frequent,[26] it is a good moment to reflect on the political economy of institutional decision-making at this level.

10.3 THE WINNERS AND THE LOSERS

The redistribution of economic resources arising out of an institutional action, such as the WHO, is not necessarily a zero-sum game nor a win–win situation for the parties involved.[27] There are, nevertheless, manifest winners and losers

[23] A. El Turabi and Ph Saynish, 'Modelling the Economic Threat of Pandemics' (Commission on a Global Health Risk Framework for the Future, 2016), 113, www.nam.edu/GHRF, accessed 25 August 2021.

[24] The obvious example are pharmaceuticals, though the radiating effect of public health decisions – especially in pandemics – can affect any number of economic sectors (such as textile companies that produce facemask prime materials or digital start-ups who create apps for the tracking of a particular virus).

[25] Klabbers, 'The Second Most Difficult Job', 271.

[26] At least two human-made phenomena will contribute to the increased frequency of pandemics: global warming and land-use change. See R. Gibb et al., 'Zoonotic Host Diversity Increases in Human-Dominated Ecosystems' (2020) 584 *Nature* 398.

[27] In the history of economic ideas, it was after *The Wealth of Nations* that the case for a win–win trade approach overcame the mercantilist notion of zero-sum international trade. For a historic analysis, see S. Pincus, 'Rethinking Mercantilism: Political Economy, the British Empire, and

when the WHO intervenes in a public health crisis. Some of these can be safely presumed. For example, pharmaceutical companies that can produce the necessary vaccine to treat a given pandemic will typically be the winners. Tourism industries in general, and airlines in particular, usually have much to lose in cases of infectious disease outbreaks.

In the case of the 2009 A1H1 outbreak there is one obvious loser: the pigs. While the misnamed 'Swine Flu' indeed transferred from pigs to humans, contact with the animals was not a source of infection – pork was safe to eat.[28] As with other respiratory disease outbreaks (like COVID-19), the A1H1 virus mutated and spilled from an animal onto humans, which meant that infection was likely from contact with other humans who were hosting the mutated virus, not the pigs in which the virus had originally mutated.[29] Little did any of this matter when, for example, Egypt decided to slaughter all the pigs in its territory (roughly 300,000 animals), while Afghanistan quarantined the only pig in the country for two months.[30]

In addition to the pig and hog slaying, the pandemic characterization prompted some significant shifts in the global meat trade. Once the WHO declared the A1HI flu virus a public health emergency of international concern (later upgraded to 'Phase 6' pandemic), Russia, China, the Philippines, Kazakhstan, Ukraine, and Ecuador all banned pork imports from Mexico and the United States. The Food and Agriculture Organization (FAO) estimated that, during 2009, global trade of meat products dropped

the Atlantic World in the Seventeenth and Eighteenth Centuries' (2012) 69 *The William and Mary Quarterly* 3.

28 The H1A1 virus, like other influenza A viruses, mutates from another animal (in this case a pig) to infect human beings. As such, pork was not the source of infection, but rather the humans (pig farmers) who hosted the original mutation. For a more technical overview, see: W. Shao et al., 'Evolution of Influenza A Virus by Mutation and Re-assortment' (2017) 18 *International Journal of Molecular Sciences* 1650.

29 C. Parrish et al., 'Cross-Species Virus Transmission and the Emergence of New Epidemic Diseases' (2008) 72 *Microbiology and Molecular Biology Reviews* 457; C. H. Schmidt, 'Swine CAFOs & Novel H1N1 Flu: Separating Facts from Fears' (2009) 117 *Environmental Health Perspectives* A394.

30 For an overview of the unnecessary slaughter of all Egyptian pigs, see S. Seef and A. Jeppsson, 'Is It a Policy Crisis or It Is a Health Crisis? The Egyptian Context: Analysis of the Egyptian Health Policy for the H1N1 Flu Pandemic Control' (2013) 14 *Pan African Medical Journal* 59. For his part, the director of the Kabul zoo, Aziz Gul Saqib, told Reuters that the pig had been unnecessarily quarantined only to quash the concern of zoo-goers who believed that the 'Swine Flu' could be contracted from swine. See P. Walker, 'Life Goes from Bad to Worse for Kabul's Only Pig', *The Guardian* (6 May 2009), www.theguardian.com/world/2009/may/06/kabul-pig-quarantined, accessed 27 August 2021.

by 4.8 per cent, while trade in pig meat contracted by 11.8 per cent.[31] Even though the FAO, WHO, and OIE (formerly the Office International des Epizooties, now the World Organization for Animal Health) went as far as to publish a joint statement in which they stated that '[i]nfluenza viruses are not known to be transmissible to people through eating processed pork or other food products derived from pigs . . . [p]ork and pork products, handled in accordance with good hygienic practices recommended by the WHO, Codex Alimentarius Commission and the OIE, will not be a source of infection,'[32] members of the WTO couched their pork-import bans in terms of sanitary and phytosanitary protection.[33] This drew immediate rebuke from the affected states, calling it lacking in 'legal or scientific basis', 'pointless' and otherwise contrary to international trade obligations.[34] Though China lifted its import ban on pork meat only a few months after, it did not continue to buy from foreign pig farmers at pre-A1H1 Pandemic volume, as it used this time to subsidise its domestic industry and stockpile large amounts of the produce.[35] In this sense, the A1H1 Pandemic afforded China the context it needed to increase its market share of pig meat.

But even if it is not a zero-sum game,[36] like an accordion, it must be squeezed on one end to produce sound at the other. It makes sense, then, to suspect that an import ban by the world's leading pig meat consumer *could* create a demand for alternative forms of animal produce. The impact of 'food

[31] 'Food Outlook: Global Market Analysis' (Food and Agriculture Organization, 2009), www.fao.org/3/ai482e/ai482e00.htm, accessed 27 August 2021. In the report, it argued that 'FAO's forecast for world pig meat trade points to a 7 percent contraction to 5.4 million tonnes in 2009, as consumer concerns related to a possible link between Influenza type A/H1N1 and swine flu are expected to depress import demand . . . International pig meat prices, which were relatively strong by the end of 2008, are expected to decline in 2009, largely reflecting a faltering global import demand. Apart from the recent outbreaks of diseases, the economic downturns, the imposition of non-tariff measures and a weakening of currencies in major import markets are all expected to drive international prices lower in 2009.'

[32] 'Joint FAO/WHO/OIE Statement on Influenza A(H1N1) and the Safety of Pork', www.oie.int/en/joint-fao-who-oie-statement-on-influenza-ah1n1-and-the-safety-of-pork/, accessed 27 August 2021.

[33] 'Summary of the Meeting of 23–24 June 2009', para 5, http://spsims.wto.org/en/SpecificTradeConcerns/View?ImsId=279, accessed 30 August 2021.

[34] These statements were made by the representatives of Mexico, the European Communities and the United States, respectively. See: 'Import Restrictions on Pork Products Relating to Influenza A/H1N1 – Extracts from SPS Committee Meeting Summary Reports', http://spsims.wto.org/en/SpecificTradeConcerns/View?ImsId=279, accessed 30 August 2021.

[35] 'China Lifts Import Ban on U.S., Canada, Mexico Pork', *Reuters* (1 December 2009), www.reuters.com/article/us-china-pork-idUSTRE5B00IW20091201, accessed 30 August 2021.

[36] For a recent study about win–win trade specifically with China, see D. Irwin, 'The Truth about Trade: What Critics Get Wrong about the Global Economy' (2016) 95 *Foreign Affairs* 84.

scares' in global supply chains, however, are much more disruptive than a model of perfect competition where one product can be replaced by a like-product. When demand for pork meat dropped, so did the demand for all associated agricultural products needed to maintain global pork trade (i.e., soybeans and corn used to feed hogs).[37] This meant that some grain-related commodity prices increased, affecting other meat industries that rely on the same commodities for feeding. In turn, this affected the global supply of live cattle, though its capacity to replace pork meat finally allowed it to increase its exports marginally and thus come out ahead from the A1H1 crisis.[38] On the other hand, for example, a recent outbreak of A1H1 flu made China once again restrict the import of certain foreign pork, and, in the process, save the Thai poultry industry from bankruptcy by increasing its exports by 60 per cent.[39]

Naturally, pharmaceutical companies came out ahead as well. Novartis, who produces the A1H1 Monovalent Vaccine, increased its stock price roughly by 24 per cent after the WHO declared the pandemic.[40] Roche, whose affiliated researchers participated in the WHO's declaration of the pandemic, saw an increase in stock price of 33 per cent.[41] GlaxoSmithKlein (GSK) – owner of the Pandemrix vaccine used for all A1H1 flu strains – saw its stock price rise by 26 per cent during the same time.[42] It is noteworthy that Pandemrix is a generic vaccine which was, in fact, patented in 2006, *before* the A1H1 influenza outbreak. Its use is only authorised once a pandemic has been officially declared by the WHO,[43] tying its financial dividends to the decisions of the seemingly technocratic Emergency Committee.[44] In this

37 R. Johnson, 'Potential Farm Sector Effects of 2009 H1N1 "Swine Flu": Questions and Answers' (Congressional Research Service of the United States 2009), 10–11 https://sgp.fas.org/crs/misc/R40575.pdf, accessed 30 August 2021.

38 W. Attanavich, B. McCarl and D. Bessler, 'The Effect of H1N1 (Swine Flu) Media Coverage on Agricultural Commodity' (2011) 33 *Applied Economic Perspectives and Policy* 241, 248.

39 P. Tanakasempipat, 'Thai Chicken Exports to China Set to Rise amid Swine Fever Outbreak' *Reuters* (19 December 2019).

40 Stock quotes taken from the Bloomberg website. See, www.bloomberg.com/quote/NOVN:SW, accessed 26 November 2021.

41 See, www.bloomberg.com/quote/ROG:SW, accessed 26 November 2021.

42 See, www.bloomberg.com/quote/GSK:US. Only in Europe, around 31 million people received a Pandemrix vaccine. See: I. Sample, 'Swine Flu Vaccine Can Trigger Narcolepsy, UK Government Concedes', *The Guardian* (19 September 2013), www.theguardian.com/society/2013/sep/19/swine-flu-vaccine-narcolepsy-uk.

43 'Pandemrix EPAR Summary for the Public', https://web.archive.org/web/20091015042718/http://www.emea.europa.eu/humandocs/Humans/EPAR/pandemrix/pandemrix.htm, accessed 31 August 2021.

44 In its European Public Assessment Report, the European Medicines Agency considers that the risks of Pandemrix are outweighed by its benefits only in situations where the WHO has officially declared a pandemic. See, 'Assessment Report for Pandemrix', www.emea.europa.eu/humandocs/Humans/EPAR/pandemrix/pandemrix.htm, accessed 26 November 2021.

context, it is worth highlighting that Article 28(j) of the WHO constitution gave the Director-General far-reaching executive power to 'combat epidemics', though Article 12 and Article 49 of the 2005 IHR now allow him to declare a public health emergency of international concern upon consultations with its Emergency Committee.[45] In other words, the characterization of a health emergency as a pandemic triggers a cascade of events that enormously profits pharmaceutical companies that have developed and stocked the relevant vaccines (and in particular GSK with its patented Pandemrix), while leaving other firms on the losing side of the competition. One of GSK competitor's – Baxter International – saw the price of its stock contract roughly by 18 per cent during the time of the A1H1 Pandemic even though they were amongst the selected providers of A1H1 vaccines.[46]

In addition to the financial wins and losses, there are some other economic costs arising out of the WHO involvement in the A1H1 outbreak. Believing that the virus had originated in Mexico, its nationals suffered particularly bitter responses. China forced healthy Mexican residents and travellers into quarantine, while Chilean authorities refused to host Mexican football teams for international competitions.[47] Its national airline – AeroMéxico – was hit particularly hard by the pandemic, forcing its owners at the time to consider a merger with its rival, Mexicana.[48] Mexico, however, was not even in the top

[45] Two features stand out from this procedure: on the one hand, the IHR are binding on all members of the Organization, and, on the other hand, the Emergency Committee is composed of members appointed entirely by the Director-General.

[46] See, www.bloomberg.com/quote/ROG:BAX. Paul Flynn, a Labour MP lamented in the British Parliament that '[t]he [UK] Government bought 23.9 million doses of vaccine from drug manufacturer GlaxoSmithKline and five million from rival company Baxter. They are still smiling. The question remains, how powerful were the tentacles of the pharmas in the WHO. Who was calling the tune?', available at https://paulflynnmp.typepad.com/my_weblog/2010/01/. The market logic, however, cuts both ways – even though Baxter provided millions of vaccines to the UK, its shareholders saw their investment contract, probably due to the comparative disadvantage with other pharmaceutical companies. GSK not only stocks anti-pandemic drugs, but its research and development expertise includes the production of medicine for respiratory infectious diseases, while Baxter's expertise lies with kidney disease-related pharmaceuticals.

[47] M. Lacey and A. Jacobs, 'Even as Fears of Flu Ebb, Mexicans Feel Stigma', *The New York Times* (4 May 2009), www.nytimes.com/2009/05/05/world/asia/05china.html, accessed 31 August 2021.

[48] 'AeroMéxico announced in late Jun-09 that it has no immediate plans to merge with rival Mexicana, despite wide speculation that a deal was planned as a way for the airline to survive the catastrophic decline in tourism caused by the economic crisis and the flu outbreak'. See: 'AeroMéxico: A US Bank's Baby' CAPA - *Centre for Aviation* (3 July 2009), https://centreforaviation.com/analysis/reports/aeromexico—a-us-banks-baby-8249, accessed 31 August 2021.

10 countries of A1H1 infections per capita, and had fewer overall infections than the United States, Brazil or India.[49]

This general overview of the redistributive effects arising from the WHO involvement in the A1H1 Pandemic gives a good sense of the sort of directions that the relevant economic resources can take. It is a game in which billions of dollars, global market shares and nationalist stereotypes are up for grabs. Naturally, the affected parties do not go gently into the good night, and pushback to the different decisions generally ensues. I discuss this backlash in Section 10.4.

10.4 BACKLASHES

There are three broadly defined areas where the WHO's handling of the A1H1 Pandemic provoked some criticism: (1) issues with nomenclature; (2) issues with transparency; and (3) issues with the science.

The most pressing issue when the A1H1 virus broke was its problematic name. In a noble attempt to avoid stigmatization, the WHO purposely tried to avoid any connection with Mexico and instead attempted to find a generic name which could be closely associated with the disease: pigs.[50] Once the needless pig slaughter and transmission misinformation followed, the WHO renamed it to A1H1 influenza virus.[51] The economic and animal damage from the misnomer, however, was already significant, as the Chicago Board of Trade's futures price for lean hogs dropped nearly 15 per cent within a week of the 'Swine Flu' announcement, equivalent to roughly 7 million dollars in lost revenue.[52] Joseph Domenech, the chief veterinary officer at the FAO, further criticised Egypt's needless slaughter of pigs, by stating that '[t]his is one of the results of this strange way of defining the disease as a swine influenza. That's why the FAO and OIE are fighting to get that name changed because it's a totally undue focus on swine'.[53]

49 'ECDC Daily Update: Pandemic (H1N1) 2009' (European Centre for Disease Prevention and Control, 2010), https://reliefweb.int/sites/reliefweb.int/files/resources/F52C202A5DE3176A492576B600098FCA-Full_Report.pdf, accessed 1 September 2021.

50 Attanavich et al., 'Effect of H1N1'.

51 M. Enserink, 'Swine Flu Names Evolving Faster than Swine Flu Itself' (2009) 324 *Science* 871.

52 'Putting H1N1 Flu in Perspective, Detailing the Economic Impact', *National Hog Farmer* (11 May 2021), www.nationalhogfarmer.com/news/0511-H1N1-flu-economic-impact, accessed 1 September 2021.

53 Ph Stewart, 'UN Agency Slams Egypt Order to Cull All Pigs', *Reuters*, 29 April 2009, www.reuters.com/article/idUSLT11250, accessed 1 September 2021.

The WHO learned its lesson from this hiccup. Pursuant to Articles 2 and 21 of the WHO constitution, the Organization has 'to establish and revise as necessary international nomenclatures of diseases' and has the power (through the Health Assembly) to adopt 'nomenclatures with respect to diseases, causes of death and public health practices'. In connection to this function and authority, the WHO produced the International Classification of Diseases (ICD, now in its 11th version). The related best practices for disease classification now explicitly forbid the use of geographical locations or animal species (such as 'Swine Flu' or 'Mexican Flu'),[54] in order to avoid negative consequences for trade and persons. The negative impact of the A1H1 misnomer, however, has left some important lessons which have affected future nomenclature procedures.[55]

In addition, some of the harshest criticism to the WHO's handling of the A1H1 Pandemic was related to the lack of transparency in its actions. Let us recall that the declaring of a public health emergency, and even more so when it gets upgraded to a pandemic, has some immediate economic effects.[56] To begin with, once a pandemic is declared, some stockpiled, generic vaccines for A1 strains of influenza are authorised for use. This is the case, for example, of GSK's Pandemrix vaccine.[57] And although the scientific community has been urging pharmaceutical companies to stock a broad range antiviral drugs,[58] large pharmaceutical companies like Pfizer have presumably taken a 'one bug, one drug' approach as pandemic-related vaccinations have little market once the crisis is held at bay.[59]

54 'World Health Organization Best Practices for the Naming of New Human Infectious Diseases', www.who.int/news/item/08-05-2015-who-issues-best-practices-for-naming-new-human-infectious-diseases, accessed 1 September 2021.

55 Nomenclature procedures, mechanisms and databases are now designed to be able to respond to the sort of misnaming in the A1H1 scenario, which has also brought more scientific awareness. See F. Konings et al., 'SARS-CoV-2 Variants of Interest and Concern Naming Scheme Conducive for Global Discourse' (2021) 6 *Nature Microbiology* 821.

56 In this specific case, the controversy surrounding the declaration of a pandemic was so extreme that it led to the unusual situation of the Council of Europe officially criticizing the World Health Organization, in what Deshman calls a case of 'horizontal review'. See A. Deshman, 'Horizontal Review between International Organizations: Why, How, and Who Cares about Corporate Regulatory Capture' (2011) 22 *European Journal of International Law* 1089.

57 The marketing authorisation for Pandemrix has now expired and no renewal has been sought, presumably for lack of demand.

58 See, for example, J. S. MacKenzie et al., 'The WHO Response to SARS and Preparations for the Future', in S. Knobler et al. (eds.), *Learning from SARS: Preparing for the Next Disease Outbreak* (National Academic Press, 2004), 42.

59 E. Dolgin, 'The Race for Antiviral Drugs to Beat COVID: and the Next Pandemic' (2021) 592 *Nature* 340.

More noteworthy, though, is the relationship between the WHO's organs (especially the Director-General and the Executive Board) and the scientific community at large. After all, 'the WHO relies to a large extent on what may be called epistemic authority – the authority that comes from knowledge and experts',[60] who are all part of the same professional, academic and social circles. It should not come as a surprise, then, that many of the members of the Emergency Committee who gave green light for the pandemic declaration had previously and simultaneously worked with pharmaceutical companies that benefitted from the WHO's decisions. It is worth noting that the IHR Emergency Committee met on nine occasions from April 2009 to August 2010. Out of its 15 members, 4 declared a conflict of interest with pharmaceutical companies: (1) Professor Arnold Monto, who had consulted for GSK, Novartis, Roche, Baxter and Sanofi; (2) Dr John Wood, who consulted for Sanofi Pasteur, Novartis, the International Federation of Pharmaceutical Manufacturers and Associations, and Powdermed; (3) Professor Maria Zambon, whose lab at the British Health Protection Agency had received funding from Sanofi, Novartis, GSK, CSL and Baxter; and (4) Professor Neil Ferguson, who had consulted for Roche, Novartis, and GSK. None of these consultancies was remunerated for more than USD 10,000.

At the time, the Organization took the risky step of maintaining the identities of the members secret in order 'to protect the committee from outside influences'.[61] Notwithstanding, later investigations showed that 'some 13 of the 29 members of the review panel are members of the International Health Regulations itself and one is the chair of the Emergency Committee. To critics that might suggest a somewhat incestuous approach'.[62] This prompted a rare and strong-worded rebuke from the WHO, stating that '[t]he world is going through a real pandemic. The description of it as a fake is wrong and irresponsible. We welcome any legitimate review process that can improve our work'.[63]

60 Klabbers, 'The Second Most Difficult Job', 277. For a more detailed account of the epistemic authority exercised by and through the WHO, see J. Klabbers, 'The Normative Gap in International Organizations Law: The Case of the World Health Organization' (2019) 16 *International Organizations Law Review* 272.

61 D. Cohen and Ph Carter, 'WHO and the Pandemic Flu "Conspiracies"', (2010) 340 *British Medical Journal* 1274, 1278. In the time since, the WHO has made these names and conflict of interest statements public on their website.

62 Ibid., 1279.

63 'Statement of the World Health Organization on Allegations of Conflict of Interest and "fake" Pandemic', https://apps.who.int/mediacentre/news/statements/2010/h1n1_pandemic_20100122/en/index.html, accessed 2 September 2021.

In addition, some significant criticism was levelled at the decision to raise the A1H1 outbreak from Phase 5 (sustained community transmission) to Phase 6 (pandemic phase). To begin with, by the time of this declaration (May 2009) only 61 deaths had been verified to have been caused by the A1H1 virus, which seemed trivial in comparison to the economic impact of the characterization.[64] To make matters worse, and after the WHO had been encouraging states to rely on a series of documents which outlined some pandemic preparedness guidelines, some member(s) of the Secretariat erased the relevant documents from the WHO's public information system and amended the definition of 'pandemic' to exclude a death-toll threshold.[65]

Both the Emergency Committee's findings and the new definition of Phase 6 – which relied exclusively in the geographical spread of the disease – were dispositive factors in the declaration of a pandemic. As pressure grew in the final months before the World Health Assembly's meeting for the WHO to revise its internal procedures in order to determine whether the declaration of the A1H1 Pandemic was in accordance with the Organization's policies, a review committee was convened to audit the decision-making process.[66] The review concluded, in its relevant parts, that '[a]though confidentiality represented an understandable effort to protect the members from external pressures, this paradoxically fed suspicions that the Organization had something to hide' and that there had been a '[l]ack of a sufficiently robust, systematic and open set of procedures for disclosing, recognizing and managing conflicts of interest among expert advisers. In particular, potential conflicts of interest among Emergency Committee members were not managed in a timely fashion by WHO'.[67] In relation to the conflict of interests, and the confusion over the definition of 'pandemic' and whether the declaration had satisfied the requirements of Phase 6, the review unequivocally stated that:

> Some commentators accused WHO of rushing to announce Phase 6 and suggested the reason was to enrich vaccine manufacturers, some of whose advance-purchase agreements would be triggered by the declaration of Phase 6. Far from accelerating the declaration of Phase 6, WHO delayed

[64] A. Kamradt-Scott, 'What Went Wrong? The World Health Organization from Swine Flu to Ebola', in A. Kruck, K. Oppermann and A. Spencer (eds.), *Political Mistakes and Policy Failures in International Relations* (Palgrave Macmillan, 2018), 199.

[65] Ibid.

[66] C. SooHoo, 'WHO to Revise Definition of Pandemic Phases amidst 2009 H1N1 Pandemic' (2009) 7 *Biosecurity and Bioterrorism: Biodefense Strategy, Practice, and Science* 117.

[67] 'Report of the Review Committee on the Functioning of the International Health Regulations (2005) in Relation to Pandemic (H1N1) 2009', 131–132, https://apps.who.int/gb/ebwha/pdf_files/WHA64/A64_10-en.pdf, accessed 1 September 2021.

> declaration until evidence of sustained community spread in multiple regions of the world was undeniably occurring. As far as the Review Committee can determine, no critic of WHO has produced any direct evidence of commercial influence on decision-making.[68]

Lastly, in relation to the science surrounding the A1H1 pandemic, it should be noted that the reference to pigs in the naming of the disease is the culprit for the relevant criticism. As discussed before, all trade-related concerns were grounded on the relationship between the A1H1 virus and swine, which was scientifically unrealistic.[69] Even though the IHR of 2005 includes an explicit awareness of the potential negative externalities of its executive decisions, markets react to WHO decisions far more sensitively than their institutional expectations.[70] The lack of scientific basis for these sanitary and phytosanitary concerns ultimately led to the issue being resolved: according to the WTO, partial resolution of this issue was communicated on 29 October 2020. Though no major trade irritants were reported at the WTO, the large gap between scientific evidence and phytosanitary restrictions imposed by China led some scholars to argue for a more robust WHO–WTO institutional collaboration.[71]

10.5 AFTERTHOUGHTS ON COVID-19

To talk about the WHO's role in global health crisis now seems to require a distinction between two epochs: pre-COVID-19 and post-COVID-19.[72] It is worthwhile recalling that the major constitutional changes to the WHO's executive powers came precisely before the A1H1 outbreak with the adoption

[68] Ibid., 133.

[69] 'Import Restrictions on Pork Products Relating to Influenza A/H1N1: Extracts from SPS Committee Meeting Summary Reports' (supra note 34); Schmidt, 'Swine CAFOs'.

[70] Article 2 of the IHR of 2005 reads in full: '[t]he purpose and scope of these Regulations are to prevent, protect against, control and provide a public health response to the international spread of disease in ways that are commensurate with and restricted to public health risks, and which avoid unnecessary interference with international traffic and trade'.

[71] See T. Mackey and B. Liang, 'Lessons from SARS and H1N1/A: Employing a WHO–WTO Forum to Promote Optimal Economic–Public Health Pandemic Response' (2012) 33 *Journal of Public Health Policy* 119.

[72] See S. Rana, 'Seismic Shifts: The COVID-19 Pandemic's Gendered Fault Lines and Implications for International Law' (2021) 39 *Australian Yearbook of International Law Online* 91; Y. Shany, 'The COVID-19 Pandemic Crisis and International Law: A Constitutional Moment, A Tipping Point or More of the Same', in M. Mbengue and J. d'Aspremont (eds.), *Crisis Narratives in International Law* (Martinus Nijhoff, 2021), 100; A. Peters, 'International Law between COVID-19 and the Next Pandemic' (2022) Research Paper No. 2022-18 *Max Planck Institute for Comparative Public Law & International Law*.

of the IHR – in particular, it granted the Director General with broad powers to handle emergencies – which were tested in 2015 with the Ebola outbreak.[73] In this sense, it was not in the context of institutional powers that the WHO's involvement in the COVID-19 crisis was different.

And yet different it was. The sheer scale of disruption of COVID-19 is on a different level of magnitude, with some models estimating a death toll between 12 and 22 million,[74] and an economic cost of 16 trillion.[75] Any other comparable emergency was either protracted (e.g. the AIDS pandemic which lasted for about 40 years) or medieval (e.g. the Bubonic Plague of the fourteenth century). Within modern health emergencies, there is no other comparable outbreak that required an institutional response of this scale.

The reactions to the WHO's declaration of the COVID-19 pandemic rang some familiar notes. As with previous outbreaks, the timing of the organization for the different phasic decisions was heavily criticized, though this time around the problem was with delay rather than prematurity, perhaps in deference to China.[76] This might well be a backlash from previous experiences – such as the A1H1 flu – where the organization seemed to have jumped the gun. In any event, an independent review organized by the WHO pursuant to the World Health Assembly's resolution 73.1 concluded that

> [T]he [WHO's] alert system does not operate with sufficient speed when faced with a fast-moving respiratory pathogen, that the legally binding IHR (2005) are a conservative instrument as currently constructed and serve to constrain rather than facilitate rapid action and that the precautionary principle was not applied to the early alert evidence when it should have been.[77]

Notwithstanding these critiques, it is important to remember that Article 2 of the IHR establishes that the Director-General must consider 'unnecessary interference with international traffic and trade' before making any determinations on the classification of an outbreak. In addition, as discussed in this

73 M. Espinal et al., 'International Health Regulations, Ebola, and Emerging Infectious Diseases in Latin America and the Caribbean' (2018) 108 *American Journal of Public Health* S466.

74 D. Adam, 'The Pandemic's True Death Toll: Millions More than Official Counts' (2022) 601 *Nature* 312.

75 D. Cutler and L. Summers, 'The COVID-19 Pandemic and the $16 Trillion Virus' (2020) 324 *Journal of the American Medical Association* 1495.

76 G. L. Burci, 'The Outbreak of COVID-19 Coronavirus: Are the International Health Regulations Fit for Purpose?', *EJIL: Talk!* (27 February 2020), ejiltalk.org, accessed 16 November 2022.

77 'COVID-19: Make It the Last Pandemic' (The Independent Panel for Pandemic Preparedness & Response), 26, https://theindependentpanel.org/, accessed 16 November 2022.

chapter, any decision made by the Director-General has an impressive radiating effect, from the capacity to bankrupt major international companies (such as commodity traders, airlines) to the immediate reshuffling of major financial resources.

Precisely because of the redistributive potential of its decisions, it is doubtful that the WHO will ever be able to react to an international crisis in a way which commentators will find entirely suitable and timely. In hindsight it might be possible to argue that it was too early with the A1H1 pandemic and too late with COVID-19, though striking the perfect balance while information rapidly flows will be an extremely difficult balancing act even after these experiences. To deepen this difficulty, it is worth remembering that, as a general rule, legal decision-making in international law relies on asymmetric information, multiple stakeholder sensitivity and general uncertainty.[78]

In this context, it is perhaps more pragmatic to reflect on the effects of this international health governance model and its implications, rather than the audacity of the organization and its Director-General in handling some of the most complex international emergencies of our time.

10.6 CONCLUSION

If the last 20 years of institutional practice of the WHO – and particularly during the COVID-19 pandemic – have taught us anything, it is perhaps that the theoretically powerful constitution of the Organization is exactly that: *theoretically* powerful. Even when expanding its mandate, the WHO has not resorted to its constitutional authority but rather to the 'undertaking of new tasks'.[79]

The A1H1 Pandemic, however, reveals an additional layer of this non-explicit exercise of authority. To be fair, both the infection rate, lethality and the economic impacts of the crisis look petty in comparison to the COVID-19 pandemic, or even the Ebola outbreak of 2014. But the disease does not need to have far-reaching or pandemic effects for the WHO to have a profound redistributive capacity. Regardless of the conclusions of the relevant reviews and audits, it is clear that the relationship between the WHO and third parties, in particular the private sector (mostly pharmaceutical companies), can muddy the ultimate purpose: safety for human life.

78 See, e.g., F. Kratochwil, *The Status of Law in World Society* (Cambridge University Press, 2014).

79 Alvarez, *The Impact*, 261.

The billions of dollars won and lost, the effects on human and animal life, as well as the WHO's self-awareness and administration in the wake of the A1H1 outbreak, show that seemingly small decisions in seemingly trivial places – such as the appointment of Emergency Committee members, or the definition of diseases and guidelines – have a real and lasting impact. If, indeed as we expect, pandemics will become more frequent and more devastating, then some thought and critique into the relevant institutional decision-making seems warranted. It is important not to forget that some of the questionable effects of the WHO decisions are entirely unintentional, inviting us to ponder whether piling onto the logistical challenges imposed by worldwide pandemics may be curbed or avoided entirely.[80]

This presents us with a choice. We can either commit to an institutional theory that cannot account for the full picture of the entanglement between organizations and the world or we can theorize about these relationships in a way that is not blind to the arrangements and organizational practices that ultimately affect third parties. Considering the sort of technocratic expertise and impeccable political shrewdness that we expect from the WHO civil servants, it might come in handy to conceive their work in a context that does justice to tension between their mission and their markets.

[80] Perhaps one of the most straightforward ways to avoid conflicts of interests between pharmaceutical companies and public health management is to restrict the patenting of pandemic vaccines, in the same vein that Jonas Salk – the inventor of the Polio vaccine – asked 'could you patent the sun?' See J. Smith, *Patenting the Sun: Polio and the Salk Vaccine* (Morrow, 1990).

11

The Problem of Applicable Law in the Contractual Relations between International Organizations and Private Parties

ORFEAS CHASAPIS TASSINIS

11.1 INTRODUCTION

While the aspired goals of international organizations remain as diverse as they have ever been, the way they go about achieving their aims is strikingly more uniform from a legal standpoint. They buy, and occasionally sell, things to help fulfill their missions; they sign rental or loan agreements; they enter into employment contracts with their staff. In short, they generally employ all the familiar legal tools that one would expect a legal person to do. And yet, there is often an impression that interactions between international organizations and private parties take place outside any legal order, in a peculiar legal void of sorts. Solidifying this impression, most international organizations seldom include clauses on applicable law in their contracts. Even when they do, the question remains as to what the legal basis for such a choice would be. Revisiting this old analytical tangle, this chapter's ambition is to chart the legal space in which interactions between organizations and private parties register, a space seemingly in-between the national and the international. To this end, this chapter seeks to unpack the legal issues surrounding the law applicable in contractual relations between international institutions and their counterparties.

Contrary to the many, and valuable in their own regard, studies that examine this problem in the practice of international organizations, the idea here is to approach the topic from first principles.[1] Accordingly, this chapter

[1] For some classic works in that regard, see C. W. Jenks, *The Proper Law of International Organization* (Oceana, 1962); F. A. Mann, 'The Proper Law of Contracts Concluded by International Persons' (1959) 35 *British Yearbook of International Law* 34; H. Batiffol,

asks how we can understand the problem by (re-)introducing to the debate first-order concepts of private international law and legal theory, rather than provide new empirical evidence as to how international organizations actually deal with this problem in their usual order of business. Drawing connections with existing puzzles, the aim here is to abstract, wherever necessary, from the presumed idiosyncrasies of international organizations, and to underline them, wherever they matter. Owing to the length of this chapter as well as the complexity at stake, the aim is to lay the issues out in the open rather than to conclusively resolve them, even though ideally a problem well-stated is a problem half-solved.

Where to start then? Part of the ambiguity surrounding the problem turns to lingering impressions that the problem of applicable law in the contractual relations of international organizations and private parties merits special treatment in at least two ways.

The first claim to special treatment draws on the lingering assumption that international organizations are indeed themselves "special" legal subjects, meaning that their "nature" should justify a different set of considerations than those that would normally apply to other legal entities. Typical examples of this are the perceived need for international institutions to be impartial actors above their members, or the idea that they are entities that operate beyond the reach of national jurisdictions. This is sometimes interpreted as suggesting that normal rules of private international law do not apply to them, especially when these lead to the application of some national law. Questioning the analytical import of these considerations, this chapter argues that the problem need not always be handled separately from that of states contracting with private parties.

A second claim to special treatment boils down to the idea that there is something inherent in the legal set up of an international organization that justifies differentiating between the various contractual relations that it partakes in. Various criteria, and resulting classifications, have been produced throughout the years, generally leading back to the idea that international organizations are set apart from other subjects, and most importantly states, by the special mission or function that they are mandated to perform. This has led some to argue that contracts are closely related to the organizations'

Problèmes des contrats privés internationaux (Association des Études Internationales, 1962); N. Valticos, 'Les contrats conclus par les organisations internationales avec des personnes privées. Rapport provisoire' (1977) 57 *Annuaire de l'Institut de droit international* 6; F. Seyersted, *Common Law of International Organizations* (Martinus Nijhoff, 2008).

function or employment contracts are to be treated differently than other types of contracts, such as, for example, the buying of stationary equipment.

Here the question lies primarily with the justification for such potentially different treatment: is it due to the particular relationship between an organization and the functions that it has been entrusted with carrying out? Or can it be explained on the basis of how more general principles and standards of private international law are to be applied in concrete cases? The chapter at hand gravitates toward the second line of approach. While theoretically one can find justifications for different treatment hardwired in an organization's constitution, most of what happens can be explained on the basis of applying, if somewhat creatively, what may otherwise appear as relatively mundane, classic notions of private international law.

Aiming to unpack these two claims to special treatment and work toward an overall clarification of the problem, this chapter proceeds as follows. Section 11.2 provides a general outline of the ideas of applicable law and party autonomy, which are normally at the epicenter of any conflict of laws analysis. This leads to two further questions which are tackled in Sections 11.3 and 11.4. Thus, Section 11.3 discusses whether international organizations and their contractual partners are free to choose the law that is to apply to their contracts. Section 11.4 explores what law should apply when international organizations do not exercise their freedom to choose the applicable law, or when that freedom is exercised beyond its recognized limits.

Before moving forward, a caveat is in order regarding the value of the practice of the organizations themselves in relation to the questions at hand. In certain cases, practice is important for a doctrinal analysis, especially if one considers the role it performs for the formation of customary international law. For example, some authors have suggested that party autonomy now enjoys customary status in public international law.[2] Naturally, this could be relevant to a discussion such as ours.

But things get more complicated when considering the practice of international organizations as such. First, there is the question of whether that practice counts toward the formation of new norms of customary international law. Even if we are inclined to count it as such, and probably rightly so, there is the question regarding the standard against which that practice is to be weighed. If, for example, the conclusion is that international organizations do

[2] For a discussion, see A. Mills, *Party Autonomy in Private International Law* (Cambridge University Press, 2018). See also A. F. Lowenfeld, 'International Litigation and the Quest for Reasonableness' (1994) 245 *Recueil de Cours* 1, 256; P. E. Nygh, *Autonomy in International Contracts* (Oxford University Press, 1999), 45.

not merit special treatment from states, or even contractual partners in general, then the practice of these institutions, even assuming that it was uniform, would be but a small drop in the ocean of state practice in that regard. Hence, it would seem that the relevance of this kind of practice is a second-order problem. Third, international organizations' practice in this field appears in fact too fragmented and often too obscure to extract general guidance from it. Finally, practice can only be relevant according to its own terms. For example, a well-established practice by certain international organizations to not include provisions on applicable law in their contracts tends to beg the question rather than answer it. All this hardly means that the practice of international organizations is inconsequential for what is examined here; it just goes to show that it needs to be put into the proper perspective.

11.2 OVERVIEW: APPLICABLE LAW AND PARTY AUTONOMY IN CONTEXT

11.2.1 *Applicable Law and Related Concepts*

The idea of applicable law refers to the laws or set of rules that are supposed to govern a legal relation. But how can we conceptualize this link between a particular body of law to a given legal relation? Standard private international law theory provides two possible answers.[3]

The first is that pairing a legal relation, including a contract, to a body of applicable law occurs through an exercise of state authority. Amongst international lawyers this is also known as part of exercising a state's so-called prescriptive jurisdiction. From this angle, the question posed is "which jurisdiction can claim that its laws govern this contract?" Often this inquiry has no single or straightforward answer. Multiple jurisdictions may have competing claims, making it unclear whose would prevail from a (real or imagined) objective point of view.

The second theory is that, at least when it comes to contracts, the source of the link between a given legal relation and a set of rules is, in the first instance, the choice made by the parties themselves. This theory is not to be confused with the idea that national jurisdictions (or, in certain cases, rules of international law) may recognize the validity of party choice. In those cases, one could argue that party choice is effective *because* it is recognized by state power. By contrast, this theory suggests that this relationship is flipped, and

[3] J. Basedow, *The Law of Open Societies: Private Ordering and Public Regulation in the Conflict of Laws* (Martinus Nijhoff, 2015), 115ff.

that party choice is grounded on some perceived natural capacity of individuals to determine the law applicable to them regardless of the confines of any particular legal system.[4]

While resolving this theoretical debate between these two schools of thought is beyond the ambition of this chapter, it is worth noting that they are not necessarily incompatible in terms of legal outcome when viewed from an objective point of view. Just as the claim of a state that its national laws should govern a given legal relation may or may not be recognized and given effect in the courts of another state, so the claim to a natural right of choosing the applicable law may or may not be denied from the perspective of a particular legal order. In both cases, the source of the claim to have a particular law apply remains theoretically intact, and in a way out of reach; it is rather that the effects of that source may or may not be recognized as valid within another legal order.

Thus, the idea of applicable law is inherently related to the concept of power, and the limits thereof, be that the power of a state to have its laws apply to a given situation or that of a party to a contractual relation to choose those rules for itself. This makes the concept of applicable law distinguishable from two related ideas: incorporation of contractual terms by reference and choice of forum.

The former concerns the case where the parties to a contract elect to include into their contract a provision to the effect that certain rules are incorporated by reference as terms of the contract. This is essentially a shorthand for drafting terms into the contract, equivalent to cutting and pasting the incorporated rules into the contract. Incorporation by reference is thus an expression of the capacity of the contractual partners to determine the contents of their contract (also known as contractual autonomy) rather than their decision to anchor it to a specific legal order. As just discussed, the latter is a manifestation of party autonomy, a concept closely related but distinct from contractual autonomy.[5] This is important to note as standard contracts of international organizations with private parties frequently include substantive references to all sorts of laws and regulations, including those of the international organization itself. When this happens, these references do not constitute "applicable law" in the sense of private international law, but rather incorporations by reference.[6]

4 Ibid., 125.
5 Mills, *Party Autonomy*, 23ff.
6 Cf E. Morlino, *Procurement by International Organizations: A Global Administrative Law Perspective* (Cambridge University Press, 2019), 279.

Choice of forum on the other hand is an expression of party autonomy and reflects the parties' choice of a forum for submitting potential disputes arising out of their contract. In practice, choices of forum in international organizations' contracts with private parties are much more common than express provisions on applicable law. It is worth noting in this regard that choice of forum and choice of applicable law are independent and may thus differ;[7] parties' choice of a forum need not necessarily be aligned with their choice of law and vice versa. Moreover, in this case too, the link between dispute and forum can be conceptualized along state-sovereignty or voluntarist lines. In the first case, the link is an expression of adjudicative jurisdiction; in the latter, it is a fundamental prerogative of the parties to choose a forum.

To sum up, party autonomy to choose the law applicable to a contract is a concept distinct from, even if related to, choice of contractual terms and choice of forum. The older theory is that party autonomy in this sense is derivative from national jurisdiction, meaning that it is effective only when a legal order recognizes it as having the power to determine the applicable law.[8] There are, however, those who argue that party autonomy in choosing applicable law is a "natural" prerogative, at least when it comes to contracts.

11.2.2 *Limits of the Classic Debate*

While in practice express choice of law agreements are given effect under the law of most states,[9] it is not hard to notice that the general theoretical outline of applicable law and party autonomy has been constructed with entities other than international organizations in mind. One could argue that, even if only state authority can effectively recognize party autonomy to choose applicable law, this is of little concern to such creatures as international organizations, who are supposed to hover above the national jurisdictions of states, and especially their member states. A similar reaction may be prompted by the idea that a contract must necessarily be anchored to a national, and thus state, law (and jurisdiction), where "state" refers to a territorial legal order.[10] This goes back to a dictum of the Permanent Court of International Justice (PCIJ)

[7] Although inferences about choice of law may be drawn from the choice of a forum. See Seyersted, *Common Law*, 478; Ph Sands and P. Klein, *Bowett's Law of International Institutions*, 6th ed. (Sweet & Maxwell, 2009), 369.

[8] As already noted within this section, there are some who argue that party autonomy is a rule of customary international law. In that sense, however, it would still be derivative or "granted" by the law, even if that law was international in nature.

[9] Mills, *Party Autonomy*, 313.

[10] Ibid., 496.

in the *Serbian Loans* case that "[a]ny contract which is not a contract between States in their capacity as subjects of international law is based on the municipal law of some country."[11] And yet, the reader may be familiar with other concepts of law that go beyond the state, most notably the idea of *lex mercatoria*. A debate endures in private international law scholarship as to whether non-state law may indeed be the law applicable to a given contract. The subject is potentially of heightened relevance for international organizations, institutions that in practice often choose some form of non-municipal law when they do include choice of law provisions in their contracts. In short, our theories of private international law have not necessarily been crafted with subjects such as international organizations in mind. The question then becomes whether we can bridge that gap by revisiting the fundamental premises that underpin our analyses of contracts concluded between states and private entities, or even between private entities as such.[12]

11.3 INTERNATIONAL ORGANIZATIONS' "RIGHT" TO PARTY AUTONOMY?

11.3.1 *The Idea of a "Right" to Party Autonomy*

In order to make sense of this conceptual landscape in relation to international organizations, we need to disambiguate the very notion of party autonomy in choosing the applicable law. Is party autonomy, as often referred to, really a "right," or is it analytically more accurate to describe it as something else?

The classic Hohfeldian analysis of the concept of "right"[13] into four fundamental legal conceptions and their correlatives can be instructive in that regard. As is well-known, Hohfeld drew a key distinction between privilege, power, right, and immunity. A privilege denotes the freedom or liberty to do something, without anyone having a corresponding duty to accommodate it. For example, I am at liberty to pick up a five-euro bill that I see lying on the pavement, but others do not have a duty to not take it themselves. By contrast,

[11] *Serbian Loans Case* (France v Yugoslavia), [1929] Publ. PCIJ Ser. A, No. 20, 41. Or, as the classic decision of the House of Lords in *Amid Rasheed Shipping Corporation Kuwait Insurance Co.* put it: "contracts are incapable of existing in a legal vacuum. They are mere pieces of paper devoid of all legal effect unless they were made by reference to some system of private law . . ." [1984] AC, 65 (Lord Diplock).

[12] See also Mann, 'The Proper Law of Contracts', 46.

[13] W. N. Hohfeld, 'Some Fundamental Legal Conceptions as Applied in Judicial Reasoning' (1913–14) 23 *Yale Law Journal* 16.

a right refers to an entitlement that corresponds to a duty of another entity. For instance, if it is my money that falls from my pocket, I have a *right* to get it and others have a duty not to take it. The third relevant concept is that of a power, that is the recognized capacity of an entity to change its legal entitlements. Someone's power corresponds to another's liability to have their legal entitlements changed. Think, for example, of the captain of a commercial flight ordering the crew and passengers to wear their seatbelts; the captain's order changes the normative situation for the crew and passengers by imposing a new duty on them, namely, to wear their seatbelts. Finally, immunity is one's freedom from the legal power or "control" of another with respect to a given legal relation. A classic example is the immunity from enforcement that states enjoy from domestic courts of other states.

When thinking about party autonomy of contractual partners, including international organizations, we should be careful to distinguish what is in fact more accurately described as a bundle of privileges, rights, and powers. In one sense, party autonomy could be seen as belonging to a category of "natural" liberties; anyone is theoretically free to write down whatever applicable law they prefer on a piece of paper. The question is whether there is a recognized power to do so, and by whom this might need to be recognized. In the absence of a specific treaty providing so[14] or a recognized rule of customary international law,[15] the answer to that question must be sought in the confines of the jurisdiction within which the problem arises. The takeaway here is that, while international organizations and their contractual partners have a general freedom to choose the law applicable to their contract, this does not necessarily correspond to a recognized, let alone "inherent," power or right to do so. In the absence of rules of international law to that effect, recognition of a

[14] See, e.g. Article 3 Rome I Regulation, that provides that "A contract shall be governed by the law chosen by the parties ... [b]y their choice the parties can select the law applicable to the whole or to part only of the contract ... [t]he parties may at any time agree to subject the contract to a law other than that which previously governed it"; See also the 1994 Mexico Inter-American Convention on the Law Applicable to International Contracts that provides in Article 7 that "[t]he contract shall be governed by the law chosen by the parties" and in Article 8 that "[t]he parties may at any time agree that the contract shall, in whole or in part, be subject to a law other than that to which it was previously subject, whether or not that law was chosen by the parties." The conceptualization of the rights of the parties to choose the law applicable as a Hohfeldian power, that is as a recognized capacity to change their legal entitlements, does not mean that there might not be limitations imposed on the exercise of that power. For example, Article 3(2) of the Rome I Regulation provides that "[a]ny change in the law to be applied that is made after the conclusion of the contract shall not prejudice its formal validity under Article 11 or adversely affect the rights of third parties."

[15] Even in those cases one could question whether these instruments create an individual entitlement as opposed to certain obligations between states.

choice of applicable law will always be relative to the forum that is called upon to decide on this question. Outside of the courts set up by organizations themselves, this forum could theoretically be a national court or an arbitral tribunal.

11.4 PARTY AUTONOMY BEFORE NATIONAL COURTS

The immunities that international organizations enjoy under international law will most often shield them in practice from appearing before national courts, but not as a matter of course from the validly exercised prescriptive jurisdiction by the state in question. The latter does not appear to contain any exception specifically regarding international organizations. This is important as, despite immunities from adjudicative jurisdiction, there are various scenarios where national courts may end up exercising jurisdiction over cases in which one of the litigants is an international organization,[16] including when an international organization itself sues a private party for non-fulfillment of a contractual obligation.[17]

Although rare, these instances pose interesting theoretical questions. National jurisdictions will most often grant a power to determine the applicable law to contractual partners. Yet, they will frequently also pose limitations or exceptions to that power.[18] For example, many legal orders impose subject matter limits to party autonomy relating to consumer, employment, or real estate contracts.[19] Others require that the law chosen by the parties must have an objective connection to their relationship[20] or reserve some safety net of public policy exceptions that apply regardless of choice of law.[21] The question here is whether there is a special reason, by virtue of one party to the contract being an international organization, that would signify a departure from the application of a states' standard rules of private international law, or at least their interpretation.

Assuming that there is no general customary rule on party autonomy as a limit to prescriptive jurisdiction, one such reason could be a member state's

[16] For studies on this, see A. Reinisch, *International Organizations before National Courts* (Cambridge University Press, 2000); A. Reinisch (ed.), *Challenging the Acts of International Organizations before National Courts* (Oxford University Press, 2010).

[17] See, e.g. K. Schmalenbach, 'Challenging Decisions of the European Schools before National Courts', in A. Reinisch (ed.), *Challenging the Acts of International Organizations before National Courts* (Oxford University Press, 2010), 178.

[18] See, e.g. Mills, *Party Autonomy*, 455–520.

[19] See, e.g. Rome I regulation.

[20] See Mills, *Party Autonomy*, 360ff.

[21] Ibid., 486ff.

obligation to recognize the independence of the organization. Several international organizations scholars have brought up similar reservations, especially in earlier studies of this topic. But here the parallel with states may put this problem into a better perspective. Just as the application of local law to a contract between an embassy of a state and a local cleaning contractor is not generally thought of as infringing upon that state's independence or makes it any less sovereign, in the same manner the application of national law does not appear to *ipso facto* render the organization any less independent. In fact, international organizations often choose national law as the applicable law to their contracts.[22] That choice generally seems to be based on the national law of the place where the contract is to be carried out.[23] There may of course be good policy reasons for those organizations to maintain the appearance that no national law is preferred over another, especially in high profile cases. Yet, as a matter of principle, there seems to be no reason to distinguish between states and international organizations in that regard. Again, concerns for operational independence (or the appearance thereof) may affect the choice of applicable law at an internal level, but neither the choice of a particular national law nor its application regardless of a choice to the contrary automatically undoes the institution's formal independence.

The question then becomes one of interpreting the obligations of a state as a member of an organization as these emanate from the latter's constituent instrument. Naturally, here the answer will depend on the constitution involved. It is possible to imagine that certain member state obligations, for example to "give every assistance in any action"[24] that an organization takes, could entail recognizing the latter's party autonomy when it comes to choosing applicable law, especially in relation to contracts that bear an elevated relation to the organization's mission. Nevertheless, this would in reality constitute a separate argument regarding the interpretation of the specific treaty in question, instead of being the default position for all international organizations regardless of circumstances.

There are two more potential complications regarding party autonomy and applicable law that may be seen as peculiar to international organizations. The first is that some provisions of private international law are not easily translatable to these institutions. Take, for example, article 8 of the Rome I Regulation that deals with employment contracts. According to

[22] Valticos, 'Rapport provisoire', 30.

[23] Sands and Klein, *Bowett's Law*, 369.

[24] See ,e.g. article 2(5) of the UN Charter: "All Members shall give the United Nations every assistance in any action it takes in accordance with the present Charter . . ."

paragraph 1 of that article, party choice can be disregarded when it derogates from the protection of the law that would otherwise be applicable to an employment contract. Paragraph 2 provides that employment contracts are "governed by the law of the country in which or, failing that, from which the employee habitually carries out his work in performance of the contract"; paragraph 3 continues that, where the applicable law "cannot be determined pursuant to paragraph 2, the contract shall be governed by the law of the country where the place of business through which the employee was engaged is situated"; and paragraph 4 concludes that "[w]here it appears from the circumstances as a whole that the contract is more closely connected with a country other than that indicated in paragraphs 2 or 3, the law of that other country shall apply."

Could such wording (and the similar wording that is often found in domestic conflict of laws provisions) accommodate the application of an organization's internal regulations when it comes to employment contracts? One could plausibly maintain that an analogy could be drawn here between "country" and "international organization,"[25] and that, even though international organizations may not enjoy a spatial dimension, in the sense of a distinct territory from where the employee carries out their work, such an employment contract would seem to be "more closely connected" (to borrow Rome I's language) to the international organization than to any country. This end-result may seem only natural to scholars of international organizations, but there indeed have been cases relating to employment contracts with international organizations where national courts have applied national law.[26]

A second reason why party autonomy may stumble in practice before a national court is a choice of non-state law as the applicable law. Traditionally domestic jurisdictions have shied away from recognizing the validity of such choices, the assumption being (at least from their perspective) that any contract has to be governed by the law of a state.[27] Although this received position has not been entirely uncontested over the years,[28] it still holds true for major jurisdictions, such as China, most of the United States, and Europe,

[25] For the conceptual justification of such an analogy, see F. L. Bordin, *The Analogy between States and International Organisations* (Cambridge University Press, 2018).

[26] E.g. Schmalenbach, 'Challenging Decisions of the European Schools', 178.

[27] Mills, *Party Autonomy*, 496. See also *Serbian Loans Case*.

[28] See, e.g. Hague Principles on Choice of Law in International Commercial Contracts 2015, whose article 3 states that: "The law chosen by the parties may be rules of law that are generally accepted on an international, supranational or regional level as a neutral and balanced set of rules, unless the law of the forum provides otherwise" (the Hague Principles were prepared by an expert group rather than government representatives, although they were later approved by the Hague Conference on Private International Law).

including where the Rome I Regulation or the older Rome Convention apply.[29] This is potentially important for international organizations when they choose non-state law to govern their contracts. Such non-state law typically includes "general principles of law,"[30] "general principles of international commercial law,"[31] or models laws such as those of UNCITRAL.[32] It would be hard to imagine a national court applying such non-state law when it would otherwise not, just because one of the contractual partners is an international organization.

11.5 PARTY AUTONOMY BEFORE AN ARBITRAL TRIBUNAL

Such complications regarding party autonomy in choosing applicable law are hardly relevant when the dispute is led before an arbitral tribunal. This is important in practice as, in most cases, contracts between international organizations and private parties will have an international arbitral tribunal as the designated forum for dispute resolution. The difference with national courts at this point is that party choices of applicable law are invariably accepted and honored by arbitral tribunals.[33] The current prevalent theories about arbitration suggest that arbitrators are inherently obligated to apply the law chosen by the parties as their authority is itself contractual.[34] In turn, the contract that gives rise to the authority of the tribunal need not, from the perspective of the

[29] See generally, Mills, *Party Autonomy*, 499–511; the prevalent academic and judicial view is that this limits the scope of the Rome Convention to only national legal systems, excluding international law. For the Rome Convention, see e.g. A. Briggs, *The Conflict of Laws* (Clarendon Press, 2002), 159; for the Rome I Regulation, see O. Lando and P. A. Nielson, 'The Rome I Regulation' (2008) 45 *Common Market Law Review* 1687. See also H. Dang, 'The Applicability of International Law as Governing Law of State Contracts' (2010) 17 *Australian International Law Journal* 133, 137–140.

[30] Valticos, 'Rapport provisoire'. See, e.g., the general terms and conditions of the FAO on applicable law: "[n]otwithstanding any specific provision herein, this Contract and any disputes arising therefrom shall be governed by general principles of law, to the exclusion of any single national system of law."

[31] See, e.g. the general terms and conditions of UNRWA, which provide that "[t]he decisions of the arbitral tribunal shall be based on general principles of international commercial law."

[32] See, e.g. International Fund for Agricultural Development, General Terms and Conditions for the Procurement of Goods, para. 32. Generally, see K.-H. Böckstiegel, 'The Application of the UNIDROIT Principles to Contracts Involving States or Intergovernmental Organizations', in Special Supplement 2002: UNIDROIT Principles of International Commercial Contracts: Reflections on their Use in International Arbitration (ICC, 2002), 52–53, who identifies at least five different alternatives (national law with a stabilization clause; general principles of law; public international law; *lex mercatoria* and trade usages; UNIDROIT principles).

[33] B. Hayward, *Conflict of Laws and Arbitral Discretion: The Closest Connection Test* (Oxford University Press, 2017), 13–14; Mills, *Party Autonomy*, 277.

[34] Mills, *Party Autonomy*, 512.

tribunal, be anchored to any system of *national* law so long as it reflects an exercise of autonomy pursuant to transnational standards.[35] In that sense, it is almost as if arbitration forms a closed system that can exist (in practice, if not in theory) "off the grid" of municipal laws that was envisaged in *Serbian Loans*.[36]

The consequence of this deference is a widespread readiness on behalf of arbitrators to accept any party choice, including non-state law, as the applicable law.[37] This is important for international organizations that, as mentioned, often choose non-national laws to govern their contracts. Whether these alternative sources qualify as "laws" is in a sense beyond the point, so long as arbitrators are prepared to treat them as such for the purposes of resolving particular disputes.

Although most of the arbitral practice involving international organizations remains unpublished due to confidentiality restrictions, there have apparently been instances where, following party agreement, non-state law has been applied. For example, Karl-Heinz Böckstiegel refers to a case of ad hoc arbitration under the UNCITRAL Arbitration Rules where Canadian claimants instituted proceedings against the United Nations (UN) with respect to claims arising out of the transport of its personnel around the globe. During the proceedings the two parties agreed that "generally accepted principles of international commercial law" were to be applied, informed by the UNIDROIT Principles. According to Böckstiegel, this was accepted by the tribunal that relied on the UNIDROIT Principles in order to define the generally accepted principles of commercial law under which it would interpret the contract.[38]

[35] Ibid., 278; E. Gaillard, *Legal Theory of International Arbitration* (Martinus Nijhoff, 2010), 35. Gaillard suggests that this view "is based on the consensus existing among States on this matter rather than on the isolated will of a given sovereign to accept the existence of this private means of dispute resolution."

[36] This is not to say that this development is altogether positive. As Horatia Muir Watt has critically remarked, international commercial arbitration "has now established itself as a largely auto-poetic, parallel, world of private justice, supposedly secreted by a self-regulating transnational merchant community." H. Muir Watt, '"Party Autonomy" in International Contracts: From the Makings of a Myth to the Requirements of Global Governance' (2010) 6 *European Review of Contract Law* 250, 254. There is, of course, still the view that international commercial arbitration must be grounded in some national jurisdiction, which in practice is that of the seat of the arbitration. See F. A. Mann, 'State Contracts and International Arbitration' (1967) 42 *British Yearbook of International Law* 1.

[37] See, e.g. ICC Arbitration Rules 2017, article 21; UNCITRAL Rules on International Commercial Arbitration, article 33; UNCITRAL Model Law on International Commercial Arbitration, article 28; 1961 European Arbitration Rules, article VII.

[38] Böckstiegel, 'The Application of the UNIDROIT Principles', 54.

11.6 APPLICABLE LAW IN THE ABSENCE OF A CHOICE BY THE PARTIES

While party choice of applicable law poses interesting theoretical questions, in practice many, if not most, contracts concluded by international organizations include no reference to any applicable law whatsoever. This was the chief finding of the empirical study conducted by the Institut de Droit International in the 1970s,[39] and still appears to hold true, especially among the UN family of organizations.[40] As already mentioned, the absence of such choice may reflect the organization's willingness to appear as equidistant from the national jurisdictions of its member states or even a genuine hesitation of predisposing a thorny question. Regardless of the reasoning behind this, the fact remains that, apparently, most contracts concluded by international organizations and private parties contain no provisions on applicable law.

A way out of this silence can be trying to infer the tacit intention of the parties. Yet, this often proves problematic in practice, as have been attempts to come up with objective criteria to that effect, including in relation specifically to contracts concluded by international organizations.[41] The most classic criterion put forward, namely that party selection of the seat of arbitral proceedings also implies party choice of law, has increasingly been recognized as "irrational and inaccurate."[42] It seems in that regard that absent an actual agreement or positive evidence of the concurrent intentions of the parties, this automatic presumption is generally not accepted.[43] This would be especially relevant to international organizations, were most often there is a complete silence regarding the question of applicable law.[44] Indeed, this does not leave much space for inferences of party intentions to be drawn.[45] What is more, in the case of some organizations there seems to be a conscious choice to *not* predetermine the applicable law.

Given that in most cases of contractual disputes between international organizations and private parties there is no provision on applicable law, the question arises as to what law is to be applied. This is a question that is difficult

39 Valticos, 'Rapport provisoire'.

40 Morlino, *Procurement by International Organizations*, 278.

41 Valticos, 'Rapport provisoire', 55–64.

42 J. Lew, L. Mistelis and S. Kröll, *Comparative International Commercial Arbitration* (Kluwer, 2003), 412, 415–416.

43 Gary Born, *International Commercial Arbitration* (Kluwer, 2014), 2636.

44 Seyersted, *Common Law*, 485; when a reference is made, it is sometimes to general principles of law, but more frequently to domestic law; see also the empirical study carried out by the Institut in 1979. See Valticos, 'Rapport provisoire', 36.

45 Born, *International Commercial Arbitration*.

to answer in the abstract. National fora will naturally apply domestic conflicts rules to determine the applicable law (provided that they have jurisdiction to hear a case involving an international organization). Arbitration also holds an endless world of possibilities depending on the specific stipulation on applicable law contained in the relevant rules setting up the dispute settlement procedures that have been agreed upon by the parties.

Dispute settlement bodies that have been set up by international organizations, of course, stand apart here. Normally these enjoy jurisdiction in relation to disputes that may arise between the organizations and their employees regarding their contracts of employment and terms of appointment. The UNIDROIT Administrative Tribunal stands out in this regard because it has jurisdiction to also hear claims arising from contractual claims with third parties, provided that they have consented to the tribunal's jurisdiction. According to the organization's statute, the Tribunal shall decide cases "by applying the provisions of the Statute and of the Regulations as well as the general principles of law" (article 7*bis*). This is an interesting provision insofar as it minimizes discretion in identifying the applicable law and excludes on its face national as well as international law. Other administrative tribunals have a much more limited jurisdiction than this, a factor that significantly narrows the rules of law that they are called upon to apply. Institutions such as the ILO Administrative Tribunal or the UN Administrative Tribunal are not tribunals of general competence in relation to potential claims under national labor laws; they only have jurisdiction to hear complaints on the nonobservance of contracts of employment of staff members or of the terms of appointment of such staff members.[46]

In practice, apart from rare cases such as the UNIDROIT's Administrative Tribunal, most instances involving contracts with third parties that include a choice of forum, will designate third-party arbitration for the settlement of potential disputes. Here again, things will invariably turn to the rules of procedure of the relevant body entrusted with setting up the arbitration.[47] The almost countless variations of provisions on applicable law in this respect can be abstracted into two broad categories: the *voie indirecte* and the *voie directe* (the "indirect" and "direct" path).[48] The *voie indirecte* means that the relevant provision entrusts the arbitrator to apply conflicts of laws rules in

46 See UNAT Statute article 2; ILOAT Statute article II. This cannot exclude theoretically the need for applying supplementary rules, relating for example to the capacity to conclude a contract or its interpretation.

47 Arbitral tribunals are generally not under an obligation to apply the conflicts rules of the state in which their seat is located.

48 Generally, see Hayward, *The Closest Connection Test*, 2.22ff.

order to identify the governing law. The *voie directe* means that the arbitrator can directly choose the law that is to apply in a certain case. Both "paths" have a restricted and an unrestricted variant, whereby the choice of the arbitrator is or is not subject to limitations.

The *voie directe* is by far the most prevalent way of dealing with the problem of applicable law in arbitral practice.[49] A popular formulation of this "direct path" is that the arbitrator shall apply "the rules that he or she determines appropriate" or "applicable." Similar formulations exist in the provisions of the UNCITRAL Rules 2010, the AAA International Arbitration Rules 1991, the ICC Rules 2012, the SCC Rules 2010, and many others.[50] Considerably less prevalent are provisions that incorporate some conflict of laws test, perhaps the most notable case here being the Swiss Rules 2012 that stipulate that the arbitrator shall apply "[T]he rules of law with which the dispute has the closest connection."

The standard formulation of the *voie directe* has been criticized for being too wide and too open to arbitral discretion, and potentially to choices made arbitrarily or at least without proper, transparent reasoning.[51] Those valid criticisms notwithstanding, the standard does not seem particularly problematic when applied to international organizations. On the contrary, it might prove more accommodating to arbitrators seeking to go beyond national laws when that would seem necessary. The problem of course is that there is a cloud of mystery as to when exactly that would be "appropriate"; international organizations and their contractual partners defer the question to arbitrators, who in turn are faced with the same problem, even as they are equipped with a wide enough discretion to not have to hammer out a conflicts test of general application. This, coupled with the fact that most arbitral awards (including those involving international organizations) are confidential, means that we can only speculate as to what goes on when a choice of the "appropriate" applicable law is to be made. This result can only be unsatisfactory from a theoretical perspective.

On the flipside, the "closest connection" test, hardwired in the provisions on applicable law of some rules of arbitration as we have seen, seems more geared toward objectivity and predictability. Of course, the two are not incompatible; indeed, one can make the argument that it is "appropriate" to apply the law with the closest connection to a dispute.[52] The closest connection test is established enough in its application to help with standard contractual relations such as the rental of offices or the provision of supplies but

49 Ibid., 2.49.

50 For a fuller list, see ibid., 2.39.

51 Ibid., 3.81-3.104; G. Cordero-Moss, 'International Arbitration and the Quest for the Applicable Law' (2008) 8 *Global Jurist* 42.

52 Hayward, *The Closest Connection Test*, 5.01ff.

also suitably open ended to accommodate the peculiarities of international organizations, allowing for the possibility that, in certain cases, the rules most closely connected to a dispute are those of the organization. These could include, for example, staff or procurement rules and regulations.[53]

11.7 CONCLUSION

It was once said that the "realm of the conflict of laws is a dismal swamp, filled with quaking quagmires and inhabited by learned but eccentric professors who theorize about mysterious matters in a strange and incomprehensible jargon."[54] International organizations' law is also often described as a field, "richly filled with paradoxes,"[55] where the limits of analytical thought can be shown. Thus, the problem presented in the present chapter lies at the intersection of two challenging, if valuable, spheres of theory and scholarship. Every country has its own rules of private international law; every arbitral tribunal its own rules and provisions on how to decide disputes; and every international organization has its own practice in concluding contracts with third parties. Amongst this plethora of variables, the need to go back to first principles is a much-needed way forward, even as it might also be a demanding one.

Such an analysis, only presented here in its general outline, can help disambiguate the problem, and potentially yield new insights. As this chapter has argued, it can be misleading to simply assert that international organizations have a general and unqualified "right" to choose the law applicable to their contracts. They do, however, appear to have an inherent freedom to do so. The exercise of this freedom produces legal effects in a given legal order depending on the provisions of the latter (including any rules of international law that may apply). In practice, given the immunities that international organizations may enjoy from domestic jurisdiction, the forum will be either commercial arbitration or an international arbitral tribunal, both having their own provisions on applicable law.

[53] This could help rationalize distinctions drawn by authors between the various contracts signed by international organizations in terms of the law that should apply to them. See e.g., Jenks, *The Proper Law*, xxxv; Batiffol, *Problèmes*, 95.

[54] W. Prosser, 'Interstate Publication' (1952–53) 51 *Michigan Law Review* 959, 971.

[55] N. Blokker, 'International Organizations and Their Members' (2004) *International Organizations Law Review* 139, 161.

12

The Private Sector and Gavi, the Vaccine Alliance

A Story of Continuous Evolution

EELCO SZABÓ*

12.1 INTRODUCTION

In studying the relationship between international organizations and the private sector, Gavi, the Vaccine Alliance's (hereinafter Gavi or the Alliance) ever evolving engagement with the private sector provides interesting examples. Gavi receives funding from private foundations and companies, it operates on markets for vaccines and related commodities and affects private actors. As a Swiss foundation, Gavi is not formally an intergovernmental organization but rather a 'quasi international organization' which has privileges and immunities in its host state (Switzerland).[1] As an alliance of partners, Gavi's founding partners, including UNICEF, the World Bank and the World Health Organization (WHO), play essential roles in many of Gavi's activities relating to the private sector. Studying Gavi's engagement with the private sector, therefore, also provides insight into the interactions of these partners with the private sector.

This contribution looks at the practical operation of those interactions with the private sector and what lessons can be drawn from them. It starts with a brief overview of how Gavi's origins were influenced by private sector-related considerations and the role of the private sector in Gavi's governance. Section 12.3 addresses the vaccine procurement model and

* The author was Director of Legal at Gavi between 2010 and 2019; this contribution is written on a personal basis.

[1] For a more detailed description of Gavi and how it operates, see, e.g. E. Szabó, 'Gavi, the Vaccine Alliance: A Unique Case Study in Partnership' (2016) 13 *International Organizations Law Review* 149; and K. Klock, 'International Public Private Partnerships as Part of the Solution to Infectious Disease Threats: Operational, Legal, and Governance Considerations', in S. Halabi et al. (eds.), *Global Management of Infectious Disease after Ebola* (Oxford University Press, 2016), 157.

Gavi and its partners' approach to 'shaping' the vaccine market. Thirdly, the relationship with the private sector other than vaccine manufacturers is described. Before some concluding remarks, the last part is dedicated to a mechanism put in place in which Gavi funds partners – international organizations and the private sector – to support countries with their immunization programmes.

12.2 ENGAGEMENT WITH THE PRIVATE SECTOR: GAVI'S HISTORY AND GOVERNANCE

12.2.1 *Gavi's Origins and Establishment Process*

Gavi's origins date back to the late 1990s – a period during which there was a growing sense that the private sector could offer solutions for, or at least contribute to, development and public health challenges. The progress of international childhood immunization programmes was stalling. This was particularly affecting children in the poorest countries who were often not fully vaccinated against deadly diseases or even went without any immunization at all. At the same time, children in richer countries were protected by expensive new vaccines but lower-income countries could not afford most of these vaccines. This 'market failure' is at the heart of Gavi's establishment.

In March 1998, the World Bank convened a summit bringing together international organizations, the CEOs (chief executive officers) of vaccine manufacturing pharmaceutical companies, foundations and non-governmental organizations to discuss how to address the stagnation in vaccine delivery and the possibilities of developing new vaccines.[2] Lidén reports that the International Federation of Pharmaceutical Manufacturers & Associations (IFPMA) representative at the summit asked '[w]hy would you expect us to invest hundreds of millions of dollars in a new AIDS vaccine when there isn't anyone even buying existing vaccines for use in developing countries?'[3] The summit concluded that the most effective way to address these 'market failures' would be to stimulate the use of new and largely unused vaccines that were either too expensive or not a priority for countries struggling to immunize children against basic childhood infections.

2 For a comprehensive account of Gavi's (and other health partnerships') history, see J. Lidén, 'The Grand Decade for Global Health: 1998–2008' (Chatham House Working Group on Governance Paper 2, April 2013), at chathamhouse.org/sites/default/files/public/Research/Global%20Health/0413_who.pdf, visited 25 January 2023.

3 Ibid., 22–23.

Task forces – including the Rockefeller Foundation, WHO, UNICEF and the World Bank – were established to design solutions for this and, at a meeting in March 1999, a global vaccine alliance was proposed. At the same time, Bill and Melinda Gates had started to become interested in investing in development through the Bill and Melinda Gates Foundation (hereinafter Gates Foundation). They were intrigued by vaccines and the impact they could achieve on saving lives. However, looking at this through a 'private sector lens' they would want to ensure that their investment would be measurable and yield tangible results and would not come to replace government funding.[4]

Nevertheless, the Gates Foundation conveyed that it might make the unprecedented amount of $750 million available to a potential alliance and invited the partners engaged in its set up to a 'proto board' meeting in July 1999. The first formal Alliance Board meeting was held in October 1999 which included – beyond representatives from 'founding partners' WHO, UNICEF, the World Bank, and the Gates Foundation – donor governments, developing countries, the pharmaceutical industry, research and technical agencies and the Rockefeller Foundation.[5] A month later, the Gates Foundation signed a grant agreement guaranteeing funding to Gavi of $750 million for a period of five years.

The Alliance was set up as an unincorporated partnership with a representative Board and a small Secretariat that was hosted by UNICEF. The Gates Foundation grant was made to a United States charity (a 501(c)(3) not-for-profit organization initially called the Global Fund for Children's Vaccines) that was established to receive tax-exempt donations from private donors based in the United States as well as other grants, and fund the procurement of vaccines and other Gavi-supported activities. The US-based Gavi charity had a separate Board and its own staff as well. From 2009, the US charity and the Alliance Board 'merged' into one Board that governed a Swiss Foundation with privileges and immunities that also became the employer of Gavi Secretariat staff previously under the UNICEF contract.

12.2.2 *Gavi's Current Governance and Conflicts of Interest Approach*

Turning to Gavi's current governance, it has already been mentioned that vaccine manufacturers had a seat on the Alliance Board from the first

[4] Ibid., 24.

[5] Global Alliance for Vaccines and Immunization, First Board Meeting (GAVI/99.02), at apps.who.int/iris/bitstream/handle/10665/66204/GAVI_99.02.pdf;jsessionid=8D9B8CBD1AB538761F15548BEB78201F?sequence=1, visited 25 January 2023.

meeting. Over time, one seat was allocated to manufacturers from industrialized countries and one for industry from developing countries. Civil society organizations and the Bill and Melinda Gates Foundation represent other private sector interests on the Gavi Board. Donor governments and implementing country governments each have five seats which are organized by constituencies. The three founding intergovernmental organizations (UNICEF, the World Bank and the WHO) each have a voting seat on the Board. The Gavi Board of today is completed by one seat for research and technical institutes, nine people sitting in their private capacity and the CEO in a non-voting capacity.

This brief historical overview reveals how much engagement with the private sector is engrained in Gavi's DNA, giving meaning to its popular characterization of 'public–private partnership'. Pharmaceutical companies provided their views on solutions to the 'market failures' that were identified, they were involved in Gavi's establishment process, and remain well represented on Gavi's Board. The Rockefeller and Gates Foundations were collaborating closely with intergovernmental organizations to establish the new alliance. And, crucially, the previously unimaginable sum in the context of global health of $750 million came from one single private source of funding – the Gates Foundation.

Even if all of Gavi's stakeholders are committed to its goal of protecting more children with vaccines that are available and recommended by the WHO, their interests in the governance and activities of a multi-stakeholder partnership are wide-ranging. Moreover, the representatives from the public and private sector tend to have different perspectives and approaches to topics. As Liliana Andonova observed, partnerships like Gavi 'became platforms through which more dynamic collaboration with industry, funders and all relevant communities could be tested'.[6] One tool for ensuring the transparency and integrity of the decision-making processes of such partnerships is through the adoption of a conflict of interests policy.

In its early years, the Alliance board provided strategic and programmatic direction whereas funding decisions were made by the board of the Gavi Fund (the US-based Gavi charity holding its funds) which was a separate and independent board of people sitting in their private capacity. Given that there were no direct financial implications for stakeholders in the Alliance Board's decisions, this meant that conflicts of interests within the Alliance Board were relatively rare. After the creation of the Swiss Foundation in 2009 when the

6 L. B. Andonova, *Governance Entrepreneurs, International Organizations and the Rise of Global Public–Private Partnerships* (Cambridge University Press, 2017).

Alliance and the charity holding the funds were merged, management of conflicts of interests took on more prominence.

As would be expected, different views on how this should be managed, in particular regarding constituencies' own interests, existed. Then Legal Counsel of the WHO Gian Luca Burci described in 2009 that the 'reliance on corporate concepts of conflict of interests had occasionally to be reconciled with the approach taken by international organizations, which are reluctant to accept that the pursuit of their constitutional mandates through their participation in partnerships may be equated to a corporate interest to be disclosed and managed'.[7] Among international organization stakeholders a view that appeared common was that they considered that only if an entity would stand to generate a 'profit' could a conflict of interests arise. Funding the intergovernmental partners of the Alliance will be further discussed in Section 12.4.

Perhaps in line with the already discussed outlook on the private sector, in a Board meeting in 2011 Board members and other members of the delegations of industrialized- and developing country vaccine manufacturers were asked to leave the room prior to the discussion on whether Gavi would be extending its funding to vaccines against diseases not previously in its portfolio and as such also did not participate in the decisions.[8] Manufacturers considered this approach unduly harsh as their contributions, for example in relation to the lead time for production, could be helpful to the discussion and they would not have been the only stakeholder group interested in whether Gavi decides to extend its funding to other vaccines.[9] There are financial implications in such decisions that may affect donors, implementing countries that may benefit from Gavi support for additional life-saving vaccines and partners may be required to provide additional assistance. When similar discussions were held in subsequent years, manufacturers would be permitted to stay in the room, make a statement and answer questions but not vote on a decision.

Over time, an approach to conflicts of interest evolved in that any organization or constituency that would receive or would have the possibility of receiving funding as a result of a Board decision would be allowed to attend the discussion and make a statement or answer questions. However, such organizations or constituencies would not be permitted to vote on decisions

7 G. L. Burci, 'Public/Private Partnerships in the Public Health Sector' (2009) 6 *International Organizations Law Review* 359, 372.

8 GAVI Alliance Board Meeting, 16–17 November 2011, gavi.org/sites/default/files/board/minutes/2011/Board-2011-Mtg-03%20-%20Minutes.pdf, visited 25 January 2023.

9 'Board members representing the developing and industrialised vaccine manufacturers expressed some dissatisfaction with not being able to fully participate in the earlier discussion regarding the new vaccine windows'; ibid.

affecting them and this would be registered in the meeting minutes. This approach aims to build on the open nature of the Alliance with different and interests viewpoints that will be important to inform decisions while being disciplined about stakeholders not being seen as voting on decisions that may affect their budget.

Engagement with the private sector is part of Gavi's founding history. Also, its approach to managing conflicts of interests in the Alliance's governance evolved from excluding the private sector from participating in discussions that may have an impact on them to allowing all governance stakeholders that may have a financial interest in a matter to participate in the discussion but not in the decision.

12.3 VACCINE SUPPLY AND 'MARKET SHAPING'

12.3.1 *Gavi's Operating Model and Initial Approach to Influence the Vaccine Market*

Gavi's mission is 'to save lives and protect people's health by increasing equitable and sustainable use of vaccines'.[10] The main tenet of Gavi delivering on its mission is that it provides funding for the purchase of vaccines that eligible countries wish to add to their immunization program. To do so, countries request Gavi to fund the addition of a vaccine to its routine immunization program. If an independent committee of experts determines that the requesting country has the requisite capacity to manage this new vaccine along with its existing portfolio, Gavi will fund the costs of procuring the vaccine and shipping it to the country. With Gavi's funding commitment, the country could use domestic procurement channels to purchase vaccines but in practice nearly all countries request UNICEF to buy vaccines on their behalf that Gavi pays for. UNICEF will only buy vaccines that meet applicable WHO quality standards.

The limited availability of funds and uncertainty of demand in low- and middle-income countries resulted in vaccine manufacturers not being sufficiently incentivized to supply vaccines to that market and, thus, children not being immunized in those countries. By aggregating the demand of all Gavi-supported countries, UNICEF – as the procurement agent of Gavi-eligible countries – with funding from Gavi leveraged larger purchasing power than countries would have been able to generate if they would need to buy their

[10] Gavi, the Vaccine Alliance Strategy 2021–2025 (updated version for 2023–2025), at www.gavi.org/sites/default/files/2022-12/Gavi-5-1-one-pager-2023-2025.pdf, visited 25 January 2023.

own vaccines. This 'bulk' approach, which also assists in providing better forecasts of future needs, aimed to create more predictability for manufacturers and to help in driving prices down, especially when comparing it to a situation where countries would have to make their own procurement arrangements. Through this centralized approach, the Alliance tried to influence the vaccine market to enable access to vaccines for the poorest children.

A first foray into bringing Alliance partners together with the goal of accelerating the development of a pneumococcal conjugate vaccine ('PCV') was the advanced market commitment pilot for PCV. The PCV advanced market commitment pilot was also aimed at incentivizing the development of PCV vaccines that meet developing country needs and bringing forward the availability of PCV vaccines for those countries. Designed from 2006 to 2008, the PCV pilot was launched in 2009 when the Governments of Italy, the United Kingdom, Canada, the Russian Federation and Norway, together with the Gates Foundation, collectively committed a total of $1.5 billion specifically for the PCV advanced market commitment pilot. Gavi was still in its early years and 'the private sector was less well recognized as a major player in international development, and there was less experience with public–private partnerships in health'.[11] These factors made the pilot very innovative for its time but also contributed to a relatively cumbersome legal structure and governance model. However, it still serves as an excellent template for public–private collaboration to achieve a health and development outcome. Different Alliance partners contributed to the arrangement. Donors provided long-term funding security. Manufacturers producing a PCV vaccine meeting specific criteria would be eligible to participate in the advanced market commitment pilot and produce life-saving vaccines. The WHO would assess whether the vaccines meet quality and safety standards. Manufacturers would need to sign 10-year contracts in which they committed to selling their vaccines at a price not exceeding $3.50 per dose. In addition, they would receive a 'top-up' payment of $3.50 per dose for the first approximately 20 per cent of doses they would supply under the 10-year contract. UNICEF managed the procurement aspects and entered into the long-term contracts (with funding from Gavi). The World Bank held donor contributions in trust and transferred funds when required as well as providing a further guarantee of donor funding by putting the donor pledges on its balance sheet.

[11] Dalberg, *Gavi PCV AMC pilot: 2nd Outcomes and Impact Evaluation* (15 October 2021), at gavi.org/sites/default/files/evaluations/Gavi-PCV-AMC-pilot-2nd-Outcomes-and-impact-evaluation-Final-report.pdf, visited 25 January 2023, 17.

12.3.2 A More Active 'Market Shaping' Approach

Apart from the PCV advanced market commitment pilot, in the first 10 years of its existence Gavi mainly relied on the 'natural market forces' of having bundled demand with little to no additional interventions. As a result, Gavi did not have the impact on reducing vaccine prices that might have been expected and hoped for. The vaccine industry and others fed back that Gavi 'could have done much more' in this area.[12] Taking this feedback into account, Gavi adopted a Supply and Procurement Strategy for 2011–2015. Through accumulated experience and a better understanding of market characteristics, the new supply and procurement strategy established priorities on supply, costs and innovation, supported by increased transparency. Tools like risk sharing agreements and volume guarantees were also introduced as part of the more active 'market shaping' agenda under the Supply and Procurement Strategy.

Some initial examples of volume guarantees that were entered into provide an interesting insight into the complementary roles of the different Alliance partners and any constraints they may have in interacting with the market. As indicated in Section 12.3.1, UNICEF conducts competitive tender processes for most Gavi-supported countries.

In April 2012, supply agreements were signed with two rotavirus manufacturers that resulted in a price reduction of two-thirds compared to before. As the Alliance's procurement agency, UNICEF entered into these agreements under which a portion of the supply was prepaid (allowing manufacturers to recoup their investments earlier and thus offer a more competitive price) and the deal period was extended to five years (giving manufacturers increased visibility which also served as an incentive to lower prices).

A year later, agreements were reached with an Indian manufacturer which agreed to making a pentavalent vaccine available at a price of almost one dollar per dose less than the average price in the year before – that is, $1.19 compared to the average price of $2.17.[13] The Gates Foundation funded technical support to the manufacturer which helped it enter the market and provide additional supply.[14] The significantly lower price-point was

[12] CEPA LLP, *Gavi Second Evaluation Report* (13 September 2010), at gavi.org/sites/default/files/document/evaluations/GAVI_Second_Evaluation_Report_2010.pdf, visited 25 January 2023, 11.

[13] 'Indian Manufacturer Cuts Price of Childhood Vaccine by 30 Percent', at gavi.org/pentavaie.lent-vaccine-30-percent-price-drop, visited 25 January 2023.

[14] M. Malhame et al., 'Shaping Markets to Benefit Global Health – A 15-year History and Lessons Learned from the Pentavalent Market' (2019) *Vaccine* X 2 100033, 5, at

established through a volume guarantee that Gavi executed in parallel to the supply agreement that UNICEF entered into based on a tender process.[15]

The roles and responsibilities of the Alliance partners involved in these initial 'market-shaping' transactions took some time and practice to crystallize. As the longstanding procurement agent for countries' vaccine programs, UNICEF might have considered that it would be the natural fit to be the vaccine 'market shaper'. However, one aspect of UNICEF's financial rules emerged that limited its ability to conclude longer term procurement contracts or purchase guarantees which could help bring prices down. To mitigate financial risks to UNICEF, it cannot enter into such long-term contracts or volume guarantees unless the funds are in UNICEF's bank account – in cash or cash-equivalent in UNICEF's determination – at the time the contract is signed. This would mean that Gavi-provided funds would be tied up for the duration of the contract or guarantee which would not be an efficient use of available resources. For Gavi to provide a guarantee (and thus assume the payment responsibility on its books) to UNICEF associated with long-term contracts, it would have needed to be accompanied by a lien on Gavi's investment, which in turn put constraints on its ability to freely manage parts of its investment portfolio.[16] Gavi then explored whether the Gavi balance sheet could be used to guarantee such orders directly to manufacturers.[17]

While over time these types of long-term commitments may not have been the most-used interventions to help ensure availability of vaccines to developing countries at reasonable prices, they do show how different types of organizations can work together on a common goal in a manner that plays to their strengths and that each alone would not be able to achieve. UNICEF's tender processes give credibility to the selection process. Gavi's balance sheet allows for additional tools to help 'market shaping' goals. The Gates Foundation engages with manufacturers aiming to enter a vaccine market to ensure they receive continued funding for product development activities. Publicly-funded organizations might not be able to offer such product development support.

In 2016, the concept of 'healthy markets' became the overarching principle of the market shaping activities of the Alliance. Under this label, the Alliance works on balancing all the elements necessary to ensure sustainable and

mmglobalhealth.org/publications/shaping-markets-to-benefit-global-health-a-15-year-history-and-lessons-learned-from-the-pentavalent-vaccine-market/, visited 27 June 2023.

[15] Ibid.

[16] GAVI Alliance Board Meeting, *Final Minutes* (12–13 June 2012), at gavi.org/sites/default/files/board/minutes/2012/Board-2012-Mtg-02%20-%20Minutes.pdf, visited 25 January 2023, 9.

[17] Ibid.

healthy market dynamics for vaccines and immunization-related products, focusing on reliable, consistent, and affordable supply as an overarching objective. These factors somewhat pull in different directions and vary per vaccine. The activities that UNICEF, Gavi and the Gates Foundation take together on this are getting more and more sophisticated. Advanced market commitments and volume guarantees also played an important role in the response to COVID-19 as part of the COVAX facility and the COVAX advance market commitment that Gavi played a coordinating role in.[18]

12.4 PRIVATE SECTOR PARTNERSHIPS

The previous sections explained how Gavi's history, mission, operating model and activities are inextricably linked to the private sector – principally vaccine manufacturers – and that its establishment was only made possible by a very large donation from a private foundation. This part addresses Gavi's evolution of engaging with the private sector other than vaccine manufacturers. Before going into the details of this evolution, a few words on the role of the Gates Foundation in Gavi and its governance.

12.4.1 *Initial Years and the Gates Foundation Role*

The Gates Foundation propelled Gavi into existence with its $750 million starting grant, which inspired others to join. As of 30 June 2022, the Gates Foundation has made commitments to Gavi for a total amount of $4.1 billion and has remained one of Gavi's largest donors.[19] As one of the founding partners of the Alliance, the Gates Foundation had and continues to have a permanent seat on the Gavi Board. This is different from, for example, the Global Fund to Fight AIDS, Tuberculosis and Malaria where private foundations are allocated one seat on the board, the occupation of which is organized through a constituency process.

More generally, the Gates Foundation is a large donor to global health and is considered to have a major footprint on the approaches decided on in global health. Much has been written about the Gates Foundation driving the agenda of global health and its organizations with an apparent preference

[18] The author worked for Gavi until the end of August 2019, i.e. before the COVID-19 pandemic and the arrangements responding to that are beyond the scope of this chapter.

[19] Donor profiles, *The Bill & Melinda Gates Foundation*, at gavi.org/investing-gavi/funding/donor-profiles/bill-melinda-gates-foundation, visited 25 January 2023.

for technological solutions and a business-oriented approach.[20] A detailed analysis of that influence goes well beyond the scope of this contribution. However, the fact that the Gates Foundation is part of Gavi's governance provides a transparency on its positions and views – and the possibility for other stakeholders to influence or disagree with those – that is perhaps lacking in relation to its contributions to intergovernmental organizations such as the WHO (of which it is also one of the largest funders). In other words, in a public–private partnership like Gavi, the Gates Foundation and other private funders, as relevant, contribute to a pool of funds that they govern and make decisions on together with other stakeholders, including sovereign donors and implementing countries. On the other hand, grant contributions that private funders make to intergovernmental organizations risk undermining the established governance processes of the intergovernmental organizations.[21]

In the first 10 years of Gavi's existence, there was only one private sector donor other than the Gates Foundation: the La Caixa Foundation started funding Gavi in 2008. The La Caixa Foundation is the international cooperation programme of CaixaBank, a Spanish bank that is one of the largest in the Eurozone. Since 2008, the La Caixa Foundation has continued to raise funds for Gavi through public, employee, and business donations.

12.4.2 A *'Matching Fund' to Entice Private Sector Donations*

In June 2011, Gavi had its first ever 'pledging' or 'replenishment' conference in London. Such conferences are used for donors to commit funding for an upcoming strategic period to create more certainty on funding to be expected during that period. The investment case associated with the upcoming strategy allows donors to track results with their funding for a given timeframe. As such, the model of a pledging conference draws from private sector logic of investing for results.

In the wake of the global financial crisis, in the run up to the 2011 pledging conference there was uncertainty whether the funding targets could be met relying only on the traditional sovereign donors and the Gates Foundation. Extending and diversifying the donor base therefore became an important

[20] See, e.g. G. Blunt, 'The Gates Foundation, Global Health and Domination: A Republican Critique of Transnational Philanthropy' (2022) 98 *International Affairs* 2039; S. Harman, 'The Bill and Melinda Gates Foundation and Legitimacy in Global Health Governance' (2016) 22 *Global Governance* 349; L. O. Gostin, *Global Health Law* (Harvard University Press, 2014), 164–166; and K. T. Storeng, 'The GAVI Alliance and the "Gates Approach" to Health System Strengthening' (2014) 9 *Global Public Health* 865.

[21] K. Daugirdas and G. L. Burci, 'Financing the World Health Organization: What Lessons for Multilateralism' (2019) 16 *International Organizations Law Review* 299, 302.

objective of the pledging conference. Together with the United Kingdom government and the Gates Foundation, Gavi launched a mechanism called the 'Matching Fund' to incentivize private donors to contribute to Gavi.[22] The UK government and the Gates Foundation together made available approximately $110 million which would be used to 'double up' eligible private sector donations to Gavi in the 2011–2015 period. Under this Matching Fund arrangement, when a private sector partner contributes an amount to Gavi, the Matching Fund – using funds made available by the UK government and the Gates Foundation – donates the same amount to Gavi. This way private sector donations generated by a company and/or its employees, customers or other partners are doubled.

The Matching Fund aimed to utilize private sector resources and know-how to broaden the support base for the immunization and increase awareness of the Gavi brand as well as to leverage consumer and employee donations to Gavi. For the private sector, the model of the Matching Fund constituted a welcome boost in increasing their contribution. Sovereign donors contribute hundreds of millions or even billions of dollars to Gavi. Private sector contributions are generally more modest even if those donations are a considerable amount for the company making them. This has been reported as a barrier for private sector donors to contribute to organizations like Gavi. The Matching Fund allows them to double their contribution which is attractive in this context. From the matching donor's perspective, it allows them to hold back some funds that are only provided if Gavi secures private sector donations creating incentives for Gavi to actively fundraise from the private sector and diversify its funding base.

12.4.3 *An Evolving Private Sector Engagement Approach*

In the initial phase of the Matching Fund, private sector contributions were mostly in cash rather than in kind. The private sector engagement approach considerably evolved in Gavi's 2016–20 strategic period. In this period, Gavi aimed to move beyond cash contributions to leverage private sector expertise and innovation for the benefit of improved immunization programming at scale. This ambition was aligned to the goals and objectives of Gavi's strategy in that period which focused more on improving vaccine coverage, health systems strengthening, sustainability and market shaping. Moreover, Gavi's expanded focus on private sector engagement was consistent with a changing global context. With the adoption of the Sustainable Development Goals (SDGs) in 2015, there was increasing recognition that all sectors have an important role to

[22] The government of the Netherlands joined the Matching Fund in 2016 and the governments of Japan and Norway made modest contributions to the programme for the 2021–2025 period.

play in advancing inclusive, sustainable development. This prompted a growing interest in how the private sector can bring solutions to development challenges.

Alongside this, there was progressive thinking in the business world about how companies can create and deliver value across different economic, social and cultural contexts. The concept of 'creating shared value' was especially influential.[23] Shared value approaches built on the principles of corporate social responsibility to highlight the interdependencies between successful businesses and 'healthy communities'. 'Inclusive business models' and 'bottom of the pyramid' approaches went further to argue that poorer, under-served populations offer large, untapped markets for growing businesses. In recent years, there has also been a focus on 'environmental and social impact and governance' as a strategy for attracting employees that wish to contribute to society and improving staff motivation and productivity.

Against this background, Gavi's evolving private sector engagement approach was implemented through three distinct modalities. First, the financial contributions modality remained as an important aspect of the approach. These financial contributions from the private sector (other than the Gates Foundation) however continue to be relatively small at about 2 per cent of Gavi's total resources before being matched. Private sector funders range from companies to foundations. Some, such as Comic Relief, which conducted televised resource mobilization campaigns in the United Kingdom, yield brand recognition for Gavi and help bring the message of the importance of immunization to the health of the poorest children while for others the value to Gavi is predominantly or even exclusively in the cash contribution. The COVID-19 pandemic and the COVAX facility that Gavi is the host of have seen a new influx of private sector financial donations including from a number of large global corporations.

A second engagement model with the private sector is referred to as the 'leveraged', 'operational' or 'expertise based' partnerships. These types of partnerships combine financial support with a mix of awareness-building campaigns and market expertise to generate demand for health services or to overcome barriers to immunization. In this model, support for immunization is often combined with other development priorities such as education, gender equality or handwashing with soap. Operational partnerships go beyond fundraising and draw on private sector expertise to advance health and development objectives such as in Gavi's case increased access to immunization. This is generally referred to as a 'shared value' approach.

[23] Mott MacDonald, *Evaluation of Gavi's Private Sector Engagement Approach 2016–2020* (15 July 2021), at www.gavi.org/sites/default/files/evaluations/Evaluation-Gavi-PSEA-Final-Report.pdf, visited 11 July 2023, 18.

An early operational partnership that attracted a lot of attention is that with the UPS Foundation and Zipline. Zipline is a company that uses drone technology to support supply chain logistics. In its initial phase, Zipline transported blood supplies for transfusions and rabies vaccines in Rwanda. The activities were extended to Ghana later. Blood transfusions and rabies vaccines were not part of Gavi's mandate. However, the potential of drone technology for last-mile vaccine delivery made it an attractive proposition for Gavi to participate in. Furthermore, like with other partnerships of this nature, the UPS Foundation contribution for the purpose of the partnership was matched through Matching Fund donations.

An operational partnership with Unilever aimed to build awareness and drive behaviour change among parents by stressing the importance of handwashing with soap and immunization to tackle the biggest child killers – pneumonia and diarrhoea. Unilever invested Euro 2.9 million and Gavi matched that so that the promotion material could be doubled and twice as many parents could be reached by the combined messaging. This raises an interesting question regarding these types of partnerships in that Gavi would be unlikely to have invested these funds in the promotion material but for the partnership with Unilever. However, given that the number of parents reached with an immunization message under this joint approach with Unilever would be much higher than Gavi would be able to achieve on its own it may be considered a worthwhile investment, especially at a time when Gavi started to become more involved in 'generating demand' to help ensure that all children are immunized.

Other operational partnerships include a project with telecommunications provider Orange in Ivory Coast that aims to increase immunization coverage through a mobile phone application that uses text and voice messages to provide vaccination information and remind parents of appointments in local languages. A partnership with Mastercard operates by storing child immunization data on a secure patient-retained digital card. These patient data are then uploaded to an electronic health information system where it replaces paper-based vaccination cards, registers and reports. The digital card could also be used for other purposes such as accessing other health information or cash transfers and other financial benefits. This project is piloted in Mauritania and Ethiopia and other countries that are eligible to receive Gavi support[24] can express an interest to join. These are

[24] Gavi focuses its support on the world's poorest countries and bases eligibility for its support on national income at an established threshold of gross national income per capita based on World Bank data, Gavi Application Process Guidelines, www.gavi.org/sites/default/files/support/ApplicationProcess_Guidelines.pdf, visited 10 July 2023, at 24.

some examples of operational partnerships and new ones keep being developed as Gavi scopes the market.

The third and final method for engaging the private sector is through 'innovation partnerships'. These partnerships are sourced through the 'Innovation through Uptake, Scale and Equity' (INFUSE) mechanism, which was launched at the World Economic Forum in 2016. INFUSE aims to create an innovation ecosystem that can assist new ideas and technologies that can radically change immunization delivery and help Gavi countries accelerate the introduction of new technology to enhance their health outcomes. Each year an INFUSE theme is chosen where technology could improve vaccine delivery. Gavi then issues a call for innovations around the theme. A panel (that includes intergovernmental partner organizations and implementing country governments) selects a number of businesses and innovators to collaborate as part of the INFUSE community on ways to improve, align and integrate their innovations. From the INFUSE community the panel selects a few of the most promising approaches – the so-called INFUSE Pacesetters. These selected businesses are connected to Vaccine Alliance partners to help take their solutions to scale. In January 2023, Gavi launched the second iteration of INFUSE – INFUSE 2.0 – which features a digital platform to simplify connections between the INFUSE community and by 2030 expects to secure more than $500 million in private investments to promote access to vaccines and immunization innovations.

A notable Gavi collaboration that emanated from the INFUSE process is with the Asia Africa Investment and Consulting (AAIC) – a Japanese growth equity fund. Under the partnership, AAIC provides up to $3 million to invest in INFUSE Pacesetters. The idea of INFUSE has always been that Gavi links selected Pacesetters to investors. There are, however, some risks with an approach where Gavi selects investment opportunities and suggests the investor to the Pacesetter. It is therefore important to set boundaries on mutual expectations and Gavi made it very clear in that context that it will not take part in investment deals and is not responsible for the outcomes of negotiations or the performance of any investment.[25] Such a 'matchmaking' approach would seem to be unusual in the realm of international organizations – even if there are no real costs to the organization and legal risks could be mitigated it seems most international organizations would still not be in a position or wish to be promoting a particular innovation including by

[25] 'Gavi and Japanese Growth Equity Fund Collaborate to Support Innovative Startups for Immunisation', at gavi.org/news/media-room/gavi-and-japanese-growth-equity-fund-collaborate-support-innovative-startups, visited 25 January 2023.

recommending investors to invest. It is notable that the AAIC investment does not appear to have been matched by the Matching Fund and AAIC does not appear on Gavi's 'donor' overview, which may be due to the fact that the investments are into the Pacesetters rather than Gavi or its countries.

Other INFUSE partnerships include a digital medical passport for children in the form of a necklace or health card operated by a not-for-profit digital health provider called Khushi Baby which allows for medical records to be always and more easily accessible to health workers. Nexleaf Analytics is another not-for-profit organization that was selected as an INFUSE Pacesetter. The Nexleaf partnership aims to create and implement a software solution that would allow Gavi and Gavi-supported countries to monitor cold chain equipment performance through wireless remote temperature monitoring. Three organizations provided funding to Nexleaf, at least one of which was matched through the Matching Fund and the project built on initiatives in Kenya, Mozambique and Tanzania.

INFUSE partners indicate that partnership with Gavi can help to raise their profile on the international stage, provide opportunities for further testing and adaptions and may facilitate entry into new product markets.[26] This may be a positive development, especially for those companies and organizations selected. However, the engagement with the private sector is a means to an end – increasing access to immunization in resource poor settings – and not an end in itself. There is limited visibility on the views from governments and partner international organizations involved in these projects and on impact data to assess whether they have a positive influence on immunization rates in those countries. One could imagine that it might be interesting for countries to have access to and be able to use cutting edge technology and innovations but the critical measure of success will be more children immunized. It may be too early to draw meaningful conclusions on these aspects.

12.4.4 *General Considerations on Private Sector Partnerships*

During the initial strategic period of the private sector engagement approach between 2016 and 2020, Gavi established 20 distinct private partnerships that leveraged private sector expertise, including new technologies. At the time of writing this contribution, Gavi's website on partnering with business had more than 30 'core partners' and close to 20 'COVAX partners' that are different

[26] Mott Macdonald, *Evaluation of Gavi's Private Sector Engagement Approach*, 13.

from the core ones.[27] When considering the time-consuming process of putting each deal in place this large number of projects is impressive. It appears that some of the projects in place have also helped in addressing some issues thrown up by the COVID-19 pandemic. However, there may be a paradox in that the large number is attractive from a resource mobilization and diversification point of view, but the significant technical and management resources involved might suggest that there may be an argument for operating a smaller portfolio with targeted interventions. To date, there appears to be insufficient impact data and country feedback to assess the impact of the operational, leveraged and innovation partnerships on Gavi's core mandate. In addition, scaling interventions up to other countries is not without challenges and can be time-consuming, especially considering the limited (human) resources available for implementation of such projects in countries. This emphasizes the importance of selecting projects that clearly address country needs.

Another aspect of private sector partnerships for Gavi and other organizations engaging with the private sector in this way is the potential for more visibility of the organization and as such increase resource commitments from sovereign donors. According to the Evaluation of Gavi's Private Sector Engagement Approach (PSEA) 2016–2022 '[t]here is some evidence to suggest the PSEA and associated partnerships may contribute to Gavi's general brand identity as a creative, innovative organization'.[28] Whether this translates into new donors becoming interested and existing donors increasing their pledges remains to be seen. Nonetheless, the available resources for international development are limited, with many organizations vying for them. In such a 'competitive field', having a reputation for being creative and innovative may well have a positive impact on generating donor (sovereign and private) interest.

Another noteworthy aspect of the INFUSE and some of the leveraged or operational partnerships already alluded to in the context of the AAIC partnership relates to the grey zone between providing a grant to a private sector entity (whether for profit or not) and providing or facilitating investments into companies. Gavi would not play the role of an investor in the sense that it would expect a monetary return on its investment. On the other hand, in some projects Gavi funds an organization's capital costs, which is different from funding the operational costs of a particular project in that arguably the

27 'Partnering with Business', at gavi.org/investing-gavi/partnering-business#types, visited 31 May 2023.

28 Ibid., 34.

company could use the investments made with Gavi's contributions for other (and/or additional) purposes than immunization.

Similarly, the exposure that partnerships with Gavi provides to some organizations could really help them in growing their business. This also brings up the concept of how valuable an international organization's brand is and what the implications of that would be. In presenting its case for collaboration with the private sector, Gavi raises several benefits for private sector organizations to engage with it, but the value of its brand is not mentioned in that context.[29] The concept of brand value is also an element in assessing which organization benefits most from the partnership. It could be argued that these are win–win partnerships given that they have a positive developmental impact as well as provide a benefit to the company beyond just recovering its operational costs. But if association with Gavi or other international organizations enhances an entity's brand and name recognition there may be scope for international organizations to assess how to leverage their positive brand equity in furtherance of their mission.

The above considerations illustrate that, in situations where the private sector contributes its expertise, this can affect companies' bottom line rather than simply being corporate social responsibility which may be involved in private sector donations. These considerations in turn raise the question of why Gavi would enter into a partnership with one organization and not another and highlight the importance of running open and transparent selection processes such as those for the INFUSE programme.

12.5 PARTNER ENGAGEMENT FRAMEWORK

As mentioned in Section 12.2, Gavi's origins go back to a group of organizations aiming to increase access to immunization – including UNICEF, WHO and the World Bank. From Gavi's inception, the role of those intergovernmental partners was to support operationalization of the Alliance strategic plans at country and global levels. In large part, those partners' support for Gavi's strategic plans was an expansion of their ongoing, core organization specific immunization mandate and efforts both at the country and global level. At the country level, the partners would provide support to governments in implementing their routine immunization programmes; such country level support is generally referred to as 'technical assistance'. Under these initial arrangements, partners would, subject to availability of funds, largely receive

[29] 'Partnering with Business', at gavi.org/investing-gavi/partnering-business, visited 25 January 2023.

the amount they would request – as those were the ones they considered as required to meet the strategy.

In 2010, a new approach for supporting the 2011–2015 Gavi Strategy was introduced that was referred to as the 'Business Plan'. Under this Business Plan, multilateral partners – primarily WHO and UNICEF (and from 2014 the World Bank also implemented activities again) – would receive Gavi funding for certain deliverables that had to align with the overall programmatic direction of Gavi's strategy. As the 'steward of donor resources', the Gavi Secretariat would oversee the multilateral partners' implementation of the business plan activities.[30] To enable progress against deliverables to be accurately measured, there was a recognition that this might require a change in the 'contractual relationships with multilateral partners'.[31]

While deliverables were key, as implemented, the Business Plan approach allowed for a great deal of flexibility and discretion in how funds allocated to (intergovernmental) partners were spent. While still accountable for the agreed-upon deliverables, this flexibility allowed partners to modify the activities to better respond to emerging or changing needs and priorities.[32] Partners at the headquarters level considered this as an important feature of supporting the overall success of the strategy and especially in supporting new vaccine applications and introductions. On the other hand, the partners' regional and country-based teams as well as other stakeholders such as national governments and the Gavi Secretariat had less visibility on what Business Plan funds were used for and how much was being provided for activities. This lack of transparency resulted in stakeholders querying how effective the accountability arrangements were under the Business Plan. With a lack of understanding of which partners were funding which activities or positions, there was a general inability to effectively monitor results and hold stakeholders accountable to milestones and deliverables.[33] In addition, substantial parts of funding to partners like WHO and UNICEF under the Business Plan ended up being used at global or regional levels.

With these considerations in mind, and at the start of a new 2016–2020 strategy that focused on dramatically improving immunization coverage and

[30] 'GAVI Alliance Strategy 2011–2015' (GAVI Alliance Board Meeting, 16–17 June 2010, Doc. 3), at gavi.org/sites/default/files/board/minutes/2010/16-june/3.GAVI%20Alliance%20Strategy%202011-2015.pdf, visited 25 January 2023.

[31] Ibid.

[32] Deloitte, *Baseline Assessment Report: Evaluation of the Technical Assistance Provided through the Gavi Partners' Engagement Framework* (July 2017), at www.gavi.org/sites/default/files/document/tca-evaluation-baseline-assessment-reportpdf.pdf, visited 11 July 2023, 10.

[33] Ibid., 12.

equity, the Alliance identified the need and opportunity to use a more bottom-up, country-driven and country focused approach for planning technical assistance to countries' immunization programmes. In 2016, the Gavi Board adopted a new approach for supporting countries and the implementation of Gavi's strategy named the Partner Engagement Framework. This new Framework for supporting countries with their technical needs was built around three principles: country-ownership, accountability and transparency. With respect to country-ownership, the new model adopted a bottom-up approach, with countries determining their needs and a substantially higher percentage of funds being spent in countries. The idea was also to increase transparency in this new model to ensure that both partners and countries would know exactly who is doing what, how much funding is allocated to each partner, what the expected deliverables are and how they are progressing. To assist in this aspect, for each component of technical assistance funded under the Partner Engagement Framework there are specific milestones that are developed in consultation with a country and for which progress is carefully monitored. This gives a country a better understanding of who is receiving what and for what purpose and their ability to hold every partner to account for outcomes that are promised and expected are enhanced.

Another aspect that was introduced in the Partner Engagement Framework was the broader range of partners available to countries to provide support. In the past such support was largely provided by the traditional partners – WHO and UNICEF in particular. The new Framework includes 'expanded' partners which can include civil society organizations, national (research) institutions or consulting service providers. Generally, these 'expanded' partners are pre-selected in accordance with Gavi's procurement rules and they can then be identified to provide specific services in a country.

The Partner Engagement Framework's aim is that the 'expanded' partners are complementing the services provided by the 'core' partners: WHO, UNICEF, the World Bank and a few others. However, the new approach does represent a shift in the dynamics of this type of funding compared to previous arrangements. Prior to the new Framework, all technical support to countries was almost exclusively provided through Gavi's traditional intergovernmental partners. Under the new Framework, countries can choose other types of institutions, including civil society organizations, research institutes or consulting service providers, to assist them. The assessment of the comparative advantage of each of the partners has in some sense resulted in the value of the contributions of intergovernmental organizations being compared to those of different types of entities. Most intergovernmental organizations do not participate in requests for proposals which would mean that their offerings would be compared to commercial or other types of service providers. While the Partner Engagement Framework does not go so far as to ask all partners to bid for certain programs, it does mean a level of comparison between the contributions of intergovernmental partners and the service offerings of other entities that may not be very common outside the Gavi context.

In addition, the principles of transparency and accountability in the Partner Engagement Framework entail that both partners and countries know exactly who is doing what and how much funding is allocated to each partner. The expected deliverables and progress towards those are also clear to all. This level of public transparency on the activities that intergovernmental organizations are conducting and the extent to which their performance against performance standards can influence the allocation of future funding in comparison to other entities is also not very common and has not always been appreciated at the headquarters of intergovernmental partners. For example, at the World Health Summit in Berlin in October 2021 in the context of challenges to WHO's coordination function the then-Chief of Staff of the WHO referred to the fact that '[WHO] is in some ways a contractor to Gavi' and that it is 'a recipient of highly earmarked funding from [the Global Fund and Gavi]'.[34]

The evolution of Gavi funding for technical assistance support to countries has slowly resulted in both private entities and intergovernmental partners being held to similar transparency and accountability standards, in particular in relation to programmatic delivery. Funders appreciate this in that it is clear what is being supported with their contributions and it helps ensure that organizations are treated in the same way regardless of their legal status. On the other hand, having public private partnerships like Gavi apply private sector performance metrics to intergovernmental organizations may not help the cohesion of the global governance system for health, as the WHO Chief of Staff alluded to in her remarks.

12.6 CONCLUSION

This contribution aimed to look at the different elements that make up the 'private' aspect of Gavi's 'public–private partnership'. Gavi's very origins lie in a 'market failure' that could only be addressed by engaging constructively with vaccine manufacturers which played a considerable role in its establishment. Moreover, not only were private funders deeply involved in the deliberations on creating Gavi, the Alliance would not have been established but for the

[34] World Health Summit, *Global Health Governance Post-Covid 19*, at youtube.com/watch?v=m9-Bh8cHIRw, visited 11 July 2023 at 1:00:15.

unprecedentedly large amount of 'seed funding' that the Gates Foundation invested. After some initial hesitation from different partners, Gavi's approach to conflicts of interest now appears to be accepted by all.

In Gavi's core business of making vaccines available to resource-constrained countries, the Alliance partners – including intergovernmental organizations – play complementary roles in trying to make as many vaccines as possible available with a given budget. Gavi and the Gates Foundation enter into transactions that might be more difficult for intergovernmental organizations or would otherwise be less efficient for the available resources if conducted by the intergovernmental partners. This shows the value of working through partnerships, in which partners have complementary roles playing to their strengths.

Gavi was initiated with private funding but its engagement with the private sector beyond vaccine manufacturers has considerably evolved. Financial contributions from private sources are now supplemented by partnerships or transactions in which private sector partners contribute to solutions to overcoming barriers to immunization in Gavi-eligible countries. These take many different forms.

A final element of Gavi's engagement with the private sector is that its funding for technical support to countries has moved from being almost exclusively intergovernmental organizations to also including private sector entities – whether for profit or with a charitable mission. In this context, the different types of partners are treated in the same way in terms of transparency and accountability and are funded from the same available resources.

Finally, it is perhaps Gavi's private sector influence that explains the prominence of the concepts of 'value for money' and 'return on investment'. This has made Gavi very effective in mobilizing resources, but the narrow approach has its detractors and may pose complexities for the balance in the international governance of global health.

13

Public–Private Cooperation in Global Security Governance

Entanglement, Infrastructure and the Affordances of Fundamental Rights

DIMITRI VAN DEN MEERSSCHE

13.1 INTRODUCTION: BLURRED BOUNDARIES/NEW COMPOSITIONS

There are many ways in which the presence and growing prominence of private actors in international public governance can be framed or understood.[1] While some portray this in the language of public–private partnerships or functional integration,[2] others, in a Marxist register, have diagnosed the work of international organizations as being guided by and serving a transnational capitalist class of private corporations and financial interests.[3] For those who approach the place of private actors within global governance with a public law sensibility, this blurring of boundaries poses particular problems

[1] I am invoking 'international public governance' in a loose manner here, referring to the multiple ways in which the work of international organizations and the authority these wield can be conceptualized. See, for example, B. Kingsbury, 'The Concept of "Law" in Global Administrative Law' (2009) 20 *European Journal of International Law* 23; A. von Bogdandy, M. Goldmann and I. Venzke, 'From Public International to International Public Law: Translating World Public Opinion into International Public Authority' (2017) 28 *European Journal of International Law* 125.

[2] See, for example, L. Andonova, *Governance Entrepreneurs: International Organizations and the Rise of Global Public–Private Partnerships* (Cambridge University Press, 2017); R. Schmidt, *Regulatory Integration across Borders: Public–Private Cooperation in Transnational Regulation* (Cambridge University Press, 2018).

[3] B. S. Chimni, 'International Institutions Today: An Imperial Global State in the Making' (2004) 15 *European Journal of International Law* 1; N. Mansouri, 'The Firm' (2022) *Völkerrechtsblog*, available at https://voelkerrechtsblog.org/the-firm/ (accessed December 2022); M. Hardt and A. Negri, *Empire* (Harvard University Press, 2000).

of power, influence and the absence of regulatory control.[4] These problematizations and the nature of our legal responses are connected to how we perceive the public and private to be tied together – contractually, transactionally, economically, culturally, ideologically, etc. In line with the ambition in this volume to theorize the ways in which international organizations engage the world (and the world engages international organizations), this chapter studies these dynamics of influence and interrelation from an infrastructural perspective: by tracing emergent – materially and relationally enacted – compositions of power and authority where the boundaries between public and private cannot easily be drawn (and where the need for doing so might dissolve).[5] 'Thinking infrastructurally', with Kingsbury, can help us observe shifts in the logic and location of global governance, while moving beyond the binary public–private divide (and the legal imagination grafted onto it).[6] Before exploring the conceptual and normative dimensions of this approach (Section 13.5), I explore different dimensions of infrastructural change in global security and their effects: infrastructures of data collection and analysis (Section 13.2), policy implementation (Section 13.3) and policy reorientation (Section 13.4). In tracing the material entanglements between international organizations and private actors in the field of global security governance, a key observation is how pre-emptive security and informational capitalism are mutually co-dependent and co-constitutive on an infrastructural level.

13.2 INFRASTRUCTURES OF DATA COLLECTION: EUROPOL AND THE ROLE OF PRIVATE PARTIES

A first case study relates to the recent amendment and expansion of Europol's mandate and how it is tied to an ongoing controversy over the institution's collection and control of vast data troves – a data 'black hole', as *The Guardian* called it.[7] This controversy was sparked by an order of the European Data

4 See J. Klabbers, 'Transforming Institutions: Autonomous International Organisations in Institutional Theory' (2017) 6 *Cambridge International Law Journal* 105, 116–117; R. Vallejo, 'After Governance? The Idea of Private Administrative Law', in P. Kjaer (ed.), *The Law of Political Economy: Transformation in the Function of Law* (Cambridge University Press, 2020), 320.

5 B. Kingsbury, 'Infrastructure and InfraReg: On Rousing the International Law "Wizards of Is"' (2019) 8 *Cambridge International Law Journal* 182; G. Sullivan, 'Law, Technology, and Data-Driven Security: Infra-Legalities as Method Assemblage' (2022) 49 *Journal of Law and Society* S31.

6 Kingsbury, 'Infrastructure and InfraReg'.

7 *The Guardian*, 'A Data "Black Hole": Europol Ordered to Delete Vast Store of Personal Data', 10 January 2022, available at www.theguardian.com/world/2022/jan/10/a-data-black-hole-europol-ordered-to-delete-vast-store-of-personal-data (accessed December 2023).

Protection Supervisor (EDPS), directed at Europol, to delete data it retained on individuals who have no established links to a criminal activity (described as a 'data subject categorization').[8] This decision concluded an investigation launched by the EDPS in 2019 into Europol's 'big data challenge',[9] which was based on the observation that the use by the organization of 'big data analytics' – the computational processing of large datasets without direct connection to pre-identified criminal activities or suspects – posed 'high risks for data subjects' and could have a 'severe impact on their fundamental rights'.[10] European Digital Rights (EDRi) – an advocacy group working to defend and advance digital rights – described this use by Europol of data mining techniques to 'identify' potential criminals as the EU's 'own Snowden scandal' – the collection and processing of big data as a form of mass surveillance.[11]

Yet, from the perspective of Europol, continued access to this data deluge is essential to develop the analytical capabilities at the heart of its pre-emptive security practices and strategies. These strategic objectives resonate, for example, in the use of new technologies in border security, where, as a study by the EU Parliament noted, 'AI algorithms ... [a]part from verifying and identifying known persons ... are also used to identify *unknown persons of interest* based on specific data-based *risk profiles*'.[12] This aligns with a much broader trend in security governance, as Gavin Sullivan summarizes, where '[p]atterns or clusters' distilled from large amounts of data are not exclusively 'aimed at targeting "known" threats [but] emerge from correlational associations ... between heterogeneous data sources algorithmically analyzed to detect previously "unknown" risks'.[13] This 'politics of possibility', to use Louise Amoore's concept,[14] is reflected in Europol's new task to 'identify[]

8 See EDPS, *Decision on the Retention by Europol of Datasets Lacking Data Subject Categorisation* (2022), available at https://edps.europa.eu/system/files/2022-01/22-01-10-edps-decision-europol_en.pdf (accessed December 2022).

9 Ibid., para. 1.2.

10 Ibid., para. 2.4. *The Guardian* reported that Europol's cache contained an astounding quantity of 'at least 4 petabytes'. See *The Guardian*, 'A Data "Black Hole"'.

11 EDRi, *The EU's Own 'Snowden Scandal': Europol's Data Mining* (2022), https://edri.org/our-work/the-eus-own-snowden-scandal-europols-data-mining/ (accessed January 2023).

12 European Parliament, *Artificial Intelligence at EU Borders: Overview of Applications and Key Issues* (2021). Cf. DG Home, *Opportunities & Challenges for the Use of Artificial Intelligence in Border Control, Migration & Security* (2020) (emphases added).

13 Sullivan, 'Law, Technology, and Data-Driven Security', S41. See also D. Van Den Meerssche, 'Virtual Borders: International Law and the Elusive Inequalities of Algorithmic Association' (2022) 33 *European Journal of International Law* 171.

14 L. Amoore, *The Politics of Possibility: Risk and Security beyond Probability* (Duke University Press, 2013).

persons ... who constitute a *high risk* for security' and hinges on an infrastructure through which 'large and complex data sets' can be accessed and analysed.[15] This is also expressed in one of the institution's key tasks: to 'collect, store, process, analyze and exchange information', which has led to some scholars labelling Europol as an 'enormous data processing agency rather than a law enforcing police office'[16] and its description in a report for LIBE (European Parliament's Committee on Civil Liberties, Justice and Home Affairs) as a 'criminal information hub' enabled by a 'computerized information system'.[17] Yet, it is precisely the collection, retention and mining of these 'large and complex data sets' – the retention of petabytes of uncategorized data, data held on people without a 'clearly established link with criminal activity' – that was the subject of the order by the EDPS.[18] In ordering Europol to delete data without appropriate categorization after a limited retention period, this formal intervention directly targeted the use of big data for purposes of 'mass surveillance and the use of predictive policing'.[19]

It is in direct response to this challenge that the legal mandate of Europol was amended in the new regulation adopted in June 2022.[20] Underlining the unique expertise of Europol in 'processing large and complex data sets',[21] the regulation, first of all, retroactively legalizes the continued storage and analysis by the organization of big data troves without appropriate data subject categorization. Article 74b now states that 'Europol may carry out a pre-analysis of [uncategorized] personal data [received before 28 June 2022] for a period of

[15] European Parliament and Council Regulation 2022/991, OJ L 169/1, Article 1. This is reflected in amended Article 4 (1) (r) of the Europol Regulation. See *Consolidated Text: Regulation (EU) 2016/794 of the European Parliament and of the Council of 11 May 2016 on the European Union Agency for Law Enforcement Cooperation (Europol)*, https://eur-lex.europa.eu/eli/reg/2016/794/2022-06-28 (accessed January 2023).

[16] S. Gless, 'Europol', in V. Mitsilegas, M. Bergström and Th Konstadinides (eds.), *Research Handbook on EU Criminal Law* (Edward Elgar, 2016), 465.

[17] LIBE, *Strengthening Europol's Mandate: A Legal Assessment of the Commission's Proposal to Amend the Europol Regulation* (2021). This report was drafted by experts Niovi Vavoula and Valsamis Mitsilegas.

[18] See EDPS, *Decision on the Retention by Europol of Datasets Lacking Data Subject Categorisation*, para. 4.9.

[19] S. Tas, 'Europol's Big Data Challenge: A Neutralisation of the European Watchdog', *The Digital Constitutionalist* (2022), https://digi-con.org/europols-big-data-challenge-a-neutralisation-of-the-european-watchdog/ (accessed January 2023). See also EDRi, 'Secret Negotiations about Europol: The Big Rule of Law Scandal', 31 January 2022.

[20] European Parliament and Council Regulation 2022/991, OJ L 169/1. In the following paragraphs, I also refer to specific articles in the consolidated Europol Regulation (referred to as 'Consolidated Regulation'). See note 15.

[21] European Parliament and Council Regulation 2022/991, OJ L 169/1, Recital 22.

up to 18 months from the date the data were first received'.[22] This retroactive legalization renders the order by the EDPS void and thereby, some argued, poses a distinct rule of law challenge.[23] With the 'amended regulation', the EDPS laments, its 'order to delete these large datasets would become ineffective'.[24] In addition to this retroactive legalization, the new regulation also provides a more structural resolution to Europol's 'big data challenge', in stipulating that the organization can conduct a 'pre-analysis' of uncategorized data – the petabytes of collected raw data targeted by the EDPS – to finds patterns, links and relations with existing criminal activity.[25] In addition, the regulation also provides legal ground for the processing of big data in the context of 'ongoing specific criminal investigation[s] within the scope of Europol's objectives'.[26] The new data processing powers reflected in Article 18 (6a) and 18a, as the Meijers Committee also argued, express a form of technological determinism, where the infrastructural affordances and demands of big data sources and processing capacities alter and expand institutional mandates and powers.[27]

Closely aligned with this storage and 'pre-analysis' of 'large and complex data sets' is the attention in the updated regulation to Europol's development of new algorithmic tools of risk assessment and analysis. As *The Guardian* observed, indeed, the new regulation would 'legalize the data cache and preserve its contents as a testing ground for new AI and machine learning

[22] Consolidated Regulation, Article 74b.

[23] Tas, 'Europol's Big Data Challenge'.

[24] EDPS, 'Amended Europol Regulation weakens data protection supervision', Press Statement, 27 June 2022.

[25] Consolidated Regulation, Article 18 (6a). See also European Parliament and Council Regulation 2022/991, OJ L 169/1, Recital 20 ('Such pre-analysis should take place prior to, and separate from, Europol's data processing for cross-checking, strategic analysis, operational analysis or the exchange of information, and after Europol has established that the data in question are relevant and necessary for the performance of its tasks'). In the LIBE report, these 'large datasets' are defined as 'datasets which, because of the volume, the nature or the format of the data they contain, cannot be processed with regular tools, but require the use of specific tools ... in particular digital forensics'. These datasets, the report notes, 'do not allow from the outset to ascertain that all the information contained in these large datasets comply with the limitations prescribed in [the regulation], with the volume of information so big that its content is often unknown until the moment when the analyst extracts relevant entities for their input into the relevant database'. See LIBE, *Strengthening Europol's Mandate*, 34.

[26] Consolidated Regulation, Article 18a. The Meijers Committee has noted in this regard that '[t]he pre-analysis of data and the processing of data in support of a specific criminal investigation are regulated by open norms that are difficult to oversee or supervise by external bodies such as the European Parliament or EDPS'. See Meijers Committee, 'Comment on Proposed Extensive Data Processing Powers for Europol', October 2021, www.commissie-meijers.nl/wp-content/uploads/2021/10/CM2114_EN.pdf (accessed January 2023), 3.

[27] Meijers Committee, 'Comment', 2.

tools'.[28] In the regulation, this resonates in 'Europol's new task to proactively monitor and contribute to research and innovation activities' which is clarified to include 'the development, training, testing and validation of algorithms for the development of tools for the use by law enforcement authorities'.[29] 'Europol should play a key role', the regulation additionally sets out, 'in promoting the development and deployment of ethical, trustworthy and human-centric artificial intelligence'.[30] This extended, proactive mandate in the field of AI development is underlined by the provisions that the automated processing of personal data – including special categories of data that reveal 'racial or ethnic origin, political opinions, religious or philosophical beliefs, … trade union membership [or a] persons' sex life or sexual orientation' – can, under specific conditions, be justified as a part of research and innovation activities (which could be understood as the development by Europol of computational tools for pre-emptive algorithmic risk assessment).[31] This extended mandate in relation to technological development also situates Europol as a focal point in relation to its member states ('Europol should play a key role in assisting Member States in developing new technological solutions based on artificial intelligence that are relevant to the achievement of Europol's objectives') and to an expanding range of external partners and private parties (as we notice in the creation of 'the EU Innovation Hub for Internal Security as a collaborative network of innovation labs').[32] Intimately intertwined with the objective to mine and analysis big data troves (through the forms 'pre-analysis'), this mandate to proactively develop new AI analytics is a crucial development in the relation of Europol to its members and the outside world.

In order to expand the data sources that Europol can use for these analytical purposes, one of the key innovations of the new regulation, central to my argument here, is that the organization now has the mandate to 'receive personal data from private parties'.[33] 'Private parties', a recital to the regulation amending Europol's mandate notes, 'hold increasing amounts of personal data, including subscriber, traffic and content data, that is potentially relevant for criminal investigations'.[34] This can relate to data held by large tech platforms, financial institutions, airline companies or online service providers. Europol, the regulation observes, 'should have measures in place to facilitate

[28] *The Guardian*, 'A Data "Black Hole"'.
[29] Consolidated Regulation, Article 4 (1) (v).
[30] European Parliament and Council Regulation 2022/991, OJ L 169/1, Recital 49.
[31] Consolidated Regulation, Articles 18 (2) (e), 30 and 33a.
[32] European Parliament and Council Regulation 2022/991, OJ L 169/1, Recitals 48–49.
[33] Ibid., Recital 32, as reflected in amended Article 26.
[34] Ibid., Recital 33.

cooperation with private parties, including with respect to the exchange of information', thereby providing a 'single point of contact' for private parties to share data sets that are scattered across multiple jurisdictions and not easily attributable.[35] In this sense, the provisions of data exchange with private parties have an explicit jurisdictional purpose: Europol's role is to receive and analyse multi-jurisdictional data with the aim of identifying and informing the relevant national authorities. Interestingly, we observe here that the spatial, material and legal disjunction between the digital infrastructures curated by private companies and the territorial jurisdiction of national law enforcement agencies generates a need for the expansion of Europol's legal mandate and the construction of a transnational infrastructure for data exchange.

The new regulation now provides Europol with a mandate to receive data directly from private parties (without member state involvement),[36] to transmit and transfer data to private parties (under specific conditions of necessity and proportionality)[37] and to request data held by private parties (via member states).[38] Importantly, Europol will also be providing the 'infrastructure ... for exchanges between the competent authorities of member states and private parties', even in relation to crimes that do not fall within Europol's objectives (in which case the institution merely serves as a data processor).[39] This is a remarkable expression of how the organization's authority and importance in transnational security governance are tied to the construction and curation of a digital infrastructure through which states, security agencies and private parties are connected. The new regulation underlines and extends these infrastructural interdependencies, which are tied to Europol's existing SIENA platform (Secure Information Exchange Network Application) and its integrated data management concept.[40] This integrated approach entails an 'architectural infrastructure' of data management where separated silos of data were replaced by 'an overarching EU database of criminal data and criminal intelligence' so that 'linkages between data and behavioural patterns may be discerned'.[41] Infrastructural design choices do not only determine Europol's

35 Ibid.

36 Consolidated Regulation, Article 26 (2).

37 Ibid., Article 26 (5).

38 Ibid., Article 26 (6b) and Recital 39.

39 Ibid., Article 26 (6c) and Recital 42.

40 European Parliament and Council Regulation 2016/794, OJ L 135/53, Recital 24.

41 LIBE, *Strengthening Europol's Mandate*, 18. Indeed, as the 2016 Europol Regulation clarifies, the purpose is to 'use new technologies to process data', to 'swiftly detect links' and to 'have a clear overview of trends', which means that 'Europol databases should be structured in such a way as to allow Europol to choose the most efficient IT structure'. European Parliament and Council Regulation 2016/794, OJ L 135/53, Recital 24.

position within the security landscape and the technological possibilities of intervention, in this sense, but also shape the affordance of legal protection – with the prospects of privacy, purpose limitation and other data protection standards being severely eroded.[42]

In a report on the proposed amendment to Europol's regulation (which has now been adopted) drafted for LIBE, this expanded mandate to directly demand, receive and transfer data from (and to) private parties has been described as 'a considerable paradigm shift from the existing powers of the agency'.[43] The new structure places the institution in direct relation with private parties, thereby circumventing member states, and, the report notes, poses 'significant risks for the protection of fundamental rights, in particular privacy and protection of personal data'.[44] This positioning of Europol as a focal point in a network between states and corporate actors reflects 'the emergence of the trend in the past years to establish direct channels of communication between law enforcement and private parties and foster a public–private partnership'.[45] These material channels, the report notes, 'fundamentally change the powers of the agency and the relationship it has with Member States'.[46] This change is not unique to Europol's engagement with private actors. In its significant Resolution 2396 from 2017 on threats of terrorism and extremism, the UN Security Council underlines the importance of digital infrastructures for pre-emptive practices of 'evidence-based risk assessments' and 'screening procedures'.[47] To this end, the resolution states, the Security Council '[e]ncourages ... cooperation with the private sector ... especially with information communication technology companies, in gathering digital data'.[48] It is through the alignment and infrastructural integration of private digital platforms with international organizations that the practices and politics of global security governance are being rewritten today.

The changes – and associated controversies – regarding Europol's mandate and pre-emptive security practices show a particular pathway by which international organizations 'engage the world'. The ever-closer cooperation and partnership with private parties, I argued, is not sustained through 'contracting

[42] LIBE, *Strengthening Europol's Mandate*, 18.

[43] Ibid., 30.

[44] Ibid. This is echoed in the analysis of Europol's new regulation by the Meijers Committee, which observed that '[w]hen Europol is empowered to process personal data directly received from private parties, these procedural and other legal requirements that protect individual rights are circumvented'. Meijers Committee, 'Comment', 4.

[45] LIBE, *Strengthening Europol's Mandate*, 30.

[46] Ibid., 26.

[47] UNSC, Resolution 2396 (2017), para. 4.

[48] Ibid., para. 21.

out' specific tasks but through the material configuration of Europol as an infrastructural focal point for the collection, analysis and distribution of data. This consolidation of Europol as a 'criminal information hub' – a 'centre of calculation' where private actors are inserted – significantly alters and extends its mandate. The associated legal problems of privacy, data protection and non-discrimination can be situated in a context of data-driven, pre-emptive security practices, where big data is algorithmically analysed to find patterns, inferences, propensities of 'high risk' behaviour and detect previously unknown threats.[49] Europol's updated regulation provides the legal architecture for precisely this mode of governance: a mandate for the storage and retention of 'large and complex datasets', a pro-active aim of developing algorithms and AI tools to 'pre-analyse' these big data sources with the aim of identifying 'high risk' individuals, and a formal integration of private parties into this emergent data ecology. This paradigm shift, as I argued, is infrastructurally enacted and it is by 'thinking infrastructurally' that the authority of Europol (in relation to states as well as affected individuals) as well as the impact on fundamental rights can be understood. As private platforms are displacing states and international organizations as privileged sites for the creation and accumulation of data about people and populations,[50] we can observe the emergence of global security infrastructures marked by what Mark Andrejevic describes as 'the blurred boundaries between state and consumer surveillance and, thus, between control, convenience, and care'.[51]

49 This displacement of the rule of law by pre-emptive practices of (algorithmic) risk assessment is underlined in K. Yeung, 'Algorithmic Regulation: A Critical Interrogation' (2018) 12 *Regulation & Governance* 505. This phenomenon is tied to a more general orientation in security practices towards the performative and materially mediated enactment of risk and the governance of unknown threats. Cf. L. Amoore, 'Risk before Justice: When the Law Contests Its Own Suspension' (2008) 21 *Leiden Journal of International Law* 847; Amoore, *The Politics of Possibility*; C. Aradau and T. Blanke, 'Politics of Prediction: Security and the Time/Space of Governmentality in the Age of Big Data' (2017) 20 *European Journal of Social Theory* 373.

50 This is important considering how, as some have argued, it was precisely this power of counting and collecting that constituted the birth of the modern state and the practice of liberal reform beyond the state. This is powerfully argued in the analysis by Guy Fiti Sinclair who connects these technologies of observation through which the Global South is rendered legible and manageable by international organizations to Foucault's theories on governmentality and biopolitics. G. F. Sinclair, *To Reform the World: International Organizations and the Making of Modern States* (Oxford University Press, 2017).

51 M. Andrejevic, 'Automating Surveillance' (2019) 17 *Surveillance & Society* 7. Gavin Sullivan has defined these 'global security infrastructures' as 'novel governance constellations that allow diverse actors (states, private platforms, international organizations, and global governance bodies) to collaborate across borders through the extraction, exchange, and interconnection of vast amounts of data for countering potential threats using AI techniques, ADM [i.e.

13.3 INFRASTRUCTURES OF IMPLEMENTATION: HASH-SHARING AND ALGORITHMIC CONTENT MODERATION

In Section 13.2, we observed how private actors are tied to contemporary infrastructures of security governance as important sites of data collection and data sharing. In this section, I map out a different mode of public–private co-operation, in which international organizations involve online platforms and corporate actors to directly implement transnational security policies. This is specifically relevant in relation to practices of countering terrorism online, or – to use the language of the UN CTC (Counter-Terrorism Committee) and CTED (Counter-Terrorism Committee Executive Directorate) – to 'counter terrorist narratives'.[52] Private actors – and particularly large online platforms – are perceived here as essential in containing the use by terrorist and violent extremist organizations of the internet for the purpose of recruitment, propaganda or the dissemination of terrorist and violent extremist content.[53] In the wake of the Christchurch mosque shootings in 2019, which had been accompanied by a white supremacist manifesto and a live-streamed video of the shooting, both of which had been widely shared on online platforms, the Christchurch Call to Action was adopted with the stated aim to 'eliminate terrorist and violent extremist content online'.[54] Remarkably, this call, initiated by New Zealand and France, did not only target states and public actors but also involved obligations for 'online service providers' to – among other commitments – 'take transparent . . . measures seeking to prevent the upload of terrorist and violent extremist content and to prevent its dissemination on social media and similar content-sharing services, including its immediate and permanent removal'.[55] To fulfil these promises, private

automated decision-making] processes, and forms of algorithmic regulation'. Sullivan, 'Law, Technology, and Data-Driven Security', S32.

[52] This is set out specifically in the 'Comprehensive international framework to counter terrorist narratives' developed by the CTC and CTED in 2017. This comprehensive framework is annexed to UNSC, *Letter dated 26 April 2017 from the Chair of the Security Council Committee established pursuant to resolution 1373 (2001) concerning counter-terrorism addressed to the President of the Security Council*, S/2017/375. This comprehensive framework to counter terrorist narratives builds on UNSC, Resolution 2178 (2014); UNSC, Resolution 2354 (2017); UNSC, Resolution 2396 (2017).

[53] This agenda is currently at the heart of the EU's regulation on the dissemination of terrorist content online and the UK's online safety bill. Cf. European Parliament and Council Regulation 2021/784, OJ L 172/79; UK Parliament, Online Safety Bill 220, 2022-23 [as amended on re-committal, in Public Bill Committee].

[54] Christchurch Call (2019), www.christchurchcall.com/assets/Documents/Christchurch-Call-full-text-English.pdf (accessed January 2023).

[55] Ibid.

platforms pledged to make 'cross-industry efforts' by 'investing in and expanding the GIFCT' – the Global Internet Forum to Counter Terrorism (a coalition of large tech corporations with the mission to 'to prevent terrorists and violent extremists from exploiting digital platforms').[56]

The emergence of this forum, and the enrolment of private actors in the struggle to 'counter terrorist narratives' more generally, has a longer lineage. In the *Comprehensive International Framework to Counter Terrorist Narratives* – developed by the CTC and CTED – the UN Security Council stressed that it 'has long noted the importance of public–private partnerships in efforts to counter incitement to commit acts of terrorism',[57] devoting an entire section of the framework to this theme. Underlining the role of ICT and social media platforms, the framework specifically stresses the need to develop novel technological tools to monitor, study, block, filter and remove terrorist content online.[58] This resonates in resolution 2396, where the Security Council stresses the need for 'cooperation with [the] private sector' in countering terrorism online, by 'developing counter-terrorist narratives and through innovative technological solutions'.[59] The Security Council further calls on 'the GIFCT to continue to increase engagement with governments' and points to the UN CTED – ICT4 Peace's initiative of Tech Against Terrorism to 'protect the internet' from terrorist use.[60] Working in close collaboration with the GIFCT network, Tech Against Terrorism – a private actor launched through UN CTED in April 2017 and implemented by the UK-based NGO QuantSpark Foundation – works 'on behalf of the UN CTED to support the global tech industry to tackle terrorist exploitation of their technologies'.

The development of 'innovative technological solutions' is central to the work of both TAT and the GIFCT. Within the context of TAT, the Terrorist Content Analytics Platform (TCAP) was developed to conduct a 'scalable automated data analysis of terrorist content including its symbolism,

56 Ibid. See GIFCT, 'About', https://gifct.org/about/ (accessed January 2023).

57 UNSC, *Comprehensive International Framework to Counter Terrorist Narratives*, S/2017/375, para. 8. The strategy summarizes that '[t]he work of the United Nations . . . in promoting public–private partnerships should be considered a core element of the comprehensive international framework to counter terrorist narratives'. Ibid., para. 14.

58 Ibid., para. 9–10. The Christchurch call equally underlined the need to develop 'technical solutions to prevent the upload of and to detect and immediately remove terrorist and violent extremist content online'.

59 UNSC, Resolution 2396 (2017).

60 Ibid. See TAT, 'About Tech against Terrorism', www.techagainstterrorism.org/about/ (accessed January 2023).

narratives, and metadata, in order to identify and classify at scale'.[61] Working with advanced technological tools of content identification (including automatic web scraping), classification (in line with an institution-specific inclusion list of terrorist organizations), automated notification of affected platforms, and the development of a 'hashing function to create an algebraic record of each content type', TCAP seeks to 'automate[] the swift detection and removal of verified terrorist content'.[62] In this chain of content moderation, TCAP sees a significant role for 'AI driven processes'.[63] The 'hashing function' to which TCAP refers is central to the GIFCT's digital infrastructure for removing online terrorist content: the 'hash-sharing database' (HSDB). The HSDB, the GIFCT states, is 'a shared, safe and secure industry database of perceptual hashes of known images and videos produced by terrorist entities on the UN's designated terrorist groups list, which GIFCT members had chosen to remove'.[64] These 'hashes', the GIFCT's Interim Executive Director and Director of Technology explain, are 'digital signatures' of image or video content that 'cannot be reverse-engineered' to the original files.[65] Access to the HSDB allows all participating platforms to rapidly and proactively review and remove terrorist content from their platforms without having to share the specific content. Considering the intractable and inherently political problem of defining terrorism and violent extremism (in contrast to, for example, opposition or political resistance), the GIFCT's initial standard for inclusion in the database – which is now being expanded – was the relation between online content and entities listed on the UN Security Council consolidated list of designated terrorist entities.[66] The HSDB, in

[61] Cf. N. Bowie, 'Terrorism Databases and Data Sets: A New Inventory' (2021) 15 *Perspectives on Terrorism* 147, 155.

[62] See Terrorist Content Analytics Platform (TCAP), 'How It Works', https://terrorismanalytics.org/about/how-it-works (accessed January 2023).

[63] TCAP, https://terrorismanalytics.org/ (accessed January 2023). This aligns with the observation that 'amidst significant technical advances in machine learning ... automated tools are not only being increasingly deployed to fill important moderation functions, but are actively heralded as the force that will somehow save moderation from its existential problems'. R. Gorwa, R. Binns and Ch Katzenbach, 'Algorithmic Content Moderation: Technical and Political Challenges in the Automation of Platform Governance' (2020) 7 *Big Data & Society*. For a more general analysis and critique of algorithmic content moderation, see T. Gillespie, *Custodians of the Internet: Platforms, Content Moderation, and the Hidden Decisions that Shape Social Media* (Yale University Press, 2018).

[64] GIFCT, 'GIFCT's Hash-Sharing Database', https://gifct.org/hsdb/ (accessed January 2023).

[65] 'The hashes used in the GIFCT hash-sharing database are "perceptual hashes" – which means visually similar content creates hashes that are mathematically close to each other'.

[66] The TCAP, more explicitly and controversially, derives this from the 'designation lists of democratic nation states'. See https://terrorismanalytics.org/policies/inclusion-policy (accessed January 2023).

other words, entails a direct response to the engagement by international organizations – with the Security Council and the EU Internet Forum leading the way – of private platforms in the international framework to counter terrorist narratives.

Tied to the standard-setting process of the UN's sanctions list,[67] the HSDB thereby allows platforms to moderate online content at an enhanced speed and scale – with large platforms reporting millions of images and videos corresponding with included hashes having been taken down automatically and quasi instantaneously.[68] The hash-sharing database thus entails an *infrastructural implementation of counterterrorism policy* enacted through the automated filtering of online content with technological tools of hashing and algorithmic content classification. As Gavin Sullivan has argued, this is a regulatory practice that works at an 'architectural level': it does not reactively respond to harmful online behaviour but proactively prevents it from manifesting.[69] This 'infrastructural' or 'architectural' mode regulation through the HSDB entails significant regulatory effects: it allows for automated forms of content moderation; aligns and amplifies the power of large online platforms in what Evelyn Douek has described as 'content cartels';[70] changes the temporal mode of intervention (from reactive to proactive); deflects the legislative demands for more stringent platform regulation; displaces definitional questions and political controversies on the notion of what constitutes terrorism (as elaborated in Section 13.4); and leads to new configurations of global governance – 'bringing', as Sullivan demonstrates, 'states and platforms, and the dynamics of global security and informational capitalism, into novel and productive relation'.[71] To grasp these changes in global security governance, I believe it is important to study digital infrastructures and technologies

67 G. Sullivan, *The Law of the List: UN Counterterrorism Sanctions and the Politics of Global Security Law* (Cambridge University Press, 2020).

68 This is also necessary in light of tightening legal obligations for online platforms. The platform governance regulations of the EU – including the EU Regulation on the Dissemination of Online Terrorist Content and the Digital Services Act – now set out a takedown period of only one hour.

69 See G. Sullivan, 'Infra-legalities: Global Security Infrastructures, Artificial Intelligence and International Law' (unpublished paper, 2023) (draft on file with author). This 'architectural' or 'design-based' regulation, as Bronwen Morgen and Karen Yeung observe, seeks to 'eliminate undesirable behaviour by designing out the possibility for its occurrence'. B. Morgan and K. Yeung, *An Introduction to Law and Regulation: Text and Materials* (Cambridge University Press, 2012), 102.

70 E. Douek, 'The Rise of Content Cartels', (2020) *Knight First Amendment Institute at Columbia University*, https://knightcolumbia.org/content/the-rise-of-content-cartels (visited 12 March 2025).

71 See Sullivan, 'Law, Technology, and Data-Driven Security', S37.

such as the HSDB or the TCAP not as passive tools employed for already existing policy agendas but as active agential forces that shape how global security problems are perceived, performed and addressed.[72] The focus hereby shifts from a study of governance *of* infrastructure to governance *by* infrastructure.[73]

Significant legal concerns have been raised regarding the workings of the HSDB as a global security infrastructure. Observing that this technology – and its corporate creation and ownership – entails a form of 'regulatory power over discourse that has never been privately possessed before', Jennifer Cobbe warns for the advent of 'algorithmic censorship' as a mode of governmentality with possibly detrimental effects for 'open and inclusive spaces for communication and discourse'.[74] Danielle Keats Citron, in a similar vein, has observed a 'censorship creep' in how detection tools for child sexual abuse material have entered a much more politically contested domain of online violent extremism.[75] Human rights scholars such as Thiago Dias Oliva, in turn, have signalled specific legal concerns related to algorithmic content moderation in relation to freedom of expression and access to information,[76] while Gavin Sullivan shows that the pre-emptive and proactive logic of the HSDB erodes the rule of law and disables legal accountability and practices of contestation and review.[77] For the purposes of this chapter, however, the key claim is that tools such as the HSDP and the TCAP display a distinct way in which international organizations engage the world: they exemplify the enrolment of corporate actors into practices of global security governance formally set out by international institutions. This enrolment is only in limited ways expressed and implemented in formal legal or institutional forms. It rather unfolds through the construction of emergent socio-technical infrastructures of implementation. In tracing these new infrastructural relations, divisions between public versus private or global versus local can no longer be taken for granted but dissolve into novel, entangled and material compositions of global regulatory power.

72 Cf. J. Bennett, *Vibrant Matter: A Political Ecology of Things* (Duke University Press, 2009).
73 See the references in note 5.
74 J. Cobbe, 'Algorithmic Censorship by Social Platforms: Power and Resistance' (2020) 34 *Philosophy and Technology* 739.
75 D. Citron, 'Extremist Speech, Compelled Conformity, and Censorship Creep' (2018) 93 *Notre Dame Law Review* 1035, 1050–1051.
76 Th Dias Oliva, 'Content Moderation Technologies: Applying Human Rights Standards to Protect Freedom of Expression' (2020) 20 *Human Rights Law Review* 607. See also B. Sander, 'Freedom of Expression in the Age of Online Platforms: The Promise and Pitfalls of a Human Rights-based Approach to Content Moderation' (2020) 43 *Fordham International Law Journal* 939.
77 Sullivan, 'Infra-Legalities'.

13.4 INFRASTRUCTURAL LOGICS: EXPERIMENTALISM AND THE SCRIPTS OF GLOBAL SECURITY GOVERNANCE

Sections 13.2 and 13.3 have pointed to the importance of public–private partnerships in the field of global security governance in relation to practices of data collection and the implementation of an international institutional agenda of countering terrorism online. In this section, I aim to trace the role of private actors, public–private partnerships and their material entanglements to the ways in which global security concerns are perceived, known, enacted and acted upon – to the changing rationalities and logics of security governance. In line with the preceding sections, I argue that these changes are best understood by situating them at a socio-technical or infrastructural level.

The role of private actors in shaping the orientation and agenda of new security practices is obvious in their direct involvement with the drafting of strategies for technology adopted. While the recent strategic report by EU DG Home on *Opportunities and Challenges for the Use of Artificial Intelligence in Border Control, Migration and Security* was drafted by Deloitte,[78] the Frontex report on *Artificial Intelligence-Based Capabilities for the European Border and Coast Guard* was written by the RAND Corporation.[79] This 'resonance' between security practices and corporate risk consultancy, as Louise Amoore has described it,[80] translates itself in the experimental, open-ended and ongoing process by which new data-driven decision-making tools are designed as a series of use cases and modules that can be iteratively 'sequenced', 'adapted' and 'plugged in'.[81] This experimental orientation is explicit in the 2025 UK Border Strategy, which states that 'the private sector must take the lead on border innovation', with the role of government being limited to 'creating an environment that encourages experimentation and technology adoption'.[82] This shift in governance logic, sparked by private actors and sustained by the recourse to new digital technologies, instantiates what Claudia Aradau described as 'experiments without protocols' – a distinct mode of governmentality that is not based on rational plans and formal causal

78 EU DG Home, *Opportunities and Challenges for the Use of AI in Border Control, Migration and Security* (2020).

79 Frontex, *Artificial Intelligence-Based Capabilities for the European Border and Coast Guard* (2020).

80 Amoore, *The Politics of Possibility*.

81 EU DG Home, *Opportunities and Challenges*, 58–59.

82 HM Government, *2025 UK Border Strategy* (2020), 29.

criteria but opens up to the space of play of machine learning models.[83] What we observe, then, is the advent in global governance of what Fleur Johns qualifies as 'an open-ended, opportunistic, now-oriented disposition [t]hat has been identified with entrepreneurship'.[84] As private actors become enrolled in (the design of) institutional practices of security governance, we see the emergence of what Johns describes as a 'lean start-up' mentality that 'favours experimentation over elaborate planning … and iterative design over traditional "big design up front"'.[85]

The effects of these emergent infrastructural logics, where adaptiveness and operational actionability figure as central concern,[86] can be observed in the different empirical spheres of Section 13.3. The 'digital forensics' envisaged and employed by Europol in its newly mandated 'pre-analysis' has an explicit orientation, in this sense, towards the iterative and open-ended detection of links, patterns and propensities in 'big data'. The importance of 'new technologies to process data' to 'swiftly detect links [and] trends' was already recognized in Europol's prior regulation,[87] and now resonates in the institutional task to pre-emptively identify 'who constitute[s] a high risk for security' and contribute to the 'development, training, testing and validation of algorithms' necessary for this task.[88] Echoing the language of corporate technology development, the design of new 'solutions based on artificial intelligence' should be supported by an 'EU Innovation Hub for Internal Security as a collaborative network of innovation labs'.[89] The infrastructural and technological developments that are inscribed in this new regulation, in short, express a distinct logic of governing security problems – a logic by which interventions are not (exclusively) guided by pre-determined formal rules and criteria (about who constitutes a risk or what the properties of deviant behaviour precisely entail) but by inferences and 'behavioural patterns' that tools of machine learning are able to distil and render actionable.[90]

[83] C. Aradau, 'Experimentality, Surplus Data and the Politics of Debilitation in Borderzones' (2022) 27 *Geopolitics* 26. The concept of 'experiment without protocol', as Claudia Aradau notes, is coined by Sarah Perret.

[84] F. Johns, 'From Planning to Prototypes: New Ways of Seeing Like a State' (2019) 82 *Modern Law Review* 833, 850. See also D. Van Den Meerssche and G. Gordon, 'Is This the Rhizome? Thinking Together with Fleur Johns' (2022) 33 *Law and Critique* 237.

[85] Johns, 'From Planning to Prototypes', 855.

[86] Cf. D. Van Den Meerssche and G. Gordon, 'The Contemporary Values of Operadiction Regimes', in I. Feichtner and G. Gordon (eds.), *Constitutions of Value* (Routledge, 2023) 236.

[87] European Parliament and Council Regulation 2016/794, OJ L 135/53, Recital 24.

[88] Consolidated Regulation, Article 4 (1) (r) and (v).

[89] European Parliament and Council Regulation 2022/991, OJ L 169/1, Recitals 48–49.

[90] Cf. LIBE, *Strengthening Europol's Mandate*, 18 (noting that '[o]perational effectiveness remains the key goal so that linkages between data and behavioral patterns may be discerned').

A similar development is noticeable in the strategic ambition of EU DG Home 'to harness AI for the benefit of borders, migration and security in Europe'.[91] At the core of this agenda is a focus on 'risk assessment' with the 'general aim to find patterns and cluster individuals for further investigation'.[92] The '[c]lassification categories' guiding this assessment, the strategy further notes, could be 'defined based on a risk threshold or specific indicators' or could be 'less pre-defined where applications are grouped based on some "learned" similarity'.[93] AI would be essential in this process to 'partition data into clusters' and to 'identify patterns which were not observed (as "strange" before)'.[94] This entails a logic of governance inherently tied to the affordances of new technological tools and infrastructures where the identification of security risks – as well as the interventions these invite – results not from fixed legal classifiers of enmity but, at least in part, from continuous and 'unsupervised uncovering of correlations'.[95] This logic resonates in the development of ETIAS (European Travel Information and Authorisation System) which relies on AI to uncover hidden correlations and craft an 'algorithm enabling profiling' to counter security-, illegal immigration- and epidemic risks.[96]

The most explicit manifestation of this changing governance logic, perhaps, relates to the GIFCT and its inclusion policy or taxonomy of what constitutes terrorist and violent extremist context.[97] In the initial stages of the forum and with the aim of finding 'common ground' with the approach taken by states and international organizations,[98] the HSDB would only include hashes associated with terrorist entities on the UN Security Council's Consolidated Sanctions List. We can observe an infrastructural alignment between the

This shift in governance logic is conceptualized and criticized, for example, in E. Isin and E. Ruppert, 'The Birth of Sensory Power' (2020) 7 *Big Data and Society*; R. Amaro, 'Machine Learning, Surveillance and the Politics of Visibility', in B. Vickers and K. Allado-McDowell (eds.), *Atlas of Anomalous AI* (Ignota, 2021); L. Amoore, 'The Deep Border', *Political Geography* (2021) 102547; L. Amoore, 'Machine Learning Political Orders' (2022) 49 *Review of International Studies* 20.

91 EU DG Home, *Opportunities and Challenges*, 6.

92 Ibid., 10.

93 Ibid., 89.

94 Ibid., 89–90.

95 Ibid., 90.

96 Council Regulation 2018/1240, OJ L 236/1, Article 33. See M. Petersmann and D. Van Den Meerssche, 'On Phantom Publics, Clusters and Collectives: Be(com)ing Subject in Algorithmic Times' (2024) 39 *AI and Society* 107.

97 See GIFCT, *HSDB Taxonomy* (2022), https://gifct.org/hsdb/ (accessed February 2023).

98 GIFCT, 'Transparency Report' (2020), https://gifct.org/wp-content/uploads/2020/10/GIFCT-Transparency-Report-July-2020-Final.pdf (accessed February 2022). On the legitimacy challenges faced by the GIFCT and the ways in which this 'content cartel' responds to those, see also Douek, 'The Rise of Content Cartels', and Sullivan, 'Infra-Legalities'.

UNSC and GIFCT, in other words, in how the technical content moderation tools of the latter encode the listing practices of the former – a dynamic of automated censorship that renders the controversies over what qualifies as terrorist content (in contrast to political criticism, for example) only more salient. Yet, as Tom Thorley (Director of Technology at GIFCT) observed, the strict reliance on this list imported a set of political and ideological biases embedded in the history of counterterrorism.[99] To overcome this problem of bias and the inability of static state-centred lists to adapt to a changing security landscape, the GIFCT undertook an initiative to broaden its hash-sharing database taxonomy.[100] In expanding the taxonomy of terrorist and violent extremist content, the list-based approach is supplemented with a method that would detect and classify content on the basis of 'behavioural indicators'.[101] The qualification of what constitutes terrorist or violent extremist content would be guided, in this sense, by the distillation of 'behavioural patterns' in real-time data aided by the use of AI. The use of machine learning for content classification differs strongly from the process of hash-matching in that actively extracts and generates features of what qualifies – on a behavioural level – as prohibited content.[102] In one of the proposed tools – the Dynamic Matrix of Extremism and Terrorism (DMET) – the idea is to 'develop models that algorithmically classify groups (or content) into categories' where 'large baskets of indicators would be associated probabilistically with each level [of extremism]' on a continuum from 'partisanship' to 'terrorism'.[103] This classification model is described as 'dynamic', 'iterative' and based on 'cognitive and behavioural cues' that translate in patterns and profiles of extremist content.[104] Interestingly, the designers of the matrix recognize that this behavioural

[99] Cyber5 Podcast, 'Combating Terrorist Messaging on the Open Internet' (2021), www.nisos.com/podcast/ep60/ (accessed February 2022). Cf. E. Saltman and T. Thorley, 'Practical and Technical Considerations in Expanding the GIFCT Hash-Sharing Database', in Global Internet Forum to Counter Terrorism, *Broadening the GIFCT Hash-Sharing Database Taxonomy: An Assessment and Recommended Next Steps* (2021), 16–17; D. Byman and Ch Meserole, 'Expanding the Hash-Sharing Database' in GIFCT, ibid., 28 ('both the U.N. list and national terrorist designation lists are not the result of independent and objective processes but instead reflect political priorities ... As a result, nearly all the hashes currently in the database refer to content linked to the Islamic State, Al-Qaeda, the Taliban, and other groups designated as terrorist organizations by the United Nations').

[100] GIFCT, ibid.

[101] GIFCT, ibid., 59.

[102] Cf. Gorwa et al., 'Algorithmic Content Moderation', 5 ('matching and classification have ... important differences; while matching requires a manual process of collating and curating individual examples ... classification involves inducing generalisations about features of many examples from a given category into which unknown examples may be classified').

[103] GIFCT, *Broadening*, 70.

[104] Ibid.

classification may flag content expressing the 'collective right to self-determination' or instantiating the exercise of fundamental rights – in which case platforms should use 'discretion'.[105] We observe how these international legal questions are now addressed by different actors and in very different terms, mediated by the global infrastructure of hash-sharing and the algorithmic processes of content identification and classification on which it hinges.[106] Yet, while recognizing the normative choices that are involved in this process, the recurring promise in the GIFCT's taxonomy expansion is to classify content in a manner that is 'agnostic to ideology' – a 'value-free modularity' that works around the intractable political problem of qualifying and addressing violent extremist content.[107]

While the current GIFCT taxonomy remains closely centred around the UN's Consolidated Sanctions List, we have now seen the initial introduction of behavioural indicators.[108] This is a conscious project of expanding the taxonomy 'iteratively', which, as Sullivan notes, entails 'an approach to regulation driven less by normative considerations than practical and infrastructural conditions'.[109] In moving beyond the 'biased' list, we can see the emergence of '[AI] processes' which rely 'on a pipeline of real-time, open-source media [to] bas[e] inclusion decisions on behavior rather than ideology or third-party designations'.[110] This shift from designated, state-based, formal lists to an expanded, adaptive taxonomy of behavioural indicators reconfigures the very notion of what terrorism entails and how it can be acted upon. In its orientation towards emergent patterns, behavioural indicators and cognitive cues, this mode of security governance clearly resonates with the ambition of Europol's algorithmic 'pre-analysis' of large and complex datasets, and the strategic aspirations by DG Home to use AI to 'find patterns and cluster individuals for further investigation'. This changing governance rationality is mediated by specific technological possibilities and infrastructural conditions where the public and private are entangled and mutually recomposed. It expresses a distinct logic, which, Fleur Johns has noted, entails an 'attentiveness to emergent patterns of all kinds' – a logic of governance that consists of 'automated dives into vast and shifting oceans of data' where possibilities are being 'worked up iteratively and inductively from the inferences that may be

[105] Ibid., 69.
[106] This is problematized in Sullivan, 'Infra-Legalities'.
[107] GIFCT, *Broadening*, 28 and 68. For a critique of this de-politicising move, see Gorwa et al., 'Algorithmic Content Moderation'; Sullivan, 'Infra-Legalities'.
[108] GIFCT, *HSDB Taxonomy*.
[109] Sullivan, 'Infra-Legalities'.
[110] GIFCT, *Broadening*, 117.

drawn from the data available, as limited or partial as those data may be'.[111] In this distinct mode of governance, Mark Andrejevic argues, the 'homogeneity of discipline is replaced by continual processes of experimentation and environmental modulation calculated to generate more data and ... anticipate and foreclose through intervention'.[112] The diagnosis of this particular governance logic is not primarily about the rising power of private actors or the tremendous opportunity for private profit in this field (although both phenomena are widely documented), but about the ways in which security problems are perceived or addressed. The relationship between international organizations and private parties, in this context, is not one of 'contracting out' public tasks: the practice of data collection and analysis that structures governance routines in the security domain now relies on private infrastructures and 'derives its animus and logic from the market'.[113]

13.5 CONCLUSION: THINKING INFRASTRUCTURALLY: THE MATERIALITY OF RULE AND AFFORDANCES OF RIGHTS

Much can be said about the technologies of security governance and infrastructures of public–private partnership canvassed in Section 13.4. We could focus our critical analyses on the expansion of organizational mandates, the synergies between informational capitalism and security governance, the change in regulatory scripts and rationalities and the associated erosion of fundamental rights. In relation to these important research strands, the intervention of this chapter is a modest one: to grasp the evolving dynamics through which international organizations 'engage the world' – along the invitation in this volume – I want to highlight the importance, as noted by Benedict Kingsbury, of 'thinking infrastructurally'.[114] This mode of thinking, I have argued, allows us to grasp salient changes in global security governance which I described by mapping emergent infrastructures of data collection, policy implementation and standard-setting in this field. It is through infrastructural changes that we see how new entanglements and compositions of public–private ordering emerge – how international organizations 'engage the world' and are materially engaged by it. This perspective opens up a distinct mode of studying the law and governance of (and by) international organizations that disrupts the traditional doctrinal dilemmas and categories within the

[111] Johns, 'From Planning to Prototypes', 850 and 853.
[112] Andrejevic, 'Automating Surveillance', 10.
[113] F. Johns, 'Governance by Data' (2021) 17 *Annual Review of Law and Social Science* 53, 62.
[114] Kingsbury, 'Infrastructures and InfraReg'.

field and holds both methodological and normative potential. In concluding, I touch briefly on both elements.

Thinking infrastructurally about the public–private partnerships that we observed in the extension of Europol's mandate or in the tasks performed by TAT and the GIFCT implies, first, a methodological reorientation to the agency and vibrancy of material and socio-technical actants. Inspired by different strands of new materialism, actor-network theory and science and technology studies, this implies an attentiveness to how material objects, sites or relations produce patterns of social ordering – how they enable and constrain institutional or political projects.[115] Rather than considering the human and non-human – the social and material – as distinct ontological zones, this implies an account of international law and global governance where latent and often invisibilized infrastructural conduits (the 'missing masses' that Bruno Latour refers to) are allowed to (re)appear on stage as active agential elements.[116] This entails what Bowker and Star described as an 'infrastructural inversion': a change in our objects of analysis from formal legal rules or institutional forms to modes of governance by infrastructure.[117]

In my view, this methodological reorientation, which is making inroads in the field of international law,[118] revolves around three dimensions. First, it urges us to recognize the agency of things: the ways in which infrastructures are not only (and never fully) defined by legal or political aspirations but also – and this is the central claim here – reshape, disrupt or displace these aspirations through their own distinct and materially mediated forms of normative ordering. This perspective invites us to approach GIFCT's hash-sharing database or Europol's 'digital forensics' of 'pre-analysis' and infrastructures for public–private data-sharing not as passive tools for already existing governance

[115] Bennett, *Vibrant Matter*; T. Lemke, *The Government of Things: Foucault and the New Materialisms* (NYU Press, 2021).

[116] B. Latour, 'Where Are the Missing Masses? The Sociology of a Few Mundane Artifacts', in W. Bijker and J. Law (eds.) *Shaping Technology/Building Society: Studies in Sociotechnical Change* (MIT Press, 1992), 225; B. Latour, 'From Realpolitik to Dingpolitik: An Introduction to Making Things Public', in B. Latour and P. Weibel (eds.), *Making Things Public: Atmospheres of Democracy* (MIT Press, 2005), 14; A. Leander, 'Locating (New) Materialist Characters and Processes in Global Governance' (2021) 13 *International Theory* 157.

[117] G. Bowker and S. Star, *Sorting Things Out: Classification and Its Consequences* (MIT Press, 1999); Sullivan, 'Law, Technology, and Data-Driven Security'; Sullivan, 'Infra-Legalities'.

[118] Kingsbury, 'Infrastructures and InfraReg'; Sullivan, 'Law, Technology, and Data-Driven Security'; Sullivan, 'Infra-Legalities'; R. Vatanparast, 'The Infrastructures of the Global Data Economy: Undersea Cables and International Law' (2020) 61 *Harvard International Law Journal Online*; J. Hohmann, 'Diffuse Subjects and Dispersed Power: New Materialist Insights and Cautionary Lessons for International Law' (2021) 34 *Leiden Journal of International Law* 585.

projects but as agential participants in emergent governance networks. Second, and related, this reorientation adopts a relational ontology where agency – including regulatory agency in global security governance – is not seen as a property of particular (institutional) actors but as 'a matter of relation, and a process that entails a potentially infinite spectrum of matter around and within us'.[119] In this sense, the a priori public–private binary cannot be maintained: we are witnessing new relational compositions in which material infrastructures perform a pivotal role.[120] Finally, thinking infrastructurally, from my point of view, also implies attention to the performative or world-making dimension of material technologies. This points to how material tools – such as those employed for sensing, ordering and translating data – enact the normative categories and forms of knowledge upon and through which they intervene (as we observed in the category of 'high risk' individuals or the very notion of 'terrorism' itself).[121] From this perspective, thinking infrastructurally would allow us to trace the socio-technical cuts between what *matters* and what is excluded from *mattering*.[122] In short, a methodological orientation towards more-than-human agency, relational ontology and performativity allows us to appreciate the active participation of technological tools and infrastructural compositions in practices of global governance – in how problems are defined, rules implemented, power assembled and distributed. I see mapping and designing these emergent compositions as a critical avenue for international (institutional) law.

In addition to a methodological reorientation, this infrastructural perspective, secondly, also entails a normative agenda. Concerns about the effect of new digital technologies of surveillance and content moderation on human

[119] Hohmann, 'Diffuse Subjects', 595; K. Barad, *Meeting the Universe Halfway: Quantum Physics and the Entanglement of Matter and Meaning* (Duke University Press, 2007), 141, 334 ('agency is not an attribute but the ongoing reconfigurings of the world. The universe is agential intra-activity in its becoming' … 'Relata do not pre-exist relations'). See also M. Petersmann, 'Response-abilities of Care in More-than-human Worlds' (2021) *Journal of Human Rights and the Environment* 102.

[120] As Gavin Sullivan argued, this perspective allows us to perceive how 'boundaries (public–private, human–machinic, legal–non-legal) [are] redrawn or stabilized through global security infrastructures'. Sullivan, 'Law, Technology, and Data-Driven Security', S37.

[121] D. Van Den Meerssche, 'International Organizations and the Performativity of Measuring States: Discipline through Diagnosis' (2018) 15 *International Organizations Law Review* 168; A. Lang, 'International Lawyers and the Study of Expertise: Representationalism and Performativity', in M. Hirsch and A. Lang (eds.), *Research Handbook on the Sociology of International Law* (Edward Elgar, 2018), 122.

[122] I am inspired here by Barad's 'agential realist elaboration of performativity', which 'allows matter its due as an active participant in the world's becoming'. In Barad, *Meeting the Universe Halfway*, 136.

rights figure prominently in the different initiatives discussed in this chapter. While the GIFCT pledges to a policy of 'countering terrorism while respecting human rights',[123] Europol's new regulation notes that the institution 'should ensure that the development, use and deployment of new technologies are guided by the principles of transparency, explainability, fairness and accountability, do not undermine fundamental rights and freedoms and are in compliance with Union law'.[124] These legal considerations relate specifically to the prevention of bias and the protection of personal data.[125] There is a risk, however, that these repeated normative commitments underestimate how the existence and exercise of human rights are tied to specific material decision-making practices. As Julie Cohen has convincingly observed: 'discourses about fundamental rights have relied on a set of unstated and unexamined assumptions about the material environment's affordance – the conditions of possibility that material environments offer for individual, collective and organizational activity'.[126] The concept of affordances is key here. Originating in design studies and environmental psychology, it has been developed in social theory to highlight how human thought and action is both enabled and conditioned by the properties of material and socio-technical settings.[127] This inspired legal scholars to stress how also the exercise of (fundamental) rights hinges on particular material configurations.[128]

Thinking infrastructurally, in this sense, allows us to critically explore how new technological tools, practices and systems impact (or erode) the exercise of human rights. What is the salience of privacy and purpose limitation principles in relation to Europol's curation and analysis of large and complex datasets or its infrastructures of integrated data management? (as signalled in Section 13.2). How do the proactive algorithmic content moderation practices enabled by the hash-sharing database influence prospects of legal review and

[123] GIFCT, 'Introducing GIFCT Working Group Output' (2022), https://gifct.org/wp-content/uploads/2022/07/GIFCT-22WG-CR-Lifecycle-1.1.pdf (accessed February 2022), 2.

[124] European Parliament and Council Regulation 2022/991, OJ L 169/1, Recital 48.

[125] Ibid.

[126] J. Cohen, *Between Truth and Power: The Legal Constructions of Informational Capitalism* (Oxford University Press, 2019), 246.

[127] As Gavin Sullivan observed, '[a]ffordances are not intrinsic properties of objects, but relationships between objects and users, "jointly determined by the qualities of the object and the abilities of the agent that is interacting"'. Sullivan, 'Law, Technology, and Data-Driven Security', S40.

[128] M. Hildebrandt, *Smart Technologies and the End(s) of Law: Novel Entanglements of Law and Technology* (Edward Elgar, 2016); J. Cohen, 'Affording Fundamental Rights' (2017) 4 *Critical Analysis of Law* 78.

redress? (as Section 13.3 analysed).[129] How can we make anti-discrimination claims against decisions that are not based on fixed normative criteria but on real-time patterns and relational associations detected in data? (as I pointed to in Section 13.4). The infrastructures of governance described in this chapter, in other words, risk to undermine the material conditions for human rights protection – to disable the affordances on which the exercise of rights has always implicitly hinged. The exercise of thinking – and acting – infrastructurally, then, aims to guide our normative attention and interventions to practices of material and socio-technical design, which are aimed at (re)opening possibilities for individual or collective legal and political action and imagination.[130] This practice of critical infrastructural design opens promising pathways for the field of international institutional law beyond its orientation towards institutional design or its preoccupation with public law analogies.

[129] Sullivan, 'Infra-Legalities' (analysing 'how the specific affordances of the hash-sharing database are altering the terrain for human rights and online speech').

[130] A promising opening in this direction was made in a recent symposium in AJIL unbound. See B. Kingsbury, 'Introduction to the Symposium on Infrastructuring International Law' (2023) 117 *AJIL Unbound* 1. There are, of course, many forms and foundations for such infrastructural interventions. I am particularly inspired by projects of critical design and fabulation, inspired, for example, by J. Austin and A. Leander, 'Designing-With/In World Politics: Manifestos for an International Political Design' (2021) 2 *Political Anthropological Research on the International Social Sciences* 83; K. Easterling, 'We Will Be Making Active Form' (2012) 82 *Architectural Design* 58; D. Rosner, *Critical Fabulations: Reworking the Methods and Margins of Design* (MIT Press, 2018).

14

Institutional Promiscuity

An Epilogue

JAN KLABBERS

14.1 INTRODUCTION

The assumption that international organizations would only need to stand in any kind of legal relationship with their member states was always based more on fiction than on fact. On some points this is rather obvious: already the early nineteenth-century river commissions served to create winners and losers, not just among their member states but mostly within their member states. Cities that lost the right to collect tolls clearly also saw a source of income dry up; cities that lost disembarking privileges likewise saw a source of income dry up. Much the same applies more generally: the regulation of telegraphic and postal communication later in the nineteenth century smoothened the flows of information considerably, allowing an enterprising individual such as Julius Reuter to establish a press agency that still exists to this day. The international ization of intellectual property protection served not so much abstract entities such as France or Italy (although perhaps that too, in an abstract sort of manner) but served mostly individuals: Victor Hugo was one of the driving forces, and for good reason, while Giuseppe Verdi is sometimes mentioned as one of the first composers who, thanks to the international protection of copyright, could actually earn a nice living from composing alone.[1]

The above suggests that there have always been winners and losers associated with international organizations; it stands to reason therefore to suggest that the relationship between international organizations and those winners and losers (be it an individual or a company or still something else) be treated as one of some legal relevance – not just to think of international organizations

[1] O. Figes, *The Europeans* (Penguin, 2019).

as a distant source of costs and benefits, but as actually having something to do with the 'authoritative allocation of values', in much the same way as the state is seen as standing in such a relationship to its population. Not all economic effects of state decisions may subject to legal regulation and judicial review, not even in the most developed administrative states; but, that said, it is generally recognized that markets rely on states, and there is thus a legally relevant connection between state and market. And this relation works typically in both directions: individuals and companies incur wins and losses from state action, while the state itself derives some of its legitimacy from providing or guaranteeing prosperity. What applies to states applies just as well to international organizations, as these do some of the regulatory work typically associated with states.

In more straightforward legal practice too, the 'vacuum assumption' was never particularly realistic. International organizations may have lacked formal international legal personality until well after the end of World War II, but this rarely stopped them from doing things which would seem to presuppose such personality. The Cape Spartel Lighthouse reportedly entered into a multilateral agreement before many other international organizations had even been created; and the various sanitary bureaus set up during the nineteenth century at the edges of Europe must have been in touch with local authorities to combat the outbreak and spread of deadly diseases. The absence of international legal personality and of treaty-making powers indicate that no other relations were expected than those with member states, but practice usually finds a way. If a treaty cannot be concluded for lack of competence, then the 'memorandum of understanding' will be invented – this is explicitly not a treaty, and thus not reliant on treaty-making powers, or even on international legal personality. And perhaps the best example is offered by none other than the International Court of Justice in its classic *Reparation for Injuries* opinion. Here it derived the UN's international legal personality, in part, from the conclusion of the treaties by the same UN. The reasoning is circular, of course – performing such acts indicates the presence of precisely that quality which is required to perform such acts – but that is not quite the point for the present purposes. The point is, rather, that the Court did not hesitate to claim that one of the treaties the UN had taken part in was the 1946 General Convention on Privileges and Immunities of the UN. Yet, upon inspection, the UN was not, and still is not, a party to that Convention. It may well be considered a beneficiary, but such would only indicate that this treaty creates rights for third parties. But the UN never was a party, which means that the Court was either careless or, possibly more likely, finishing a thought: the thought that it is unlikely that an entity such as the UN, designed as the centre of the legal and political universe after a devastating world war, would not be capable of participating in international relations.

To even state the possibility of a UN unable to act internationally is to state its absurdity, and yet a similar absurdity played out around the creation of the EU at Maastricht, in the early 1990s. Since the EU had not expressly been endowed with international legal personality, some felt that it could not be considered to be an international legal person (and some were delighted with this conclusion, mistakenly believing it seemed to safeguard national sovereignty).[2] Yet, such reasoning bordered on the nonsensical: surely, an entity with an official foreign policy and powers related to combating international crime and migration (in no particular order) could not be devoid of international legal personality – at least for those who feel that international legal personality is a threshold for acting on the international level. How else to implement a foreign policy? How else to give effect to migration decisions?

The vacuum assumption, in other words, has always been a myth. For many though, it appeared a useful myth. International organizations and their leadership and staff (if they would ever reflect on these things) were happy enough: the vacuum assumption entailed, amongst others, that they could only be held accountable by their member states, which in practice means they are rarely, if ever, held to account. Member states, likewise (if they would ever reflect on these things) were happy enough: they remained in full control of their creatures, without having to fear interference by victims, judges or other stakeholders – this makes life so much easier. And if neither organizations nor their member states ever question received wisdom (and academics feel they should not question what they think constitutes 'practice', however misguided), then a grand 'coalition of the unwilling' all but guarantees that the law remains stuck in a time-warp going back to the late nineteenth, early twentieth century.

14.2 SOME RAMIFICATIONS

This volume has demonstrated abundantly that the vacuum assumption no longer holds – if it ever did. International organizations, so the volume demonstrates, constantly interact with entities other than their member states. They interact with non-member states; with cities; with each other; with international sports associations; with large consultancy firms; with the private

[2] See, further, J. Klabbers, 'Presumptive Personality: The European Union in International Law', in M. Koskenniemi (ed.), *International Law Aspects of the European Union* (Martinus Nijhoff, 1998), 231.

sector, as well as with others. Gavi, the Vaccine Alliance, is an intriguing example, bringing together international organizations, states and private funders. An even more intriguing example perhaps is (was?) the Contact Group on Piracy off the Somali Coast, established to implement a Security Council mandate and involving not just states and international organizations, but also trade unions (of seafarers), church associations and the largest shipping insurer in the form of Lloyd's of London. Whatever the formal legal status of the Contact Group (whether an international organization or a mere 'governance mechanism' of uncertain provenance), it clearly brought international organizations such as the EU, NATO and the IMO together with a wide variety of other actors – other than (member or participating) states and other international organizations.

The volume further demonstrates how such interactions may take place, zooming in on the private sector. International organizations, so the volume makes clear, procure goods and services from the private sector; they do so in ways that are strictly legally regulated and in doing so they help shape the very markets in which they operate. They are funded by private actors, including philanthropic foundations. They not only procure goods and services, they also have their own services and goods to sell, and such relations may demand a further explanation in terms of contract law.

These are not novel observations per se. In 2013, a group of international relations scholars noted that international organizations were 'opening up' to the world by making provision for contacts with each other and what were referred to as 'transnational actors'.[3] International organizations had, in fact, already been doing this for quite some time, for instance in the form of accepting observers, in particular perhaps from civil society.[4] And many international organizations have developed rules or guidelines with respect to whose funding or donations they can accept or who they can do business with – clear signs of regulating engagement with the external world.[5]

The question remains though what this means for international organizations law. Clearly, the classic assumption according to which the only legal relationship of relevance was that between the organization and its member

[3] J. Tallberg et al. (eds.), *The Opening Up of International Organizations* (Cambridge University Press, 2013).

[4] See, e.g. N. Sybesma-Knol, *The Status of Observers in the United Nations* (Vrije Universiteit, 1981).

[5] The most well-known of these are the WHO's rules, known as the Framework of Engagement with Non-State Actors (FENSA). For discussion, see A. Berman, 'Between Participation and Capture in International Rule-Making: The WHO Framework of Engagement with Non-State Actors' (2021) 32 *European Journal of International Law* 227.

states has little traction, but then what? If we should not look at international organizations solely as agencies set up by member states to do things for those member states, then what should be put in its place?

What complicates the puzzle further is that, as a matter of fact, the classic assumption fails not because it is inaccurate, but because it is incomplete, meaning that some of it needs to be rescued: the baby should not be thrown out together with the bathwater. After all, international organizations are typically set up by member states to do things for member states – it is just that this is not even scratching the surface of what they do and, thus, cannot be the only legal relationship that matters.

Be that as it may, at a bare minimum the 'vacuum assumption' should be discarded, for lacking any correspondence with empirical reality. A properly grounded law of international organizations can no longer afford to think of only the 'organization–member' dynamic; it needs to 'open up', all the more so at a time when international organizations are often criticized for being untouchable and unaccountable.[6] The criticism, after all, stems directly from this untenable vacuum assumption.

It would be much better to accept that international organizations are characteristically set up by states, but rapidly (albeit to varying degrees) become political agents in their own right, in much the same way that domestic administrative agencies are usually not solely associated with central government. There is, after all, little qualitative difference – other than matters of scope – between a national radio frequencies board and an international frequencies board; between a national pandemic-declaring health agency and an international one; between a national river commission and an international river commission or even between a domestic development bank and an international development bank.

An international organizations law reflective of this state of affairs – the largely administrative task of many international organizations – will come to realize that international organizations are political operators in their own right. Their work needs funding; elementary fairness demands that they need to play by market rules in much the same way domestic agencies do; and their decisions and acts come with winners and losers – and not just among member-states.

And if that is realized, then it should no longer be near-automatic to just accept that international organizations can expand their competences and

6 The literature is voluminous. See, e.g. C. Ferstman, *International Organizations and the Fight for Accountability: The Remedies and Reparations Gap* (Oxford University Press, 2017); G. Hirschman, *Accountability in Global Governance* (Oxford University Press, 2020).

activities seemingly at will, without any form of scrutiny. It would entail that a decision to grant a particular international organization some privileges and immunities may well become a matter of calm contemplation, without anyone immediately proclaiming that the global common good is undermined. It may be a brilliant idea to protect health organizations and their staff against interference by domestic authorities but, surely, the same does not immediately apply to military or security officials.

Starting from the idea that international organizations do not only relate to their member states may also help to stimulate thinking about how they should be set up internally. As it is, the law of international organizations lacks the intellectual resources to address questions of relations between organs of the same organization, typically borrowing somewhat loosely from domestic 'separation of powers' arguments – if at all. And likewise, whatever international organizations may stand for, they are also employers, sometimes of fairly large numbers of people. While there is a lot of jurisprudence on specific legal questions, little principled thinking has gone into the role of international organizations as employers – likely because, under the vacuum assumption, such a role is hardly deemed to be of much relevance.

But most visibly, the putative accountability of international organizations towards third parties cannot be addressed in any meaningful way as long as the 'vacuum assumption' applies: in a conception where no third parties are considered relevant, no issues of accountability can possibly arise. *Quod erat demonstrandum*. There is merit in not succumbing to the knee-jerk reflex of blaming international organizations for all the perils one encounters;[7] but, by the same token, the total incapacity of the international legal order to devise a working accountability system (beyond accountability to the member states, that is) is not a very desirable situation either.

14.3 FINAL REMARKS

This volume has provided a first overview of how international organizations interact with the outside world – with a particular emphasis on relations with the private sector – and what this may entail for the governing legal framework. The volume hardly exhausts the matter. Not only are there at least 300 international organizations in existence at any given moment (empirically, therefore, this volume only scratches the surface), it is also plausible to

7 J. Klabbers, 'Responsibility as Opportunism: The Responsibility of International Organizations', in S. Besson (ed.), *Theories of International Responsibility Law* (Cambridge University Press, 2022), 119.

suggest that different organizations may require different approaches. The work of the multilateral development banks, for instance, will affect local populations differently than those of, for example, humanitarian organizations. Military alliances such as NATO may kill people in ways that are unlikely to apply to organizations active in the field of communications, such as the Universal Postal Union. And academic institutions (whether the European University Institute or the European Molecular Biology Laboratory) will operate in ways different from food security organizations.

It is useful to recognize that international organizations are not just 'international', but that they are 'organizations' too, in much the same way as is the local fire department, municipal social security office or provincial board of education. Looked at from such an angle, it will become clear that international organizations, like all organizations, tend to do three things: they regulate; they monitor and manage what they regulate; and, in doing so, they allocate costs and benefits among stakeholders. It was long thought that only member states counted as stakeholders, but it is hoped that this volume has demonstrated that this assumption is no longer tenable, if it ever was.

Bibliography

This bibliography does not list newspaper articles, blog posts and the like.

Abbott, K., 'Public Private Partnership', in *Max Planck Encyclopedia of International Law* (Oxford University Press).

Abbott, K. and B. Faude, 'Hybrid Institutional Complexes in Global Governance' (2022) 17 *Review of International Organizations* 263.

Abbott, K., J. Green and R. Keohane, 'Organizational Ecology and Institutional Change in Global Governance' (2016) 70 *International Organization* 247.

Abbott, K. and D. Snidal, 'Why Do States Act through Formal International Organizations' (1998) 42 *Journal of Conflict Resolution* 3.

Abbott, K. et al. (eds.), *International Organizations as Orchestrators* (Cambridge University Press, 2015).

Adam, D, 'The Pandemic's True Death Toll: Millions More than Official Counts' (2022) 601 *Nature* 312.

Adams, B. and J. Martens, *Fit for Whose Purpose? Private Funding and Corporate Influence in the United Nations* (Global Policy Forum, 2015).

Akande, D., 'The Legal Nature of Security Council Referrals to the ICC and Its Impact on Al Bahir's Immunities' (2009) 7 *Journal of International Criminal Law and Justice* 333.

Alter, K. and S. Meunier, 'The Politics of International Regime Complexity' (2009) 7 *Perspectives on Politics* 13.

Alvarez, J. E., 'A BIT on Custom' (2009) 42 *New York University Journal of International Law and Politics* 17.

The Impact of International Organizations on International Law (Martinus Nijhoff, 2017).

International Organizations as Law-Makers (Oxford University Press, 2005).

Amaro, R., 'Machine Learning, Surveillance and the Politics of Visibility', in B. Vickers and K. Allado-McDowell (eds.), *Atlas of Anomalous AI* (Ignota, 2021).

Amburgey, T. and H. Rao, 'Organizational Ecology: Past, Present, and Future Directions' (1996) 39 *Academy of Management Journal* 1265.

Amoore, L., 'The Deep Border' (2021) *Political Geography* 102547.

'Machine Learning Political Orders' (2022) 49 *Review of International Studies* 20.

The Politics of Possibility: Risk and Security Beyond Probability (Duke University Press, 2013) .

'Risk before Justice: When the Law Contests Its Own Suspension' (2008) 21 *Leiden Journal of International Law* 847.

Andenas, M. and I. H.-Y. Chiu, *The Foundations and Future of Financial Regulation: Governance for Responsibility* (Routledge, 2014).

Andonova, L., *Governance Entrepreneurs: International Organizations and the Rise of Global Public–Private Partnerships* (Cambridge University Press, 2017) .

Andrejevic, M., 'Automating Surveillance' (2019) 17 *Surveillance & Society* 7.

Aradau, C., 'Experimentality, Surplus Data and the Politics of Debilitation in Borderzones' (2022) 27 *Geopolitics* 26.

Aradau, C. and T Blanke, 'Politics of Prediction: Security and the Time/Space of Governmentality in the Age of Big Data' (2017) 20 *European Journal of Social Theory* 373.

Arnold, P., 'Disciplining Domestic Regulation: The World Trade Organization and the Market for Professional Services' (2005) 30 *Accounting, Organizations and Society* 299.

Attanavich, W., B. McCarl and D. Bessler, 'The Effect of H1N1 (Swine Flu) Media Coverage on Agricultural Commodity' (2011) 33 *Applied Economic Perspectives and Policy* 241.

Aust, A., 'The Theory and Practice of Informal International Instruments' (1986) 35 *International and Comparative Law Quarterly* 787.

Aust, H. P., *Das Recht der globalen Stadt – Grenzüberschreitende Dimensionen kommunaler Selbstverwaltung* (Mohr Siebeck, 2017).

'Shining Cities on the Hill: The Global City, Climate Change and International Law' (2015) 26 *European Journal of International Law* 255.

Aust, H. P. and J. Nijman (eds.), *Research Handbook on International Law and Cities* (Edward Elgar, 2021).

Aust, H. P. and A. Rodiles, 'Cities and Local Governments: International Development from Below?', in R. Buchanan, L. Eslava and S. Pahuja (eds.), *The Oxford Handbook on International Law and Development* (Oxford University Press, 2023), 207.

Austin, J. and A. Leander, 'Designing-With/In World Politics: Manifestos for an International Political Design' (2021) 2 *Political Anthropological Research on the International Social Sciences* 83.

Aziz, D., 'Global Public–Private Partnerships in International Law' (2012) 2 *Asian Journal of International Law* 339.

Bäckstrand, K. and J. Kuyper, 'The Democratic Legitimacy of Orchestration: The UNFCCC, Non-State Actors, and Transnational Climate Governance' (2017) 26 *Environmental Politics* 764.

Bäckstrand, K. et al., 'Non-State Actors in Global Climate Governance: From Copenhagen to Paris and Beyond' (2017) 26 *Environmental Politics* 561.

Bantekas, I. et al., *UNCITRAL Model Law on International Commercial Arbitration: A Commentary* (Cambridge University Press, 2020).

Barad, K., *Meeting the Universe Halfway: Quantum Physics and the Entanglement of Matter and Meaning* (Duke University Press, 2007).

Barber, B., *If Mayors Ruled the World: Dysfunctional Nations, Rising Cities* (Yale University Press, 2013).
Barnett, M. and M. Finnemore, *Rules for the World: International Organizations in Global Governance* (Cornell University Press, 2004).
Basedow, J., *The Law of Open Societies: Private Ordering and Public Regulation in the Conflict of Laws* (Martinus Nijhoff, 2015).
Batiffol, H., *Problèmes des contrats privés internationaux* (Association des Études Internationales, 1962).
Bederman, D., 'The Souls of International Organizations: Legal Personality and the Lighthouse at Cape Spartel' (1996) 36 *Virginia Journal of International Law* 275.
Beigbeder, Y., *The World Health Organization* (Martinus Nijhoff, 1998).
Bennett, J., *Vibrant Matter: A Political Ecology of Things* (Duke University Press, 2009).
Benvenisti, E, 'Upholding Democracy amid the Challenges of New Technology: What Role for the Law of Global Governance?' (2018) 29 *European Journal of International Law* 9.
Berman, A., 'Between Participation and Capture in International Rule-Making: The WHO Framework of Engagement with Non-State Actors' (2021) 32 *European Journal of International Law* 227.
Besson, S., 'Democratic Representation within International Organizations: From International Good Governance to International Good Government' (2022) 19 *International Organizations Law Review* 489.
Reconstruire l'ordre institutionnel international (Collège de France, 2021).
Betsill, M. and H. Bulkeley, 'Cities and the Multilevel Governance of Climate Change' (2006) 12 *Global Governance* 141.
Biggins, J. and C. Scott, 'Resolving the Gaps: Embedding Isda in States' Responses to Systemic Risk', in N. Dorn (ed.), *Controlling Capital, Public and Private Regulation of Financial Markets* (Routledge, 2016), 157.
Blank, Y., 'The City and the World' (2006) 44 *Columbia Journal of Transnational Law* 875.
'Localism in the New Global Legal Order' (2006) 47 *Harvard International Law Journal* 263.
Block, F. and B. Somers, *The Power of Market Fundamentalism: Karl Polanyi's Critique* (Harvard University Press 2014).
Block-Lieb, S. and T. Halliday, *Global Lawmakers: International Organizations in the Crafting of World Markets* (Cambridge University Press, 2017).
Blokker, N., 'International Organizations and Their Members' (2004) 1 *International Organizations Law Review* 139.
Blunt, G., 'The Gates Foundation, Global Health and Domination: A Republican Critique of Transnational Philanthropy' (2022) 98 *International Affairs* 2039.
Böckstiegel, K.-H., 'The Application of the UNIDROIT Principles to Contracts Involving States or Intergovernmental Organizations', in H. G. Naón and R. Briner (eds.), *Special Supplement 2002: UNIDROIT Principles of International Commercial Contracts: Reflections on their Use in International Arbitration* (ICC, 2002), 51.
Bodansky, D., J. Brunnée and L. Rajamani, *International Climate Change Law* (Oxford University Press, 2017).

von Bogdandy, A., 'The Idea of European Public Law Today', in P. Huber, S. Cassese and A. von Bogdandy (eds.), *The Max Planck Handbooks in European Public Law: Volume I: The Administrative State* (Oxford University Press, 2017), 1.

von Bogdandy, A., M. Goldmann and I. Venzke, 'From Public International to International Public Law: Translating World Public Opinion into International Public Authority' (2017) 28 *European Journal of International Law* 125.

Boisson de Chazournes, L., 'Les Relations Entre Organisations Régionales et Organisations Universelles' (2010) 347 *Recueil des Cours* 79.

Bordin, F. L., *The Analogy between States and International Organisations* (Cambridge University Press, 2018).

Bordin, F. L., et al., *Final Report of the ILA Study Group on the International Law of Regional Organizations* (International Law Association, 2024).

Born, G., *International Commercial Arbitration* (Kluwer, 2014).

Borowicz, M., 'Contracts as Regulation: The Isda Master Agreement' (2021) 16 *Capital Markets Law Journal* 72.

Borsi, U., 'Municipalisme et internationalisme' in *Mélanges Hauriou* (Sirey, 1929), 81.

Börzel, T. and Th. Risse, 'Governance without a State: Can It Work?' (2010) 4 *Regulation and Governance* 13.

Boussebaa, M., 'Global Professional Service Firms, Transnational Organising and Core/Periphery Networks', in L. Seabrooke and L. Henriksen (eds.), *Professional Networks in Transnational Governance* (Cambridge University Press, 2017), 233.

Bowie, N., 'Terrorism Databases and Data Sets: A New Inventory' (2021) 15 *Perspectives on Terrorism* 147.

Bowker, G. and S. Star, *Sorting Things Out: Classification and Its Consequences* (MIT Press, 1999).

Bradford, A., *The Brussels Effect: How the European Union Rules the World* (Oxford University Press, 2020).

Bradley, M., *The International Organization for Migration: Challenges, Commitments, Complexities* (Routledge, 2020).

Brierly, J. L., *The Law of Nations*, 6th ed. (Clarendon Press, 1963).

Briggs, A., *The Conflict of Laws* (Clarendon Press, 2002).

Bromley, P. and W. Powell, 'From Smoke and Mirrors to Walking the Talk: Decoupling in the Contemporary World' (2012) 6 *Academy of Management Annals* 483.

Brown, H., 'And the Next Director-General of WHO Is . . .' (2006) 368 *The Lancet* 1757.

Brunnée, J. and S. Toope, *Legitimacy and Legality in International Law: An Interactional Account* (Cambridge University Press, 2010).

Bull, B., M. Bøås and D. McNeill, 'Private Sector Influence in the Multilateral System: A Changing Structure of the World Governance?' (2004) 10 *Global Governance* 481.

Burci, G. L., 'Public/Private Partnerships in the Public Health Sector' (2009) 6 *International Organizations Law Review* 359.

Cafaggi, F., 'New Foundations of Transnational Private Regulation' (2011) 38 *Journal of Law and Society* 20.

Cantelon, H. and M. Letters, 'The Making of the IOC Environmental Policy as the Third Dimension of the Olympic Movement' (2000) 35 *International Review for the Sociology of Sport* 294.

Carodenuto, S. and B. Cashore, 'Can Non-State Regulatory Authority Improve Domestic Forest Sustainability? Assessing Interactive Pathways of Influence in Cameroon' in S. Wood et al. (eds.), *Transnational Business Governance Interactions: Advancing Marginalized Actors and Enhancing Regulatory Quality* (Edward Elgar, 2019), 207.

Chimni, B. S., 'International Institutions Today: An Imperial Global State in the Making' (2004) 15 *European Journal of International Law* 1.

Citron, D, 'Extremist Speech, Compelled Conformity, and Censorship Creep' (2018) 93 *Notre Dame Law Review* 1035.

Clinton, C. and D. Sridhar, *Governing Global Health* (Oxford University Press, 2017).

Cobbe, J., 'Algorithmic Censorship by Social Platforms: Power and Resistance' (2020) 34 *Philosophy and Technology* 739.

Cogan, J. K., 'Cities in the Shadow of International Institutional Law' (2021) 18 *International Organizations Law Review* 133.

'Financing and Budgets', in J. K. Cogan, I. Hurd and I. Johnstone (eds.), *Oxford Handbook of International Organizations* (Oxford University Press, 2016), 903.

'International Organizations and Cities', in H. P. Aust and J. Nijman (eds.), *Research Handbook on International Law and Cities* (Edward Elgar, 2021), 158.

Cohen, D. and Ph. Carter, 'WHO and the Pandemic Flu "Conspiracies"' (2010) 340 *British Medical Journal* 1274.

Cohen, J., 'Affording Fundamental Rights' (2017) 4 *Critical Analysis of Law* 78.

Between Truth and Power: The Legal Constructions of Informational Capitalism (Oxford University Press, 2019).

Collins, R. and N. White (eds.), *International Organizations and the Idea of Autonomy* (Routledge, 2011).

Collste, G., '"Where You Live Should Not Determine Whether You Live": Global Justice and the Distribution of COVID-19 Vaccines' (2022) 15 *Ethics and Global Politics* 43.

Conrad, S., *Globalgeschichte* (Beck, 2013).

Cordero-Moss, G., 'International Arbitration and the Quest for the Applicable Law' (2008) 8 *Global Jurist* 42.

Craig, P., *EU Administrative Law*, 3rd ed. (Oxford University Press, 2018).

Crawford, J., *Brownlie's Principles of Public International Law*, 9th ed. (Oxford University Press, 2019).

Curtin, D. and P. Leino, 'In Search of Transparency for EU Law-Making: Trilogues on the Cusp of Dawn' (2017) 54 *Common Market Law Review* 1673.

Cutler, D. and L. Summers, 'The COVID-19 Pandemic and the $16 Trillion Virus' (2020) 324 *Journal of the American Medical Association* 1495.

Dadwood, F. S. et al., 'Estimated Global Mortality Associated with the First 12 Months of 2009 Pandemic Influenza A H1N1 Virus Circulation: A Modelling Study' (2012) 12 *The Lancet Infectious Diseases* 687.

Dang, H., 'The Applicability of International Law as Governing Law of State Contracts' (2010) 17 *Australian International Law Journal* 133.

Daugirdas, K., 'International Organizations and the Creation of Customary International Law' (2020) 31 *European Journal of International Law* 201.

'Review: Advanced Introduction to the Law of International Organizations, Written by Jan Klabbers' (2016) 13 *International Organizations Law Review* 396.

Daugirdas, K. and G. L. Burci, 'Financing the World Health Organization: What Lessons for Multilateralism?' (2019) 16 *International Organizations Law Review* 299.

De Vree, J. K., *Political Integration: The Formation of Theory and Its Problems* (Mouton, 1972).

Del Sarto, R., 'Normative Empire Europe: The European Union, Its Borderlands, and the Arab Spring (2015) 54 *Journal of Common Market Studies* 215.

Deshman, A., 'Horizontal Review between International Organizations: Why, How, and Who Cares about Corporate Regulatory Capture' (2011) 22 *European Journal of International Law* 1089.

Dias Oliva, Th., 'Content Moderation Technologies: Applying Human Rights Standards to Protect Freedom of Expression' (2020) 20 *Human Rights Law Review* 607.

Dijkzeul, D., 'Not Just States or the Secretary-General: The Emergence of UNOPS as a New UN Organization', in J Oestreich (ed.), *International Organizations as Self-Directed Actors: A Framework for Analysis* (Routledge, 2012), 195.

Dogliani, P., 'European Municipalism in the First Half of the Twentieth Century: The Socialist Network' (2002) 11 *Contemporary European History* 573.

Dolgin, E., 'The Race for Antiviral Drugs to Beat COVID – and the Next Pandemic' (2021) 592 *Nature* 340.

Donaldson, M. and B. Kingsbury, 'Power and the Public: The Nature and Effects of Formal Transparency Policies in Global Governance Institutions', in A. Bianchi and A. Peters (eds.), *Transparency in International Law* (Cambridge University Press, 2013), 502.

Dorn, A. and R. Cross, 'Flying Humanitarians: The UN Humanitarian Air Service', in A. Dorn (ed.), *Air Power in UN Operations: Wings for Peace* (Ashgate, 2014), 101.

Douek, E., 'The Rise of Content Cartels' (2020) *Knight First Amendment Institute at Columbia University*, https://knightcolumbia.org/content/the-rise-of-content-cartels (visited 12 March 2025).

Downie, Ch., 'Competition, Cooperation, and Adaptation: The Organizational Ecology of International Organizations in Global Energy Governance' (2022) 48 *Review of International Studies* 364.

Dunoff, J., 'Is Sovereign Equality Obsolete? Understanding Twenty-First Century International Organizations' (2012) 43 *Netherlands Yearbook of International Law* 99.

Easterling, K., 'We Will Be Making Active Form' (2012) 82 *Architectural Design* 58.

Eilstrup-Sangiovanni, M., 'Death of International Organizations. The Organizational Ecology of Intergovernmental Organizations, 1815–2015' (2020) 15 *Review of International Organizations* 339.

Enserink, M., 'Swine Flu Names Evolving Faster than Swine Flu Itself' (2009) 324 *Science* 871.

Espinal, M. et al., 'International Health Regulations, Ebola, and Emerging Infectious Diseases in Latin America and the Caribbean' (2018) 108 *American Journal of Public Health* S466.

Fassbender, B., *The United Nations Charter as the Constitution of the International Community* (Martinus Nijhoff, 2009).

Faude, B., *Von Konkurrenz zu Arbeitsteilung: Komplexität und Dynamik im Zusammenspiel internationaler Institutionen* (Campus, 2015).

Ferstman, C., *International Organizations and the Fight for Accountability: The Remedies and Reparations Gap* (Oxford University Press, 2017).

Fidler, D., 'The Future of the World Health Organization: What Role for International Law?' (1998) 31 *Vanderbilt Journal of Transnational Law* 1079.

'International Law and Global Public Health' (1999) 1 *University of Kansas Law Review* 1.

Figes, O., *The Europeans* (Penguin, 2019).

Fransen, L., and G. LeBaron, 'Big Audit Firms as Regulatory Intermediaries in Transnational Labor Governance' (2019) 13 *Regulation and Governance* 260.

Frowein, J., 'The United Nations and Non-Member States' (1970) 25 *International Journal* 333.

Gaillard, E., *Legal Theory of International Arbitration* (Martinus Nijhoff, 2010).

Gaspari, O., 'Cities against States? Hopes, Dreams and Shortcomings of the European Municipal Movement, 1900–1960' (2002) 11 *Contemporary European History* 597.

Gehring, Th. and B. Faude, 'A Theory of Emerging Order within Institutional Complexes: How Competition among Regulatory International Institutions Leads to Institutional Adaptation and Division of Labor' (2014) 9 *Review of International Organizations* 471.

Gibb, R. et al., 'Zoonotic Host Diversity Increases in Human-Dominated Ecosystems' (2020) 584 *Nature* 398.

Gillespie, T., *Custodians of the Internet: Platforms, Content Moderation, and the Hidden Decisions that Shape Social Media* (Yale University Press, 2018).

Gless, S., 'Europol', in V. Mitsilegas, M. Bergström and Th. Konstadinides (eds.), *Research Handbook on EU Criminal Law* (Edward Elgar, 2016), 465.

Glynn, J. J., 'The Development of British Railway Accounting: 1800–1911' (1984) 11 *The Accounting Historians Journal* 103.

Golia Jr, A. and A. Peters, 'The Concept of International Organization', in J. Klabbers (ed.), *The Cambridge Companion to International Organizations Law* (Cambridge University Press, 2022), 25.

Gorwa, R., R. Binns and Ch. Katzenbach, 'Algorithmic Content Moderation: Technical and Political Challenges in the Automation of Platform Governance' (2020) 7 *Big Data & Society*.

Gostin, L. O., *Global Health Law* (Harvard University Press, 2014).

Gött, H., 'Interactions between International Organizations: Approaching a Neglected Governance Dimension' (2020) 17 *International Organizations Law Review* 75.

Graham, E. R., 'Money and Multilateralism: How Funding Rules Constitute IO Governance' (2015) 7 *International Theory* 162.

Grant, T., *Admission to the United Nations: Charter Article 4 and the Rise of Universal Organization* (Martinus Nijhoff, 2009).

Green, J., *Rethinking Private Authority: Agents and Entrepreneurs in Global Environmental Governance* (Princeton University Press, 2014).

'Transnational Delegation in Global Environmental Governance: When Do Non-State Actors Govern?' (2018) 12 *Regulation and Governance* 263.

Grigorescu, A., 'Transparency of Intergovernmental Organizations: The Roles of Member States, International Bureaucracies and Nongovernmental Organizations' (2007) 51 *International Studies Quarterly* 625.

Gulbrandsen, L., 'Public Sector Engagement with Private Governance Programmes: Interactions and Evolutionary Effects in Forest and Fisheries Certification', in A. Nollkaemper et al. (eds.), *Smart Mixes for Transboundary Environmental Harm* (Cambridge University Press, 2019), 211.

Gulbrandsen, L. and G. Auld, 'Contested Accountability Logics in Evolving Nonstate Certification for Fisheries Sustainability' (2016) 16 *Global Environmental Politics* 42.

Gupta, A., 'Transparency under Scrutiny: Information Disclosure in Global Environmental Governance' (2008) 8 *Global Environmental Politics* 1.

Haftel, Y. and T. Lenz, 'Measuring Institutional Overlap in Global Governance' (2022) 17 *Review of International Organizations* 323.

Hale, R., 'Bargaining, Duress, and Economic Liberty' (1943) 43 *Columbia Law Review* 603.

Hale, Th., 'The Role of Sub-State and Non-State Actors in International Climate Processes' (2018) *Chatham House Research Paper*.

Hale, Th. and Ch. Roger, 'Orchestration and Transnational Climate Governance' (2014) 9 *Review of International Organizations* 59.

Hancher, L. and M. Moran, 'Organizing Regulatory Space', in L. Hancher and M. Moran (eds.), *Capitalism, Culture, and Economic Regulation* (Clarendon Press, 1989), 271.

Hannan, M., *Organizational Ecology* (Harvard University Press, 1989).

Hannan, M. and J. Freeman, 'The Population Ecology of Organizations' (1977) 82 *American Journal of Sociology* 929.

Hardt, M. and A. Negri, *Empire* (Harvard University Press, 2000).

Harman, S., 'The Bill and Melinda Gates Foundation and Legitimacy in Global Health Governance' (2016) 22 *Global Governance* 349.

Hawkins, D. et al., 'Delegation under Anarchy: States, International Organizations and Principal-Agent Theory', in D. Hawkins et al. (eds.), *Delegation and Agency in International Organizations* (Cambridge University Press, 2006), 3.

Hayward, B., *Conflict of Laws and Arbitral Discretion: The Closest Connection Test* (Oxford University Press, 2017).

Herman, L., 'Neither Takers nor Makers: The Big-4 Auditing Firms as Regulatory Intermediaries' (2020) 25 *Accounting History* 349.

Herrhausen, A., *Organizing Peacebuilding: An Investigation of Interorganizational Coordination in International Post Conflict Reconstruction Efforts* (Peter Lang, 2009).

Hildebrandt, M., *Smart Technologies and the End(s) of Law: Novel Entanglements of Law and Technology* (Edward Elgar, 2016).

Hildyard, N., '"Infrastructure" and the Big 4: Public–Private Partnerships, Corridors, and the Expansion of Capital', in Ch. Hurl and A. Vogelpohl (eds.), *Professional Service Firms and Politics in a Global Era* (Palgrave MacMillan, 2021), 197.

Hirschman, G., *Accountability in Global Governance* (Oxford University Press, 2020).

Hohfeld, W. N., 'Some Fundamental Legal Conceptions as Applied in Judicial Reasoning' (1913–14) 23 *Yale Law Journal* 16.

Hohmann, J., 'Diffuse Subjects and Dispersed Power: New Materialist Insights and Cautionary Lessons for International Law' (2021) 34 *Leiden Journal of International Law* 585.

Hooghe, L., *Measuring International Authority: A Postfunctionalist Theory of Governance*, Vol. III (Oxford University Press, 2017).

Hooghe, L., T. Lenz and G. Marks, *A Theory of International Organization* (Oxford University Press, 2019).

Hurl, Ch. and A. Vogelpohl (eds.), *Professional Service Firms and Politics in a Global Era* (Palgrave MacMillan, 2021).

Irwin, D., 'The Truth about Trade: What Critics Get Wrong about the Global Economy' (2016) 95 *Foreign Affairs* 84.

Isin, E. and E. Ruppert, 'The Birth of Sensory Power' (2020) 7 *Big Data and Society*.

Jain, N., *Perpetrators and Accessories in International Criminal Law: Individual Modes of Responsibility for Collective Crimes* (Hart, 2014).

Jenks, C. W., *The Proper Law of International Organization* (Oceana, 1962).

Jessup, Ph., *Transnational Law* (Yale University Press, 1956).

Jiang, S., 'Serving the National on the Global Plane: Disentangling Chinese Cities' Practice of International Law' (2022) 15 *Urban Research & Practice*.

Johns, F., 'From Planning to Prototypes: New Ways of Seeing Like a State' (2019) 82 *Modern Law Review* 833.

'Governance by Data' (2021) 17 *Annual Review of Law and Social Science* 53.

Johnson, T., *Organizational Progeny* (Oxford University Press, 2014).

Jones, C., Y. Temouri and A. Cobham, 'Tax Haven Networks and the Role of the Big 4 Accountancy Firms' (2018) 53 *Journal of World Business* 177.

Jordan, A. et al., 'Governing Climate Change Polycentrically: Setting the Scene', in A. Jordan et al. (eds.), *Governing Climate Change: Polycentricity in Action?* (Cambridge University Press, 2018), 3.

Kalaitzake, M., 'Accounting for Success: The Big Four as Allies of Finance in Post Crisis Regulatory Reform' (2019) 21 *Business and Politics* 297.

Kamradt-Scott, A., 'What Went Wrong? The World Health Organization from Swine Flu to Ebola', in A. Kruck, K. Oppernann and A. Spencer (eds.), *Political Mistakes and Policy Failures in International Relations* (Palgrave Macmillan, 2018), 199.

Kamto, M., 'Le rôle des "accords et organismes régionaux" en matière de maintien de la paix et de la sécurité internationales à la lumière de la Charte des Nations Unies et de la pratique internationale' (2007) 111 *Revue générale de droit international public* 771.

Kanie, N. et al., 'Introduction: Global Governance through Goal Setting' in N. Kanie and F. Biermann (eds.), *Governing through Goals: Sustainable Development Goals as Governance Innovation* (MIT Press, 2017), 1.

Kavanagh, M., R. Singh and M. Pillinger, 'Playing Politics: The World Health Organization's Response to COVID-19', in S. Greer et al. (eds.), *Coronavirus Politics* (University of Michigan Press, 2021), 34.

Kelsen, H., *The Law of the United Nations: A Critical Analysis of Its Fundamental Problems* (Stevens and Sons, 1950).

Kennedy, D, 'The Stakes of Law, or Hale and Foucault' (1991) 15 *Legal Studies Forum* 327.

Kentikelenis, A., Th. Stubbs and L. King, 'IMF Conditionality and Development Policy Space, 1985–2014' (2016) 23 *Review of International Political Economy* 543.

Keohane, R., *After Hegemony: Cooperation and Discord in the World Political Economy* (Princeton University Press, 1984).

Kingsbury, B., 'The Concept of "Law" in Global Administrative Law' (2009) 20 *European Journal of International Law* 23.

'Infrastructure and InfraReg: On Rousing the International Law "Wizards of Is"' (2019) 8 *Cambridge International Law Journal* 182.

'Introduction to the Symposium on Infrastructuring International Law' (2023) 117 *AJIL Unbound* 1.

Kingsbury, B., N. Krisch and R. Stewart, 'The Emergence of Global Administrative Law' (2005) 68 *Law and Contemporary Problems* 15.

Kirmse, S, 'Sleepy Side Alleys, Dead Ends and the Perpetuation of Eurocentrism' (2014) 25 *European Journal of International Law* 307.

Klabbers, J., 'An Accidental Revolution: The ILO and the Opening Up of International Law', in T. Halonen and U. Liukkunen (eds.), *International Labour Organization and Global Social Governance* (Springer, 2020), 123.

'The EJIL Foreword: The Transformation of International Organizations Law' (2015) 26 *European Journal of International Law* 9.

'The Emergence of Functionalism in International Institutional Law: Colonial Inspirations' (2014) 25 *European Journal of International Law* 645.

'Governance by Academics: The Invention of Memoranda of Understanding' (2020) 80 *Zeitschrift für ausländisches öffentliches Recht und Völkerrecht* 35.

'Interminable Disagreement: Reflections on the Autonomy of International Organisations' (2019) 88 *Nordic Journal of International Law* 111.

An Introduction to International Institutional Law, 2nd ed. (Cambridge University Press, 2009).

An Introduction to International Organizations Law, 4th ed. (Cambridge University Press, 2022).

'The Life and Times of the Law of International Organizations' (2001) 70 *Nordic Journal of International Law* 287.

'The Normative Gap in International Organizations Law: The Case of the World Health Organization' (2019) 16 *International Organizations Law Review* 272.

'Notes on the Ideology of International Organizations Law: The International Organization for Migration, State-Making, and the market for Migration' (2019) 32 *Leiden Journal of International Law* 383.

'Presumptive Personality: The European Union in International Law', in M. Koskenniemi (ed.), *International Law Aspects of the European Union* (Martinus Nijhoff, 1998), 231.

'Reflections on the International Telecommunication Union: International Organizations as Epistemic Structures', in A. Bianchi and M. Hirsch (eds.), *International Law's Invisible Frames* (Oxford University Press, 2021), 200.

'Responsibility as Opportunism: The Responsibility of International Organizations', in S. Besson (ed.), *Theories of International Responsibility Law* (Cambridge University Press, 2022), 119.

'The Second Most Difficult Job in the World: Reflections on COVID-19' (2020) 11 *Journal of International Humanitarian Legal Studies* 270.
'Sources of International Organizations' Law: Reflections on Accountability', in S. Besson and J. d'Aspremont (eds.), *Oxford Handbook of the Sources of International Law* (Oxford University Press, 2017), 987.
'Sui Generis? The European Union as an International Organization', in D. Patterson and A. Södersten (eds.), *A Companion to European Union Law and International Law* (Wiley, 2016), 3.
'Towards a Political Economy of International Organizations Law' (2023) 20 *International Organizations Law Review* 82.
'Transforming Institutions: Autonomous International Organisations in Institutional Theory' (2017) 6 *Cambridge International Law Journal* 105.
Treaty Conflict and the European Union (Cambridge University Press, 2008)
'Two Concepts of International Organization' (2005) 2 *International Organizations Law Review* 277.
'What Role for International Organizations in the Promotion of Community Interests? Reflections on the Ideology of Functionalism', in E. Benvenisti and G. Nolte (eds.), *Community Interests across International Law* (Oxford University Press, 2018), 86.
Klabbers, J. and P. Koutrakos (eds.), 'An Anatomy of Autonomy' (2019) 88 *Nordic Journal of International Law* (special issue).
Klamer, A, *Speaking of Economics: How to Get in the Conversation* (Routledge, 2007).
Klock, K., 'International Public Private Partnerships as Part of the Solution to Infectious Disease Threats: Operational, Legal, and Governance Considerations', in S. Halabi et al. (eds.), *Global Management of Infectious Disease after Ebola* (Oxford University Press, 2016), 157.
Koivisto, I., 'The IMF and the "Transparency Turn"' (2016) 25 *Minnesota Journal of International Law* 381.
Konings, F. et al., 'SARS-CoV-2 Variants of Interest and Concern Naming Scheme Conducive for Global Discourse' (2021) 6 *Nature Microbiology* 821.
Kosovac, A., M. Acuto and T. L. Jones, 'Acknowledging Urbanization: A Survey of the Role of Cities in UN Frameworks' (2020) 11 *Global Policy* 293.
Koutrakos, P., *EU International Relations Law* (Hart, 2006).
Kranke, M., 'Exclusive Expertise: The Boundary Work of International Organizations' (2022) 29 *Review of International Political Economy* 453.
'Pathologies of a Different Kind: Dysfunctional Interactions between International Organizations' (2022) 2 *Global Studies Quarterly* 1.
Krasner, S., (ed.), *International Regimes* (Cornell University Press, 1983).
Kratochwil, F., *Praxis: On Acting and Knowing* (Cambridge University Press, 2018).
Rules, Norms and Decisions (Cambridge University Press, 1989).
The Status of Law in World Society (Cambridge University Press, 2014).
Lachimia, A., *Tied Aid and Development Aid Procurement in the Framework of EU and WTO Law: The Imperative for Change* (Hart, 2013).
Lagrange, E., 'Les relations entre les organisations internationales', in M. Vellano (ed.), *Il Futuro delle Organizzazioni Internazionali: Prospettive Giuridiche* (Scientifica, 2015), 131.

Lando, O. and P. A. Nielson, 'The Rome I Regulation' (2008) 45 *Common Market Law Review* 1687.

Lang, A., 'International Lawyers and the Study of Expertise: Representationalism and Performativity', in M. Hirsch and A. Lang (eds.), *Research Handbook on the Sociology of International Law* (Edward Elgar, 2018), 122.

Latour, B., 'From Realpolitik to Dingpolitik: An Introduction to Making Things Public', in B. Latour and P. Weibel (eds.), *Making Things Public: Atmospheres of Democracy* (MIT Press, 2005), 14.

'Where Are the Missing Masses? The Sociology of a Few Mundane Artifacts', in W. Bijker and J. Law (eds.) *Shaping Technology/Building Society: Studies in Sociotechnical Change* (MIT Press, 1992), 225.

Laurenti, J., 'Financing', in T. G. Weiss and S. Daws (eds.), *Oxford Handbook on the United Nations*, 2nd ed. (Oxford University Press, 2018), 250.

Leander, A., 'Locating (New) Materialist Characters and Processes in Global Governance' (2021) 13 *International Theory* 157.

Lee, T., 'Global Cities and Transnational Climate Change Networks' (2013) 13 *Global Environmental Politics* 108.

Leino, P., 'Transparency, Participation and EU Institutional Practice: An Inquiry into the Limits of the "Widest Possible" EUI Working Paper Law 2014/3' (2014), at EUI website: https://cadmus.eui.eu/handle/1814/30580 (visited 13 March 2025).

Lemke, T., *The Government of Things: Foucault and the New Materialisms* (NYU Press, 2021).

Lenaerts, K., '"In the Union We Trust": Trust Enhancing Principles of Community Law' (2004) 41 *Common Market Law Review* 317.

Lenger, F., *Metropolen der Moderne. Eine europäische Stadtgeschichte seit 1850* (Beck, 2013).

Lew, J., L. Mistelis and S. Kröll, *Comparative International Commercial Arbitration* (Kluwer, 2003).

Lidén, J., 'The Grand Decade for Global Health: 1998–2008' (Chatham House Working Group on Governance Paper 2, April 2013).

Liefferink, D. and R. Wurzel, 'Environmental Leaders and Pioneers: Agents of Change?' (2017) 24 *Journal of European Public Policy* 951.

Littoz-Monnet, A. (ed.), *The Politics of Expertise in International Organizations: How International Bureaucracies Produce and Mobilize Knowledge* (Routledge, 2017).

Lowenfeld, A. F., 'Cuba', in *Max Planck Encyclopedia of Public International Law* (Oxford University Press).

'International Litigation and the Quest for Reasonablensess' (1994) 245 *Recueil de Cours* 1.

MacKenzie, J. S. et al., 'The WHO Response to SARS and Preparations for the Future', in S. Knobler et al. (eds.), *Learning from Sars: Preparing for the Next Disease Outbreak* (National Academic Press, 2004), 42.

Mackey, T. and B. Liang, 'Lessons from SARS and H1N1/A: Employing a WHO–WTO Forum to Promote Optimal Economic-Public Health Pandemic Response' (2012) 33 *Journal of Public Health Policy* 119.

Malhame, M. et al., 'Shaping Markets to Benefit Global Health: A 15-year History and Lessons Learned from the Pentavalent Market' (2019) *Vaccine* X 2 100033.

Maniglier, P. et al., 'Bachelard and the Concept of Problematic' (2012) 173 *Radical Philosophy* (special issue).
Mann, F. A., 'The Proper Law of Contracts Concluded by International Persons' (1959) 35 *British Yearbook of International Law* 34.
'State Contracts and International Arbitration' (1967) 42 *British Yearbook of International Law* 1.
Marchegianno, G., 'The Juristic Character of the International Commission of Cape Spartel Lighthouse' (1931) 25 *American Journal of International Law* 339.
Mathiason, J., *Invisible Governance: International Secretariats in Global Politics* (Kumarian Press, 2007).
Matsushita, M. et al., *The World Trade Organization. Law, Practice, and Policy*, 3rd ed. (Oxford University Press, 2015).
May, C., *The World Intellectual Property Organization: Resurgence and the Development Agenda* (Routledge, 2007).
Mazower, M., *Governing the World: The History of an Idea* (Penguin, 2012).
Meidinger, E., 'The Administrative Law of Global Private–Public Regulation: The Case of Forestry' (2006) 17 *European Journal of International Law* 47.
'Forest Certification and Democracy' (2011) 130 *European Journal of Forest Research* 407.
Miller, S., *The Moral Foundations of Social Institutions* (Cambridge University Press, 2010).
Mills, A., *Party Autonomy in Private International Law* (Cambridge University Press, 2018).
Mitrany, D., *A Working Peace System* (Royal Institute for International Affairs, 1943).
Momani, B., 'Professional Management Consultants in Transnational Governance', in L. Seabrooke and L. Henriksen (eds.), *Professional Networks in Transnational Governance* (Cambridge University Press, 2017), 245.
Morgan, B. and K. Yeung, *An Introduction to Law and Regulation: Text and Materials* (Cambridge University Press, 2012).
Morgenstern, F., *Legal Problems of International Organizations* (Grotius, 1986).
Morlino, E., 'Engaging with International Organizations: A Tale of Love and Darkness' (2024) 21 *International Organizations Law Review* 460.
Procurement by International Organizations: A Global Administrative Law Perspective (Cambridge University Press, 2019).
Muir Watt, H., '"Party Autonomy" in International Contracts: From the Makings of a Myth to the Requirements of Global Governance' (2010) 6 *European Review of Contract Law* 250.
Müller-Mall, S., *Legal Spaces: Towards a Topological Thinking of Law* (Springer, 2013).
Murphy, C., *International Organization and Industrial Change: Global Governance since 1850* (Polity, 1994).
Murphy, S., 'Reflections on the ICJ Advisory Opinion on Kosovo: Interpreting Security Council Resolution 1244 (1999)', in M. Wood and M. Milanovic (eds.), *The Law and Politics of the Kosovo Advisory Opinion* (Oxford University Press, 2015), 134.
Neamtu, B. and D. Dragos, 'Freedom of Information in the European Union: Legal Challenges and Practices of EU Institutions', in D. Dragos, P. Kovac and A.

Marseille (eds.), *The Laws of Transparency in Action: A European Perspective* (Palgrave MacMillan, 2019), 11.

Nesi, G., 'The Shifting Status of Cities in International Law? A Review, Several Questions and a Straight Answer' (2021) 30 *Italian Yearbook of International Law* 17.

Nouwen, S., 'Exporting Peace? The EU Mediator's Normative Backpack' (2022) 1 *European Law Open* 26.

'Return to Sender: Let the International Court of Justice Justify or Qualify International-Criminal-Court Exceptionalism Regarding Personal Immunities' (2019) 78 *Cambridge Law Journal* 595.

Novosseloff, A., 'La coopération entre l'Organisation des Nations Unies et les institutions européennes de sécurité: principes et perspectives' (2001) 2 *Annuaire français de relations internationales* 594.

Nygh, P. E., *Autonomy in International Contracts* (Oxford University Press, 1999).

Oberthür, S., 'Reflections on Global Climate Politics Post Paris: Power, Interests and Polycentricity' (2016) 51 *International Spectator* 80.

Osterhammel, J., *Die Verwandlung der Welt: eine Geschichte des 19. Jahrhunderts* (Beck, 2009).

Otlet, P., 'Un projet grandiose' de Cité Internationale', in W. Whyte (ed.), *Ghent Planning Congress 1913: Premier Congrès international et exposition comparée des Villes* (UIV, 1913), 237.

Parrish, C. et al., 'Cross-Species Virus Transmission and the Emergence of New Epidemic Diseases' (2008) 72 *Microbiology and Molecular Biology Reviews* 457.

Partiti, E., 'Orchestration as a Form of Public Action: The EU Engagement with Voluntary Sustainability Standards' (2019) 25 *European Law Journal* 94.

Payre, R. and P. Y. Saunier, 'A City in the World of Cities. Lyon, France; Municipal Associations as Political Resources in the Twentieth Century', in P. Y. Saunier and S. Ewen (eds.), *Another Global City. Historical Explorations into the Transnational Municipal Movement* (Palgrave Macmillan, 2008), 69.

Peters, A., 'International Law between COVID-19 and the Next Pandemic' (2022) Research Paper No. 2022-18, *Max Planck Institute for Comparative Public Law & International Law.*

'Towards Transparency as a Global Norm', in A. Bianchi and A. Peters (eds.), *Transparency in International Law* (Cambridge University Press, 2013), 534.

Petersmann, M., 'Response-abilities of Care in More-than-Human Worlds' (2021) 12 *Journal of Human Rights and the Environment* 102.

Petersmann, M. and D. Van Den Meerssche, 'On Phantom Publics, Clusters and Collectives: Be(com)ing Subject in Algorithmic Times' (2024) 39 *AI and Society* 107.

Peterson, J., *Timeline: An Abbreviated History: The Origins of the Big Eight, and How They Shrank to Four* (Emerald, 2017).

Pincus, S., 'Rethinking Mercantilism: Political Economy, the British Empire, and the Atlantic World in the Seventeenth and Eighteenth Centuries' (2012) 69 *The William and Mary Quarterly* 3.

Poggi, G., *The Development of the Modern State: A Sociological Introduction* (Stanford University Press, 1978).

Polanyi, K., *The Great Transformation: The Political and Economic Origins of Our Time*, 2nd ed. (Beacon Press, 2001).

Portmann, R., *Legal Personality in International Law* (Cambridge University Press, 2010).

Prosser, W., 'Interstate Publication' (1952–53) 51 *Michigan Law Review* 959.

Pulkowski, D., 'Structural Paradigms of International Law', in T. Broude and Y. Shany (eds.), *The Shifting Allocation of Authority in International Law* (Hart, 2008), 51.

Rana, S., 'Seismic Shifts: The COVID-19 Pandemic's Gendered Fault Lines and Implications for International Law' (2021) 39 *Australian Yearbook of International Law Online* 91.

Raustiala, K. and D. Victor, 'The Regime Complex for Plant Genetic Resources' (2004) 58 *International Organization* 277.

Reinisch, A. (ed.), *Challenging the Acts of International Organizations before National Courts* (Oxford University Press, 2010).

'Decisions of the European Patent Organization before National Courts', in A. Reinisch (ed.), *Challenging Acts of International Organizations before National Courts* (Oxford University Press, 2010), 137.

International Organizations before National Courts (Cambridge University Press, 2000).

Revers, H., *IULA 1913–1963. The Story of the First Fifty Years of International Municipal Co-operation* (International Union of Local Authorities, 1963).

Rosenberg, E., 'Transnationale Strömungen in einer Welt, die zusammenrückt', in E. Rosenberg (ed.), *Geschichte der Welt 1870–1945: Weltmärkte und Weltkriege* (Beck, 2012, Zettel transl.), 815.

Rosenne, S., 'United Nations Treaty Practice' (1954) 86 *Recueil des Cours* 275.

Rosner, D., *Critical Fabulations: Reworking the Methods and Margins of Design* (MIT Press, 2018).

Ruffert, M., 'Transboundary Cooperation between Local or Regional Authorities', in *Max Planck Encyclopedia of International Law* (Oxford University Press).

Sadurska, R. and C. Chinkin, 'The Collapse of the International Tin Council: A Case of State Responsibility?' (1990) 30 *Virginia Journal of International Law* 845.

Sanchez-Graells, A., 'Transparency in Procurement by the EU Institutions', in K.-M. Halonen, R. Caranta and A. Sanchez-Graells (eds.), *Transparency in EU Procurements* (Edward Elgar Publishing, 2019), 82.

Sander, B., 'Freedom of Expression in the Age of Online Platforms: The Promise and Pitfalls of a Human Rights-Based Approach to Content Moderation' (2020) 43 *Fordham International Law Journal* 939.

Sands, Ph. and P. Klein, *Bowett's Law of International Institutions*, 6th ed. (Sweet & Maxwell, 2009).

Saunier, P. Y., 'Introduction', in P. Y. Saunier and S. Ewen (eds.), *Another Global City. Historical Explorations into the Transnational Municipal Movement* (Palgrave Macmillan, 2008), 1.

'Les voyages municipaux américains en Europe 1900–1940. Une piste d'histoire transnationale' (2003) 15 *Jahrbuch für Europäische Verwaltungsgeschichte* 267.

'Sketches from the Urban Internationale, 1910–1950: Voluntary Associations, International Institutions and US Philanthropic Foundations' (2001) 25 *International Journal of Urban and Regional Research* 380.

Schermers, H. G. and N. Blokker, *International Institutional Law: Unity within Diversity*, 5th ed. (Martinus Nijhoff, 2011).

International Institutional Law: Unity within Diversity, 6th ed. (Martinus Nijhoff, 2018).

Schmalenbach, K., 'Challenging Decisions of the European Schools Before National Courts', in A. Reinisch (ed.), *Challenging the Acts of International Organizations before National Courts* (Oxford University Press, 2010), 178.

Schmidt, C. H., 'Swine CAFOs & Novel H1N1 Flu: Separating Facts from Fears' (2009) 117 *Environmental Health Perspectives* A394.

Schmidt, R., 'The Carbon Footprint of the Games: International Climate Change Law and the Olympics' (2020) 114 *AJIL Unbound* 362.

'Local Practices: Transnational Solutions? The Role of Host Cities in the Cyclic Process of Environmental Regulation in the Context of Sports', in S. Wood et al. (eds.), *Transnational Business Governance Interactions* (Edward Elgar, 2019), 77.

'Protecting the Environment through Sports? Public–Private Cooperation for Regulatory Resources and International Law' (2017) 28 *European Journal of International Law* 1341.

Regulatory Integration across Borders: Public Private Cooperation in Transnational Regulation (Cambridge University Press, 2018).

Schneider, J. W., *Treaty-Making Power of International Organizations* (Droz, 1959).

Schulz, M., 'Internationale Institutionen', in J. Dülffer and W. Loth (eds.), *Dimensionen internationaler Geschichte* (Oldenbourg, 2012), 211.

Scott, J., 'Extraterritoriality and Territorial Extension in EU Law' (2014) 62 *American Journal of Comparative Law* 87.

Scott, J. B., 'The Fifth International Conference of American States' (1923) 17 *American Journal of International Law* 518.

Seef, S. and A. Jeppsson, 'Is It a Policy Crisis or It Is a Health Crisis? The Egyptian Context: Analysis of the Egyptian Health Policy for the H1N1 Flu Pandemic Control' (2013) 14 *Pan African Medical Journal* 59.

Sen, A., *On Ethics and Economics* (Blackwell, 1987).

Sending, O. J., *The Politics of Expertise: Competing for Authority in Global Governance* (University of Michigan Press, 2017).

Seyersted, F., *Common Law of International Organizations* (Martinus Nijhoff, 2008).

Shany, Y., 'The COVID-19 Pandemic Crisis and International Law: A Constitutional Moment, a Tipping Point or More of the Same, in M. Mbengue and J. d'Aspremont (eds.), *Crisis Narratives in International Law* (Martinus Nijhoff, 2021), 100.

Shao, W. et al., 'Evolution of Influenza A Virus by Mutation and Re-assortment' (2017) 18 *International Journal of Molecular Sciences* 1650.

Shore, Ch. and S. Wright, 'How the Big 4 Got Big: Audit Culture and the Metamorphosis of International Accountancy Firms' (2018) 38 *Critique of Anthropology* 303.

Sinclair, G. F., *To Reform the World: International Organizations and the Making of Modern States* (Oxford University Press, 2017).

Singer, M., 'Jurisdictional Immunity of International Organizations: Human Rights and Functional Necessity Concerns' (1995) 36 *Virginia Journal of International Law* 53.

Slaughter, A.-M., *A New World Order* (Princeton University Press, 2004).
Smith, J., *Patenting the Sun: Polio and the Salk Vaccine* (Morrow, 1990).
Smith, M. P., *Transnational Urbanism: Locating Globalization* (Blackwell, 2001).
Smith, W., and D. R. Kaplowitz, 'Cuba', in J. Krieger (ed.), *The Oxford Companion to Politics in the World* (Oxford University Press, 1993), 206.
SooHoo, C., 'WHO to Revise Definition of Pandemic Phases amidst 2009 H1N1 Pandemic' (2009) 7 *Biosecurity and Bioterrorism: Biodefense Strategy, Practice, and Science* 117.
Stephen, M., 'Legitimacy Deficits of International Organizations: Design, Drift, and Decoupling at the UN Security Council' (2018) 31 *Cambridge Review of International Affairs* 96.
Stone, R., *Controlling Institutions: International Organizations and the Global Economy* (Cambridge University Press, 2011).
Storeng, K. T., 'The GAVI Alliance and the "Gates Approach" to Health System Strengthening' (2014) 9 *Global Public Health* 865.
Sullivan, G., 'Infra-legalities: Global Security Infrastructures, Artificial Intelligence and International Law' (unpublished paper, 2023).
The Law of the List: UN Counterterrorism Sanctions and the Politics of Global Security Law (Cambridge University Press, 2020).
'Law, Technology, and Data-Driven Security: Infra-Legalities as Method Assemblage' (2022) 49 *Journal of Law and Society* S31.
Swiney, C., 'The Urbanization of International Law and International Relations: The Rising Soft Power of Cities in Global Governance' (2020) 41 *Michigan Journal of International Law* 227.
Sybesma-Knol, N., *The Status of Observers in the United Nations* (Vrije Universiteit, 1981).
Szabó, E., 'Gavi, the Vaccine Alliance: A Unique Case Study in Partnership' (2016) 13 *International Organizations Law Review* 149.
Tallberg, J. et al. (eds.), *The Opening Up of International Organizations* (Cambridge University Press, 2013).
Talmon, S., 'Article 2(6)', in B. Simma et al. (eds.), *The Charter of the United Nations: A Commentary* (Oxford University Press, 2012), 252.
Taylor, A., 'Controlling the Global Spread of Infectious Diseases: Toward a Reinforced Role for the International Health Regulations' (1997) 33 *Houston Law Review* 1327.
Tesner, S. with G. Kell, *The United Nations and Business: A Partnership Recovered* (Macmillan, 2000).
Teubner, G. and P. Korth, 'Two Kind of Legal Pluralism: Collision of Transnational in the Double Fragmentation of the World Society', in M. Young (ed.), *Regime Interaction in International Law: Facing Fragmentation* (Cambridge University Press, 2012), 23.
Thorstensen, V., D. Ramos and C. Muller, 'The "Missing Link" between the WTO and the IMF' (2013) 16 *Journal of International Economic Law* 353.
Toly, N., 'Transnational Municipal Network in Climate Politics: From Global Governance to Global Politics' (2008) 5 *Globalizations* 341.
Tushnet, M., *The New Constitutional Order* (Princeton University Press, 2003).

Tzanakopoulos, A., 'Transparency in the Security Council', in A. Bianchi and A. Peters (eds.), *Transparency in International Law* (Cambridge University Press, 2013), 367.

Urueña, R., 'Después de la fragmentación: ICCAL, derechos humanos y arbitraje de inversiones', in A. von Bogdandy et al. (eds.), *El constitucionalismo transformador en América Latina y el derecho económico internacional. De la tensión al diálogo* (Universidad Nacional Autónoma de México Instituto de Investigaciones Jurídicas, 2018), 59.

'Hacia Un Espacio Jurídico Latinoamericano: El Diálogo Internacional Judicial En La Protección de Los Derechos Humanos En América Latina', in J. Martín y Pérez de Nanclares (ed.), *El diálogo judicial internacional en la protección de los derechos humanos fundamentales* (Universidad de Salamanca, 2019), 419.

'Interaction as a Site of Postnational Rule-Making: A Case Study of the Interamerican System of Human Rights', in E. Fahey (ed.), *The Actors of Postnational Rule-Making: Contemporary Challenges of European and International Law* (Routledge, 2015), 133.

'Interaction between International Organizations', in J. Klabbers (ed.), *The Cambridge Companion to International Organizations Law* (Cambridge University Press, 2022), 222.

'Temporariness and Change in Global Governance' (2014) 45 *Netherlands Yearbook of International Law* 19.

Vallejo, R., 'After Governance? The Idea of Private Administrative Law', in P. Kjaer (ed.), *The Law of Political Economy: Transformation in the Function of Law* (Cambridge University Press, 2020), 320.

Valticos, N., 'Les contrats conclus par les organisations internationales avec des personnes privées. Rapport provisoire' (1977) 57 *Annuaire de l'Institut de droit international* 6.

Van den Bossche, P., *The Law and Policy of the World Trade Organization*, 5th ed. (Cambridge University Press, 2021).

Van Den Meerssche, D., 'International Organizations and the Performativity of Measuring States: Discipline through Diagnosis' (2018) 15 *International Organizations Law Review* 168.

'Virtual Borders: International Law and the Elusive Inequalities of Algorithmic Association' (2022) 33 *European Journal of International Law* 171.

Van Den Meerssche, D. and G. Gordon, 'Is This the Rhizome? Thinking Together with Fleur Johns' (2022) 33 *Law and Critique* 237.

'The Contemporary Values of Operadiction Regimes', in I. Feichtner and G. Gordon (eds.), *Constitutions of Value* (Routledge, 2023), 236.

Van Eysinga, W. J. M., *Ontwikkeling en inhoud der Nederlandsche tractaten sedert 1813* (Martinus Nijhoff, 1916).

Van Krieken, P. and D. McKay (eds.), *The Hague: Legal Capital of the World* (Springer, 2005).

Vatanparast, R., 'The Infrastructures of the Global Data Economy: Undersea Cables and International Law' (2020) 61 *Harvard International Law Journal Online*.

Wei, D., *Linking Non-State Action with the U.N. Framework Convention on Climate Change* (Center for Climate and Energy Solutions, 2016).

Weiler, J. H. H. and A. P. Müller, 'Everything Must Change so that Everything Can Remain the Same (G. Tomasi di Lampedusa): The CJEU and the Temporal Dissonance of Europe "Then" and "Now"' (unpublished paper).
Wen, W. and A. Sonnerfeldt, 'The Interplay between Global Accounting Firms and National Institutional Contexts: The Establishment of the Big Four in China from 1978 to 2007' (2022) 27 *Accounting History* 95.
Wenham, C., M. Eccleston-Turner and M. Voss, 'The Futility of the Pandemic Treaty: Caught between Globalism and Statism' (2022) 98 *International Affairs* 837.
Wickremasinghe, C., The Jurisdictional Immunities of International Organisations and Their Officials. Doctoral Thesis, London School of Economics, 2003.
Widdows, K., 'Security Council Resolutions and Non-Members of the United Nations' (1978) 27 *International and Comparative Quarterly* 459.
Wilkins, D., and M. Esteban Ferrer, 'The Integration of Law into Global Business Solutions: The Rise, Transformation, and Potential Future of the Big Four Accountancy Networks in the Global Legal Services Market' (2018) 43 *Law and Social Inquiry* 981.
Wright, A., *Cataloging the World: Paul Otlet and the Birth of the Information Age* (Oxford University Press, 2014).
Wurm, J., 'Asking National Courts to Correct Over-Flight Charges of Eurocontrol', in A. Reinisch (ed.), *Challenging Acts of International Organizations before National Courts* (Oxford University Press, 2010), 157.
Wurzel, R., D. Liefferink and D. Torney, 'Pioneers, Leaders and Followers in Multilevel and Polycentric Climate Governance' (2019) 28 *Environmental Politics* 1.
Wynes, S., 'Covid-19 Disruption Demonstrates Win–Win Climate Solutions for Major League Sports' (2021) 55/23 *Environmental Science & Technology* 15609.
Yao, J., *The Ideal River: How Control of Nature Shaped the International Order* (Manchester University Press, 2022).
Yeung, K., 'Algorithmic Regulation: A Critical Interrogation' (2018) 12 *Regulation & Governance* 505.
Young, O., 'Institutional Linkages in International Society: Polar Perspectives' (1996) 2 *Global Governance* 1.
Zammit, A., *Development at Risk: Rethinking the UN-Business Partnerships* (South Centre, 2003).
Zemanek, K., *Das Vertragsrecht der internationalen Organisationen* (Springer, 1957).

Index

Printed in the United Kingdom by TJ Clays Ltd.